AFFORDABLE HOUSING AND PUBLIC–PRIVATE PARTNERSHIPS

Law, Property and Society

Series Editor:
Robin Paul Malloy

The Law, Property and Society series examines property in terms of its ability to foster democratic forms of governance, and to advance social justice. The series explores the legal infrastructure of property in broad terms, encompassing concerns for real, personal, intangible, intellectual and cultural property, as well as looking at property related financial markets. The series is edited by Robin Paul Malloy, and book proposals are welcome from all interested authors.

Robin Paul Malloy is E.I. White Chair and Distinguished Professor of Law at Syracuse University College of Law, USA. He is Director of the Center on Property, Citizenship, and Social Entrepreneurism. He is also Professor of Economics (by courtesy appointment) in the Maxwell School of Citizenship and Public Affairs, Syracuse University. Professor Malloy writes extensively on law and market theory and on real estate transactions and development. He has authored six books (one now in its third edition and another in its second edition), and edited five additional books. He has also written more than 25 scholarly articles, and contributed to 12 other books. His recent books include: LAW AND MARKET ECONOMY (2000, in English and translated into Spanish and Chinese); LAW IN A MARKET CONTEXT (2004); and REAL ESTATE TRANSACTIONS 3RD (with James C. Smith, 2007).

Affordable Housing and Public–Private Partnerships

Edited by

NESTOR M. DAVIDSON
University of Colorado Law School, USA

ROBIN PAUL MALLOY
Syracuse University, USA

Routledge
Taylor & Francis Group
LONDON AND NEW YORK

First published 2009 by Ashgate Publishing

Published 2016 by Routledge
2 Park Square, Milton Park, Abingdon, Oxfordshire OX14 4RN
711 Third Avenue, New York, NY 10017, USA

First issued in paperback 2016

Routledge is an imprint of the Taylor & Francis Group, an informa business

British Library Cataloguing in Publication Data
Affordable housing and public–private partnerships. --
(Law, property and society)
1. Housing policy--Great Britain. 2. Public-private sector cooperation--Great Britain.
I. Series II. Davidson, Nestor M. III. Malloy, Robin Paul, 1956-
363.5'0941-dc22

Library of Congress Cataloging-in-Publication Data
Affordable housing and public–private partnerships / edited by Nestor M. Davidson and Robin Paul Malloy.
p. cm. -- (Law, property and society)
Includes bibliographical references and index.
ISBN 978-0-7546-7720-8 (hardback)
1. Housing--Law and legislation--United States. 2. Housing--Finance--Law and legislation--United States. 3. Housing policy--United States. I. Davidson, Nestor M. II. Malloy, Robin Paul, 1956-

KF5730.A38 2009
344.73'063635--dc22

2009011267

ISBN 13: 978-1-138-25317-9 (pbk)
ISBN 13: 978-0-7546-7720-8 (hbk)

Contents

List of Contributors

Susan D. Bennett Professor of Law, Washington College of Law, American University.

Barbara Bezdek Professor of Law, University of Maryland School of Law.

Nestor M. Davidson Associate Professor, University of Colorado School of Law.

Michael Diamond Professor of Law, Georgetown University Law Center and Director of Georgetown's Housing and Community Development Clinic.

Lorna Fox O'Mahony Reader, Durham Law School, Durham University (UK).

Tim Iglesias Professor of Law, University of San Francisco School of Law.

Robin Paul Malloy E.I. White Chair and Distinguished Professor of Law, College of Law, Syracuse University.

Peter W. Salsich, Jr McDonnell Professor of Justice in American Society, Saint Louis University School of Law.

James Charles Smith John Byrd Martin Professor of Law, University of Georgia.

List of Contributors

Editors' Preface

Affordable housing is critical to all communities. People need places to live, places that provide shelter and places that provide a sense of "home," and how to meet those needs in a time of economic crisis is one of the most pressing issues facing our nation today. With distressing statistics about rising cost burdens, increasing foreclosure rates, rising unemployment, falling wages, and widespread homelessness, building affordable housing will remain one of our most pressing social policy problems for years to come.

Although affordable housing law and policy stands at the forefront of national debates about community and the economy, serious attention to cutting-edge housing issues by legal scholars remains lacking. Consequently, we have undertaken this book with the goal of addressing broad questions of housing law, policy, and practice, with a primary emphasis on how best to approach the public–private partnerships through which most affordable housing is now built, operated, and maintained.

The book begins with Michael Diamond's assessment of policy choices regarding the conflicts of competing goods in housing markets. Diamond puts front and center one of the most difficult aspects of engaging the private sector to produce and preserve affordable housing; the balancing of consumer demands for housing and its affordability. Diamond explores a variety of pragmatic, but ultimately unresolved, approaches to balancing the incommensurables that pervade housing policy, offering a plea for policymakers and housing practitioners to make the choice between priorities more self-consciously.

In Chapter 2, Tim Iglesias broadens the horizon by mapping the increasing focus on public–private partnerships through the lens of what he describes as our pluralist housing ethics. These ethics paradigms—which variously understand housing as an economic good, as home, as a human right, as a source of social order, and as an element in a functional land use system—all provide insights into how to balance the potential benefits and harms posed by the right of public–private partnerships. Iglesias argues that this trend could build support for increased subsidies, foster creativity in developing housing, and change perceptions of affordable housing in legal and policy debates. As Iglesias highlights, however, without appropriate care, public–private partnerships could yield the opposite outcomes.

Building on scholarship highlighting the potential for value creation by lawyers in ordinary business transactions, Nestor Davidson, in Chapter 3, argues that housing lawyers have unique potential to translate complex regulatory regimes into workable private ordering arrangements, adding "value" in a very broad sense of the word. Better understanding the regulatory translation work that deal lawyers in affordable housing undertake can help refocus policymakers and practitioners on this often hidden aspect of housing policy.

Chapter 4 begins an exploration of specific policy interventions that have the potential to improve the development of affordable housing. In this chapter, Michael Diamond argues for tenant ownership as a new model of Low Income Housing Tax Credit development, recognizing that tax credits represent the primary subsidy mechanism for the creation and preservation of affordable housing. This new resident participation, Diamond concludes, carries great potential benefits not only for residents, but for their communities and could serve as a model for a variety of other housing programs.

Peter Salsich, in Chapter 5, turns from the best-established to the newest form of production subsidy in his exploration of the recently authorized National Housing Trust Fund. This new fund, the first significant housing program created in over two decades, has the potential to generate a paradigm shift in housing production and preservation policy. Highlighting both the public–private partnerships and the innovative federal–state–local relationships that the new fund will enable, Salsich provides a roadmap for improving and broadening a variety of collaborative efforts that are so vital to implementing housing policy.

In Chapter 6, Barbara Bezdek argues for a solution to the displacement and loss of community that often marks the landscape of public–private housing partnerships. In this chapter, Bezdek explores community equity shareholding as a way for vulnerable community members faced with redevelopment to participate in decision-making about the character of the redevelopment and at the same time receive an entitlement to profits from the redevelopment. Through special purpose entities created for this purpose, community equity has the potential to instantiate social and geographic community as a novel form of ownership.

Focusing on a similar set of challenges posed by urban renewal, Susan Bennett, in Chapter 7, proposes the use of social impact statements to respond to the needs of residents facing redevelopment-generated upheaval. These statements would evaluate how all residents measure their investment in their community, capturing values that transcend the supposed fair market value of home. These measurements, Bennett argues, have great potential to provide both a practical tool to broaden meaningful involvement in redevelopment and a new measure for just compensation in eminent domain.

Chapter 8 takes a step back from programmatic development concerns to highlight a critical background concern underlying so many aspects of housing policy. Too often, Lorna Fox O'Mahony argues, housing policy promotes homeownership with insufficient attention to a legal context that fails to protect those residents, particularly those at greatest risk from foreclosure. Mapping out the breadth of losses that accompany repossession, Fox O'Mahony offers significant insights into what she calls the affective value of home and its vulnerability in contemporary housing policy.

Robin Paul Malloy, in Chapter 9, highlights another shortcoming in contemporary single-family housing policy in the failure to provide any national standards for inclusive design for the mobility impaired. Malloy points to the significant number of individuals with physical disabilities denied access to the bulk of newly constructed housing in the United States, a policy choice partly generated by concerns about affordability. Given this, Malloy argues that the choice between accessibility and affordability is not irreconcilable, and suggests pragmatic approaches to achieve both.

Finally, in Chapter 10, Jim Smith concludes with an exploration of timely lessons about the vulnerability of our affordable housing stock. Using disaster planning for public housing as a case study, Smith argues that housing practitioners need to pay greater attention to long-term asset management. This emphasis on risk management, insurance, replacement reserves, and other seemingly mundane considerations in reality holds important lessons for the responsible long-term stewardship of affordable housing assets across the entire array of programs.

With these contributions, this book captures some of the most important challenges, and explores some of the great potential, of affordable housing and public–private partnerships. Affordable housing is receiving renewed policy attention in the wake of a global economic crisis tied fundamentally to failures in housing markets. This book approaches critical issues in housing policy—particularly at the intersection of public and private efforts—from a variety of directions, helping advance this vital national conversation about the central human need for housing.

Nestor M. Davidson
Associate Professor
University of Colorado Law School
Boulder, Colorado 80309
303-735-5294
nestor.davidson@colorado.edu
www.colorado.edu/law

Robin Paul Malloy, J.D., LL.M.
E.I. White Chair and Distinguished Professor of Law
Director, Center on Property, Citizenship, and Social Entrepreneurism
College of Law, Syracuse University
Syracuse, NY 13244
315-443-3559
rpmalloy@law.syr.edu
www.law.syr.edu/rpm

Acknowledgements

We thank Dean Hannah Arterian for her support of the Center on Property, Citizenship, and Social Entrepreneurism at Syracuse, and Dean David Getches and Associate Dean Dayna Matthew for supporting the Workshop on Affordable Housing and Public Private Partnerships: The Intersections of Housing, Property, and Real Estate, held (as a joint project of Syracuse and Colorado) in October 2007 at Colorado Law School. It is this workshop that gave rise to AFFORDABLE HOUSING AND PUBLIC–PRIVATE PARTNERSHIPS. We also extend our thanks and appreciation to Kristin A. Urbach and Sheila Welch for their valuable assistance in the preparation of this book.

For Clare Huntington
NMD

Dedicated to all the people at Catholic Charities of Syracuse who give of themselves to provide housing, shelter, and support services to the neediest members of our community
RPM

Chapter 1
Affordable Housing and the Conflict of Competing Goods: A Policy Dilemma

Michael Diamond

My purpose in this chapter is twofold; first to set out some broad concepts related to affordable housing production; and second, to note some of the dilemmas associated with governmental housing policy. In particular, I want to discuss what I have called *the conflict of competing goods*, that is, the conflict between various housing goals that most people would agree, at least in the abstract, are socially and morally desirable. The conflict arises because, in a world of finite resources, it is impossible to maximize for each of the competing goals. Society, therefore, is put to the choice among incommensurables. The question is how to make the choice. In this chapter, unfortunately, my goal is limited to pointing out the conflicts and suggesting some of the ways society has, or might, attempt a resolution of these conflicts. Since each of the methods I mention has significant flaws, identifying or creating the perfect resolution will have to wait for future authors.

To begin, there is a wide range of goals that might underlie the promotion of affordable housing and I would like to discuss some of them. Many are obvious while others are much less so, often visible only upon close analysis. Let me suggest some of the major goals sought to be accomplished by policymakers and by advocates of decent, affordable housing. Among the obvious ones are the provision of shelter and the potential creation of wealth.

Perhaps less obvious goals are the growth in psychological well-being due to a resident's sense of "home" and its resulting stability,[1] the improved physical health of the homeowner's family,[2] the resident's increased participation in civic society,[3] and the improved educational performance of their children.[4] Another goal might be to achieve racial and economic integration in order to allow a wider

1 J. Peter Byrne & Michael Diamond, *Affordable Housing, Land Tenure, and Urban Policy: The Matrix Revealed*, 34 Fordham Urb. L.J. 527, 550 (2007).

2 Office of the Surgeon General, Healthy People: The Surgeon General's Report on Health Promotion and Disease Prevention 6 (United States Public Health Service 1979).

3 *See* Jeffrey James Minton, *Rent Control: Can and Should It Be Used to Combat Gentrification?*, 23 Ohio N.U. L. Rev. 823, 835 (1997); *see also* William H. Simon, *Social-Republican Property*, 38 UCLA L. Rev. 1335, 1360–61 (1991).

4 J. Peter Byrne, *Two Cheers for Gentrification*, 46 How. L.J. 405, 423–24 (2003).

range of residents to partake of the benefits often associated with mixed race and/or mixed income communities, such as greater cultural diversity, more and better municipal services, greater social amenities and the social connections that might lead to better employment opportunities.[5] Still others might be to enhance housing accessibility for those with disabilities,[6] to create environmentally friendly housing,[7] or to preserve the historical and cultural value of the property.[8]

The provision of shelter is probably the most fundamental aspect of affordable housing policy. Yet as of 2005, the Department of Housing and Urban Development estimated a shortage of nearly six million units of affordable housing in the nation and this estimate applies only to worst case needs.[9] The shortage of decent affordable housing is actually much greater than this and the shortage is growing.[10] To add to the problem, the private market, under current conditions, has only a limited ability to produce sufficient units to make up the deficit or even to stem the increasing gap. The shortfall results in such societal problems as homelessness, overcrowding, inadequate conditions, and the payment by many households of a disproportionate amount of their income for housing.

Moreover, in the current economic climate, there does not seem to be a viable way to construct sufficient numbers of new affordable units. High land costs, significant local resistance to affordable housing units being placed in certain communities and current political priorities all militate against new construction. So do the economics of unsubsidized units, particularly the limited ability of the poor to pay the actual costs of decent, newly constructed housing. Thus, some attention has been given by policymakers to rehabilitation of existing units. While some of the problems associated with new construction, for example, the placement of affordable housing units, are reduced by calling for rehabilitation of existing units, many other problems, including escalating land costs, persist. In addition, other issues, such as the potential entrenchment of concentrated poverty, may be exacerbated by rehabilitating units to house the poor in existing low income communities.

---

5 *Id.*

6 Robert G. Schwemm, *Barriers to Accessible Housing: Enforcement Issues in "Design and Construction" Cases Under the Fair Housing Act*, 40 U. Rich. L. Rev. 753, 756 (2006).

7 *See* Green Building Act of 2006, D.C. Code § 6-1451.01 (Supp. 2007).

8 *See* National Historic Preservation Act, 16 U.S.C § 470 (2000).

9 *Affordable Housing Needs: A Report to Congress on the Significant Need for Housing*, 2007 United States Department of Housing and Urban Development, Office of Policy Development and Research 14.

10 *See Affordable Housing Needs: A Report to Congress on the Significant Need for Housing*, 2007 United States Department of Housing and Urban Development, Office of Policy Development and Research 14; *see also Affordable Housing Needs: A Report to Congress on the Significant Need for Housing*, 2005 United States Department of Housing and Urban Development, Office of Policy Development and Research 14.

Because of these realities, government policy has had to create incentives for the construction and rehabilitation of affordable units. While there is wide variety in the form of the incentives, they cluster around direct subsidy payments to owners or renters,[11] income and real estate tax forbearance,[12] zoning concessions,[13] and land write-downs.[14] Unfortunately, because the goals associated with affordable housing policy are so varied, the overall array of policies is incoherent and, in many cases, contradictory. Policies favoring one goal often work, presumably unconsciously, in opposition to others. This characterizes the conflict of competing goods.

One set of conflicting goals that I mentioned earlier is the competition between the provision of decent, affordable shelter and the creation of wealth for homeowners. While each of these goals is laudable, they cannot each be maximized in any particular project. To the extent society seeks to preserve an affordable housing unit for the long term, it must restrict the wealth that an owner can derive from the sale or rental of that property. To the extent the owner is able to demand full market value for the unit, it would likely be too expensive, either as a purchase or as a rental, for a low income resident. However, if the owner is restricted from deriving maximum financial benefit from the property, that owner's wealth creation is restricted, often severely. If the owner does sell the property subject to the restriction, the net proceeds may not be sufficient to buy another unit in the unsubsidized market.

This begs the question of who is the intended beneficiary of governmental housing subsidy programs. It might be the resident who is lucky enough to get the subsidy, either the difference between the market rent and what the resident actually has to pay for the unit or the difference between what a buyer had to pay for the unit and the amount he or she could sell it for. In the homeownership model, the subsidy might be captured by the individual resident which might give that resident the capital to escape poverty. On the other hand, such a sale would take the particular unit out of the pool of affordable housing forever, leaving potential future residents and society one more step away from closing the affordability gap.

Alternatively, the beneficiary could be a class composed of all potential current and future low income residents. This is not unlike what many Native American

---

11 For example, the Housing Choice Voucher Program, available at http://www.hud.gov/offices/pih/programs/hcv.

12 Norman Alpert, *Property Tax Abatement: An Incentive for Low Income Housing*, 11 Harv. J. On Legis. 1 (1973).

13 Nico Calavita, Kenneth Grimes & Alan Mallach, *Inclusionary Housing in California and New Jersey: A Comparative Analysis*, 8 Housing Pol'y Debate 109, 123 (1997).

14 Melvyn R. Durchslag, *Property Tax Abatement for Low-Income Housing: An Idea Whose Time May Never Arrive*, 30 Harv. J. On Legis. 367, 373 (1993).

groups believe about natural resources, including land.[15] They believe each person is merely a steward of such resources for all future generations, using what he or she needs and leaving the rest for those yet to come. To protect subsequent users of the property, a deed restriction could be used to limit the equity that each successive owner could take from the sale of the property. In this way, society would be able to preserve the pool of affordable units available to future eligible residents. The cost of such a policy, however, is to leave low income homeowners in these units without the tool that is most likely to raise their living standard; the equity from their home. When residents leave an equity restricted homeownership unit, will they have the wherewithal upon the sale of their unit to purchase a comparable unit in the unsubsidized market?

Another conflict concerning the rehabilitation of existing units is the question of de-concentrating poverty. The literature is replete with examples of the social problems in communities with very high concentrations of very low income residents.[16] To the extent society desires to de-concentrate poverty and to create mixed income neighborhoods, the result will also be to break up existing communities and to dissolve the ties and local networks that are fundamental to the well-being of many people. On the other hand, to leave high concentrations of poverty intact is to risk misery for many residents of such neighborhoods and further social deterioration. Efforts to repair existing high concentration communities would require very large expenditures while offering only uncertain outcomes. For example, efforts to attract higher income residents to the re-developed, formerly low income areas risks the type of gentrification that results in the involuntary displacement of the lower income residents. The displaced residents often have very limited prospects as to where to move. They often go to other communities with high poverty concentrations or they create new such areas as the influx of lower income residents results in the departure of many current moderate or middle income residents.

Since these policy conflicts have received a good deal of attention in several scholarly outlets, I would like to discuss some of the other, less obvious, policy conflicts. Two have recently created difficulties for affordable housing development in the District of Columbia and have implications for doing so nationally. One is the requirement that projects funded, in whole or in part, by the local government include, at a minimum, 5 percent of the units developed be fully accessible to persons with handicaps. The second is that such buildings include environmentally sound elements, that is, they utilize "green" materials and techniques in their construction. A third conflict is a bit more abstract. It deals with the relationship between historic preservation and the provision of affordable housing. This

15 Paul H. Carlson, The Plains Indians 111 (1998).

16 *See, e.g.*, Karen Seccombe, *Families in Poverty in the 1990s: Trends, Causes, Consequences, and Lessons Learned*, 62 Journal of Marriage and the Family 1094, 1103–4 (Nov. 2000); Matthew R. Lee, *Concentrated Poverty, Race, and Homicide*, 41(2) The Sociological Quarterly 189, 190–94 (Spring 2000).

conflict arises very graphically when buildings in historic districts, although not themselves historically noteworthy, are to be renovated for the purpose of creating decent and affordable housing for the poor. The historic designation requires that the renovations be done in compliance with the historic nature of the district. This means the materials and designs utilized must be compatible with the historic norm. In many cases, compliance causes the cost of the renovation to rise dramatically.

To put these issues into context, let me refer to a recent experience I had with a client. Not too long ago, I represented a resident association in purchasing the building, which was in one of the poorest neighborhoods in the District of Columbia, in which the members resided.[17] The association wished to purchase the building, renovate it, and then convert it into an affordable cooperative. As the association developed plans for the acquisition and renovation of the property, we began estimating the cost associated with these plans. We determined that the only way the residents could afford the project would be to finance the acquisition and renovation through programs operated by the District of Columbia's government.[18] Since the loan terms available from the government were so favorable, borrowing from the City would reduce the financing costs of the project significantly in comparison to the costs associated with a market rate loan. The City loan, however, came with a range of requirements including a deed restriction mandating long-term affordability, the requirement to provide a fully accessible unit in the 15-unit building, and a variety of "green" elements.

Each of these requirements, accessibility, environmental soundness, and historic preservation (which was an issue in another building in which I worked), are laudable elements of public policy. Most would agree, I think, that people with handicaps should be able to participate in all elements of civic society without unnecessary barriers that limit their access to societal involvement and to the broad range of housing available to others. Similarly, most would agree that protecting the environment is a worthwhile goal and that society should take steps to do so. Finally, many who consider the question would say that it is important for society and communities to recognize and preserve their history and culture, including through the maintenance of the traditional appearance of historic neighborhoods. The problem, of course, is that achieving these goals has costs. The costs are not merely the expenditure of additional funds, although all of these goals involve costly elements. There are also opportunity costs associated with each choice society makes. Each choice, as with many policy choices, involves costs to other

17 Such a series of events was possible due to the District of Columbia's Tenant Opportunity to Purchase Act (TOPA), D.C. Code § 42-3404.02 *et seq.* (2001), which gives tenants in buildings that the owner wishes to sell the opportunity to purchase them, often with financing provided by the District's Department of Housing and Community Development (DHCD).

18 DHCD operates a variety of very low interest rate, long-term loan programs. In addition, the terms of the loan can be negotiated to create a great deal of flexibility. This allows many projects that appear not to be feasible to be completed at an affordable cost.

laudable social goals in that they reduce resources available to satisfy such other goals.

Let us examine in turn each of the conflicts I mentioned. The requirement of accessibility, particularly in renovations of existing structures, often involves retrofitting structural elements that increase significantly the cost of housing. For example, in the short narrative I presented earlier, the building had no elevator and an entrance way that required one to go up or go down one flight of stairs to gain access to the units, none of which was on ground level. The stairways were not wide enough to permit a stairway lift to be added. Of the various ways to comply with the City's accessibility requirement, only one would preserve the semblance of affordability, yet even that method involved enormous cost.

The residents chose to reconfigure the building by constructing a ramp from the public sidewalk to the side of the building and then along the side of the building to a newly constructed exterior entrance into a unit that had to be built, essentially from scratch, to accommodate the width and amenity requirements of accessibility. This was accomplished by reconfiguring space in what had been the utility room in the basement. This required moving the heating plant and electrical panel to another area of the basement. The cost of making these changes added about 15 percent, or more than $10,000, to the cost of each unit. The income of the residents, which ranged from about $13,000 per year to approximately $35,000, could barely manage the additional monthly burden caused by these changes. And after shouldering this additional load, and despite serious efforts to fill the unit with a person in need of accessible housing, the association has not attracted even a single inquiry from a person in need of such a unit. The cost of constructing the accessible unit, as well as the cost of having the unit remain unoccupied, is borne by the residents of that building through higher monthly housing costs. To the extent that residents, including those with handicaps, have low or very low incomes, the increases in cost associated with accessibility put enormous pressure on the element of affordability, the very purpose of the renovation in the first place.

Similarly, the goal of environmentally friendly buildings also may conflict with the goal of affordability. Green elements and construction are often more expensive than their conventional counterparts, sometimes considerably more expensive. While the up front capital costs of installing green elements in a building are often recaptured by lower operating costs over the life of the project, where affordability is a goal, the question is whether the operating savings in any particular year exceed the increased financing costs for the installation of the green elements. If not, the effect of going green is to increase the current cost of housing for the poor, a cost they can ill afford to absorb. Of course, there are gains to society from using more environmentally friendly materials and techniques but, to a great extent, the costs of doing so are placed upon the poor while the environmental benefits are shared by society as a whole.

The third conflict, that of historic preservation and affordability, arose in the context of another building. In order to do the renovations planned by the residents, the building had to comply with the historic district's architectural guidelines. This meant that the exterior had to be maintained in the same architectural style in which it had been built. This became a problem, for example, when new, energy efficient windows were to be installed. There was no standard window that complied with the historic guidelines. Thus, the windows had to be custom made in order to comply with the historical requirements. The same was true of interior moldings which could not be purchased as a stock item. They had to be specially milled. Again, the very high cost of meeting these requirements was borne by the residents, although it is possible, if not probable, that none of them felt that they benefited from the historic preservation.

The concept of competing goods is not new. Forty years ago, Garrett Hardin wrote a well-known essay entitled "The Tragedy of the Commons."[19] Hardin posited a world with finite resources and needs that exceed the ability or willingness of societies to meet them. He asked the question how ought society to choose between competing needs and how should it pay for the needs that are given priority. While Hardin was concerned with the problem of population growth and the ability of the world to provide for the growing population, his conceptual framework is relevant here. How shall we choose, in the universe of varying goals for housing policy, among the large number of competing goods where each cannot be maximized in any particular situation? How shall we allocate the costs of the choices we ultimately make?

There are many theories of how to make the selection among competing goals and I would like to discuss just a few of them. One such theory, public choice,[20] suggests that individuals will be motivated by their own self-interest regardless of what they might consider the greater societal good. In democracies, where the will of a majority is thought to be the best method for deciding political priorities, the poor are generally at a serious disadvantage. They, almost by definition, lack the political power to achieve their ends. This is true even if one assumes that those ends are held in common among the poor, itself a questionable assumption. Thus, the added costs imposed by implementing these societal goods may fall directly on the poor, while the benefits are distributed more widely through society, a classic free-rider problem.

But just what is one's self-interest? If everyone pursues his or her own interest, how do we account for policies supporting affordable housing? A cynical response might be that the public provides just enough affordable housing to prevent more serious social disruptions. It also might be that the policies in place keep affordable housing mostly cabined in poor neighborhoods, away from the middle class citizens who support such policies. These possibilities suggest a touch of altruism used in service of a more concealed self-interest. Another possibility is less cynical. Policy may be the result of people choosing to do the right thing. This "right thing"

19 Garrett Hardin, *The Tragedy of the Commons*, SCIENCE, Dec. 13, 1968, at 1243.

20 Thomas Romer & Howard Rosenthal, *The Elusive Median Voter*, 12 JOURNAL OF PUBLIC ECONOMICS 143–70 (1979).

could arise from a Habermasian discourse,[21] the result of which elucidates the appropriate choice. This type of discourse hearkens to the civic republican tradition of participatory democracy.[22] Both Habermas and civic republicanism offer the opportunity for participation by those typically excluded by public choice theory. This model, however, offers only a procedural framework within which decision-making can take place. It allows discussion, reasoning, and, perhaps, compromise. It does not, however, solve the problem of greater resources or power by one of the discoursing sides. Moreover, there are countless numbers of "right things" and in our current economic situation, doing one right thing may preclude doing some other right thing. We may be in a zero-sum game in which to favor one goal is to deprive another. How should we choose between affordability and accessibility or environmental soundness? Between wealth creation and preservation? I know what I would choose, and why. I also know that others will have sound arguments for different choices. The problems caused by these conflicts sound in morals, politics, and economics. So much of the decision is based on who we are and what we have been brought to believe. I think back to the Rawlsian model put forward in his classic "A Theory of Justice."[23] What would our housing policy look like if the policymakers were all shrouded by the veil of ignorance? What if they did not know who they were or where they stood in society? In such a case, self-interest would be irrelevant because the policymakers would not be aware of what that interest might be. While I admire the purity of Rawls' model, I am not sure it gets us any closer to deciding, in our world of finite resources, which of the several competing goods should be chosen or to articulating a formula that would help us decide. We must, as Hardin reminds us, make commensurable the incommensurable.

My goal in this chapter, however, has not been to delve into moral or political philosophy but, rather, to point out the incommensurables in current housing policy. Without committing significant new resources to affordable housing, a very unlikely occurrence in today's world, these incommensurables will arise in many housing situations. Neither the policymakers, nor many practitioners, however, seem cognizant of the conflicts which present both policy and practice problems. On the one hand, policymakers need to choose, consciously, what goals to prioritize among the many conflicting ones in affordable housing. On the other hand, practitioners need to be able to maneuver between these goals to achieve satisfactory ends for their clients. In addition, we need, as a society, to understand where the costs and benefits of our policy choices actually lie. On the assumption that knowledge may lead to power, being aware of and understanding these conflicts and the allocation of their costs is the first step toward a coherent and effective program of affordable housing development.

21 *See, e.g.*, Jurgen Habermas, between facts and norms: contributions to a discourse theory of law and democracy (1998).

22 *See, e.g.*, Derek Heater, What is Citizenship? 44–79 (1999).

23 John Rawls, A Theory of Justice (1971).

Acknowledgements

The author would like to thank his friend and colleague Peter Byrne for ongoing assistance in developing and refining this project and the participants in the *Affordable Housing and Public–Private Partnerships: The Intersection of Housing, Property, and Real Estate* at the University of Colorado Law School, particularly Robin Malloy and Nestor Davidson, for their comments and support. I also want to thank Aaron Schmitz for very able research assistance.

Chapter 2

Our Pluralist Housing Ethics and Public–Private Partnerships for Affordable Housing

Tim Iglesias

While affordable housing[1] has been produced through a variety of public–private partnerships (PPPs) for many decades,[2] this fact is garnering new and increasing attention by legal and policy analysts.[3] This chapter considers how this new

1 In the chapter, "affordable housing" is defined as housing that is legally restricted for the use of persons or households who meet specific income requirements.

2 "Subsidized housing provides a fertile field of examination [of relational contracting] because policymakers, program managers, and private providers have been tinkering with the structures of privatization in that context for decades …" Nestor Davidson, *Relational Contracts in the Privatization of Social Welfare: The Case of Housing*, 24 Yale L. & Pol'y Rev. 263, 264 (2006) [hereinafter Davidson, *Relational Contracts*]. Examples of affordable housing developments often categorized as "PPPs" include: (1) developments in which government provided subsidies either directly (such as in HUD's programs Section 202 or Section 811) or indirectly (through the Low Income Housing Tax Credit (LIHTC) program) to private housing developers (whether for-profit or non-profit); (2) developments in which local government provided regulatory relief (for example, fee waivers) or regulatory incentives (for example, density bonuses) to private housing developers; (3) developments in which local governments provided infrastructure, subsidy and/or land to private sector developers in redevelopment projects; and (4) traditional public housing developments which are redeveloped by private developers through the HOPE VI program. *See also* U.S. Department of Housing and Urban Development (HUD), *Guidebook: Building Public-private Partnerships to Develop Affordable Housing* (Hud-1583-cpd, May 1996), *available at* http://www.ezrc.hud.gov/offices/cpd/affordablehousing/library/modelguides/1583.cfm (last visited May 6, 2008).

3 Examples of this, besides the conference itself, include: Angela M. Christy, *Revitalizing Public-Private Partnerships (Chair's Message)*, 9 J. of Affordable Housing and Community Development Law 207 (2007); Land Centre, *The Role of Public-Private Partnerships in Producing Affordable Housing: Assessment of the U.S. Experience and Lessons for Canada, available at* http://landcentre.dreamhosters.com/?q=node/4336 and http://www.cmhc.ca/publications/en/rh-pr/socio/socio047.pdf (last visited May 6, 2008) (report examining how public–private partnerships (PPPs) have emerged in the United States as a delivery vehicle for the provision of affordable housing).

attention may affect the future of America's affordable housing movement[4] through the lens of our pluralist housing ethics.[5] After defining a "housing ethic," this chapter briefly explains our five housing ethics and reflects on our housing ethics pluralism. Then, after analyzing the PPP phenomenon using this framework, the chapter concludes that development of affordable housing through the form of PPPs presents important and even historic opportunities for affordable housing development but also substantial risks.[6] Specifically, the proliferation of affordable housing PPPs could engender increased subsidies, continued experimentation with creative methods of developing affordable housing, improved public perceptions of affordable housing, and, most importantly, a fundamental repositioning of "affordable housing" in legal and policy debates. However, this phenomenon could also lead to the opposite outcomes.

"Housing ethics"[7] are organizing principles (or paradigms) that have shaped the whole range of housing issues (from financing, production, and siting to the use of housing) at the federal, state, regional, and local levels. More specifically, a "housing ethic" is an organizing principle that affects American housing law and policy by directing attention to certain kinds of facts and issues as relevant and important for policy and decision-making. It may be pre-reflective or consciously employed. It enables a certain kind of discourse with its own concepts and vocabulary. Beyond just categorizing the world, each ethic incorporates a normative dimension; it is poised toward decision and action in a value-laden way.

There are five distinct, decipherable, and stable housing ethics deeply embedded in American housing policy and law that influence current housing law and policy

4 The chapter defines the affordable housing movement as non-profit affordable housing developers, the wide range of affordable housing advocates (for example, community organizations, architects, and so on), and civil rights attorneys who work in the field.

5 The housing ethics framework was first explicated in Tim Iglesias, *Our Pluralist Housing Ethics and the Struggle for Affordability*, 42 Wake Forest L. Rev. 511 (2007) [hereinafter Iglesias, *Pluralist Housing Ethics*].

6 Others, including Nestor Davidson, *supra* note 2 at 269–83, have discussed the challenges to efficiency and accountability posed by the development of affordable housing through public–private partnerships. This chapter focuses on the opportunities and risks to the broader affordable housing movement posed by PPPs.

7 The phrase "housing ethic" is modeled on Professor Fred Bosselman's use of the term "environmental ethic" in his article which spawned a significant literature on that topic, Fred Bosselman, *Four Land Ethics: Order, Reform, Responsibility, Opportunity*, 24 Envtl. L. 1439 (1994). The conceptual object of this investigation could have been named otherwise. This chapter takes no position on the issue of whether the housing ethics function as rhetorical devices, framing devices, ideologies, or separate rationalities (with the potential for bounded rationality), or some combination of these. This issue is left to future scholarship.

through an ongoing social dialogue.[8] They are: (1) Housing as an Economic Good, (2) Housing as Home, (3) Housing as a Human Right, (4) Housing as Providing Social Order, and (5) Housing as One Land Use in a Functional System.[9] Each housing ethic is now briefly explained.[10]

The *Housing as an Economic Good* ethic directs our attention to the fact that most housing is financed, produced, and distributed by the private market. For many Americans, their house is their largest single investment and one of their largest monthly expenditures. Fortunes are regularly made and lost in the housing market. Therefore, this ethic focuses our attention on economic principles as critical to the formation of good housing law and policy. This familiar ethic is evidenced in real estate transactions law and a wide range of policies at all levels of government. From the perspective of this ethic, any proposed legal rule or policy affecting housing should be scrutinized on the basis of how this proposal will affect investment in housing development, applications for housing development permits, residential property values, and related economic consequences.

The *Housing as Home* ethic concentrates on the fact that homes are *special* spaces for the people who live in them.[11] There they create their lives, their families, and

---

8 This is an interpretative claim that places housing law and policy under one conceptual roof by identifying the deeper structures of American housing law and policy. Conference co-participant and keynote speaker Michael R. Diamond has addressed a related but distinct issue in J. Peter Byrne & Michael Diamond, *Affordable Housing, Land Tenure, and Urban Policy: The Matrix Revealed*, 34 Fordham Urb. L.J. 527, 528 (2007) ("This article attempts to organize and clarify the relationships among various goals of subsidized housing policy and the elements of programs adopted to meet them") [hereinafter Byrne and Diamond, *Matrix Revealed*].

9 "Housing as a focal point for self-governance" may be an additional emerging housing ethic. Currently, approximately 50 million Americans live in some form of "common interest community" ("CIC") in which housing ownership is linked to membership and voting rights in a self-governing body. Community Assn's Inst., An Introduction to Community Association Living 2–3, 35 (2003), *available at* http://www.regenesis.net/community_association_living.pdf (last visited May 6, 2008). Some argue these developments enable community formation, social capital building, and citizenship skill building. Dell Champlin, *The Privatization of Community: Implications for Urban Policy*, 32 J. Econ. Issues 595 (1998) (discussing the economic and social reasons favoring CICs); Robert H. Nelson, *Pro-Choice Living Arrangements*, Forbes, June 14, 1999, at 222. Others argue that CICs are the latest form of exclusion and represent privatization of government. Edward J. Blakely & Mary Gail Snyder, Fortress America: Gated Communities in the United States 44 (1997). *See generally* Symposium, *AALS Common Interest Communities Symposium*, 37 Urb. Law. 325 (2005) (illustrating the various perspectives on CICs). In the author's view, while these forms of housing are well-grounded in law, it is premature to determine whether or not they will create a new housing ethic.

10 Interested readers will find much more extensive expositions of each housing ethic in Iglesias, *Pluralist Housing Ethics*, *supra* note 5, at 518–82.

11 Another conference participant, Lorna Fox, has written extensively on this topic in the United Kingdom context, for example, Lorna Fox, Conceptualising Home: Theories,

their very selves. Therefore, this special space must be protected and expectations deriving from it should receive legal recognition. This ethic is expressed in a wide range of laws and policies generally benefiting current residents of housing. By and large, these laws and policies concern non-economic rights and privileges affecting safety, freedom, and privacy, including the Fourth Amendment of the United States Constitution.[12] This ethic inquires of any proposed rule or policy: How will this proposal affect domestic privacy, security, household composition, and related values?

The *Housing as a Human Right* ethic contends that adequate, safe, and affordable housing is critical to proper human development. Such housing enables individuals to be healthy, to take advantage of educational opportunities, to be productive members of the workforce, and to form nurturing families. Because housing is fundamental to proper human flourishing, this ethic urges that all people should have rights to housing protected by law. This ethic is expressed in the widespread adoption of the implied warranty of habitability as well as by more selective adoption of just cause eviction ordinances and rent control policies. And it was addressed (although not embraced) in the important case *Lindsey v. Normet*.[13] The question it asks of any new proposal is: How will this proposal affect access to and tenure in safe, decent housing?

The *Housing as Providing Social Order* ethic notes that the relative location of housing, types of housing, and who lives in them—our housing settlement patterns—create a social order. Where and among whom we live structures important parts of our lives. Therefore, housing law and policy should respect and promote "good communities," including by respecting who people want to associate with in their neighborhoods. Evidence of this ethic's effects on our housing law and policy include "Jim Crow" laws, racial and classist restrictive covenants, exclusionary zoning cases (for example, the famous Mount Laurel cases), and the enactment of fair housing law.[14] This ethic continually asks: How will this proposal affect *who* will live in "my community"?

The *Housing as One Land Use in a Functional System* ethic draws our attention to the fact that housing is only one of many land uses that are necessary for a healthy city. And housing, like any land use, may have both positive and negative externalities. Therefore, housing law and policy should be conscious and deliberate about financing, producing, designing, and siting housing, considering

---

LAWS AND POLICIES (2007).

12 Professor Ben Barros has summarized many of these laws and policies in D. Benjamin Barros, *Home as a Legal Concept*, 46 SANTA CLARA L. REV. 255 (2006).

13 Lindsey v. Normet, 405 U.S. 56 (1972) (refusing to recognize an individual right to housing under the Due Process and Equal Protection Clauses of the Federal Constitution).

14 *See, e.g.*, DOUGLAS S. MASSEY & NANCY A. DENTON, AMERICAN APARTHEID (1993); James Kushner, *Apartheid in America: An Historical and Legal Analysis of Contemporary Residential Segregation in the United States*, 22 HOW. L.J. 547 (1979) (extensive analysis focusing on role of government and courts in causing segregation).

its relationships to other land uses in the relevant geographical unit. The marks of this ethic on our law and policy include comprehensive planning law, subdivision law, much of environmental law, and numerous cases, for example, *Home Builders v. City of Napa*.[15] The primary concern of this ethic is: How will any housing law or policy affect infrastructure and schools, the jobs–housing balance and the environment?

The relationships among the five housing ethics are complex. The housing ethics are not consistently aligned with any particular interest group. Each ethic is not monolithic; there are several versions or strands of each ethic. For example, versions of the Housing as an Economic Good ethic vary depending upon each one's interpretations of housing markets and appropriate role for government policy towards them.[16] Each ethic can support more than one social value, for example, the Housing as One Land Use in a Functional System ethic can be concerned with efficiency, environmental quality, and affordability. One or more of the five housing ethics often combine with each other in support of a particular legal rule or policy. A policy or law is most stable when supported by several housing ethics.[17] The ethics also function as reciprocal constraints on each other. For example, effects on the cost of housing (Housing as an Economic Good ethic) are raised as a criticism to policies that would ensure habitability (Housing as a Human Right ethic).

---

15 Home Builders Ass'n of Northern California v. City of Napa, 108 Cal. Rptr. 2d 60 (Ct. App. 2001) (recognizing the functional importance and value of affordable housing for the city in upholding an inclusionary zoning ordinance against a facial regulatory takings claim).

16 *See* Iglesias, *Pluralist Housing Ethics*, *supra* note 5, at 523–5.

17 For example, the promotion of homeownership—America's most enduring housing policy over the last 50 years—probably derives its stability from the fact that it can be supported by one version of all five of our housing ethics. The asset-building aspect of homeownership incorporates the Housing as an Economic Good ethic by focusing on a house as a good investment. Obviously, the economic interests of builders, realtors, and financial institutions also help explain the popularity of the policy. Homeownership appeals to the Housing as Home ethic by reassuring homeowners of their privacy rights and fueling imaginations about positive subjective meanings associated with "homes." There is a hint of the Housing as a Human Right ethic in calls for government to regulate in such a way that makes the "American Dream" possible for all. Homeownership is consistent with the Housing as Providing Social Order ethic by its inference that: "You've really (only) made it in this society when you own your own home." The element of mobility that sometimes accompanies the American Dream presumes a hierarchically arranged set of neighborhoods in which one climbs from a good house in one neighborhood to a better house in a "better neighborhood." And homeownership is consistent with the Housing as One Land Use in a Functional System ethic in the association of single-family houses in suburbs as good, safe places for raising children. The "American Dream" of homeownership is so powerful in part because it seamlessly weaves together versions of all of America's housing ethics.

The combination of the five housing ethics with these dynamics results in a "housing ethics pluralism" in which American housing law and policy supports numerous, diverse goals and interests but not in a consistent or coherent way.[18] Thus our housing ethics pluralism helps account for the past and current muddle of our housing law and policy.[19]

Coexistence among the housing ethics has been the norm historically in America, and is likely to persist. However, there is a potential for temporary or limited hegemony by one or more ethics. In the last few decades, two particular versions of housing ethics have been rising and arguably dominant: a deregulatory version of Housing as an Economic Good and a racial and classist exclusionary version of the Housing as Providing Social Order ethic.

The deregulatory version of Housing as an Economic Good is founded on the view that our housing affordability problem is caused by the cumulative effect of government regulations raising the production costs of housing. The proposed solution is to deregulate. On this view, government subsidies for housing become unnecessary if government lets the markets work.[20] The racial and classist exclusionary version of the Housing as Providing Social Order ethic is regularly expressed in continued exclusionary zoning and Not-In-My-Back-Yard opposition to proposed affordable housing development.[21] These two particular versions of

---

18 Any particular policy, legal rule or program can pit the ethics against each other; or certain versions of them can combine to support it; or proponents may try to use one ethic's power to support their policy which primarily serves another ethic. *See, e.g.*, Megan J. Ballard, *Legal Protections for Home Dwellers: Caulking the Cracks to Preserve Occupancy*, 56 SYRACUSE L. REV. 277, 277 (2006) (employing Housing as Home ethic arguments to promote adoption of new housing rights for tenants).

19 Numerous publications describe this muddle. *See, e.g*, R.A. Hays, *Housing America's Poor: Conflicting Values and Failed Policies*, 28 J. OF URBAN HISTORY 369–81 (2002); Rachel G. Bratt, *Nonprofit Developers and Managers: The Evolution of their Role in U.S. Housing Policy*, *in* SHELTER AND SOCIETY: THEORY, RESEARCH, AND POLICY FOR NONPROFIT HOUSING (C. Theodore Koebel ed., 1998); Bishwapriya Sanyal, *Beyond the Theory of Competitive Advantage: Political Imperatives of the Government-Nonprofit Relationship*, *in* SHELTER AND SOCIETY: THEORY, RESEARCH, AND POLICY FOR NONPROFIT HOUSING (C. Theodore Koebel ed., 1998). Professors Bryne's and Diamond's article implicitly explains the muddle as either the result of policymakers naively ignoring inherent tradeoffs, or as a failure to achieve a more comprehensive policy that deliberately and rationally takes the tradeoffs into account. Byrne and Diamond, *Matrix Revealed*, *supra* note 8, at 528–30, 611. In contrast, in the author's view, the confusion and unclarity of our housing policy is largely due to the dynamics of our housing ethics pluralism.

20 Note that in contrast to this view, even the National Association of Home Builders supports government housing subsidies including the federal mortgage interest deduction and other types of subsidies under some circumstances. *See, e.g.*, National Association of Home Builders, Government Support for Affordable Housing, *available at* http://www.nahb.org/generic.aspx?genericContentID=79486 (last visited April 19, 2008).

21 While facially discriminatory housing policies are now illegal, substantial racial/ethnic housing discrimination still exists. These laws and policies have left a legacy of

housing ethics are in profound conflict with the stability and flourishing of the affordable housing movement.

In response, the affordable housing movement has articulated different versions of each of these ethics, analyzing our chronic housing crisis as an effect of various market failures justifying governmental regulation,[22] and promoting an "inclusionary" Housing as Providing Social Order ethic through laws and policies (such as federal fair housing law) designed to integrate neighborhoods and cities.[23]

Due to our persistent housing ethics pluralism, America is not likely to ever have a completely coherent, efficient, and equitable housing policy.[24] Therefore, the affordable housing movement needs to *survive* our housing ethics pluralism by successfully resisting the attempted hegemony of a deregulatory version of Housing as an Economic Good and a racial and classist exclusionary version of the Housing as Providing Social Order ethic. It also needs to adapt so as to *thrive* in our housing ethics pluralism, for example, by expanding its appeal to a version of each of the ethics. As explained below, affordable housing development by PPPs offers opportunities for both surviving and thriving in our housing ethics pluralism, but also presents risks for the affordable housing movement.

Gauging the prospects of PPP development for affordable housing using the housing ethics framework, it is important to define PPP in affordable housing development. PPP is an ambiguous, value-laden, and potentially ideological term. There is now a vast literature debating the meaning of "public–private partnerships" and discussing their benefits and costs.[25] For some, "PPP" is only a marketing label pragmatically employed to promote a particular housing development deal.

---

widely recognized class and race segregated neighborhoods and communities. It is hard to underestimate the influence of these past laws and policies on current attempts to promote affordable housing that would have the effect of increasing racial and class integration. In addition, ongoing legal and public acceptance of class-based housing patterns poses a formidable challenge to affordable housing development.

22 *See, e.g.*, National Housing Institute, *Our Housing Markets Don't Work*, SHELTERFORCE MAGAZINE, May/June 2001. *See* Byrne and Diamond, *Matrix Revealed, supra* note 8, at 530–31 ("… [I]t is widely accepted that the market will not provide housing that meets community standards.")

23 In addition, the housing movement has begun to rely more on the Housing as One Land Use in a Functional System ethic and less on the Housing as a Human Right ethic. See discussion *infra* at notes 62–69 and accompanying text.

24 This conclusion appears to conflict with the implicit hope of such a policy evinced by Professors Byrne and Diamond in *Matrix Revealed, supra* note 8.

25 *See, e.g.*, Stephen H. Linder, *Coming to Terms With the Public-Private Partnership: A Grammar of Multiple Meanings*, AMERICAN BEHAVIORAL SCIENTIST 35–51 (1999); Nick Beerman, *Comment: Legal Mechanisms of Public-Private Partnerships: Promoting Economic Development or Benefiting Corporate Welfare*, 23 SEATTLE U. L. REV. 175 (1999); Angela M. Christy, *Revitalizing Public-Private Partnerships (Chair's Message)*, 9 J. OF AFFORDABLE HOUSING AND COMMUNITY DEVELOPMENT LAW 207 (Spring 2007).

Consequently, for these the term "PPP" has no real consistent substance. Others embrace a narrow economic view, assuming housing is only a private economic good and assuming the market is always the best provider. On this view, PPP is merely one form of "privatization," a one-way movement transferring traditional governmental duties or operations to the private market.[26] This view reduces the scope of PPP options to the types of subsidy that government might provide for-profit housing producers.

Broader definitions of PPPs open up a wide variety of options. For the purposes of this chapter, I adopt a broad functional definition of a PPP (drawn largely from Marc Mihaly)[27] as a cross-sectoral[28] collaboration involving shared allocation of resources, risk,[29] and/or other activities/roles and responsibilities usually based upon relative skills, competencies or other circumstances[30] to achieve a combination of public and private goals.[31]

---

26 The sale of public housing units to tenants without any future affordability requirements is an example of such uni-directional privatization. *See, e.g.*, Robert Pear, *Panel Urges Sale of Public Housing*, New York Times, November 11, 1987, *available at* http://query.nytimes.com/gst/fullpage.html?res=9B0DE6D81F3DF932A25752C1A961948260 (last visited May 5, 2008).

27 Marc B. Mihaly, *Public-Private Redevelopment Partnerships and the Supreme Court: Kelo v. City of New London*, 7 Vt. J. Envtl. L. 41 (2005/2006) [hereinafter Mihaly, *Public-Private Redevelopment Partnerships*].

28 I include any combination of the following three sectors: governments, the market, or civil society (including religious organizations and non-profits).

29 The types of risk that can be allocated among the parties include: (1) market risk (the risk that rental and sales markets will change); (2) development risk (the risk of losing money, for example, sunk costs in predevelopment costs); (3) regulatory risk (the risk that the project will not get its needed discretionary land use approvals); and (4) construction risk (that cost overruns will be high). Mihaly, *Public-Private Redevelopment Partnerships*, *supra* note 27, at 59–60.

30 Mihaly, *Public-Private Redevelopment Partnerships*, *supra* note 27, at 51–2, 58.

31 Each of the PPPs listed *supra* in note 2 could be understood within this definition. These collaborations are usually memorialized in legally enforceable agreements. My definition is an example of what Professor Davidson terms "the pragmatic approach." Davidson, *Relational Contracts*, *supra* note 2, at 269. A similar definition appears in Shelter and Society: Theory, Research, and Policy for Nonprofit Housing (C. Theodore Koebel ed., 1998). The chapter entitled *Public-Private Partnerships for Affordable Housing: Definitions and Applications in an International Perspective* offers several definitions of PPPs including "full partnerships" as a form of inter-sectoral cooperation distinguished by "shared responsibilities, joint decision-making and mutual commitment of resources." *Id.* at 42. Similarly, the Encyclopedia of Housing entry for "Public/Private Housing Partnership" defines a PPP as a partnership "in which private persons or entities carry out specific programs or projects in conjunction with public agencies, sharing control and using both private and public resources." The Encyclopedia of Housing 448–9 (Willem Van Vliet ed., 1998). The Encyclopedia defines a "partnership" as "a voluntary association of two or more

The primary opportunities that the PPP development of affordable housing offers to the affordable housing movement are: (1) increasing subsidies; (2) expanding the scope of experimentation with methods of developing affordable housing; (3) changing public perceptions of affordable housing; and (4) repositioning affordable housing in legal and policy debates.

Developing affordable housing under the rubric of PPPs might increase the amounts of subsidies available from government and also private parties.[32] Elected officials who have been skeptical of government production of affordable housing, and particularly those who focus on the limited but widely publicized failures of the public housing program, may lend more support to affordable housing development if financing, production, and/or management were performed jointly by the public and private sectors. This view may help explain the enactment and continuing vitality of the federal Low Income Housing Tax Credit (LIHTC) program that currently provides the largest federal subsidy for affordable housing development.[33] Successful PPP models such as the Vermont

persons or entities who agree to carry out a business together, with mutual participation in profits and benefits." *Ibid.*

32 … [I]n a time of diminishing federal and other governmental resources, we need to rely on the market and other forces for larger scale answers. Inclusionary zoning in strong markets, tax increment financing, larger foundations using the financial power of their endowments for social purposes and tapping into individual and family foundations that will see an exponential transfer of wealth over the next 10 years. In short, we need to stabilize the public part of the public/private partnership and greatly expand the private part until this country has the will to properly address its human needs.

Bart Harvey, *Building Alliances at All Levels*, 144 Shelterforce Magazine, November/December 2005, *available at* http://www.nhi.org/online/issues/144/buildingalliances.html (last visited January 12, 2008).

33 Under the LIHTC program, private investors exchange equity investments in affordable housing developments for federal income tax credits. For a brief explanation of how the LIHTC program works, *see* Adam McNeely, *Improving Low Income Housing: Eliminating the Conflict Between Property Taxes and the LIHTC Program*, 15 J. Affordable Housing & Community Dev. L. 324, 325—9 (2006). "Whether from a syndicator or directly from the developer, corporations purchase about 70 percent of the tax credits awarded nationwide through the LIHTC." Citing Eric A. Smith, *Low-Income Housing Tax Credit Basics*, 3 J. Fin. Plan. 114, 116 (2000).

Housing and Conservation Board,[34] the Georgia Quality Growth Partnership,[35] and Neighborhood Assistance Programs[36] may be replicated more broadly. In the wake of federal withdrawal since the early 1980s, state and local governments have significantly increased their involvement in affordable housing development, including by providing resources and by joining in various PPPs.[37] The need for "workforce housing"—affordable housing for teachers, nurses, municipal workers (such as police officers and firefighters), and other workers—has attracted the attention of chambers of commerce, employers (for example, the Silicon Valley Manufacturing Group), and others. Wealthy private individuals, corporations or foundations may offer more resources for affordable housing development in PPP funding mechanisms such as The Housing Trust of Santa Clara County.[38]

---

34 "The Vermont Housing and Conservation Board is an independent, state-supported funding agency providing grants, loans and technical assistance to nonprofit organizations, municipalities and state agencies for the development of perpetually affordable housing and for the conservation of important agricultural land, recreational land, natural areas and historic properties in Vermont." For more information, visit Vermont Housing & Conservation Board, http://www.vhcb.org/ (last visited January 12, 2008). "To anyone concerned with both affordable housing and open space, the 12-year-old Vermont Housing and Conservation Trust Fund is seen as a model." Miriam Axel-Lute, *A Meeting of Movements*, 103 Shelterforce Magazine, January/February 1999.

35 Founded in March, 2000, The Georgia Quality Growth Partnership (GQGP) has grown to more than 30 organizations. These partners each contribute time, in kind services, or financial resources to foster Partnership efforts. GQGP Toolkit, http://www.dca.state.ga.us/toolkit/toolkit.asp (last visited April 19, 2008).

36 "Now in use by 11 states—Connecticut, Delaware, Florida, Indiana, Kansas, Maryland, Missouri, Nebraska, Pennsylvania, Virginia, and West Virginia—with legislation pending in at least two others, neighborhood assistance programs (NAPs) provide tax credits to businesses that contribute (cash, materials, staff) to community-based non-profit organizations, often targeting low-income people and communities" including for affordable housing development. Carol Wayman, *Neighborhood Assistance Programs*, Shelterforce Magazine, January/February 1997.

37 In Shelter Burden, Professor Ed Goetz of the University of Minnesota focuses on the local government "response to federal cutbacks in housing in the 1980–1990 decade. During this period, he estimates that increased state and local governmental spending on low- and moderate-income housing made up approximately one-third of the loss of federal aid." W. Dennis Keating, *The Housing Affordability Crisis: Progressive Responses*, Book Review: Edward G. Goetz, Shelter Burden: Local Politics and Progressive Housing Policy (Temple University Press 1993), Shelterforce Magazine, March/April, 1994, *available at* http://www.nhi.org/online/issues/books/74.html (last visited January 12, 2008). PPPs was one of the four models of local low-income housing delivery systems that Professor Goetz analyzed.

38 "The Housing Trust of Santa Clara County is a catalyst to develop specific, desperately needed housing in Santa Clara County through an innovative blend of corporate and community investors." For more information, visit The Housing Trust of Santa Clara County, http://www.housingtrustscc.org/ (last visited January 12, 2008). *Public-Private*

The promotion of affordable housing development as PPPs will enable and encourage affordable housing providers to continue experimenting creatively with various versions of PPPs. As the majority in the *Kelo* case recognized, PPPs can create "a whole greater than the sum of its parts."[39] There is still much to be explored in the fractionalization of property rights and in combining the various roles and responsibilities of private and public partners towards different private and public goals.[40] For example, municipalities are now partnering with non-profit developers in establishing "community housing trusts," a strategy previously implemented by non-profits alone.[41] In this regard, an important unresolved question is: Are PPPs with non-profits in housing substantially distinct and better at achieving some public purposes than PPPs with for-profit actors?[42] If so, this

---

Partnership Announces Loan Fund to Create Affordable Housing in Louisiana, PHILANTHROPY NEWS DIGEST, April 26, 2007, *available at* http://foundationcenter.org/pnd/news/story.jhtml?id=176500022 (last visited January 12, 2008). San Francisco Mayor Gavin Newsom toured public housing with very wealthy individuals to solicit money for rehabilitation. Heather Knight, *Newsom Taking Rich on Tours of Housing for Poor: He Seeks Donations to Rebuild Projects*, SAN FRANCISCO CHRONICLE, August 29, 2007, at A1. For an example of a successful cross-sectoral partnership between the for-profit and non-profit sectors, *see* Scott Anderson, *Building Partnerships for a Better Tomorrow*, 3(5) THE CAMPAIGN FOR AFFORDABLE HOUSING NEWSLETTER (The Campaign for Affordable Housing, Los Angeles, CA), September 10, 2007, at 3 (describing Habitat for Humanity's longstanding partnership with the Whirlpool corporation).

39 Kelo v. City of New London, Conn. et al., 125 S. Ct. 2655, 2665 (2005). Other commentators understand housing PPPs in a similar way. *See, e.g.*, Richard Steinberg, *The Theory of the Nonprofit Sector in Housing*, *in* SHELTER AND SOCIETY: THEORY, RESEARCH, AND POLICY FOR NONPROFIT HOUSING 35 (C. Theodore Koebel ed., 1998) ("Housing partnerships may create synergistic benefits and costs, providing a whole different from its parts").

40 For a taste of this discussion *see* Mihaly, *Public-Private Redevelopment Partnerships*, *supra* note 27; Davidson, *Relational Contracts*, *supra* note 2.

41 Once exclusively a tool for grassroots activists seeking to change local policies, the community land trust

> (CLT) is increasingly being adopted by local governments facing urgent housing-affordability needs. ... [M]unicipalities as different as Irvine, Calif., Chicago, Ill., Sarasota County, Fla., Austin, Texas, Delray Beach, Fla., Highland Park, Ill., Las Vegas, Nev., and Chaska, Minn., have taken the lead in creating their own CLTs. This trend represents an important evolution of the CLT model and a significant rethinking of the goals and roles of municipal government in promoting and preserving affordable housing.

Rick Jacobus & Michael Brown, *City Hall Steps In*, 149 SHELTERFORCE MAGAZINE, Spring 2007, *available at* http://www.nhi.org/online/issues/149/cityhall.html (last visited May 6, 2008).

42 *See* Rocky Tarantello, *Affordable Housing Through Non-Profit/Private-Public Partnerships*, BUSINESS NETWORK, Fall 1998, *available at* http://findarticles.com/p/articles/mi_qa3681/is_199810/ai_n8823514_(arguing non-profits and local governments are "natural partners").

could lead to expansion of the Third Sector in which consumer housing prices are not subject to market forces.[43]

It is no secret that affordable housing has a huge public relations problem. This difficulty is often discussed under the rubric of "exclusionary zoning" and/or the Not-In-My-Back-Yard ("NIMBY") phenomenon.[44] One intriguing opportunity of greater public recognition of affordable housing development as a PPP is whether it can be used to change negative public perceptions of affordable housing.

Affordable housing has strong historical and actual links to poverty and "race."[45] Lately, however, the media and many policymakers have been recognizing that our chronic affordable housing crisis actually affects a wide range of working families with "good jobs."[46] Yet, deeply engrained images of public housing failures combined with unsympathetic stereotypes of the expected occupants obstruct the adoption of more favorable policies. These perceptions hinder the affordable housing movement's attempt to get more subsidies, to improve local siting policies, and to deal with local opposition to proposed affordable housing

---

43 *See* Shelter and Society: Theory, Research, and Policy for Nonprofit Housing (C. Theodore Koebel ed., 1998); The Affordable City: Toward a Third Sector Housing Policy (John Emmeus Davis ed., 1994); Property and Values: Alternatives to Public and Private Ownership (Charles Geisler & Gail Daneker eds., 2000) (Chapters 10–12 focus on housing).

44 "Right now, the face of public housing is the face of people on the dole who have no legitimate rights to that assistance. That's not true. That doesn't describe public housing, so it's a big job of education. The face of housing assistance programs is that it's a pork-barrel that feeds rich developers. The fact is that many programs that involve public-private partnerships are quite effective in delivering good products, but the public image is it is just a big scam for rip-off artists. We have to educate the public as to what's been going on."

Interview by Chester Hartman with Bill Apgar, Executive Director, Harvard's Joint Center for Housing Studies, *in* Shelterforce Magazine, July/August 1995 (William C. Apgar, Jr. is Executive Director of Harvard's Joint Center for Housing Studies). *See also* Tim Iglesias, *Managing Local Opposition to Affordable Housing: A New Approach to NIMBY*, 12 J. of Affordable Housing & Community Development Law 78, 79–83 (2002) (discussing exclusionary zoning and NIMBY). Note that the relatively recent change from using the terms "low-income housing" or "low-cost housing" to using the term "affordable housing" has its roots in a recognition of this problem.

45 This chapter uses the term "race" recognizing that it is a social construct. *See* Ian F. Haney Lopez, *The Social Construction of Race: Some Observations on Illusion, Fabrication and Choice*, 29 Harv. C.R.-C.L. L. Rev. 1 (1994).

46 Joint Center for Housing Studies of Harvard University & Center for Workforce Preparation of the U.S. Chamber of Commerce, *Strengthening our Workforce and our Communities Through Housing Solutions*, Report on Making the Connection … Housing and Workforce Development: A National Leadership Forum (2006), *available at* http://www.jchs.harvard.edu/publications/markets/wh05-1_workforce_housing_report.pdf; Carol A. Bell, *Workforce Housing: The New Economic Imperative?*, 4(2) Fannie Mae Housing Facts & Findings, *available at* http://www.fanniemaefoundation.org/programs/hff/v4i2-workforce.shtml.

developments. These perceptions and attitudes are hard to replace.[47] Yet more (and more positive) public attention may be drawn to affordable housing constructed under a PPP arrangement because the private sector partners may have an interest in gaining public attention for their roles. And they may have more expertise in attracting and sustaining public attention for their achievements. This kind of positive, sustained, and careful attention to affordable housing due to the PPP form may demonstrate how appropriately designed and professionally managed affordable housing is an asset to a community and address affordable housing's public relations problem.[48]

An exciting and even historic opportunity presented by the PPP model is its potential to reposition affordable housing in American housing policy and law.[49] Currently "affordable housing" is ideologically framed as special pleading for individual "welfare rights" for unpopular populations and/or as a government redistribution program.[50] Perhaps PPPs of affordable housing can reposition affordable housing as promoting a *public* interest in pragmatic community development.[51] By emphasizing the important public *and* private interests served in affordable housing production (further discussed below), a greater focus on affordable housing development as PPP could serve an important educative function to numerous important audiences, including local elected officials and policymakers, the media, and the general public.

In particular, a broad functional approach to PPPs raises the potential for more constructive conversations and debates about the relative roles of government, the private for-profit sector, the non-profit sector, and even more broadly, civil society

---

47 Contemporary non-profit affordable housing is largely indistinguishable from market-rate housing. *See, e.g.*, Good Neighbors: The Design of Affordable Family Housing (Michael Pyatok, Tom Jones & William Pettus eds., 1995). However, this similarity renders it relatively *invisible* to the public. Ironically, due to its relative invisibility, the newer versions of affordable housing have a limited capacity to replace the past images that continue to occupy the public's imagination.

48 *See* The Campaign for Affordable Housing, "The Campaign for Affordable Housing is a national, nonpolitical nonprofit organization dedicated to dispelling the negative stereotypes surrounding affordable housing. … The Campaign is solely dedicated to the message that affordable housing is an asset to our communities and that citizens who understand its value must take action to support its creation." *See* The Campaign for Affordable Housing, About Us: About the Campaign, *available at* http://www.tcah.org/about_us.cfm (last visited May 5, 2008).

49 To a large extent, the fulfillment of this opportunity would be the cumulative effect of success in each of the previously described opportunities. Another historic opportunity posed by PPPs is their potential for reforming and revitalizing governance structures, but that topic is beyond the scope of this chapter.

50 *See supra* note 44.

51 The more recent emphasis by the affordable housing movement on the Housing as One Land Use in a Functional System ethic also helps counter this tendency. *See* discussion, *infra* at notes 62–69 and accompanying text.

in responding to our chronic housing crisis.[52] By its own terms a PPP in affordable housing development points beyond neoclassical economics' facile assumption of a "pure public" sector and a "pure private" sector which underlies some critiques of government involvement in the housing sector. Lamenting the misunderstanding of PPPs in the redevelopment context by the United States Supreme Court in the *Kelo* case,[53] Professor Marc Mihaly notes that public and private roles are no longer separate but are commingled.[54] This failure to understand is "poignant because much of this entire sea change in land use comes at the urging of thoughtful conservatives who have spearheaded, intellectually and in practice, the movement to remake government in ways that imitate qualities found in the private sector, and to bring to government land-use planning an understanding of economies and the operation of markets."[55]

As more legal and policy analysts and other opinion-leaders come to understand how PPPs work and to appreciate the breadth of possibilities in affordable housing development through various kinds of PPPs, the policy environment for affordable housing could improve. The formation, funding, and operation of PPPs in affordable housing require the parties to construct a collaboration across sectors in which parties play different roles but work together to develop and operate affordable housing. The process of defining, negotiating, publicly explaining, and implementing affordable housing development through PPPs may undercut the old categories and spur more sophisticated insight into relationships between the public sector, the market, and other elements of civil society. For their part, experienced non-profit developers of affordable housing have learned the importance of market principles and considerations. And the collaboration of some for-profit developers with their non-profit counterparts has engendered mutual respect. Acknowledging together that the successful development of affordable housing that truly serves community needs over the long term is a complex enterprise which PPP collaboration can enhance could help policy debates move beyond simplistic "government" versus "market" categories. This overdrawn distinction is impossible to sustain in the actual practice of PPPs.

The *public* values achieved by government promotion of homeownership have been consistently and widely recognized.[56] Deeper engagement with PPP

52 This analysis assumes that the vexed question of whether the lack of affordable housing is caused by overregulation of the market or by market failures is not irresolvable, and that in the pragmatic structuring of PPPs to produce affordable housing this sometimes ideological conflict can be finessed or avoided.

53 Kelo v. City of New London, 545 U.S. 469 (2005).

54 Mihaly, *Public-Private Redevelopment Partnerships*, *supra* note 27, at 42 ("… [T]he very nature of land development in the city center has evolved, altering both public and private roles, erasing traditional boundaries between what is a public use and what is a private use, and between what is government owned and what is privately owned").

55 *Id.* at 61.

56 The typical public benefits cited as a result of homeownership include "good citizens, stable neighborhoods and strong communities." William M. Rohe, Shannon Van

development of affordable housing and further research might similarly reveal and affirm the public goals served by *all* housing, and specifically affordable housing.[57] The PPP discussion might make the longstanding and important public/governmental roles and interest in *all* housing development both more explicit and better understood.[58] Depending upon how broadly one defines "public" and "private" roles, arguably nearly all housing development in America is PPP; affordable housing is just more explicitly so. For example, the federal government

---

Zandt & George McCarthy, *The Social Benefits and Costs of Homeownership: A Critical Assessment of the Research* 3 (Joint Center for Housing Studies of Harvard University, Low-Income Homeownership Working Paper Series LIHO-01.12, October 2001), *available at* http://www. jchs.harvard.edu/publications/homeownership/liho01-12.pdf. *See generally* D. Benjamin Barros, *Home as a Legal Concept*, 46 SANTA CLARA L. REV. 255 (2006). Some commentators, however, have argued that the dominant focus on homeownership amounts to an unjustified bias against rental form of tenure. Nicolas P. Retsinas & William Apgar, *Opinion: Homeownership Should Not be Sole Barometer of Housing Success*, MASSACHUSETTS HOUSING PARTNERSHIP NEWS, July 15, 2005, *available at* http://www.mhp.net/homeownership/news.php?page_function=detail&mhp_news_id=22.

57 For example, *see* Byrne and Diamond, *Matrix Revealed, supra* note 8 (articulating social goals served by affordable housing and calling for more research). The argument is that while affordable housing is not a "public good" in the technical economic sense of the term, it at least has certain significant positive externalities that ground a public interest in ensuring its development and preservation. In *Home Builders Association of Northern California v. City of Napa*, a California Court of Appeal recognized the social value of affordable housing when it upheld an inclusionary zoning ordinance against a facial regulatory takings claim. Home Builders Association of Northern California v. City of Napa, 90 Cal. App. 4th 188 (1st Dist. 2001), *cert. denied*, 535 U.S. 954 (March 25, 2002). The court wrote:

> City, like many other localities in California, has a shortage of affordable housing. This shortage has negative consequences for all of City's population, but causes particularly severe problems for those on the lower end of the economic spectrum. Manual laborers, some of whom work in the region's wine or leisure industries, are forced to live in crowded, substandard housing. There is a large and growing population of homeless, including many families and teenagers. Workers from low-income families increasingly are forced to live greater distances from their places of employment, which causes increased traffic congestion and pollution.

Id. at 191.

58 Consistent with this, Steinberg explains how housing is not just a private good and articulates five ways in which housing is different from many other goods: (1) society's interest in providing "a minimum standard of occupancy for all," not equality of outcomes; (2) "housing is rife with externalities," for example, NIMBY; (3) the "long lags in supply adjustments"; (4) the "ownership/rental choice in housing"; and, (5) "housing policy is used to regulate the overall economy." Richard Steinberg, *The Theory of the Nonprofit Sector in Housing*, *in* SHELTER AND SOCIETY: THEORY, RESEARCH, AND POLICY FOR NONPROFIT HOUSING 35 (C. Theodore Koebel ed., 1998). *See also* Robin Paul Malloy, *Inclusion by Design: Accessible Housing and Mobility Impairment* , 60 HASTINGS L.J. 699 (2009).

played a crucial role in the creation of both the 30-year mortgage and the secondary mortgage markets.[59] Affordable housing advocates have long argued that the federal mortgage interest deduction (America's largest "housing program" measured by dollars) ought to be considered a housing subsidy.[60] And some courts have held that the development of affordable housing is a "public purpose."[61] Recognition of the public role in *all* housing development could blunt the force of arguments characterizing affordable housing as merely another welfare program for underprivileged (and possibly unworthy) populations. Then with affordable housing repositioned in this way, public involvement in affordable housing development will appear as normal and uncontroversial as our government's commitment to homeownership.

For the affordable housing movement to take full advantage of this opportunity to reposition affordable housing in American housing law and policy, these understandings of PPP could be combined with a de-emphasis on the Housing as a Human Right ethic and a greater emphasis on the Housing as One Land Use in a Functional System ethic. This housing ethic is particularly compatible with the PPP development model. And it draws attention away from individual "welfare" rights

---

59 Federal government action made 30-year mortgages possible which in turn significantly expanded the market for home purchases and also created the government enterprises Fannie Mae and Freddie Mac (now quasi-public) which formed the secondary market for mortgages that significantly expanded access to homeownership and created new, lucrative housing investment opportunities. *See* Kent W. Colton, *Housing Finance in the United States: The Transformation of the U.S. Housing Finance System*, Joint Center for Housing Studies at Harvard University (2002), *available at* http://www.jchs.harvard.edu/publications/finance/W02-5_Colton.pdf.

60 Chester Hartman, *The Case for a Right to Housing*, 9 Housing Pol'y Debate 223, 235 (1998) ("The various homeowners' income tax deductions provide the federal government's only true (civilian) housing entitlement 'program': All homeowners are entitled to deduct from their taxable income base virtually all mortgage interest and all property taxes …") *See* Peter Drier, *The New Politics of Housing*, 63 J. of the American Planning Association 5, 9 (1997) ("The federal tax code allows all homeowners to deduct mortgage interest payments from their income taxes. Whether it is labeled a 'subsidy' or a 'tax expenditure,' the homeowner deduction cost the federal government over $53.3 billion in 1995 alone.") Of course, defenders argue that the tax deduction is not a "subsidy." Some argue that although it is only a statutory policy, it should be considered as a "right" because it is treated as politically inviolable entitlement.

61 Utah Housing Finance Agency v. Smart, 561 P.2d 1052 (1977) (upholding state legislation establishing state housing finance agencies from state constitutional claims recreating public debt, lending state credit, and using public funds for private activities). "The legislature therefore specifically declares it a public purpose for the State to cooperate with private institutions to increase the amount of reasonably available financing for the construction, purchase, and rehabilitation of decent, low and moderate income housing." *Id.* at 1053. And, *see* Home Builders Association of Northern California v. City of Napa I, *supra* note 57.

to housing toward what might be called "social rights to housing opportunities."[62] This ethic can help neutralize affordability's historical association with divisive poverty and race issues. Certain versions of this ethic challenge (implicitly at least) stereotypes about what kind of people need and qualify for affordable housing, highlighting that workers in "good jobs" also both need and qualify for it.[63]

To some extent, the affordable housing movement has engaged in this shift in the last 20 years. This change is evidenced in the recent focus on "workforce housing," inclusionary zoning ordinances, commercial linkage fee programs, and mandatory "housing elements" as part of comprehensive plans, all of which present affordable housing as one necessary land use for a workable community rather than as a human right. These policies can be understood as "developmental policy" for cities, rather than as "redistributive policy" as many past housing programs are perceived.[64] This helps to extricate affordability from its excessive entanglement with stereotypes associated with poverty and race.[65] In addition, each of these policies can be fairly characterized as examples of "social rights to housing opportunities." In a social right to housing, government owes a legal obligation to the community, and the law provides a private right of action against the government to ensure fulfillment of that duty.[66] However, a successful plaintiff's relief is not an individual claim to a housing unit, but rather an injunction

---

62 This point does not diminish the fact that the affordable housing movement's historical reliance on the Housing as a Human Right ethic has generated critically important individual housing rights and policies. Yet, in the view of the author, this ethic is unlikely to be as useful in the foreseeable future due to courts' reluctance to interpret law expansively to recognize individual housing rights and legislatures' reluctance to expand what are perceived as "welfare rights" for individuals. It should also be noted that there are strong and enduring tensions between affordability and some environmentalist versions of the Housing as One Land Use in a Functional System ethic. And it is uncertain whether this ethic can support affordability for very low income households, including homeless people.

63 Of course, the struggle about affordability is: how far does the "workforce" definition go? Does it include low-wage workers in hotels, restaurants, and private homes who are needed for a city to work?

64 *See* Victoria Basolo, *Explaining the Support for Homeownership Policy in US Cities: A Political Economy Perspective*, 22 Housing Studies 99 (2007) (making a similar distinction about local government policies favoring homeownership). Of course, developers and landowners may still perceive and oppose such policies as redistributive.

65 This is not to deny the historical fact that many policies harming affordability were embraced and broadly accepted because alternative policies would largely benefit members of a disfavored race or class. Nor is it to deny that the statistical correlation between race, poverty, and the need for affordable housing is, in part, an effect of such previous policies. The point here is to argue that currently negative stereotypes continue to plague affordable housing policies and proposed developments when in the current situation affordability problems extend well beyond those communities.

66 Professor Bo Bengtsson addresses a similar concept regarding Swedish housing law in Bo Bengtsson, *Housing as a Social Right: Implications for Welfare State Theory*, 24(4) Scandinavian Political Studies 255–75 (2001) (copy on file with author).

requiring the city to follow the law requiring it to take actions which will benefit the community.[67] State legislatures and city governments are more likely to enact social rights to affordable housing because they do not commit themselves to large open-ended financial commitments.[68] Courts are more comfortable enforcing these rights because this exertion of judicial power seems more consistent with separation of powers doctrines—to the degree they are mandating expenditures, they are only expenditures that the government has already committed itself to.[69] The resulting housing rights would be a patchwork, but that is only realistic given our housing ethics pluralism.

A crucial benefit of such repositioning of affordable housing in American law and policy could be stability in affordable housing policy, such as that enjoyed by homeownership policies.[70] A policy or law is most stable when supported by several housing ethics. Affordability *can* be consistent with some version of each of the housing ethics. Greater attention to affordable housing development as PPP could help move in that direction. Affordability is consistent with versions of the Housing as an Economic Good ethic, including those that emerge from pragmatic collaborations between the public sector, the market, and civil society expressed in affordable housing PPPs. Increasing the number, type, and visibility of such collaborations and the consequent broader participation of the private sector in creating affordable housing opportunities more deeply anchors affordability in the Housing as an Economic Good ethic because of the participation of the private sector itself. The Housing as Home ethic is largely indifferent to affordability, but nothing in this ethic would deny someone a home because of her income. This ethic could be mustered to support affordable housing PPPs that expand opportunities for

67 The term "social right to housing" should be distinguished from the common expression "social housing" which refers to either government-supplied or government-subsidized housing, especially in Europe.

68 While the size of a state's financial commitment for mandating local government planning that includes planning for affordable housing is not insubstantial, it is small relative to funding the subsidies required for meeting housing needs founded upon individual housing rights.

69 To be effective, of course, the "social rights to housing opportunities" strategy must include broad legal standing for complainants and sufficient legal resources to enforce such rights. An administrative complaint option would also be useful. *See* Ben Field, *Why Our Fair Share Housing Laws Fail*, 34 Santa Clara L. Rev. 35, 50–51 (1993); Brian Augusta, Comment, *Building Housing from the Ground Up: Strengthening California Law to Ensure Adequate Locations for Affordable Housing*, 39 Santa Clara L. Rev. 503, 513–14 (1999). Attorney's fees awards to parties prevailing over a government defendant would also be appropriate and useful. *See, e.g.*, Mike Geniella, *Ruling Favors Housing Lawsuit: Mendocino County Must Pay $70,000 in Legal Fees*, Santa Rosa Press Democrat, September 28, 2005 (reporting attorney's fees award for successful lawsuit under California's housing element law).

70 For a discussion of the stability of U.S. housing policies promoting homeownership, *see supra* note 17.

families to experience the benefits of "home," whether as homeowners or renters.[71] Of course, the Housing as a Human Right (affordability's natural "home" ethic) can support any policy that provides housing to those in need as PPPs certainly do. Our established Housing as Providing Social Order ethic is largely hostile to affordability, but competing inclusive visions of community could promote affordable housing as integral to a healthy community. PPP affordable housing development can foster these inclusive visions because the public spectacle of government, private for-profit business, and other segments of civil society working together to create affordable housing legitimates the resulting community and its diverse membership. Finally, the Housing as One Land Use in a Functional System ethic supports affordability when it is seen as functionally necessary and as an asset to the community. Extended commitments of time, money, and organizational resources by businesses, chambers of commerce, and a wide range of other collaborators to produce affordable housing in a PPP can testify to its necessity and value for a community.

As is frequently the case, the risks are in some substantial measure the flip-side of the opportunities. The primary risk associated with potential expansion of subsidies for affordable housing development through PPPs is their possible contraction. PPPs in affordable housing development could become a victim of their own success. This could happen, for example, if Congress perceived the amount of resources from state and local governments and private sources dedicated to affordable housing PPPs as justifying a further reduction in federal commitments. The affordable housing movement could address this risk by continuing to educate the public, decision-makers, and the media about the success of PPPs, the continuing need for affordable housing, and the continuing need for a strong federal government role.

The other side of the fact that PPPs create synergistic wholes that are "greater than the sum of their parts"[72] is that PPPs raise complex efficiency, public accountability, and contracting issues.[73] Developers need to be open to continued multiplicity of production methods and strategies using PPPs' potential for fractionalizing property rights. However, with any substantial experimentation comes failure. Some PPPs will fail, and some will fail miserably and, possibly, in a very public manner.[74] If affordable housing PPPs are widely perceived as inefficient,

71 *See, e.g.*, Megan J. Ballard, *Legal Protections for Home Dwellers: Caulking the Cracks to Preserve Occupancy*, 56 SYRACUSE L. REV. 277, 277 (2006) (employing Housing as Home ethic arguments to promote adoption of new housing rights for tenants).

72 *See supra* note 39.

73 See Davidson, *Relational Contracts*, supra note 2.

74 Connie Susilawati & Lynne Armitage, *Do Public Private Partnerships Facilitate Affordable Housing Outcome in Queensland?*, 2004 AUSTRALIAN PROPERTY JOURNAL 184 (2004) (Proceedings 11th European Real Estate Society Conference, Milan, Italy) (finding that the program failed to produce any affordable housing units because of inappropriate design).

ineffective, or unaccountable, then the attempt to reposition affordable housing through them will fail; and the hope of changing negative public perceptions of affordable housing will be disappointed and may even backfire.[75]

To guard against this risk, the affordable housing movement should strive to make affordable housing PPPs as efficient and politically accountable as possible, given the public goals.[76] For example, the Corporation for Supportive Housing has addressed this issue head-on with several evaluative studies demonstrating supportive housing's relative economic efficiency to other housing and treatment options for homeless people.[77] There are signs that the leadership of the affordable housing movement is concerned about this problem.[78] And national intermediaries supporting affordable housing development, such as the Local Initiatives Support Corporation, regularly contribute to this work.[79] Ultimately, this may require

---

75 For example, the LIHTC program would be a politically vulnerable type of PPP. Ironically, the LIHTC program, which was heralded as a market-oriented reform to our national housing policy, is probably the least efficient means of subsidizing housing because of its high transaction costs. *See, e.g.*, Sagit Leviner, *Affordable Housing and the Role of the Low Income Housing Tax Credit Program: A Contemporary Assessment*, 57 Tax Law. 869, 878—81 (2004). However, despite the fact of its well-documented economic inefficiency, the LIHTC program consistently garners broad and powerful political support. This result may be explained by the fact that those transaction costs represent income for lawyers, bankers, and accountants, all traditionally politically powerful groups.

76 Professor Davidson's article, *Relational Contracts*, *supra* note 2, addresses the inherent difficulty in this task.

77 *See* Corporation for Supportive Housing (CSH), Research and Evaluation: Using Evidence to Advance Systems Page, http://www.csh.org/index.cfm?fuseaction=page.view Page&pageID=3749&nodeID=81 (last visited May 6, 2008).

78 In the "Chair's Message" introducing the Spring 2000 issue of the *Journal of Affordable Housing and Community Development Law*, Angela Christy expresses concerns about: the lack of cooperation and coordination among a multitude of players in affordable housing transactions; that deals are unnecessarily complex and expensive; growing conflicts between developers and governmental entities (for example, regarding supportive housing); and an adversarial approach between HUD and private partners leading to increased litigation. She then calls for needed reforms. And she offers the Interagency Stabilization Group that the Twin Cities created as an example of good collaboration.

79 *See, e.g.*, Local Initiatives Support Corporation (LISC), Organizational and Professional Development Programs, http://www.lisc.org/section/areas/sec5 (last visited January 12, 2008). U.S. Department of Housing and Urban Development, *Building Public-private Partnerships to Develop Affordable Housing*, 1583 HUD Community Planning and Development (May 1996), *available at* http://www.ezrc.hud.gov/offices/cpd/affordablehousing/library/modelguides/1583.cfm. Working under HUD contract, four national technical assistance providers—The Enterprise Foundation, The National Development Council, The Local Initiatives Support Corporation and The Community Builders—worked to create "local affordable housing partnerships, supporting strategic planning for affordable housing, increasing the production and availability of suitable, affordable housing and improving the capacity of community-based development

developing a more sophisticated definition and analysis of "efficiency" that accounts for what might be called the "double-bottom line" of these programs serving both private and public goals.[80]

Just as affordable housing PPPs open up the potential for broader and deeper conversations about the relative roles of government and the market in affordable housing production, the dialogue could get caught up in "market fundamentalism"—the view that *a priori* always and everywhere markets are better than government.[81] Some free-market promoters want to use PPP as a means/rhetorical device to criticize government, for example, PPP as merely a form of privatization.[82] This definition of PPPs limits their goals to "private" ones, excluding *public* values and goals served by PPPs. It makes affordable housing PPPs a part of a wholesale privatization policy rather than an alternative to wholesale deregulation. This chapter articulated the counter argument. To manage this risk, the affordable housing movement must engage vigorously in the public conversation defining the meaning and purpose of PPPs to include achieving both private and public goals. At the same time, the affordable housing movement must be open to deregulation where it makes sense, for example, in reducing zoning and planning restrictions imposed by local governments on market-affordable housing types (for example, manufactured housing and secondary units).[83]

Finally, there is another risk overshadowing any optimistic scenario. In order for the affordable housing movement to take advantage of these opportunities, there will need to be some substantial unity in its response to them. PPPs in affordable housing development challenge affordable housing advocates to agree on what it is they are seeking in PPPs, but as discussed above, the term "PPP" is

---

organizations (CHDOs) to develop affordable housing and participate in local partnerships." *Id.*

80 *See* Byrne and Diamond, *Matrix Revealed*, *supra* note 8 at 612 (calling for more research and analysis concerning the "efficiency" of affordable housing programs); and *see* Davidson, *Relational Contracting*, *supra* note 2.

81 *See, e.g.*, Fred Block, *Reframing the Political Battle: Market Fundamentalism vs. Moral Economy*, http://www.longviewinstitute.org/projects/moral/sorcerersapprentice (last visited January 12, 2008).

82 In defining "privatization," E.S. Savas, a prominent privatization advocate, writes:

> The term "public-private partnership" is particularly malleable as a form of privatization. It is defined broadly as an arrangement in which a government and a private entity, for-profit or non-profit, jointly perform or undertake a traditionally public activity … Despite its ambiguity, "public-private partnership" is sometimes a useful phrase because it avoids the inflammatory rhetoric of "privatization" on those ideologically opposed.

E.S. Savas, Privatization and Public-Private Partnerships, http://www.cesmadrid.es/documentos/Sem200601_MD02_IN.pdf (last visited May 5, 2008).

83 *See* Tim Iglesias, *State and Local Regulation of Particular Types of Affordable Housing*, *in* The Legal Guide to Affordable Housing Development (Tim Iglesias & Rochelle E. Lento eds., 2005).

ambiguous. Affordable housing development through PPPs poses many difficult issues to the diverse and sometimes divided affordable housing movement.[84] What definition(s) of "public–private partnership" should it advocate? What public goals for PPP collaborations should it pursue and with what partners? Which regulatory strategies and subsidy programs should it promote?[85] What types of developments (homeownership or rental, mixed use or single use, mixed income or 100 percent affordable) should be prioritized? What should be the role of the local community in which a new development will be sited?

Overall, in the author's estimation, the potential opportunities offered by PPPs for affordable housing development make the risks worth taking. To date, the affordable housing movement has proven relatively adept at conceiving, initiating, and implementing PPPs. While some advocates are skeptical of PPPs (or at least specific PPPs),[86] many have embraced them.[87] The challenge will be to identify through practice which PPPs most effectively promote affordable

84 "'Public-Private Partnerships' has become a popular buzzword over the past two decades. Whether they are successful, who pays, and who benefits have been the subject of considerable debate." W. Dennis Keating, *Encouraging Middle-Class Homeownership in NYC*, Shelterforce Magazine, July/August 1998 Reviews (book review of Charles J. Orlebecke, New Life at Ground Zero: New York, Homeownership, and the Future of American Cities (The Rockefeller Institute Press 1997)).

85 One particularly intriguing possibility is whether affordable housing produced pursuant to inclusionary zoning ordinances which include regulatory relief and/or subsidy can be appropriately characterized as "public–private partnerships." The author will address this possibility in future scholarship. Inclusionary zoning ordinances are typically enacted by local governments. For more information, *see Inclusionary Zoning: The California Experience*, 3(1) NHC Affordable Housing Policy Review (National Housing Conference, Washington, D.C.), February 2004, *available at* http://www.nhc.org/pdf/pub_ahp_02_04.pdf.

86 Mitch Kahn, *Paradise Lost*, 138 Shelterforce Magazine, November/December 2004 (book review of J.S. Fuerst, When Public Housing Was Paradise: Building Community in Chicago (University of Illinois Press 2004)) (arguing that when PPPs work they do so because they are following the same policies that a properly run government housing project would); "Housing advocates have long questioned the efficacy of paying for-profit developers to operate low-income housing [under the federal Section 8 program] …" Rachel G. Bratt, *A Withering Commitment*, Shelterforce Magazine, July/August 1997; Norman Krumholz, *The Reluctant Hand: Privatization of Public Housing in the U.S.* (criticizing the HOPE VI program), http://www.uic.edu/cuppa/cityfutures/papers/webpapers/cityfuturespapers/session1_4/1_4reluctanthand.pdf (last visited January 12, 2008); *Letters, The Myth of the Double Bottom Line*, 127 Shelterforce Magazine, January/February 2003, *available at* http://www.nhi.org/online/issues/127/letters.html. *See also* criticisms of the LIHTC program, including for its inefficient use of public funds, *supra* note 75.

87 "The consistent leadership of local elected officials in support of public/private partnerships and system building make Santa Fe a model for other cities trying to respond to seemingly intractable housing needs." Peter Werwath, *Words into Action: A New Housing*

housing and then to unite around advocating for those forms[88] while maintaining the historically favored form of PPPs in affordable housing development—direct government subsidies.

Acknowledgements

I am grateful to Robin Malloy and Nestor Davidson for organizing an intellectually stimulating and community-creating conference and for inviting me to attend. I also appreciated the many insightful comments I received from Nestor Davidson and other conference participants.

Delivery System for Santa Fe, SHELTERFORCE MAGAZINE, March/April 1996, *available at* http://www.nhi.org/pdf/EnterpriseRelease1106.pdf.

88 Drawing on the lessons of these cases, and from previous research, [the National Housing Institute] outlines steps the federal government can and should take to create effective partnerships with state and local governments and the thousands of community-based organizations (CBOs) dedicated to saving affordable housing and rebuilding the communities in which low- and moderate-income Americans live. By studying these successful partnerships, NHI aims to help guide future efforts to save affordable housing.

National Housing Institute, Shelterforce Online, *Saving Affordable Housing: Introduction*, http://www.nhi.org/ online/issues/90/intro.html (last visited January 12, 2008).

Chapter 3
The Value of Lawyering in Affordable Housing Transactions

Nestor M. Davidson

Introduction

Affordable housing can be many things to many people—a fundamental right, a critical source of shelter, a contested locus of community. But we tend not to think about affordable housing as much in one of its most pragmatic aspects, as a realm of dealmaking. Yet with the government relying increasingly on private developers and investors, non-profit entities, and others, affordable housing has become a realm of complex public–private transactions that often involve sophisticated structuring with myriad layers of subsidies for new construction and preservation. As a result, much of housing policy now takes shape in the interstices of financing documents, partnership agreements, long-term undertakings, and other tools of sophisticated transactional practice.

Focusing on this public–private transactional dynamic brings to the fore the central—and largely unheralded—role that deal lawyers play in affordable housing. This role is poorly understood, despite a significant literature that scholars have developed to examine private-sector transactional lawyering. Beginning with the work of Ronald Gilson 25 years ago,[1] scholars have argued that business lawyers have the potential in conventional transactions to increase the value of deals by structuring to respond to a variety of common transaction costs.[2] As Gilson phrased it, lawyers have unique potential to "make the [deal] pie grow larger rather than merely to help to carve it up."[3]

Although deal lawyers in public–private housing transactions can transaction-cost engineer in the sense Gilson identified, lawyers also have the potential to add "value" in a very different sense of the word. Housing lawyers can add value as well through deal structuring that responds to the public policy goals that the private sector has been engaged to advance. Housing lawyers thus approach deals

1 *See* Ronald J. Gilson, *Value Creation by Business Lawyers: Legal Skills and Asset Pricing*, 94 YALE L.J. 239, 241 (1984). For an overview of the development of the transactional value-creation literature, *see* Nestor M. Davidson, *Values and Value Creation in Public-Private Transactions*, 94 IOWA L. REV. 937, 945–51 (2009).

2 Gilson, *supra* note 1, at 255.

3 *Id.* at 308.

through a double lens, engineering transactions to balance traditional economic value creation with public policy goals that cannot easily be captured in pure economic terms—transactional objectives that respond as much to market *failure* as to market requirements. In short, housing lawyers can add value in no small part through the difficult task of translating their clients' and the government's policy goals into the practical mechanisms of private ordering.[4]

This chapter explores this policy translation function for housing deal lawyers, arguing that understanding this role can help guide the work of policymakers, housing program participants, and housing lawyers themselves. Accordingly, the chapter first outlines the public–private transactional aspects of affordable housing, discussing how such deals vary from their more private-sector-oriented counterparts. It then reviews the literature on value creation in transactional law, including an emerging emphasis on the role of lawyers in managing regulatory constraints. Finally, building on this framework for evaluating lawyering in housing deals, the chapter explores consequences that might flow from better recognizing this unique type of value creation.

Public–Private Partnerships in Affordable Housing

Public–private partnerships have long been deployed to deliver an array of public services,[5] particularly in the social-services arena.[6] This trend has deep roots and is increasingly marking affordable housing policy. Providing housing for people in need has long been the responsibility of an amalgam of private-sector forces and public initiatives, but has come to be increasingly dominated by programs that seek to leverage private-sector resources and expertise for public goals.

Engaging the private sector in the provision of public services has generated some measure of controversy. Skeptics raise concerns about democratic accountability, inherent conflicts of interest undermining the quality of the services provided, competition undermining the public sector, and a weakening of the rule of law. On the other side, proponents tout private-sector involvement for the potential it

---

4 Although this chapter focuses on the role of private-sector attorneys in housing transactions, public-sector attorneys also play an important role in public–private partnerships. Moreover, although this chapter examines the work of deal lawyers in public–private housing transactions, this is not to minimize the important work that lawyers perform in a variety of other related roles, including community organizing and grassroots advocacy. *See, e.g.*, Ann Southworth, *Business Planning for the Destitute? Lawyers as Facilitators in Civil Rights and Poverty Practices*, 1996 Wis. L. Rev. 1121.

5 Public–private partnerships cover a variety of relationships. *See* United States General Accounting Office, Public-Private Partnerships: Terms Relating to Building and Facility Partnerships 1 (1999). Unlike public contracting, in public–private partnerships the recipient of the relevant good or service is the public, not the government.

6 *See* Lester M. Salamon, Partners in Public Service: Government-Nonprofit Relations in the Modern Welfare State (1995).

carries to enhance the efficiency of public services and the advantages of drawing on the experience of a greater variety of service providers.[7] Whatever the merits of these arguments, it is undeniable that the government is increasingly drawing upon the private sector to deliver public services. For a variety of reasons, this has been a less contentious development in the affordable housing arena than in many other areas of service provision. This is not to accept uncritically all aspects of public–private partnerships in housing or in other areas, but recognizing their ascendancy does provide an opportunity to focus the discourse on how to maximize their potential and the appropriate institutional structures through which to do so.[8]

With recognition of the limitations of public–private partnerships, then, it is possible to map out how such partnerships typically arise in affordable housing.[9] In housing partnerships, the private sector develops, owns, and operates the housing, but some or all of the financing is public. On the supply side, then, federal, state, and local governments engage private developers, lenders, equity investors, and others to create and operate housing that is affordable at below-market-rate rents or for sale on an income-restricted basis. On the demand side, subsidies typically come through rental vouchers and supply- and demand-side programs often work in tandem.[10] Subsidies can take the form of grants or loans, waivers of fee requirements, and other soft subsidies, or, increasingly, indirect subsidy through tax credits for equity investors in Low Income Housing Tax Credit transactions.[11]

---

7 *See* Nestor M. Davidson, *Relational Contracts in the Privatization of Social Welfare: The Case of Housing*, 24 Yale L. & Pol'y Rev. 263, 269–76 (2006).

8 Scott Cummings has argued that lawyering in programs that ameliorate conditions that might generate demand for broader social change carries the potential to undermine the very causes such lawyering seeks to serve. *See* Scott L. Cummings, *Community Economic Development as Progressive Politics: Toward a Grassroots Movement for Economic Justice*, 54 Stan. L. Rev. 399 (2001). This is a valid concern, but in the context of affordable housing, fundamental change—such as a universal entitlement to a minimum level of housing—seems unlikely. Given that, and given the fact that governmental entities are increasingly turning to public–private partnerships in housing, this chapter asks how best to understand the role of the lawyer in that context.

9 *Cf.* Tim Iglesias, *Our Pluralist Housing Ethics and the Struggle for Affordability*, 42 Wake Forest L. Rev. 511, 589 (2007).

10 Single-family housing, particularly for-sale housing, also forms part of affordable housing policy, but given that this sector of the market is untenable for many of those served by core affordable housing programs, this chapter focuses primarily on multifamily rental housing.

11 For good overviews of various subsidy mechanisms, *see* The Legal Guide to Affordable Housing Development (Tim Iglesias & Rochelle E. Lento, eds, 2005), particularly Chapter 7 (Rochelle E. Lento, *Federal Sources of Financing*), Chapter 8 (Peter Salsich, *State Sources of Housing Finance*), and Chapter 9 (Rick Judd & Barbara E. Kautz, *Local Government Financing Powers and Sources of Funding*). The newest source of federal funding is the recently enacted National Housing Trust Fund, which will provide an opportunity for new models of public–private partnerships. For details, *see* Peter W. Salsich, Jr., *The National Housing Trust Fund: A Challenge and an Opportunity for Creative Public-Private Partnerships*, *infra* Chapter 5.

Another model of public–private partnership in affordable housing, expansively understood (and more controversial), involves housing and other public benefits provided by developers and others in exchange for favorable regulatory treatment. This can arise from inclusionary zoning or project-specific agreements, and has become a central part of urban redevelopment and large-scale development of any kind in many communities.

Housing deals often require layers of subsidy, particularly in projects that serve very low and extremely low income residents. Each subsidy stream carries particular requirements for structure, residents, affordability periods, and other variables. Each subsidy also involves a particular set of generally detailed regulations and related requirements. The more subsidy layers a project requires—and the more public and private entities involved—the more legal coordination becomes critical.

In terms of orientation to the public goals at issue, private entities—both for-profit and non-profit—that get involved in this sector of the affordable housing market run the gamut from relatively disinterested to deeply committed. An example at one end can be found with certain Low Income Housing Tax Credit investors who participate purely for the economics (a one-for-one tax credit), whose concern with program goals largely revolves around compliance. At the other end of the spectrum are the myriad of non-profit housing providers whose mission is to provide affordable housing and often related services. These entities include everything from the smallest community-based church group with a few units to the kinds of sophisticated national non-profit entities managing portfolios in the thousands of units that have emerged in the past two decades. For all of these entities—even largely indifferent investors—the "deal" involves more than simply the economics and the threshold decision to participate in any public–private partnership reflects at least some understanding of the public goals involved.

Another notable feature of public–private partnerships in affordable housing is the role of the public as the recipient of the mix of goods and services that below-market rate renting represents. Many transactions that do not directly involve consumers take place with cognizance of the ultimate consumer served by those transactions. In public–private partnerships, however, the public nature of the final "product" tends to bring a range of stakeholders to the table and involve political considerations that can be more muted in purely private transactions. These stakeholders and considerations in turn shape the expectations and risk profiles of the participants.

From the government's perspective, the fact that housing is a relatively durable asset changes the nature of the public–private relationship. When a public subsidy incentivizes the private sector to generate affordable housing or to convert a housing asset that was serving market-rate tenants, the time-horizon of the public commitment can often be measured in decades, if not longer. This can be true of other public–private partnerships involving hard assets, but is generally less true compared to other areas of social welfare. This extended public commitment, which has proven controversial for private providers at times,[12] creates incentives and practical problems that intertwine the government and the private sector into long-term, ongoing interactions that have to be understood—and accounted for in deal structuring—from the outset.

Models of Deal Lawyering

If affordable housing is increasingly the realm of transactional law, how can we best understand what lawyers do in such transactions? Generally speaking, lawyers often stand at the center of many significant commercial transactions. Deal lawyers serve a range of practical roles that include business and legal negotiator, document drafter, information gatherer, coordinator, and legal counselor. In all of these capacities, it is fair to ask whether—and how—lawyers benefit the transaction and why other professionals (or clients themselves) could not as easily or more efficiently perform the same, often quite costly, tasks.

In attempting to answer these questions, Ronald Gilson's framework is a useful starting point.[13] Gilson began with the proposition that in the absence of transaction costs, parties would reach agreement—would price the asset that is the subject of a deal and, by extension, the other material terms of the transaction—with perfect information.[14] In this transactional environment, there would be no need for lawyers or any other third-party intermediaries. In the real world, of course, transaction costs are pervasive, with parties having different time-horizons and expectations about the future, as well as significantly different information

12 A notable area of policy development and litigation involves the problem of time-limited affordability requirements. Many housing programs make an explicit bargain with the private sector: utilize public subsidies to develop housing that will be below market for a period of time—30 years, for example, in many Low Income Housing Tax Credit transactions—at which point you will be able to take that building to market-rate housing. Congress and HUD have attempted in a variety of ways to mitigate the impact of this initial bargain (with owners resisting some of these attempts), and ever-longer affordability periods are becoming common, but this remains a controversial aspect of contemporary housing policy.

13 The economic orientation of much of the value-creation literature can limit the breadth of its insights, as Mark Suchman has argued. *See* Mark C. Suchman, *Translation Costs: A Comment on Sociology and Economics*, 74 Or. L. Rev. 257 (1995) (discussing cultural norms, power relations, and developmental dynamics as alternative explanatory inputs into business lawyering absent from economic accounts). Nonetheless, the framework that Gilson and his successors have laid out is valuable in considering the work of housing lawyers.

14 Gilson derived this transaction-cost-free baseline from the financing concept of the Capital Asset Pricing Model, which presumes that capital assets will be priced based on market forces, a world that would make the cost of any third-party intermediary a loss to the transacting parties. *See* Gilson, *supra* note 1, at 251.

about all of the inputs to the transaction and ability and incentives to gather that information. To these barriers, Robert Mnookin and others have added the reality that parties can behave irrationally in negotiating and tend to bring incentives to any transaction to act strategically, undermining the potential for mutual gain.[15]

It is in the gap between the unreal assumption of perfect transacting by rationally acting parties and the transaction-cost-filled world of imperfect information and strategic behavior that lawyers have the potential to add value. Business lawyers, in Gilson's term, serve as "transaction-cost engineers," devising mechanisms through which market imperfections—primarily heterogeneous expectations and information costs—can be unearthed and structured around.[16] Lawyer-facilitated cooperative bargaining can thus create more valuable transactions by recognizing that solving transactional failures saves deals that would otherwise collapse, lowers the overall cost of a deal, and shifts the focus of negotiations away from potentially destructive distributional bargaining that engenders mistrust and opportunism.[17]

Recently, scholars have begun to add a new dimension to this picture of lawyers as transaction-cost engineers. Gilson dismissed the potential for value creation from what he described as "manipulation of a regulatory system,"[18] arguing that most business lawyers operate "in a world in which regulation has made few inroads," and thus where the "critical rule of law is that a court will enforce whatever the lawyer writes."[19] In the modern transactional world, however, managing regulatory constraints may be as important, if not more important, to the

---

15 *See* Robert H. Mnookin, Scott R. Peppet & Andrew S. Tulumello, Beyond Winning: Negotiating to Create Value in Deals and Disputes 127–55 (2000); Ronald J. Gilson & Robert H. Mnookin, *Foreword: Business Lawyers and Value Creation for Clients*, 74 Or. L. Rev. 1, 10–13 (1995) (reviewing strategic behavior and psychological barriers to transacting).

16 Gilson, *supra* note 1, at 255.

17 There is an important empirical question that suggests a note of caution in taking too rosy a view of Gilson's description of value creation, namely the *relative* value to a client of the gains from value-creating lawyering versus the distributional consequences to that client from participating in the kind of cooperative behavior that Gilson highlights. *Cf.* Edward A. Bernstein, *Law & Economics and the Structure of Value Adding Contracts: A Contract Lawyer's View of the Law & Economics Literature*, 74 Or. L. Rev. 189, 195 (1995) (practicing lawyers "who are properly concerned only with the well being of their clients, frequently fail to understand that a reduction in joint costs can benefit their client perhaps because, in practice, many actions that increase the value of a transaction as a whole decrease the value of a transaction to one of the parties"). In other words, if the increase in the size of the pie yields less than the benefits to keeping a larger slice of a smaller pie, then a client has every incentive to act strategically or otherwise add to total costs—short of killing a deal—to capture that relative advantage.

18 Gilson, *supra* note 1, at 244.

19 *See id.* at 247. Edward Bernstein has challenged the assumption of costless enforcement, *see* Bernstein, *supra* note 17, noting that "legal system" costs are themselves pervasive.

value lawyers can create than non-regulatory transaction costs.[20] The paradigm of the private client largely indifferent to regulation is now more of the exception than the rule, if it ever was predominant. And in that regulatory world, even the most seemingly mundane private transaction takes place under regulatory constraints with potential regulatory consequences.

David Schizer, for example, has identified what he describes in the tax-planning context as "frictions," constraints on transactional structure that derive from accounting rules, securities regulation, and other legal regimes.[21] Schizer argues that tax planners are more or less successful in working around targeted tax laws, depending in no small measure on the effect of these non-tax legal constraints. Victor Fleischer has argued more broadly that lawyers engage in what he calls "regulatory cost engineering," where lawyers "driv[e] a wedge between the economics of a deal and its treatment for legal or regulatory purposes."[22] Fleischer acknowledges that this descriptive claim raises potentially significant normative implications, as regulatory cost engineering can potentially pit private benefit against social cost.[23]

Operating in regulation-influenced transactional contexts can create a tension, moreover, for lawyers between what David Dana has identified as a "client-service" model of lawyering as opposed to a "public-service" model. The former focuses on zealous advocacy of a client's goals above all else, while the latter emphasizes the lawyer's role as agent of a legal system whose ends may transcend—or conflict—with their client's interests.[24] Taking the realm of environmental compliance as an example, Dana argued that for lawyers drawn to the public service model, a number of forces conspire to give primacy to client service over the often vague and complex demands of any modern regulatory system.

This is a sobering cautionary note for lawyers serving the private sector, and a marker for what might be different when client interests and the public interest are more closely aligned, as we shall see. Despite this appropriate concern,

20 Victor Fleischer has pioneered the shift in the transactional-value literature towards understanding the increasing importance of regulatory constraints. *See, e.g.*, Victor Fleischer, *The MasterCard IPO: Protecting the Priceless Brand*, 12 Harv. Neg. L. Rev. 137 (2007); *see also* Steven Schwarcz, *Explaining the Value of Transactional Lawyering*, 12 Stan. J.L. Bus. & Fin. 486, 492–3 & n.36 (2007) (discussing Fleischer's conception of regulatory cost engineering).

21 *See* David M. Schizer, *Frictions as a Constraint on Tax Planning*, 101 Colum. L. Rev. 1312 (2001).

22 Fleischer, *supra* note 20, at 138. Fleischer gives the example of the MasterCard initial public offering, which was structured to include "reverse" dual-class voting that reduced formal voting control for member banks (while retaining an effective veto). This structure, Fleischer argues, flipped the usual pattern of insider control in dual-class voting, but did so to reduce the member banks' antitrust exposure. *Id.* at 150.

23 *Id.* at 155.

24 *See* David Dana, *Environmental Lawyers and the Public Service Model of Lawyering*, 74 Or. L. Rev. 57 (1995).

however, transaction-cost and regulatory-cost engineering perspectives ultimately suggest a salutary role for transactional attorneys, overcoming barriers that clients may not understand or appreciate to maximize the value of mutually beneficial exchange.[25]

Regulatory Translation in Affordable Housing

Given the complexity of transactions in the context of public–private housing partnerships and the unusual nature of the client, the range of responsibilities—and the concomitant potential for adding value—of the housing deal lawyer is different in important ways from what is required of their more purely private-sector-oriented counterparts. Attorneys in this setting add value not just by transaction-cost and regulatory-cost engineering, but also by serving as the critical bridge between the government and the private sector. The "value" a transactional lawyer can create in these kinds of public–private transactions thus goes beyond managing the kinds of primarily information-cost-related barriers that Gilson identified or responding to the kinds of regulatory constraints that Fleischer noted. Lawyers in this context are instead undertaking what can be called "regulatory translation."[26]

Private lawyers come to this task with a variety of tools to translate policy goals—both abstract and concrete—into the terms of private agreement: risk allocation, information management, and the basic structures of reciprocal obligation over time. These tools allow solutions to a different kind of information-cost failure than found in the private sector, namely the inevitable informational challenges that the government engenders by engaging the private sector in public programs. If transaction-cost engineering is an exercise in moving deals closer to hypothetical perfect market conditions, then changing the predicate assumption from a perfect market benchmark to a benchmark shaped in many ways by public responses to market failure correspondingly changes the role of the lawyer in adding value. The mechanics of the task may be similar, with lawyers identifying opportunities and challenges from the differential information and expectations of the parties, but those differences are endemic to the different sectors, public and private, from which the partners approach any transaction.

---

25 It is important to note that the paradigm of value creation from transaction-cost engineering may underestimate the "value" that can arise from transaction costs themselves, as David Driesen and Shubha Ghosh have noted. *See* David M. Driesen & Shubha Ghosh, *The Functions of Transaction Costs: Rethinking Transaction Cost Minimization in a World of Friction*, 47 Ariz. L. Rev. 61, 88 (2005). To identify the potential for value creation generically from reducing transaction costs should not, accordingly, minimize the value of friction itself.

26 For further discussion of the nature of regulatory translation, *see* Davidson, *supra* note 1.

In translating public-policy goals into the ordinary, if important, matrix of contractual language, transactional lawyers in affordable housing deals have to capture values that may be non-commodifiable or that might run counter to what would otherwise inform the market price of the asset. Policy goals include not just providing safe and decent below-market-rate shelter, which would be challenging enough, but also giving residents voice and stability, providing a locus for other social services, creating economic opportunity, and mitigating the impacts of the concentration of poverty, among others.

In affordable housing, conflicts between private incentives and public goals are inevitable, as in any transactional environment. However, just as lawyers can engineer private transactions to recognize such conflicts and create mechanisms to add value in solving them, transactional lawyers in housing can add value by clearly anticipating such conflicts and structuring the framework of the parties' interaction to emphasize the alignment of interests over points of conflict. Gilson called this cooperative bargaining, and the potential for similar structuring in public–private partnerships is even more pervasive.

The presence of public subsidies, moreover, alters private parties' risk profiles. Risk is inevitable in any deal, and will be factored into return in a well-structured transaction. Many elements of typical housing programs, however, are designed to minimize the risk of failure and maximize the long-term stability of the public benefit. Unlike private-sector actors in market transactions, then, the public investment in this context means that certain risks become less acceptable or must be managed differently than in purely private transactions. Deal lawyers must accordingly translate that fact into mechanisms for ensuring the long-term viability of a project and, ideally, long-term commitment on the part of the government to support that viability.

Ultimately, because public–private partnerships are designed to benefit not the direct parties involved but rather those members of the public who will live in the housing produced or preserved, those interests become entwined in the latitude given to private providers.[27] This has two primary consequences. Political considerations become unavoidable, although deals can be structured to moderate the impact that such considerations might have. This is not to argue that political considerations are inherently illegitimate or inappropriate to factor into the implementation of public programs. There are positive and negative aspects to factoring in public participation and it is hard in many situations to separate beneficial involvement from naked rent seeking. The practical problem, however, is how to translate the potential for policy changes into a long-term set of mutual obligations. Conversely, accountability on the part of the provider is equally fundamental.

---

27 *Cf.* Robin Paul Malloy, Law in a Market Context: An Introduction to Market Concepts in Legal Reasoning 220 (2004) (discussing agency costs that arise when non-profit entities provide public goods and service, notably the conflicts that arise when organizational intermediaries filter choices that clients might otherwise make directly).

More immediately, the interests of the members of the public to be served are appropriately a constant factor to be considered. Agencies have tried a variety of methods to ensure meaningful participation, including tenant rights and subsidies for tenant organizations, among others. Tenant involvement remains, however, an aspect of transactional practice that often lingers primarily in the background. These challenges play out in the ordinary language of the deal documents that frame housing deals.

It is difficult to quantify the "value" in a broad sense that transactional lawyers add in regulatory translation. Gilson, for his part, pointed out that evidence of value creation is discernible in deal documents. Gilson thus highlighted a number of examples in a typical asset-purchase agreement that demonstrated how lawyers in practice engineer transaction costs, citing earnout provisions, representations, warranties, indemnifications, and legal opinions as tools to manage expectations and informational and other costs.[28]

Similarly, one can see evidence of regulatory translation in some of the more common provisions of typical affordable housing transactions. These provisions involve translating what can often be difficult, and in the context of multiple subsidy streams, conflicting regulatory requirements into obligations that are understandable and that can be framed in terms of the allocation of risks between the parties. To give one example, in Low Income Housing Tax Credit transactions, it is typical to see elaborate provisions for payments to investors in the case of "recapture" or similar adverse tax events, given that investors are generally subject to a 15-year window of tax-credit recapture risk. These provisions manage the differential horizon and incentives facing tax credit investors—often passive entities with little interest in actively intervening over the life of a project—and tax credit developers and owners.

For non-profit developers, moreover, the IRS has suggested constraints on their ability to offer strong indemnities to for-profit investors, even in the service of the accepted charitable mission of providing affordable housing. One common resulting structure caps the exposure to the non-profit developer to the economic value coming out of the deal. This gives investors some protection—and aligns the interests of the developer and investor over the period of risk—while protecting the ongoing viability of the non-profit. This kind of creative structure bears a family resemblance to the kinds of structures that Gilson highlighted as solving heterogeneous-expectation problems in private transactions, but deal lawyers in the housing context must mold those solutions to the realities of the programs at issue.

Such transactional engineering in the face of programmatic and policy constraints is pervasive: housing transactions often include provisions that cover third-party rights, primarily for tenants; that require notification of the government and governmental approval at key turning points in the life of a project or reserve regulatory authority to the government; or that impose relatively open-ended

28 *See generally* Gilson, *supra* note 1, at Part III.

"quality" standards on the housing.[29] Third-party rights can be understood as mechanisms to define the obligations of private owners and landlords in a way that balances their expectations with the need for tenant security. Oversight mechanisms similarly balance private flexibility with the need to protect the core public benefit at issue, both in terms of preserving affordability but also in terms of preserving the physical asset itself. And quality or similar open-ended obligations on the nature of management recognize the risk of opportunism at the same time as acknowledging the challenge of specifying with any level of detail the variety and complexity of obligations this can entail.

This by no means exhausts the universe of provisions distinctive to housing deals that frame the terms of engagement for long-term public–private interactions, but does give a sampling of regulatory translation in action. Each of these typical provisions in the end represents a solution to a potential barrier to the various interests involved, public and private, reaching a mutually beneficial outcome. Because lawyers are capable of rendering these interests in the terms of agreement, even with provisions that are at times open ended, deals are created and made more "valuable" in the broadest sense of the word.

Housing Lawyering in a New Light

Gilson noted that lawyers are often seen as more of a hindrance than a help to deals—at worst, "deal killers whose continual raising of obstacles … ultimately causes transactions to collapse under their own weight."[30] If, as many clients assume, lawyers are true transaction costs, then their use may be hard to justify and even more so in transactions that involve scarce public resources. Anecdotally, critiques of transactional lawyering as adding unjustified costs ring as true, if not more so, for clients in affordable housing, especially where transactions exist on narrow margins and subsidies are perennially limited.

However, where deal lawyers add value through engineering deals to translate regulatory complexity, there is concomitant value in doing so self-consciously. Gilson noted the competition that lawyers face from other potential market participants, as there is nothing traditional or inherently "legal" about the type of transaction-cost engineering that he identified.[31] By contrast, where lawyers are operating in transactional environments shaped by regulatory goals, such as public–private housing deals, Gilson's comparison has less force. Because the involvement of the government is expressed through complex legal requirements, with public entities setting the terms of private transacting, there is no escaping the centrality of lawyers to what in other contexts would tend to be non-legal aspects

29 *See* Davidson, *supra* note 7, at 288–93 (discussing contractual provisions in affordable housing transactions).

30 Gilson, *supra* note 1, at 242.

31 *See id.* at 295.

of a transaction. In this way, lawyers are not just leveraging their unique capability to understand and render comprehensible the mass of governmental constraints attached to most subsidies (as much as can be done) to take on additional tasks as drafters or negotiators or the like; they are instead adding value by operating simultaneously in the world of private transactional structures and public policies expressed through regulatory language.

Housing lawyers can also add value by leveraging the experience of working on one challenging regulation-driven transaction to other such transactions. It is hardly cost effective for most participants in the housing arena—a policy area that often involves the long-term management of significant hard assets—to invest in the information necessary to understand evolving regulatory requirements that affect only a fraction of their portfolio or that represent only a marginal risk. Housing lawyers, by contrast, can and do develop expertise, the costs of which can be spread across multiple clients.

Recognizing this market niche, however, does not mean that housing lawyers should exploit that advantage to capture more value from a transaction than they add or than other potential participants might more efficiently provide. If a client or a less costly third-party professional can more efficiently play a role that deal lawyers now do, it is incumbent upon deal lawyers to cede that role—not out of some altruistic regard for their clients (although that should not be dismissed), but rather because the overall value to clients—and to the public—can be increased by more targeted specialization.

One cultural aspect that marks transactional lawyering in affordable housing is that attorneys seem open to sharing knowledge, document forms, and experience working with the various agencies that fund housing. The members of the American Bar Association's listserv for affordable housing and community development law regularly engage in ongoing discussions of arcane regulatory questions and an ethos seems to prevail that is hard to imagine in, say, the world of structured finance or mergers and acquisitions.[32] Deal lawyers in this context share insights and provide detailed feedback on regulatory interpretation (and the extent to which such interpretation has been accepted by agencies and market participants).

One can speculate that this is because attorneys see reciprocal advantage to be gained by this exchange of knowledge, but it is at least possible that this ethos has developed because of an awareness among housing deal lawyers that there is an important aspect of their work that is much closer to David Dana's public service model than the kinds of conflicts Dana associated with the client service model in heavily regulated sectors of the economy. Dana argued that where regulatory constraints were clear and draconian, there would be no conflict between what

32 This is an anecdotal impression, to be sure, and cannot be proven empirically without study of comparative contexts. There are certainly a number of contexts in legal practice where lawyers offer each other continuing legal education, and regulatory and other legal knowledge is considered something of a common stock. Suffice it to say that deal lawyering in affordable housing does tend to foster a culture of mutual support.

client service and public service would demand of a lawyer. Dana rightly pointed out that this is rarely, if ever, the case.[33] But in public–private housing transactions, the potential for an alignment of interest between private goals and public policy seems much more achievable.

Understanding the value that transactional lawyers add to public–private transactions has implications for clients as well. This perspective can lead clients to develop in-house expertise where that is appropriate, as many players in the housing arena have done, but also to be less reluctant to engage attorneys when the necessity for regulatory translation is most acute. And given the potential to develop expertise that transcends any given client, housing providers can understand the potential for cost saving that such leveraging might provide.

One aspect of client attitudes toward deal lawyers in public–private partnerships may stem from the connection between the need for regulatory translation and the concomitant provision of that service by lawyers. In other words, law creates complications that lawyers conveniently step in to solve,[34] and in working to translate regulatory requirements for private clients, lawyers could be seen as shifting value from the private sector to the government and undermining public incentives for transparency and consistency. This concern is appropriate, but somewhat misplaced. Regulatory complexity is an inevitable cost of involvement in public–private partnerships and the question is how best to manage that complexity.

The rise of public–private partnerships also underscores that there are risks inherent in the professionalization of the affordable housing industry. As investors and developers move away from the kind of bottom-up responses that retain responsiveness to community and other intangibles, housing can become like any other commodity. Balancing this risk on the other side is the reality that public resources are scarce and professionalization may help stretch those resources in creative ways. Engaging the private sector also has the potential to increase the constituency invested in housing as a policy sphere.

Finally, if lawyers can structure deals to bring public goals in line with private incentives, the process can work the other way as well. Transactional lawyers can conversely structure deals to help the government achieve its goals through the language of private law in a way that can be hard for agencies steeped in policy to manage effectively. This is not to suggest that policymakers or government attorneys lack sophistication about their private counterparts, but rather that there is value to be added for the public by transactional attorneys who operate in both worlds.

Given that governments at all levels have found it in the public interest to engage the private sector in serving the public, facilitating the regulatory translation function of deal lawyering can yield significant benefits. The Department of Housing and Urban Development, for example, has attempted in recent years to

33 *See* Dana, *supra* note 24, at 59–60.

34 *Cf.* Gilson, *supra* note 1, at 246–7.

foster what former HUD General Counsel Keith Gottfried described as regulatory transparency in its dealings with the housing bar.[35] More can be done by all agencies involved in housing to make the implementation of public programs through the medium of private transactional law more efficient, whatever the content of the regulatory requirements the government finds necessary for the public interest.

Agencies in general can understand that public–private partnerships cannot simply involve the imposition of public goals on private participants, no matter how willing or enthusiastic those participants are. There are direct costs to regulatory complexity and those costs are not borne exclusively (or perhaps primarily) by the private entities that serve the public in these partnerships. Given the types of assets involved in the housing context, initial deal structures have long-term effects, which means that government entities no less than their private counterparts have to pay careful attention to asset management over time. It is through the obligations that lawyers craft to align long-term incentives and interests that the public interest is advanced.

Returning to the question of private deal-lawyer economies of scope, is it unlikely to be in the government's interest to have to undertake the work of matching general regulatory goals to the vast array of specifically situated private entities who will be engaged in advancing those goals. Translation by lawyers in the context of specific transactions—information that can be taken to scale by those lawyers—seems an appropriate intermediate solution.

In public–private housing partnerships, ultimately, both sides have to recognize the consequences of interrelating between two cultures. The world of public subsidies is grounded in budget cycles, public scrutiny, political risk, and changing policy priorities. Take the problem of appropriation risk. Often an important aspect of the financial viability of given development is a form of project-based rental subsidy. However, project-based Section 8 subsidies are typically limited by the proposition that Congress must appropriate funds for the subsidy on an annual basis. Congress has never failed to renew the subsidy, but the risk exists nonetheless that an important aspect of the financial viability of a project rests on political grounds. Lawyers manage this risk—again a question of heterogeneous information and expectation between public and private actors—by a variety of means, but the important point is that it does not in the end hold up transactions.

In sum, lawyers can add value in affordable housing deals by understanding and translating the goals of the private sector, the public sector, and the recipients of housing. This translation function melds law, finance, public policy, and culture—an amalgam that deal lawyers are uniquely situated to manage.

35 *See, e.g.*, Keith E. Gottfried, General Counsel, United States Department of Housing and Urban Development, Remarks at the National Settlement Services Summit (June 14, 2006) (discussing regulatory transparency).

Conclusion

The rise of public–private partnerships has brought transactional lawyers into a central role in affordable housing policy. We can, and should, continue to debate the appropriate program structures to best deliver critically needed affordable housing, all the more so in times of economic crisis. But given the centrality of public–private partnerships to contemporary affordable housing, it is critical to understand that many such partnerships take fundamental shape through transactional law.

Understanding the potential that housing lawyers have to translate complex regulatory regimes into the practical world of dealmaking can help such lawyers as well as their clients and the public sector that has engaged their clients to maximize the value of these partnerships in the broadest sense of the word. Just as lawyers in purely private transactions can recognize hidden barriers—and hidden opportunities for mutual gain—so too can lawyers in the public–private transactions at the heart of contemporary housing policy craft deal structures and the relationships that flow from these deal structures in ways that enhance the overall benefits of the transaction. At their best and most creative, this is just what we should be asking of housing lawyers, and just what they are capable of delivering.

Acknowledgements

The author wishes to thank participants in the 2007 *Workshop on Affordable Housing and Public–Private Partnerships* for helpful comments on this chapter. Portions of this chapter are adapted from *Values and Value Creation in Public-Private Transactions*, 94 Iowa L. Rev. 937 (2009), and appear with permission of the Iowa Law Review.

Chapter 4

Another Model of Low Income Housing Tax Credit Development: Building Housing and Building Capacity

Michael Diamond

This publication derives from a workshop whose theme was "Affordable Housing and Public–Private Partnerships: The Intersection of Housing, Property, and Real Estate." My particular concern at the workshop and in this chapter is the intersection of affordable housing, poverty and community. I am also interested in the ways in which law and lawyers have addressed and, in the future, might address these issues. As has been amply discussed over the years, poverty is the result of many factors and is composed of many elements.[1] Lawyers have long been prominent in the battle against poverty but the law itself has, inadvertently or not, been as much a cause as a cure for the problems of poverty. I believe that to combat poverty and to alleviate at least some of its insidious effects, lawyers must take a broader view of the nature of poverty and of their own role in the struggle to combat it.

I have focused on housing as a core element in poverty because housing is central to people's lives and affects many aspects of their existence beyond the mere provision of shelter.[2] Among these, housing creates the possibility of wealth creation, provides the situs for family and social life, affects one's sense of identity, health, and well-being, and has a major impact on educational prospects and attainment.[3] I have been interested in housing for all of these reasons, but my interest here is about the political possibilities of housing. By this I mean the opportunity housing offers to residents for organization, for capacity building, for participation in civic activities, and for social and political interaction.[4] These opportunities offer the potential to create and maintain community institutions that

---

1 Sheldon Danziger & Peter Gottschalk, America Unequal 92–110 (1995). The authors point to the shift towards single female headed households, a slow rate of economic growth between the 1970s to 1990s, and the slow rate of increase in the mean income level as significant factors of increased poverty.

2 J. Peter Byrne & Michael Diamond, Affordable Housing, Land Tenure and Urban Policy: The Matrix Revealed, 34 Fordham Urb. L.J. 527, 527–31 (2007) [hereinafter Byrne and Diamond, Matrix Revealed].

3 *Id.* at 527.

4 *Id.* at 574–80.

can acquire and wield power on an ongoing basis.[5] I believe that such institutions must be in the forefront of the struggle against poverty and subordination and are essential to the success of that struggle.

This view of housing as a central element in the struggle against poverty has motivated me over the years to explore the idea of preserving affordable housing for low income residents through tenant ownership of that housing. Through tenant ownership, the residents, both current and future occupants of the property, can control its destiny and therefore, in a not insignificant way, a part of their own. Through ownership of their building they can, to a degree, control costs, prioritize needs, select incoming co-owners, and, in the process, recognize and develop skills in themselves that may be transferred into other areas of their lives. Moreover, through their ownership, they may serve as symbols of what is possible and, in a more immediate sense, have an impact on the conditions in the community in which they reside.[6]

Of course, to make tenant ownership work requires support from many quarters including, not insignificantly, from the government, both on the local level and nationally. While many states and local jurisdictions actively support affordable housing and some support the idea of tenant ownership,[7] the federal government has been less supportive. In fact, the federal government is no longer in the business of producing affordable housing.[8] While the federal government used to produce significant numbers of public housing units, the public housing program had fallen into disuse in many areas and into disrepute in the public's consciousness. This withdrawal from the production arena has resulted, in part, in the severe shortage of adequate, affordable housing for low income families.

Instead of direct production, for several years now the federal government's housing policy on the supply side has been to encourage private enterprise to produce affordable housing.[9] One of the main aspects of this approach has been

5 *Id.* at 596–601.

6 Michael Diamond, *Community Economic Development: A Reflection on Community, Power and the Law*, 8 J. SMALL & EMERGING BUS. L. 151, 166–7 (2004).

7 *See, e.g.*, the Illinois Tenants Union, http://www.tenant.org/about.htm (last visited September 12, 2008); the National Alliance of HUD Tenants, http://www.saveourhomes.org (last visited September 12, 2008); and the Housing Crisis Center, http://www.hccdallas.org/index1.html (last visited September 12, 2008).

8 KENT W. COLTON, HOUSING IN THE TWENTY-FIRST CENTURY: ACHIEVING COMMON GROUND 220–21 (2003).

9 On the demand side, there are various subsidy programs, the most prominent of them, other than the income tax deductions for homeowners of mortgage interest and real estate taxes, being the Housing Choice Voucher program. This program was formerly known as the § 8 program. It subsidizes recipients by providing the difference between 30 percent of the recipient's income and the rent for an acceptable unit, so long as the rent does not exceed a federally set cap.

the Low Income Housing Tax Credit program (LIHTC).[10] Through this program more than 1.4 million units of low income housing have been built or renovated between 1987 and 2004.[11] Low income residents often benefit from this program by obtaining decent housing at affordable rents. Depending on the sponsor of a particular development, the residents might also have the opportunity to obtain various social services and amenities such as an after-school program or a computer lab. Rarely, however, do residents participate in the decision-making concerning the property and its operation. My goal in this chapter is to offer a model for giving residents significant involvement in every aspect of the development and operation of a tax credit property. I will argue that doing so is beneficial to all concerned. Moreover, while the context for the model is a tax credit development, I will argue that it is, in many ways, a usable model in several other situations.

In the first part of this chapter I will describe the tax credit regime and the typical tax credit ownership vehicle, a limited partnership comprised of investors as limited partners and a developer, either non-profit or for-profit, as the general partner. In the second part, I will present a different model for the ownership of the property in which the residents of a building that will undergo tax credit renovation participate in all phases of the project. The third part will include a discussion of the benefits to the residents and, indirectly, to the community in which they live, to be derived from resident participation. In the conclusion, I will suggest the possibility of expanding the model to areas other than tax credit transactions with the expectation that the benefits of resident participation can be obtained in these other areas as well.

The Tax Credit Program

Section 42 of the Internal Revenue Code was added in 1986. It essentially offers tax credits, that is, a dollar for dollar reduction of a taxpayer's tax liability, in exchange for private investment in the construction or redevelopment of affordable housing.[12] There are two different programs under which an owner of property may be awarded these credits.[13] As I mentioned above, the LIHTC program has produced a total of more than 1.4 million units of affordable housing since 1987, by far the largest federal

10 26 U.S.C. § 42 (2008). The program offers taxpayers significant tax benefits in exchange for their investment in low income housing development.

11 HUD USER Data Sets, U.S. Department of Housing and Urban Development, Low-Income Housing Tax Credits, http://www.huduser.org/datasets/lihtc.html (last visited November 16, 2007).

12 Housing is considered affordable if a family would spend no more than 30 percent of their income on housing. *See Affordable Housing Needs 2005: Report to Congress*, 2007 U.S. Department of Housing and Urban Development, Office of Policy Development and Research 23.

13 26 U.S.C. § 42(b) (2008) provides for a 9 percent credit and a 4 percent credit. The 9 percent credit is available for otherwise eligible projects that are not federally subsidized. The 4 percent credit is for projects that have other federal subsidy. For this purpose,

affordable housing development program since the inception of Low Income Housing Tax Credits. The operation of this program involves great complexities that are largely beyond the scope of this chapter. What I do want to explore, however, is the effect on a tax credit development and on the residents of such a development of the ongoing, in-depth involvement of those residents in the planning and implementation of the project and the subsequent operation of the renovated building.

Since tax credits are allocated only to owners of property, the form of ownership must be one that permits tax write-offs to pass through directly to the business owners. Most of the investors are individuals or companies that are not otherwise involved with the affordable housing business, and will not be involved in the planning, implementation or operation of the project in which they invest. They therefore demand, as a prerequisite for investing, protection from the liabilities that might arise from the construction and operation of the property. The ownership vehicle that has traditionally been chosen is a limited partnership (although today a limited liability company would appear to be the more efficient vehicle).[14] The developer would be the general partner and manager of the project and the investors would be the limited partners with no role in the project's management. The general partner's liability would be unlimited but the limited partners enjoy limited liability.[15] The developer typically receives no more (and often less) than 1 percent of the profits, losses, and credits from the venture while the investors will receive the balance, typically 99.9 percent.

Because of the tax risks associated with these projects,[16] the investors will require that the general partner be experienced in real estate development in general and in tax credit development and operations in particular. Moreover, they normally require that the developer provide them with financial guarantees against losses that may occur due to the recapture of the credits. Thus, in addition to being experienced, the general partner must have financial resources sufficient to protect the investors in the event that the general partner's management results in unexpected tax liabilities for the investors.

The financing of a tax credit development involves, in addition to the normal equity and debt calculation typical in any proposed real estate development, a

---

financing with tax exempt bonds qualifies as federally subsidized and the use of such bonds generally accompanies the 4 percent credit.

14 A limited liability company offers all the tax and liability features desired by the investors along with great flexibility in governance. Nevertheless, attorneys for investors are often uncomfortable with this relatively recent form of doing business and often insist upon the more familiar limited partnership. As we will see in the second part of this chapter, when a tenants' association is involved in the ownership structure, that discomfort can lead to a much more complex ownership entity.

15 So long as a limited partner does not engage in the management of the project, his or her liability will be limited to the amount he or she invested.

16 The main risk is the recapture of previously claimed credits together with the interest and penalties associated with the resulting underpayment of taxes for the years in which the recaptured credits had been claimed.

calculation of the amount that might be contributed by investors seeking tax write-offs. The amount of write-off, and thus an approximation of the amount of capital that might be invested, is calculated by determining the eligible basis of the property,[17] which will establish how much credit will be available to investors,[18] and then multiplying that number by the then current market rate for credits.[19] This will tell the developer approximately how much he or she will receive from the sale of the credits.[20] Since the contribution by investors to obtain access to the credits is an equity investment, it need not be repaid to the investors and works as a reduction of the amount needed to be borrowed to finance the project. That, in turn, results in lower financing costs. Developers, therefore, will evaluate the use of tax credits for a project by determining whether the net inflow of dollars from investors will make a financially viable project more profitable, permit a greater degree of rehabilitation than could otherwise be had with conventional financing, or make a financially questionable project feasible.[21]

The agreement between the investors and the developer will be memorialized in a limited partnership agreement. The agreement limits the general partner's activities to those that are consistent with the LIHTC guidelines and sets out the organizational parameters of the partnership. The negotiation of this document is important because, in many ways, it can allocate control of the operations of the development by restricting the general partner in ways that the limited partners could not, without jeopardizing the limited liability status of the investors, once the partnership is created. It is through this agreement that the residents, acting

17 The basis includes the cost of the building plus certain other depreciable or amortizable costs times the percentage of the project that will be used to house eligible residents.

18 For example, if the eligible basis of a property is $10,000,000, the 4 percent credit program (there is also a 9 percent program) would give the investors approximately $4,000,000 of credit over ten years available in installments of $400,000 per year. If investors were paying $0.85 per dollar of credit, they would pay $3,400,000 for the $4,000,000 of credit.

19 There is a market for credits that functions as any other market. To the extent that there is a great supply of comparable investments, the demand for credits would fall and so would their price. Recently, the price for credits was more than 95 cents per dollar of credit. An interesting question is whether the participation of residents, thereby deviating from the standard model of tax credit deals, affected the price investors were willing to pay for the credits in this deal. This is a question to which I will return later in this chapter.

20 There are other calculations, such as what percentage of the units will be tax credit eligible and what the actual rate of credit will be for the investors that affect the final amount to be contributed.

21 Investors, of course, will calculate the value of the potential tax credits and against the risks of losing the credits against the risks and rewards of other available investments. This will determine whether the individual investor is interested in a deal and, if so, the amount he or she is willing to invest in the activity. The calculation is made without regard to the return of the investment capital.

through a tenants' association, can have a major influence on the structure and operations of the project.

Tenant Involvement in the Development Process

I and others have written elsewhere about the significance of participation by low income residents in the life of their communities and in their buildings.[22] The same benefits of participation apply to projects financed with tax credits. The involvement of residents has the potential to enhance the physical development of the property, its ongoing operations and to increase the capacity and social capital of the residents. Nevertheless, very few tax credit projects involve residents in a significant, much less an ownership, capacity. In this section I will discuss resident involvement in the planning of a project, their participation in its management, and their ability to obtain title to the property at the expiration of the tax credit compliance period.[23] In discussing these issues, I will also explain what I think are the benefits to the developer in agreeing to the residents' proposal.

Project Planning

Several years ago, a tenant in a building in the District of Columbia received a notice from the building's owner that he intended to sell the building and had a buyer ready to purchase, subject only to the residents' rights pursuant to the District's Tenant Opportunity to Purchase Act (TOPA).[24] TOPA requires that when an owner of residential rental property in the District desires to sell the property, the owner must give the residents a bona fide opportunity to purchase it.[25] The notice sent by the owner informed the residents of his intent to sell, gave information about the third party buyer and the contract the owner had with the third party, and gave the residents the opportunity to purchase the building. The building has 136

---

22 *See generally* U.S. Department of Housing and Urban Development, *Community Building in Public Housing: Ties that Bind People and Their Communities* (1997); Byrne and Diamond, *Matrix Revealed*, supra note 2; Michael Diamond & Aaron O'Toole, *Leaders, Followers and Free Riders: The Community Lawyer's Dilemma When Representing Non-Democratic Client Organizations*, 31 Fordham Urb. L.J. 481 (2004); Duncan Kennedy, *The Limited Equity Coop as a Vehicle for Affordable Housing in a Race and Class Divided Society*, 46 How. L.J. 85 (2002); Georgette C. Poindexter, *Who Gets the Final No? Tenant Participation in Public Housing Redevelopment*, 9 Cornell J.L. & Pub. Pol'y 659 (2000).

23 As a practical matter, there must be tax credit compliance for 15 years from the time the property is put into service under the tax credit program. After that, the limited partnership disposes of its asset, the property, and dissolves. The property normally then goes to the developer/general partner based on a formula established in the partnership agreement.

24 D.C. Code §§ 42-3404.02 *et seq.* (2001).

25 D.C. Code §§ 42-3404.02(a) (2001).

units and was selling for $6.5 million. It is in a neighborhood that had traditionally been African American with a mix of working class and lower income residents. The neighborhood, however, was rapidly gentrifying due to the construction of a new Convention Center and the amenities that would accompany its completion, particularly a hotel, restaurants, and shops that would cater to those attending events at the Center. Many of the long-term residents of the neighborhood and of the building feared that they would be forced out of their homes.

When the residents received the notice, they organized a tenants' association and hired an attorney. Together, they reviewed their options under the statute. The association could purchase the building itself and develop it as an affordable rental, a cooperative or a condominium. It could form a partnership with a third party developer of its choice and assign its right to purchase to the developer in exchange for various concessions, such as guaranteed rents, participation in management or relocation benefits, that they could agree upon in advance. Finally, it could sell its rights for cash and its members could either leave the building or remain as renters under a new owner. The latter choice was not really considered because the association had as one of its goals the preservation of affordable housing in the neighborhood and the ability of any resident who wanted to remain in the building to be able to do so.

The resident association made an initial decision to pursue their opportunity to purchase the building. Doing so preserved their rights but did not commit them actually to complete the purchase. The attorney presented the association with information about the process of purchasing the building, about available financing, about third party developers, and about operating a building once it was purchased. The residents, who typically earned 60 percent or less of the area median income, had no prior experience with purchasing property and were disconcerted by the price asked by the owner. They feared they could neither raise the required financing nor operate the building should they be able to acquire it. Moreover, the building would need millions of dollars of renovation in order to be brought into compliance with the local housing code and made more modern and efficient. When all was said and done, the residents were looking at a project that would probably cost between $15,000,000 and $20,000,000, numbers that were beyond comprehension for many of them.

They decided that their best chance to develop the property in a manner that preserved affordability and gave them the opportunity to participate meaningfully in the process was to work with a developer. They interviewed several large and well-respected non-profit developers with experience in affordable housing. In conversations with these developers, the idea of using Low Income Housing Tax Credits was proposed. The use of the credits would bring in much needed equity to reduce the amount of debt the project would have to carry. This, in turn, would lower the financing costs of the project. The tradeoff for the influx of equity, however, would be the loss of some control by the residents.[26]

After a great deal of debate and consideration, the residents decided to go ahead with a development using tax credits. While they were concerned about the loss of control, it was, at least in part, their concern about their inability to manage the project that brought them to the third party developers in the first place. Moreover, the loss of control need not be complete. While tax credit projects typically did not have significant resident involvement in their planning or implementation, they also typically did not have the reality of residents being able to control who could purchase the property. The leverage provided by TOPA concerning the acquisition of a desirable piece of property allowed the residents to negotiate a high degree of involvement in the development. With this possibility at the forefront of their strategy, the residents narrowed the field of potential partners and began negotiating with them. They eventually made a choice and began the process of creating the relationship they desired.

A word would be useful here about the motivations of the developer. There are several reasons why the developer would go along with this, admittedly highly unusual and, to a great extent, more problematic, deal. While I do not know how the developer prioritized these reasons, let me suggest a few, in no particular order, that the developer would consider important. As I mentioned earlier, the developer was a non-profit organization. Its mission was to preserve affordable housing and this project provided an opportunity to preserve a significant number of affordable units from what otherwise would have become an upper income condominium project in a rapidly gentrifying neighborhood. Moreover, tax credit developments typically offer developers a significant fee for their efforts, generally just under 15 percent of the total development costs of the project. In this project, because of TOPA, if the developer wanted to be involved, it had to make concessions to the residents or they would go elsewhere to obtain a developer.

Setting the Terms of the Deal

The residents had several goals they wanted to achieve in any agreement to assign their right to purchase the building. Among them was the desire to participate in the planning of the project, to be engaged in its management, and to be able to have title to the building at the end of the compliance period. These goals served two overriding purposes: to have an improved yet affordable living situation and to gain capacity as individuals and as a group. As a consequence of gaining capacity, the residents hoped to have an effect on their personal lives, their building, their

26 As mentioned earlier, the investors in a tax credit deal would require that there be an experienced developer serving as a general partner and that the developer have control of all issues pertaining to the continued eligibility to receive credits. That meant that the residents would have to give up a good deal of authority to the developer if they wished to pursue a tax credit development.

neighbors, and their community. They hoped, in other words, to create a durable institution that would be both a bellwether of resident rights and a model of what a determined group can achieve.[27]

On the other side of the table, the developer's goals were to produce affordable housing, a goal it had in common with the residents, and to do so efficiently and in compliance with the tax credit rules, particularly since the developer would be required to guarantee to investors that they would receive the expected credits. The developer also desired to make money from its development and operation of the project. It feared that tenant involvement would jeopardize these goals by slowing the process, making it more expensive, and scaring investors into investing less capital or worse, not investing at all.[28] To add to its concern, the developer had no experience with resident groups as partners. While it had good relations with residents in buildings it owned and operated as rentals, it never had to deal with residents as business equals.

Negotiating the Partnership Agreement

The developer had expressed a willingness in principle to form a partnership with the resident association but it had not really considered the dimensions of that relationship. Nevertheless, it was surprised at the expectations of the residents and somewhat resistant to them. To begin with, the residents wanted their association to be a co-general partner with the developer in the limited partnership that would own the property. In that role, while they were willing to give the developer final say on any issue that affected the provision of the tax benefits to the investors, on other issues it wanted considerable input, and on some, total control.

For example, the residents wanted to, among other things, help to structure the financing, participate in the renovation planning, and pick the management company. They also wanted to be involved in tenant selection (provided the potential tenants were tax credit eligible), participate in planning social and educational programs for residents, develop house rules, and participate in selecting a security company. Due to the reluctance of the developer to engage so deeply with the residents, the negotiation of the agreement was difficult and time-consuming. It involved an education for both the resident leadership and the developer. The developer learned that the residents had capabilities and insights that were valuable and, at least to the developer, totally unexpected. It also learned of the residents' commitment to the project and to participating in it, and of the hard work the residents were willing to put into completing it and making it successful. In fact, meetings took place regularly, often several times a week, until a deal was hammered out.

The education obtained by the residents was multifaceted. An obvious outcome was that they began to learn about housing development and finance. They

27 Byrne and Diamond, *Matrix Revealed*, *supra* note 1, at 596–601.

28 The developer guaranty helped ease any concerns the investors might have had about the degree of resident participation. It left the pricing of the credits at essentially what it would have been in a deal without the resident participation.

learned how hard it is to develop and run a successful project and of the skill and commitment of the developer. They learned that their homes were also the main asset of a business that they would help to operate and the heavily intertwined nature of these factors. More subtly, however, the residents learned about their own capacity and about partnership in a sophisticated undertaking.

As these lessons were being learned, often after acrimonious interactions, the relationship settled into a more trusting and productive one. A partnership agreement was negotiated with compromises acceptable to each party. For instance, the residents participated fully in all aspects of the development and assisted in structuring the financing. The developer retained final say only to the extent that the tax credit regulations or significant budgetary constraints were involved. Renovation plans were to be jointly developed and monitored. The residents interviewed architects and general contractors and participated in the negotiation of their contracts. The residents would pick the management company from among a group acceptable to the developer. The residents would also be responsible for preparing house rules.

Another major element of the partnership agreement involved the disposition of the property after the end of the tax credit compliance period. At that point, the limited partner investors would want to terminate the partnership and move on. The residents wanted the building back. The developer was the least certain element. It was in the business of buying and operating affordable housing and this property was both sound and in a gentrifying neighborhood. Its value could be expected to increase over time. On the other hand, the developer had a mission of preservation of affordable housing and the development of resident capacity.

The resolution of this issue was very favorable to the residents. At the end of the compliance period, and the liquidation of the partnership, the resident association would take title to the building in exchange for its assuming the existing debt on the property, paying the transaction costs of liquidating the partnership and paying any exit taxes, most likely to be capital gains, incurred by the other partners. Thus, for what would amount to a relatively small outlay of cash, which could be obtained by refinancing the debt on the property or by taking a second mortgage, the residents could secure a very valuable asset. Their goal would be to convert the property to some form of homeownership, a cooperative or a condominium, that would preserve affordability while giving individual residents a financial stake in the property.[29]

---

29 Interestingly, the developer has recently changed its business model. It is no longer willing to permit subsequent resident groups to obtain the property on the same terms as described herein. It has said that in order to preserve its own capital base, it needs to own the property. When faced with the prospect that tenant groups using TOPA to initiate tax credit projects would not work with this developer, the developer modified its position to suggest that it would be willing to discuss a split of the equity between the tenant association and the developer (that is, the association would have to pay more to obtain the building with

The final element of the agreement was the splitting of the developer's fee. The total fee was substantial, being a total of 12 percent of the acquisition cost and 15 percent of the total development cost other than acquisition.[30] The parties negotiated an 80/20 split of the approximately $3 million fee. The fee would be paid over several years as the equity from the investors was paid in.[31] The residents decided that to protect its share of the fee for future use, particularly the need for funds at the end of the compliance period, they would set up a fund in the nature of a trust. They created such a fund that was to be managed by a financial professional who would invest the principal in a prudent, income-producing manner. The association provided for its ability to use a limited amount of the annual income of the fund to cover various current expenses. The balance would be held for use when the property was transferred to the association.

Developing the Property

Once the agreement was signed, the parties moved on to the process of developing the property. They worked on creating a pro forma for the development with the goal of maximizing the eligible basis of the property. The higher the basis, the more credit would be available and the greater the capital contributions of the investors. The parties found various ways to increase basis including increasing the level of renovation to be done. Of course, the higher the cost of the transaction, the higher the rents would have to be to support the project. Also, the higher the cost, the higher the fee to the developer. This created a series of conflicts that had to be resolved by the parties. A resolution could be found through careful planning of the project's financing.

The residents, along with the developer, decided to seek funding from various sources, including heavily subsidized loans from the District of Columbia's Department of Housing and Community Development (DHCD).[32] Of course, there would be the equity contribution of the investors and, given the tax credit program

---

the excess going to the developer) or the developer would have to be guaranteed a new developer's fee for any redevelopment of the property after the compliance period expires.

30 This is the maximum percentage allowed by the LIHTC rules and is the standard fee taken by developers of such projects. The percentages are the same regardless of whether the project involves a large dollar amount or a small one. Therefore, the fee does not necessarily correspond to the amount of work a developer puts into a particular project. As there is a potential bonus above the cost of labor, overhead, and profit and risk factors, the surplus may add significantly to the cost of the project, thereby increasing tenant rents beyond what is necessary to keep developers interested in undertaking such deals.

31 Investor contributions usually come in installments as certain benchmarks are met. The entire contribution would be paid by the time the buildings had been substantially renovated, usually a period of several years after the tax credit deal was finalized with the investors.

32 This agency is the conduit for the U.S. Department of Housing and Urban Development's (HUD) Community Development Block Grant and HOME funds. It also administers the District's Housing Production Trust Fund program.

they intended to use, there would be tax exempt municipal bonds issued by the District's Housing Finance Agency.[33] The bonds, though carrying an interest rate that was below market, were still a relatively expensive item. The DHCD loans can carry very low interest rates, occasionally as low as half of 1 percent over 40 years. If such a loan were available and was blended with the bonds and equity, the overall effective interest rate on the total project would be manageable. Nevertheless, the parties also sought to acquire or maintain existing governmental subsidies such as Section 8[34] rent subsidies and Section 236[35] mortgage interest reduction payments. Each of these efforts was ultimately successful, allowing for a total development cost of about $22 million but retaining affordability for all residents. Of the 136 residents who lived in the building at the start of the process, more than 125 remained when the process was completed.

The resident association engaged in a variety of other activities such as interacting with the architect, the contractor, various financial institutions, and, of course, with the developer. Partnership meetings between the developer and the association occurred weekly, while development team meetings, including the residents, their lawyers, the contractor architect, and the developer, usually occurred every two weeks. Other meetings occurred as needed (but the need was constant). The members of the board made and followed through on a heavy commitment of time and energy, which commitment continued long after the project was completed. For example, there were regular meetings with the developer and the management company concerning the operation of the building. There were also regular meetings with the residents to keep them informed of what was going on in the building and to get their input on decisions that needed to be made about operations and ongoing improvements.

Benefits Derived from Resident Participation

The benefits that have been derived from resident participation in the development of this project can be categorized into three main areas: improvement of building conditions; improved conditions in the community; and personal development. While there have been significant benefits in each of these areas, there have also been several unfavorable aspects of that participation. In this section, I will discuss these aspects and attempt to educe some lessons for subsequent transactions.

---

33 The agency issues the bonds to investors, often the same investors who purchase the credits, and uses the proceeds from the bond sale to issue a mortgage to the property owner.

34 *See* 42 U.S.C. § 1437f(a) (2000).

35 *See* 12 U.S.C. § 1715z-1 (2000).

Improvements in the Building

Once the relationship between the parties was established, they turned their attention to the physical redevelopment of the building. The building had obvious needs such as a new roof, upgraded electrical and plumbing systems, and more modern heating and cooling. There were a variety of other needs of the residents beyond those required for health and safety or code compliance. For example, the residents desired a community area where they could hold tenant-wide meetings, celebrations, educational programs, and community events. They designed an area on the lower level that would accommodate a large crowd and built in a kitchen, restrooms, and storage space. They also created a secure first floor office for the tenants' association where the board of directors could hold meetings and where corporate records could be kept. Residents also helped to design the facade of the building and its entry area.

The residents were also concerned about the disruptions that would be caused by the construction activities at the property. The residents and developer had decided that construction would go on with residents in place. This decision had been reached due to the residents' desire not to have to move out of the property and then to move back and by the cost savings for the project of not having to pay for relocation and for excess rent payments elsewhere. In order to make this disruption palatable, the residents and developer created a plan in which development would occur on a floor at a time. The residents and developer created a hospitality suite on the lower level where the community room had been built. They installed chairs, couches, tables, computers with internet access, televisions, and VCRs, provided books and games, and made the space available to tenants whose floor was being worked on at the time. The construction plan was to do all in-unit work on a tight schedule so that unit functions such as electricity and plumbing, heating and cooling, would not be available during the day but would be restored each evening when the tenant returned to the unit. While the process was inconvenient and messy (and engendered a good deal of griping), it was completed successfully with a significant cost saving to the project.

As life in the building stabilized, the residents developed a set of house rules, rules for the day-to-day life of the building. They provided, among other things, regulations about pets, noise, access to the community room, and guests. They imposed penalties for violations that escalated from warnings to expulsion, and became more severe depending on the gravity or frequency of the violation. These rules were developed by the association's leadership after consultation with the general membership. When a final draft was ready, it was presented to the membership for a vote. The rules have been incorporated by reference into the leases in the building and are binding on all tenants and their guests.

As time went on, the residents had problems with the management company and the security company. In each case, the personnel of the management and security companies were not doing their jobs and were not treating the leadership of the tenants' association as a part of the ownership structure of the property. After several meetings with the leadership of the tenants' association, the non-profit developer, and executives of each of the companies, the management company created a new set of operating guidelines for dealing with the tenants' association and the security company was replaced.

Security, however, continued to be a major problem. While the neighborhood was gentrifying, there were still significant elements of gang and drug activity in the area. This was a particular problem in the building, in part because higher income buildings in the neighborhood could afford a greater number of full-time security personnel on the premises. Thus, the drug sales and violence gravitated to the less well-secured buildings. The residents were particularly concerned about the activity in and around the building. They pressured management to identify those residents letting unauthorized people into the building or who were engaged in illegal activity, and to proceed against them in court. They pressured the security company to do identity checks of everyone who entered the building. Picture ID cards were given to residents and guests had to identify themselves with a picture ID, say who they were visiting, and sign in.

This latter requirement caused some negative response by some of the tenants who did not want to show IDs to the security personnel. Several building-wide meetings were held to address these concerns, with many residents wanting even stronger measures imposed to restore safety and order to the premises. The residents then started interacting with the Metropolitan Police and the U.S. Attorney's office to get their assistance in resolving the security problems. They were successful in having the police and U.S. Attorney attend meetings at the property and beef up patrols in the area and in the building itself.

These efforts have helped to keep out strangers who used the building to buy, sell or use drugs, and for the purpose of general loitering. They did not, however, completely solve the problem. The residents then sought to have the elevators and the entry to the first floor apartments (which gave access to the stairways in the building) protected by swipe card access from the entrance area of the building. Again over objection by some residents, these changes were implemented after building-wide meetings were held to discuss and, ultimately, to approve the modifications.

The results of the efforts by residents were to create a desired renovation in a way that met residents' needs; to improve the day-to-day life in the building; to add social and service amenities to the property; and to improve the security of the residents. These improvements were the result of resident initiatives. They were accepted, even welcomed, by the developer in part because of the merits of the initiatives but also because of the contractual role played by the residents. The role gave them the right not only to propose initiatives but also to have them implemented. This right, in turn, gave them greater access to and involvement with the developer who came to recognize the resident association as a true partner in the operation of the building.

Community Improvement

There have also been several beneficial effects for the local community as a whole. An obvious one is that the greater involvement of the local law enforcement agencies in the life of the building has had a spillover effect for the area surrounding the building. More police patrols and greater involvement in the neighborhood has led to fewer incidents and a lower level of violence. Moreover, other property owners and tenants' associations as well as local community groups have observed the improvements at the property and sought to become involved in a broader effort to reduce crime and increase safety for their buildings and for the community as a whole. This has led to collaborations between several tenants' associations and building owners over a variety of issues in the community.

This collaboration was initiated by a suggestion made by the leader of the tenants' association during one of the regular meetings with the developer and management company. Each participant in that meeting agreed to make contact with other entities in the neighborhood (for example, other buildings managed by the management company or owned by the developer and local organizations and tenant groups) to begin to meet to discuss neighborhood issues. They also agreed to contact the local city council member and invite him to meet with the local residents to discuss these issues.

The resident association has also established an after-school program and a summer camp for children in the building. While it is currently limited to the children of residents, the plan is either to open the programs up to other neighborhood children or to assist other buildings in creating similar programs, and to establish a collaboration among the different buildings and programs in order to enrich all of them. These programs have worked well and are staffed by a combination of professionals (whose salaries were budgeted in the original development plan) and volunteers from the building. In addition, there is a computer lab and a seniors program that, again, are planned to be expanded or replicated in neighboring buildings. Finally, the community room in the building has been used for meetings of organizations engaged in alcohol and substance abuse self-help. These programs have been opened to a wider community participation and are not limited just to residents of the building.

Conclusion

To a great extent, it is too soon to tell what effect the resident association will have on the neighborhood as a whole. It may even be too soon to make a definitive prediction on the benefits to be derived by the building and its residents. Preliminary indications, however, are positive. This is not to say that there are not problems, often significant ones, in the building. For example, there is always a concern for the economics of the situation. The goal is to provide affordable housing and that means keeping the rents within the means of the residents. This is in some conflict with the ambitious nature of the programs and social services that the residents want for themselves and their neighbors. The association, in conjunction with their developer/partner, has begun applying for grants to accomplish some of their goals without straining their budget.

There is also the problem of resident disinterest or free-riding. Not enough people are fully engaged and many others are not engaged at all. For the time being, there is a critical mass sufficient to carry out the program design, but will there be adequate leadership when the current group of leaders moves on? Can a second or subsequent generation of leaders have the same commitment to participation as those who went through the development process? Do they need that level of commitment or, now that the major activities have been undertaken and major goals accomplished, is a lesser level of dedication sufficient?

Interestingly, and in some conflict with the previous observation, there is a problem of fictionalization within the group. There are two groups vying for power within the building and, while each has the best interests of the group in mind, they are very different in approach. Nevertheless, much of this situation is based on personality. Leadership is very visible in the building and in the community. Because of this visibility, the leaders have drawn fire from other residents and neighbors. Some have claimed that the leadership is now the owner of the building or that leaders have misappropriated funds. While neither allegation is true, these and other claims take their toll on the leaders who occasionally wonder whether the successes are worth the time and trouble associated with them. Burn out in such an intense activity is a real concern.

Beyond these problems, however, stands a fully renovated building with significant tenant input concerning all aspects of management. There has been preservation of 136 units of affordable housing in a very hot downtown housing market. In addition, there is a large body of residents who have grown in terms of capacity, self-confidence, and social capital. This has been accomplished by creating a hybrid model between traditional rental housing and tenant ownership. It is a model that has the potential for significant rewards, albeit at some costs. It is also a model that can be replicated in situations other than tax credit deals. Two such situations come immediately to mind.

The first is a situation where the sponsor of affordable rental housing has a mission-driven position that supports tenants. Many such sponsors already involve residents in choosing and providing various social services on the property. This relationship could easily be expanded, by contract or otherwise, into giving tenants a role in management. The role might be merely advisory or, in some cases, might be decisional. The effects of this type of involvement are to create better understanding and a tighter bond between residents and sponsor and, in many cases, I believe, a better run building.

The second area in which this model might be utilized is a bit more contentious. I have speculated for many years about the benefits of using such a model in the context of settling landlord–tenant matters when one of the parties to the action is a tenants' association. In many such cases, where a landlord is seeking rent and the residents have withheld it because of poor conditions in the building, the case is settled with the landlord promising to make repairs and the residents paying over some of all of the withheld rent. My speculation goes to what are the possibilities of including some tenant involvement in management as part of the settlement.

Of course, this possibility would require a motivated tenant group and ongoing professional assistance. Both of these prerequisites are far from certain elements of any situation. Unlike tenant ownership situations, the residents in a landlord–tenant dispute will be less likely to see the long-term benefits of participation. The need for organizing, which is present in all tenant involvement situations, will not have the added spur of owning the building to assist the landlord–tenant organizer. Moreover, since the effort to improve conditions through a rent strike is relatively short-lived (as opposed to the purchase and renovation of a building), the ability to train residents in the skills needed to perform is more limited. This is exacerbated by the paucity of lawyers who would be available for such efforts. Legal services and legal aid lawyers, even assuming they had the necessary skills, are already constrained by the press of caseloads. Will they be able to devote the needed time and effort to such esoterica?

I believe the results to date of tenant involvement warrant its continuation in ownership situations and in tax credit deals. I would like to see the model expanded into the friendly and not-so-friendly rental situations, as well. For that to happen there must be support from local governments. Among the policy changes that would support these efforts would be:

- the enactment of tenant opportunity to purchase statutes
- the provision of funds for purchase or for technical assistance
- a requirement that owners bargain in good faith with tenant associations
- an overall willingness to explore new and, perhaps, exotic methods to deal with the problems of inadequate and unaffordable housing.

With these policies in place and with a body of tenants and professionals willing to explore alternative housing strategies, there is a place for the concept of tenant involvement in the provision of decent, affordable housing that the residents, the owners, and the community can be proud of.

Acknowledgements

The author would like to thank my colleague and friend, Peter Byrne, who provided great encouragement and support in the early stages of this project, and the participants in the *Affordable Housing and Public–Private Partnerships: The Intersection of Housing, Property, and Real Estate* workshop at the University of Colorado Law School. Robin Malloy and Nestor Davidson, in particular, provided valuable comments and assistance in the completion of this chapter. I also want to acknowledge the fine research assistance of Aaron Schmitz.

Chapter 5
The National Housing Trust Fund: A Challenge and an Opportunity for Creative Public–Private Partnerships

Peter W. Salsich, Jr

Introduction

"Marvin, what do we do now?"[1]

With that nervous question, Robert Redford, the newly elected long shot senatorial candidate in the 1972 hit movie *The Candidate*, made the point that election to office was only the beginning. To be successful, the election winner had to accomplish something while in office.

"I would rather support a mediocre idea with an excellent implementation plan, than an excellent idea with a mediocre implementation plan," stressed billionaire investor Wilbur Ross in describing his approach to determining which troubled companies have the potential to be revitalized.[2]

Both quotes emphasize the importance of implementation as the key to success with new ventures.

An implementation challenge faces advocates and supporters of the newly created National Housing Trust Fund (NHTF).[3] Buried deep in the several-hundred-page bill, approved July 30, 2008[4] in response to the subprime mortgage foreclosure crisis and its after-effects,[5] are two little noticed[6] but potentially

1 The Candidate (Warner Bros. 1972).

2 *NPR Morning Edition: Wilbur Ross: Finding His Calling* (NPR radio broadcast September 15, 2008), *available at* www.npr.org.

3 Housing and Economic Recovery Act of 2008, Pub. L. No. 110-289, § 1131, 122 Stat. 2654 (2008) (adding new sections 1337–1339 to the Federal Housing Enterprises Financial Safety and Soundness Act of 1992 (12 U.S.C. § 1301 *et seq.*)).

4 *Id.*

5 *Infra* notes 20–24 and accompanying text.

6 For example, the *Wall Street Journal* and the *Washington Post* coverage of final passage of the bill in the Senate did not mention the Housing Trust Fund. Damien Paletta, *Housing Bill Relies On Banks to Take Loan Losses*, Wall St. J., July 28, 2008, at A3; Lori Montgomery and Paul Kane, *Housing Bill Won't "Perform Miracles,"* Washington Post, July 27, 2008, at A1. The *New York Times* listed the Housing Trust

significant new programs, the National Housing Trust Fund and the Capital Magnet Fund.[7] Scheduled to be funded by an allocation of a small percentage (4.2 basis points/dollar) of the "unpaid principal balance of [Fannie Mae and Freddie Mac's] total new business purchases,"[8] the funds, when fully implemented in 2012,[9] are expected to provide an estimated $800 million – $1 billion each per year for affordable housing development, preservation, rehabilitation or purchase of rental and for-sale housing, primarily for extremely low income (30 percent or less of area median income) and very low income (50 percent or less of area median income) households,[10] groups long neglected by federal housing policies.[11]

The new housing trust fund legislation presents two opportunities: (1) for a paradigm shift in federal housing production and preservation policy; and (2) for improving and broadening the collaboration necessary for successful implementation of housing policy. As the first new federal program in a generation providing direct financial assistance for housing production and preservation, it begins the restoration of a balance in federal housing policy between direct and indirect[12] financial support, and between support for rental as well as home ownership. Rather than an administration-backed, top-down initiative, the new trust fund legislation is the culmination of over 15 years of grass roots organizing and advocacy,[13] solid evidence of the potential, and the importance, of grass roots

---

Fund at the end of a summary of the Housing Bill, but did not mention it in its main story. David M. Herszenhorn, *Congress Sends Housing Relief Bill to President*, N.Y. Times, July 27, 2008, at 12, 16.

7 Housing and Economic Recovery Act of 2008, *supra* note 3, at § 1131. The Capital Magnet Fund is described briefly *infra*, but will not be discussed further.

8 *Id.* at § 1331(b) (adding new § 1337(a) (1) & (2)).

9 For the first three years, the funds will be allocated on a sliding scale to repayment of bonds issued to pay for FHA costs in implementing the HOPE for Homeowners refinancing program, Housing and Economic Recovery Act of 2008, *supra* note 3, at §§ 1401–1404.

10 National Housing Trust Fund, Memo to Members, *Victory: House Passes Housing Trust Fund Act*, 12 Nat'l Low Income Housing Coalition. 40, at 3 (October 12, 2007).

11 The Low Income Housing Tax Credit (LIHTC) targets households in the 50–60 percent of median income ranges. I.R.C. § 42(g) (2000).

12 The LIHTC relies on the indirect approach of offering tax credits in return for equity investments in qualified housing developments. *Id.* at §§ 38 & 42(a) and (b) (2000).

13 The National Low Income Housing Coalition (NLIHC) put together a 50-state coalition of more than 100 "state partners" and 5600 "organizations and local leaders" that supported the housing trust fund proposal. NLIHC, *National Housing Trust Fund News*, http://www2398.ssldomain.com/nlihc/template/page.cfm?id=75 (last visited October 17, 2008). Modeled after a state and local housing trust fund concept developed in the 1980s by Mary Brooks, Director of the Housing Trust Fund Project, Center for Community Change, http://www.communitychange.org/housing-trust-funds/ (last visited June 9, 2008), the first national legislation was introduced in 1994. H.R. 5475, 103d Cong. (2d Sess. 1994); Nancy Bernstine & Irene Basloe Saraf, *New Rental Production and the National Housing Trust Fund Campaign*, 12 J. of Affordable Housing and Community Development Law 389, 390 (2003). Of course, one person's grass roots coalition is another person's special interest

inclusion in the development of housing policy. The NHTF offers a flexible tool that housing advocates and providers can use at the local level to complement and enhance existing housing programs.

While the NHTF is established as a block grant in the tradition of the Community Development Block Grant (CDBG),[14] Housing Development Action Grant (HODAG),[15] and HOME Investment Partnership (HOME)[16] programs, trust fund monies are not subject to annual Congressional appropriations as are the other block grant programs. Rather, the funding is intended to be "permanent" in the sense that the Highway Trust Fund is "permanent."[17] The housing trust fund program is intended to maximize local choice with respect to fund recipients, as well as amount and use of available funds, subject to a needs-based distribution formula to be developed by the Department of Housing and Urban Development (HUD)[18] and state-prepared allocation plans.[19]

The ink had barely dried on the President's signature approving the massive housing bill containing the trust fund provisions when excessive turmoil in worldwide financial markets triggered by the mortgage foreclosure crisis led the government to take extraordinary steps, including assuming control of the operations of Fannie Mae and Freddie Mac.[20] When even this action and the rescue of the American International Group (AIG), the world's largest insurance company,[21] failed to quell the turmoil in the financial markets, Congress enacted

---

group. But special interest groups generally are thought of as groups seeking something for themselves. For the most part, the state partners for the NLIHC were not seeking benefits for themselves but rather for persons in their communities who did not have the resources to participate in local housing markets and needed assistance to obtain decent shelter.

14 42 U.S.C. § 5301 and ff (2000).

15 42 U.S.C. § 1437o(d) (1988), repealed in 1990, Pub. L. 101-625, title II, 289(b), Nov. 28, 1990, 104 Stat. 4128.

16 42 U.S.C. § 12741 (2000).

17 26 U.S.C. § 9503 (2000).

18 Housing and Economic Recovery Act of 2008, *supra* note 3, at § 1338(c)(3)(B). HUD has 12 months from the date of enactment to develop the allocation formula. *Id.*

19 *Id.*, at § 1338(c)(5)(A) & (g)(2)(C).

20 Henry M. Paulson, Jr, Secretary, U.S. Treasury Dept., Statement on Treasury and Federal Housing Finance Agency Action to Protect Financial Markets and Taxpayers (September 7, 2008), *available at* http://www.ustreas.gov/press/releases/hp1129.htm; James B. Lockhart, Director, Federal Housing Finance Agency, Statement of FHFA Director James B. Lockhart (September 7, 2008), *available at* http://www.ofheo.gov/media/statements/FHFAStatement9708.pdf (announcing that FHFA, acting under authority granted in the Housing and Economic Recovery Act of 2008, § 1101*et seq*., has placed Fannie Mae and Freddie Mac into conservatorship with FHFA acting as conservator "to operate the enterprises until they are stabilized").

21 Press Release, Board of Governors of the Federal Reserve System (September 16, 2008), *available at* http://www.federalreserve.gov/newsevents/press/other/20080916a.htm (authorizing the Federal Reserve Bank of New York to lend up to $85 billion to AIG under § 13(3) of the Federal Reserve Act, 12 U.S.C. § 343 [as added by act of July 21, 1932 (47

a $700 billion rescue plan authorizing the Secretary of the Treasury to acquire subprime mortgages and other "troubled assets" from financial institutions in an effort to restore liquidity to the credit markets.[22]

As a result of these actions, questions arose concerning the future of the new trust funds.[23] The National Low Income Housing Coalition (NLIHC), the leading advocate for the NHTF, stressed in response to these concerns that the funding formula is "based on [Fannie Mae's and Freddie Mac's] volume of new business, not profits," that contributions to the NHTF "can be suspended by the regulator [the Federal Housing Finance Agency]" if the contributions are considered "detrimental to the health" of Fannie Mae and Freddie Mac, and that the delay in funding the NHTF "hopefully" will enable the government's response to the current crisis to "restore confidence" in the agencies "so that contributions to the National Housing Trust Fund will be possible" by the time they are scheduled to be activated.[24] While it may be some time before a final rescue plan is implemented, this chapter will assume that Fannie Mae and Freddie Mac (or any successors) will continue to play an important role in the secondary mortgage market.

Following a brief summary of the new trust fund legislation in the second part of this chapter, the third part will examine implementation issues emanating from the distribution formula that the Department of Housing and Urban Development (HUD) will develop and the allocation plans that states will prepare. Experience with a special block grant program to aid the state of Louisiana recover from the ravages of Hurricanes Katrina and Rita will form the basis of this discussion. The fourth part will discuss the potential of Community Preservation Funds and Community Land Trusts to become key players in local public–private partnerships through use of trust fund monies as seed money. The chapter will conclude with a recommendation that special attention and care should be given to the implementation question, both because of the potential that good implementation plans have to attract additional investment,[25] and to respond to anticipated future attacks[26] on the dedicated fund concept that is at the heart of the housing trust fund program.

Stat.715); and amended by acts of August 23, 1935 (49 Stat. 714) and December 19, 1991 (105 Stat. 2386)]).

22 Emergency Economic Stabilization Act of 2008, P.L. 110-343, § 101 (2008); Edmund L. Andrews, *Vast Bailout Plan is Proposed in Bid to Stem Economic Crisis*, N.Y. Times, September 19, 2008, at A1.

23 *See, e.g.*, National Housing Trust Fund, *What Fannie and Freddie Crisis Means for NHTF*, 13 Nat'l Low Income Housing Coalition 35, at 1 (September 5, 2008).

24 Id.

25 Wilbur Ross, *supra* note 2.

26 NLIHC, *supra* note 23.

The New Trust Fund Programs[27]

Housing Trust Fund

Section 1131 of the Housing and Economic Recovery Act establishes two trust funds, a HUD-managed Housing Trust Fund to support "production, preservation, and rehabilitation" of rental housing and housing for homeownership,[28] and a Treasury Secretary-managed Capital Magnet Fund to support a "competitive grant program to attract private capital" for affordable housing and related economic development and community service activities.[29]

Initially, the main source of capital for the two trust funds will come from Fannie Mae and Freddie Mac, as each agency is required to "set aside an amount equal to 4.2 basis points for each dollar of the unpaid principal balance of its total new business purchases." Twenty-five percent of the funds generated by this formula are to be deposited in a reserve fund to support FHA mortgage foreclosure relief efforts.[30] The balance is allocated, 65 percent to the Housing Trust Fund and 35 percent to the Capital Magnet Fund.[31] Most importantly, both funds can also receive additional monies by appropriation, transfer or credit "under any other provision of law."[32] Although HUD and Treasury have day-to-day fund management responsibilities, the Director of the new oversight agency, FHFA,[33] has supervisory responsibilities to insure that fund allocations do not cause financial instability, undercapitalization or other interference with the enterprises, and to prohibit the

27 An earlier version of the description of the trust fund legislation appeared in Peter Salsich, *National Affordable Housing Trust Fund Legislation: The Subprime Mortgage Crisis Also Hits Renters,* 16 GEO. J. POV. L. & POL. (forthcoming 2009) and is used with permission.

28 Housing and Economic Recovery Act of 2008, *supra* note 3, at § 1131, adding § 1338 to the Federal Housing Enterprises Financial Safety and Soundness Act of 1992, 12 U.S.C. § 1301 *et seq*. Section 131 "builds on the basic tenets of S. 2523," the National Affordable Housing Trust Fund Act of 2008, introduced by Senator John Kerry, D-Mass. Letter from Sheila Crowley, President and CEO, NLIHC, to John Kerry, United States Senator from Massachusetts (June 5, 2008), *available at* www.nhtf.org.

29 Housing and Economic Recovery Act of 2008, *supra* note 3, at § 1131, adding § 1339.

30 *Id.* at § 1337(e).

31 *Id.* adding § 1337. As noted earlier, *supra* note 23 and accompanying text, concerns were raised during the debate over the Emergency Economic Stabilization Act. Supporters stressed that a dedicated source of funding is not an earmark and the statutory emphasis on new business of Fannie and Freddie make the programs relevant as the secondary mortgage market is restructured. National Housing Trust Fund, *NHTF Falsely Characterized in Debate on Bail-Out Bill*, 13 NAT'L LOW INCOME HOUSING COALITION 39, at 1 (October 3, 2008).

32 *Id.* at §§ 1338(a) and 1339(a).

33 *Supra* note 20.

enterprises from passing their costs onto mortgage originators.[34] Housing Trust Fund and Capital Magnet Fund monies may not be used to support economic development projects in which eminent domain is used to acquire private property that will be transferred to another private entity.[35]

Full implementation of the Housing Trust Fund's basic purpose, making grants to states for production and preservation of rental units and increased homeownership opportunities for extremely low income (ELI) and very low income (VLI) households, has been postponed for three years.[36] Funds will be allocated during the first three years of operation in declining percentages to reimburse FHA for costs associated with proposed refinancings to prevent foreclosures.[37] Beginning in 2010, funds not allocated to foreclosure relief efforts will be distributed as grants to states or state-designated agencies such as state housing finance agencies, state housing and community development entities, tribally designated housing entities, "or other qualified instrumentalit[ies]."[38] Distributions will be made in accordance with a needs-based formula to be developed by HUD that includes the sum of four ratios: (i) the ratio of the shortage of standard rental units that are "affordable and available to extremely low-income renter households" in the state to the national shortage of such units; (ii) the ratio of the shortage of similar units for very low income renter households; (iii) the ratio of extremely low income renter households living with incomplete kitchen or plumbing facilities, or more than one person per room, or paying more than 50 percent of income for housing costs; and (iv) the ratio of very low income renter households living with the same housing concerns, multiplied by the relative cost of construction in the state measured against national costs.[39]

States or state-designated entities and grantees will be required to prepare allocation plans that are based on "priority housing needs" and are consistent with established comprehensive housing affordability strategies (CHAS).[40] Allocation plans must provide that funding priority will be based on "geographic diversity," ability to undertake activities in a "timely manner," extent and duration of affordable rents for ELI families, extent to which other funds will be used, and the "merits" of a particular proposal.[41] Eligible activities include "production, preservation and rehabilitation," as well as operating costs, of rental housing, with at least 75 percent of the funds required to benefit ELI families and 25 percent to

34 Housing and Economic Recovery Act of 2008, *supra* note 3, at § 1337(b) and (c).

35 *Id.* at § 1337(f).

36 *Id.* at § 1338(a).

37 *Id.* at § 1338(b) (100 percent in calendar year 2009, 50 percent in 2010, and 25 percent in 2011).

38 *Id.* at § 1338(c).

39 *Id.* at § 1338(c)(3)(B).

40 42 U.S.C § 12705 (2000).

41 Housing and Economic Recovery Act of 2008, *supra* note 3, at § 1338(c)(5)(A) & (g)(2)(C).

benefit VLI families, and homeownership opportunities for ELI and VLI first-time homebuyers who have completed a financial education and counseling program from an approved counseling agency,[42] but only 10 percent of trust fund monies can be used for homeownership support.[43] Eligible grant recipients include both for-profit and non-profit organizations which demonstrate experience, financial and organizational capacity, ability, familiarity with the requirements of other housing programs, and provide assurances of compliance with program and statutory standards.[44]

Capital Magnet Fund

The Capital Magnet Fund established by the Act will utilize its 35 percent share of the GSE fund allocation[45] for a "competitive grant program to attract private capital for and increase investment in" affordable housing for ELI, VLI, and LI (low income) families, as well as economic development activities or community service facilities, "which in conjunction with affordable housing activities implement a concerted strategy to stabilize or revitalize a low-income area or underserved rural area."[46] Eligible grantees include Treasury-certified community development financial institutions and non-profit affordable housing development or management organizations.[47]

Grants from the fund may be used to provide loan loss reserves, to capitalize revolving loan, affordable housing or economic development loan funds, or to make risk-sharing loans,[48] all of which "shall be reasonably expected" to result in developments that leverage the grant funds by at least a ratio of 10 to 1.[49] Funds are to be distributed under the principle of "geographic diversity," defined as metropolitan and underserved rural areas in every state "that meet objective criteria of economic distress," including such factors as the percentage of low income families or the extent of poverty, rates of unemployment or underemployment, extent of blight and disinvestment, and projects which target ELI, VLI and LI families "in or outside a designated economic distress area."[50]

---

42 *Id.* at § 1338(c)(7)(A) & (B). Section 132 of the Act creates a new financial education and counseling grant program in the Treasury Department.

43 *Id.* at § 1338(c)(9)(A).

44 *Id.* at § 1338(c)(8).

45 *Id.* at § 1339.

46 *Id.* at § 1339(c). Day care centers, workforce development centers, and health care centers are included as examples of community service facilities.

47 *Id.* at § 1339(e).

48 *Id.* at § 1339(f).

49 *Id.* at § 1339(h)(3).

50 *Id.* at § 1339(h)(2).

Funding Link to Fannie Mae and Freddie Mac

The funding link to Fannie Mae and Freddie Mac is based on the extremely significant role Fannie Mae and Freddie Mac play in the residential secondary mortgage market, as those two agencies held or guaranteed approximately 50 percent of the outstanding $1 trillion residential loan portfolio at the time of the July 2008 legislative enactment.[51] While the amount to be available upon full implementation in 2012[52] is quite small in comparison to current federal housing programs,[53] it is understandable in view of the subprime mortgage foreclosure crisis that triggered a restructuring of Fannie Mae and Freddie Mac and a massive Congressional rescue package.[54] Advocates also hope to persuade Congress, by effective use of the funds, to increase the size of the funds through a statutory provision authorizing receipt of additional monies "under any other provision of law."[55]

The new legislation is controversial, both because of its emphasis on providing support for extremely low income households, and because of the fact that it by-passes the regular appropriations process. Supporters point to the fact that the public housing production program[56] and the Section 8 new construction/substantial rehabilitation program,[57] both of which have been dormant for over 25 years, are the only federally supported housing production programs that would reach extremely low income households. Because extremely low income households do not have the resources to compete effectively in private housing markets, nor the political strength of households with greater resources who have succeeded in institutionalizing housing assistance programs such as the mortgage interest

51 Julie Creswell, *Long Protected by Washington, Fannie and Freddie Ballooned*, N.Y. Times, July 12, 2008, at A1.

52 During the first three years of operation, contributions scheduled to go to the Housing Trust and Capital Magnet Funds will be diverted in part to cover the costs of implementing new authority for the Federal Housing Administration (FHA) to insure refinancing mortgage loans as part of a foreclosure prevention program created by the Housing and Economic Recovery Act of 2008, *supra* note 3, at § 1338.

53 In 2007, expenditures for public housing and Section 8 assistance totaled approximately $28 billion. Executive Office of the President, Office of Management and Budget, *Department of Housing and Urban Development*, *in* Budget of the United States Government: Fiscal Year 2009, at 77 (2008).

54 Emergency Economic Stabilization Act of 2008, *supra* note 22.

55 Housing and Economic Recovery Act of 2008, *supra* note 3, at § 1131, adding new §§ 1338(a) and 1339(a). Supporters of the NHTF see it as the first step toward a new national goal of producing 1.5 million new or preserved housing units for ELI and VLI households over a ten-year period. Housing Commission on Financial Services, National Affordable Housing Trust Fund Act of 2007, Report 110-362, at 15 (October 2, 2007).

56 United States Housing Act of 1937, ch. 896, Title I (codified at 42 U.S.C. §§ 1437 and ff (2000)).

57 42 U.S.C. § 1437f (terminated in 1983, Pub.L. 98-181, § 209(a)(1)).

tax deduction,[58] a "permanent" program free from the political uncertainties of the appropriations process is necessary to secure predictable funding, trust fund supporters argue.[59]

Emergency Block Grant for Municipal Foreclosure Response

In addition to the new trust funds, the legislation includes an emergency, one-time $4 billion infusion of CDBG funds designed to enable cities to respond to the foreclosure crisis through "the redevelopment of abandoned and foreclosed upon homes and residential properties."[60] Responding to statutory requirements for speed, HUD announced allocations under a statutory funding formula to identify states and localities "with the greatest need," as that may be evidenced by "the number and percentage of" (1) home foreclosures, (2) homes financed by subprime mortgage loans and (3) homes in default or delinquency.[61] Fund recipients have until April, 2010, 18 months from the mandatory date of distribution, [62] to use the money for acquisition and redevelopment of "abandoned and foreclosed homes and residential properties.[63]

An Opportunity to Rethink the Federal Role in Housing Production and Preservation

The NHTF legislation offers the federal government an opportunity to rethink its role in housing production and preservation, but from a different perspective. For over 20 years, the centerpiece of federal housing production policy has been the Low Income Housing Tax Credit (LIHTC) enacted in 1986.[64] With enactment of the LIHTC, federal housing policy shifted from direct support for housing production

58 I.R.C. § 163 (2002). The revenue foregone as a result of the mortgage interest tax deduction and other tax concessions offered home owners approached an estimated $130 billion in 2007. Budget Of The United States, *supra* note 53, Analytical Perspectives 294 tbl.19-2 (2008) (tax expenditures).

59 *See, e.g.*, the website for the National Housing Trust Fund, http://www.nhtf.org/template/page.cfm?id=40 (last visited October 21, 2008).

60 Housing and Economic Recovery Act of 2008, *supra* note 3, at § 2301. A small portion of the $4 billion appropriation, $180,000,000, is set aside for homeownership counseling. *Id.* at § 2305.

61 Id. at § 2301(b) (3). Brian Sullivan, *Preston Allocates Nearly $4 Billion to Stabilize Neighborhoods in States and Localities Hard-Hit by Foreclosure: HUD Plans Housing Summit to Explain New Neighborhood Stabilization Plan*, HUD News Release No. 08-148 (September 26, 2008), available at http://www.hud.gov/news/release.cfm?content=pr08-148.cfm.

62 *Id.* at § 2301(b) (2) & (4).

63 *Id.* at § 2301(c)(1).

64 I.R.C. § 42, added Pub. L. 99-514, Title II, § 252(a), 100 Stat. 2189 (October 22, 1986), as amended (2000).

and preservation to indirect support for such production and preservation through tax credits offered to investors, and has remained so ever since.[65] The LIHTC program is managed by the Internal Revenue Service (IRS)[66] rather than the Department of Housing and Urban Development (HUD) and is administered in a decentralized fashion by state housing agencies.[67] Direct support to the producers of affordable housing has been limited to relatively small capital grants for public housing,[68] a short-lived housing development grant program (HODAG),[69] and a targeted housing block grant program, HOME Investment Partnerships (HOME), enacted in 1990.[70]

In summary, the NHTF legislation redirects housing policy toward populations not targeted by the LIHTC and other programs, and offers a chance to rethink the nature of participation (both public–private and federal–state–local) in the implementation of that policy. The permanent nature of NHTF funding sources greatly enhances the ability of housing advocates and providers to fashion successful programs through collaboration, experimentation, and long-term planning.

Implementation Through National Regulations and State Plans

Implementation[71] issues abound with the NHTF, as with any new program. They may be grouped as follows. (1) "Getting out of the ground issues—government side," such as delay, administrative costs of approving specific uses of funds, avoiding fraud. (2) "Getting out of the ground issues—private side;" how is implementation tied to overall economic health, or to the health of the housing economy? (3) Political power battles—are the "wrong" people/projects/activities being funded? (4) Thoroughness issues—are trust fund dollars going to make a difference in communities? If so, by whose standards will this be determined? (5) Operational issues—how will the operational funding gap, so big a problem with public housing, be addressed in trust fund-supported developments? (6) Evaluation issues—by what standards will success or failure be determined? Who will be the judge?

65 The prime example of a tax-based housing policy is the collection of tax deductions available to home owners, including the mortgage interest tax deduction, I.R.C. § 163, the state and local real property tax deduction, I.R.C. § 164, and the deduction for casualty losses, I.R.C. § 165, as well as the exclusion of up to $250,000 ($500,000 for married couples) of gain on the sale of the principle residence, I.R.C. § 121.

66 I.R.C. § 42(n) (2000). Internal Revenue Service regulations of the LIHTC are located at 26 C.F.R. § 1.42-0 & ff.

67 I.R.C. § 42(h) (2000).

68 42 U.S.C. §§ 1437c(a)(2) (2000).

69 42 U.S.C. § 1437o (enacted in 1983 and repealed in 1990).

70 42 U.S.C. § 12741 and ff (2000).

71 I am indebted to my colleague, Nancy Walsh, for this list of implementation issues.

These questions should be addressed in the national regulations governing accountability of trust fund monies distributed to states and localities,[72] as well as the state allocation plans required before funds are distributed to local entities.[73] The nature and tone of these regulations and allocation plans will be critical factors in the initial success as well as the long-term growth of the two trust funds. Experience with funds to help victims of Hurricanes Katrina and Rita in New Orleans and the rest of Louisiana offers a caution with respect to the approach to be taken in drawing up these regulations and allocation plans.

Almost three years to the day Hurricane Katrina struck, Hurricane Gustav bore down on a New Orleans that had not fully recovered from Katrina as "much of the city remain[ed] a wasteland."[74] Some families who had been evacuated after Katrina to trailer parks established by the Federal Emergency Management Agency (FEMA) away from the flooded coastal areas were facing homelessness because they were required to leave the FEMA trailers after high levels of toxic formaldehyde were discovered in the trailers.[75]

While Hurricane Katrina confronted federal, state, and local officials with an unprecedented emergency, the fact that New Orleans was far from restored three years later triggered much soul-searching and an unflattering comparison with China's Olympic Games venues.[76] New Orleans dodged a bullet when Hurricane Gustav weakened considerably before landfall west of the city, but officials cautioned against complacency.[77]

One example of the difficulties encountered in responding to the devastation caused by Katrina offers a cautionary tale for the implementation of the NHTF. The Road Home program,[78] an $8.1 billion federal grant to the state of Louisiana called the "largest housing aid program in American history,"[79] had fallen far short of its potential three years after the funds for the program were appropriated by

72 Housing and Economic Recovery Act of 2008, *supra* note 3, at § 1337(e).

73 *Id.* at § 1337(c)(5).

74 Nicolai Ouroussoff, *Reflections: New Orleans and China*, N.Y. Times, September 14, 2008, at WK 1.

75 Deepa Fernandes, *Three Years After Hurricane Katrina, Homelessness Looms*, Mother Jones, August 28, 2008, *available at* www.motherjones.com/cgi-bin/print_article.pl?url.

76 Ouroussoff, *supra* note 74 ("the tragedy of New Orleans is not just about governmental disregard for the welfare of the city's inhabitants. It is about a lost opportunity.")

77 John Schwartz, *Gustav Was No Katrina, But Next Time …*, N.Y. Times, September 7, 2008, at WK 3.

78 The name, the Road Home, was coined by Kathleen Blanco, the governor of Louisiana at the time.

79 Adam Nossiter, *After Fanfare, Hurricane Grants Leave Little Mark*, N.Y. Times, August 31, 2008, at 15 (examining the impact of $3.3 billion allocated to New Orleans).

Congress.[80] A study by the RAND Gulf States Policy Institute for the Louisiana Recovery Authority, the state agency responsible for overseeing implementation of the Road Home program through grants to individual homeowners,[81] found that "[a]lthough some applications have been processed in a timely manner, the overall timeliness of the grantmaking process has not been consistently good or predictable."[82]

As noted by the RAND study, the application process was particularly complicated, having as many as 12 stages including "paperwork, interviews and detailed correspondence," as well as "fingerprinting and photographing of applicants, and punctilious checks of ownership documents that in many cases were hard to come by."[83] Delays in distribution of funds to individual homeowners, resulting in large part from the complicated application process, were substantial. The average wait for cash grants was "about 250 days …; many had waited well over a year."[84]

The 12-stage application procedure appeared to be based, at least in part, on concerns over the possibility, even likelihood, that ineligible persons would seek the grant money or that persons who received grants would squander the money on expenditures other than the rehabilitation of their homes.[85] In short, applicants were

80 *Id.*, citing the work of the RAND Corporation, Rick Eden & Patricia Boren, Timely Assistance: Evaluating the Speed of Road Home Grantmaking (2008).

81 Louisiana Recovery Authority Act, Acts 2006, 1st Ex. Sess., No. 5, § 2 (codified at LSA – R.S. 49 §§ 220.1- 220.7).

82 Eden & Boren, *supra* note 80, at xii.

83 Nossiter, *supra* note 79 (citing Eden & Boren at 7).

84 Eden & Boren, *supra* note 80, at xiii. In appropriating the funds in June 2006, Emergency Supplemental Appropriations Act for Defense, the Global War on Terror, and Hurricane Recovery, 2006, H. R. 4939, Pub. L. No. 109-234, 120 Stat. 472-473 (June 15, 2006), Congress provided that cash grants were to be made to individual homeowners "based on a house's value before the storm and the extent of the damage, minus insurance payments and other grants already received." Nossiter, *supra* note 79.

85 Nossiter, *supra* note 79. In the Emergency Supplemental Appropriations Act, Congress included the requirement that "the Secretary [of HUD] shall establish procedures to prevent recipients from receiving any duplication of benefits and report quarterly to the Committees on Appropriations with regard to all steps taken to prevent fraud and abuse …" *Supra* note 84, at 120 Stat. 473.

not trusted to abide by the rules.[86] In fact, very little fraud has been reported.[87] But many people have encountered frustrating and ultimately unnecessary delays.[88]

These observations are not made to single out the problems Louisiana officials encountered in responding to one of the most devastating natural disasters in U.S. history, but rather to suggest that officials in HUD and the states can draw useful lessons from this experience in developing the regulations and application plans to implement the NHTF programs. Perhaps the most important lesson is to trust the people at the local level and not burden the allocation system with excessive regulatory steps beyond those necessary to provide an accounting of the use of the funds.

In another context, the Supreme Court of Utah made a relevant observation about trust:

> The fear of local governments abusing their delegated powers as a justification for strict construction of those powers is a slur on the right and the ability of people to govern themselves ... [W]e simply do not accept the proposition that local governments are not to be trusted with the full scope of legislatively granted powers to meet the needs of their local constituents.[89]

The St Louis Post-Dispatch made a similar point in an editorial concerning land acquisition activities in a low income neighborhood in St Louis by a suburban St Louis developer. In noting that, because of the size and complexity of the project, "eminent domain would appear to be unavoidable," the Post editorialized that

---

86 A key part of the complicated application process was the verification step. Applicants had to prove ownership of the homes they sought to rebuild. In many cases, hurricane victims had inherited their property but title was never formally changed. Without some evidence of the change in title, applicants could not prove ownership. Email from John Ammann, Director, Saint Louis University Law Clinic, to the author (October 13, 2008). Mr Ammann and members of his staff have led SLU law students to New Orleans during semester and spring break periods to assist applicants in the title verification process. *See also*, David Hammer, *Road Home Deadlines Are Rescinded; Thousands of Applicants Have Encountered Technical Obstacles*, New Orleans Times-Picayune, August 28, 2008, at 1 (reporting on the rescission of deadlines to resolve legal issues that threatened to overwhelm a legal-aid consortium assisting applicants).

87 Nossiter, *supra* note 79. However, an audit by the Inspector General of HUD did find evidence that funds had been dispersed to ineligible persons or to persons whose eligibility was not adequately supported. *OIG Finds Eligibility Problems in Louisiana's Road Home Program*, 36 Housing & Development RPTR. No. CD-17 [Current Dev.], at 527 (September 1, 2008) (reporting on HUD audit report, 2008-AO-1005), *available at* www.hud.gov/offices/oig.

88 Eden & Boren, *supra* note 80, at 1.

89 State v. Hutchinson, 624 P. 2d 1116, 1121 (Utah 1980) (rejecting challenge to Salt Lake County ordinance requiring local candidates for elective office to file campaign statements and disclose campaign contributions).

"[the developer's] best strategy is to trust the people by sharing information and listening to constructive criticism."[90]

Over the past 30 years or so, state and local governments have gained valuable experience in making decisions regarding the allocation of limited housing and community development funds. The NHTF program is designed to draw on that experience and use the seed money potential of the new trust funds to restart a production program geared to working people in the bottom quartile of the current service economy.

National Support for Creative State and Local Housing Programs

Passage of the Housing and Economic Recovery Act of 2008, with the Housing Trust and Capital Magnet Trust Funds included,[91] climaxed a 20-year legislative struggle with odds as long as those faced by Mr Redford's character in *The Candidate*.[92] Advocates for a National Housing Trust Fund had long sought it as a way to re-energize federal housing policy with a greater focus on the housing needs of the lowest-income cohort of America's households.[93] Their model was based on the state and local housing trust fund concept developed by the Housing Trust Fund Project of the Center for Community Change and operating in at least 43 states with close to 600 separate city, county or state housing trust funds.[94]

A National Housing Trust Fund is not meant to be a return to the top-down, Washington-dictated housing programs of the 1940s–1970s, whose poster children were the Public Housing and the Section 8 New Construction/Substantial Rehabilitation programs.[95] While Public Housing and Section 8 New Construction/Substantial Rehabilitation continue to provide thousands of units of decent and affordable rental housing, no new production funds have been authorized for these

90 *Our View: Trust the People*, St Louis Post-dispatch, September 15, 2008, at A16.

91 Housing and Economic Recovery Act, *supra* note 3.

92 The Candidate, *supra* note 1.

93 For discussion of the NHTF movement, *see* Laura Schwarx, Comment, *The 2007 National Affordable Housing Trust Fund Act: A National Fund for a National Need*, 17 J. of Affordable Housing and Community Development Law 393, 398–9 (2008); Bernstine & Saraf, *supra* note 13; Beth Parr, Note, *Almost Home: Policy and Politics in the Campaign for a National Housing Trust Fund*, 11 Geo. J. Pov. L. & Pol. 321 (2004).

94 The Housing Trust Fund Project began in 1986 as an effort to provide information and technical assistance to groups seeking to establish housing trust funds. Center for Community Change, Housing Trust Fund Project, www.communitychange.org/our-projects/htf/housing-trust-funds/ (last visited November 7, 2008).

95 For a history of the public housing program, with a special focus on the Boston Housing Authority, *see* Lawrence J. Vale, From the Puritans to the Projects: Public Housing and Public Neighbors (2000), and Lawrence J. Vale, Reclaiming Public Housing: A Half Century Of Struggle In Three Public Neighborhoods (2002).

programs since the advent of the LIHTC.[96] Rather than return to those centralized models of housing production assistance, the NHTF is designed to provide a regular, predictable, and "permanent"[97] source of funds that will supplement state and local housing efforts that emphasize the supply side of the housing equation.

Given the relatively long incubation period, the relatively small amount of initial funding, and the emphasis on the housing needs of extremely low income (30 percent or less of area median income—$15,000/year/family of four) and very low income (50 percent or less of area median income—$25,000/year/family of four)[98] households, effective use of the Housing Trust and Capital Magnet Funds will require careful analysis of local housing needs and the possibilities of leveraging other resources with monies available through the trust funds. Examples of state and locally managed programs that could benefit from Housing Trust Fund support include state and local housing trust funds, community preservation funds and community land trusts (CLTs).

State and Local Housing Trust Funds

As noted earlier, an extensive network of state and local housing trust funds has developed in the past quarter century. A myriad of revenue sources are used to operate state housing trust funds, with the real estate transfer tax[99] (11 states) and the land records recording fee[100] (seven states) the most common.[101] The "objective of flexibility" is a noteworthy component of state housing trust funds, as a wide variety of eligible activities, including "new construction, rehabilitation/preservation, acquisition, serving special populations, and permanently supportive housing," as well as 13 other activities such as down payment assistance, transitional housing, homeless services, and rental assistance, are featured in the state programs.[102]

96 LIHTC, *supra* note 64.

97 While the initial funding source, "an amount equal to 4.2 basis points for each dollar of the unpaid principal balance of [Fannie Mae and Freddie Mac's] total new business purchases," Housing and Economic Recovery Act, *supra* note 3, at § 1337(a) (1) & (2), is not subject to Congressional appropriations, the problematic status of Fannie and Freddie, *see, e.g.*, Sudeep Reddy, *Fannie, Freddie Woes Vex Experts and Leave U.S. Hard Choices*, WALL ST. JOURNAL, August 25, 2008, at A2, plus the fact that Congress can always revisit, revise, and repeal legislation, casts doubt on the idea of a "permanent" program.

98 For these examples, the estimated 2007 national median income of $50,700 is used. Alemayehu Bishaw & Jessica Semega, *Income, Earnings, and Poverty Data from the 2007 American Community Survey* 3, U.S. CENSUS BUREAU (August 2008).

99 A real estate transfer tax, also known as a documentary stamp tax, is a tax on the "privilege of transferring title." 35 ILL. COMP. STAT. 200/31-10 (2006).

100 Missouri, for example, allocates $3.00 of its land recording fees to the state housing trust fund. MO. ANN. STAT. § 59.319.2-3 (West 2007).

101 Center for Community Change, *supra* note 94, HOUSING TRUST FUND PROGRESS REPORT 6 (2007).

102 *Id.* at 10.

Many county and city trust funds assist similar activities with revenues garnered through sources such as voter-approved housing bond issues (Austin, Texas), electronic filing of property tax disclosure forms (Indianapolis), surplus casino revenues (Milwaukee), and tax increments (Anaheim, California).[103]

Community Preservation Funds

Community preservation funds (CPFs) are "dedicated perpetual environmental fund[s]" that enable communities to purchase land for environmental purposes such as preservation of open space, protection of water quality, and creation of community parks.[104] The CPFs are also used to acquire land for affordable housing initiatives.[105] CPFs are described as "facilitators" enabling landowners to sell fee title or the development rights from their land to local public entities for fair market value.[106] The primary sources of monies for CPFs include real estate transfer fees on the sale of houses above the median sale price in the community (New York),[107] and a surcharge on real property expressed as a percentage, currently "not more than 3 per cent," of the annual real estate tax levy (Massachusetts).[108]

The Joint Center for Housing Studies of Harvard University has recommended the establishment of CPFs as "mission driven entit[ies]" capable of participating in the foreclosure sale market "with the goal of creating affordable housing and stable communities rather than simply maximizing profits."[109] The subprime mortgage foreclosure crisis has affected cities as well as individual homeowners and lenders going through the foreclosure process.[110] Large-scale foreclosures threaten to

---

103 *Id.* at 16.

104 Citizens Campaign for the Environment (NY), Campaigns: Community Preservation Funds, www.citizenscampaign.org/campaigns/cpf.asp (last visited September 29, 2008).

105 Community Preservation Coalition (MA), The Community Preservation Act, www.community preservation.org/index.cfm (last visited September 29, 2008).

106 Citizens Campaign, *supra* note 104.

107 *Id.*; Town of Southampton, Community Preservation Fund, www.town. southampton.ny.us/listing.ihtml ?myid=1957&id=170&cat=Land%20Ma (last visited November 6, 2008) (describing the Town of Southampton, New York's CPF, which in its first decade of operation generated over $243 million and purchased title or development rights to more than 2400 acres within the Town limits).

108 Mass. Gen. Laws ch. 44B, §§ 3–7 (2000); Community Preservation Coalition, *supra* note 105.

109 Harvard Joint Center for Housing Studies, America's Rental Housing: The Key to a Balanced National Policy 23 (2008).

110 See, e.g., David Streitfeld & Gretchen Morgenson, *Building Flawed American Dreams: Helping Low-Income Families Buy Homes and Watching the Failures*, N.Y. Times, October 19, 2008, at 1; Tim Logan, *Renters Often Become the Forgotten Victims*, St Louis Post-Dispatch, June 20, 2008, at B1; Rich Brooks & Constance Mitchell Ford, *The United*

pull down entire neighborhoods and vast swatches of cities.[111] For example, Cleveland, Ohio, has been hit so hard with subprime mortgage foreclosures that it has repeatedly been the headline on foreclosure stories.[112]

Commentators have noted that cities tend to react to such large-scale foreclosures by either letting speculators acquire the properties at foreclosure sales and dispose of the property, seeking profits in the process, or acquiring such units themselves in order to demolish them, clear the land, and seek development of new housing units.[113] As a third alternative, the Joint Center recommends that cities participate in the foreclosure sale process[114] through CPFs organized as not-for-profit corporations whose mission is to "capture a significant share of good-quality housing … [being offered to the highest bidder at foreclosure sales]."[115]

The Joint Center also noted that several national not-for-profit organizations, NeighborWorks America, Enterprise Community Partners, Inc., the Housing Partnership Network, and the Local Initiatives Support Corporation, with assistance from the Ford and MacArthur Foundations, have collaborated to sponsor the National Community Stabilization Trust, which is designed to assist local communities "to acquire distressed Real Estate Owned (REO) properties[116] from national servicers and investors and to finance and rehabilitate them in a manner that promotes community stabilization and affordable housing."[117] Local CPFs could be created or expanded by cities using funds from the National Housing Trust Fund, coupled with funds from local and state housing trust funds. These

---

States of Subprime; Data Show Bad Loans Permeate the Nation; Pain Could Last Years, WALL ST. J., October 11, 2007, at A1.

111 ALAN MALLACH, TACKLING THE MORTGAGE CRISIS: 10 ACTION STEPS FOR STATE GOVERNMENT 6 (2008).

112 Margot Carmichael Lester, *Sign of the Times—Five Cities Bringing New Life to Abandoned Sites*, DEVELOPER, August 11, 2008, *available at* www.developeronline.com/sign-of-the-times-five-cities-turning (noting that, in the process of recording Cleveland's troubles, commentators have dubbed it "the Cleve").

113 For example, Margot Lester's entry on the Developer blog, *id.,* features the "5 in 5" program of Buffalo, New York Mayor Byron Brown—demolition of 5000 of the city's approximately 10,000 abandoned structures in five years, and Cleveland, Ohio's goal of demolishing 1000 abandoned houses in 2008 following demolition of 800 in 2007. A response to her entry stated that the demolition strategy featured was "insane … Vacant buildings need to be reoccupied, by any means necessary. Failing that, buildings need to be stabilized so that they can persist until new uses and needs arise." Posting of Jon Seward in response to Lester (August 19, 2008, 9:05 a.m.). *Id.*

114 HARV. JOINT CTR., *supra* note 109.

115 *Id.* at 23.

116 REO properties are those that have gone through the foreclosure sale process and have been purchased by the entities that were holding or servicing the loans that went into default.

117 NeighborWorks America, *National Community Stabilization Trust to be Established by NeighborWorks America and Other Nonprofit Organizations*, AUGUST NEIGHBORWORKS ALERT, www.nw.org (last visited August 29, 2008).

entities could collaborate with the new Stabilization Trust and bid on foreclosed properties in order to enable them to be preserved and restored to the local housing market, or banked until the local market recovered.

The primary source of initial funding for CPFs organized to participate in the foreclosure sale process likely will be the $3.9 billion emergency CDBG funds appropriated in 2008.[118] But those funds will not be sufficient to enable affected cities to resolve all their problems with residential abandonment. When the NHTF trust funds are fully operational in 2010, an allocation of housing fund revenues could enable CPFs to continue to support local, neighborhood-based reclamation projects.

Community Land Trusts

Community land trusts (CLTs) are an increasingly popular device for implementing affordable housing and neighborhood preservation programs. Blending the trust concept of separate legal and equitable title with the long-term ground lease, CLTs enable a particular community to control the use of land while permitting individuals to have an ownership or controlling stake in the housing they occupy.[119] CLTs are organized as not-for-profit corporations who take title to land, then transfer control of that land to housing developers, neighborhood organizations or individuals who agree, through the terms of a long-term ground lease, to use the land in a particular manner.[120] Originally developed as a technique for preserving farm land and a rural way of life,[121] CLTs attracted attention as a potential way to provide permanently affordable housing in cities[122] at a time in the late 1980s and 1990s when hundreds of thousands of federally subsidized housing units appeared

118 Housing and Economic Recovery Act of 2008, *supra* note 3, at § 2301.

119 David M. Abromowitz, *Community Land Trusts and Ground Leases,* 1 J. of Affordable Housing and Community Development Law 2, at 5 (1992).

120 *Id.* For a comprehensive discussion of the CLT's role in home ownership, *see* Julie Farrell Curtin & Lance Bocarsly, *CLTs: A Growing Trend in Affordable Home Ownership,* 17 J. of Affordable Housing and Community Development Law 367 (2008).

121 John Emmeus Davis & Rick Jacobus, The City-clt Partnership: Municipal Support For Community Land Trusts 4 (Lincoln Institute of Land Policy 2008); Daniel Fireside, *Community Land Trust Keeps Prices Affordable—For Now and Forever,* YES! Magazine, Fall 2008 ("environmentalist Rick Carbin formed the Vermont Land Trust in the late 1970s to preserve open space as developers bought up farms"), *available at* www.yesmagazine.org/article.asp?ID=2834.

122 David Abromowitz uses the term "preserving housing affordability *for the long term.*" David M. Abromowitz, *An Essay on Community Land Trusts: Toward Permanently Affordable Housing, in* Property And Values: Alternatives To Public And Private Ownership 213, 214 (Charles Geisler & Gail Daneker eds., 2000) (emphasis added). Davis and Jacobus identify over 200 CLTs in 41 states in 2008, *supra* note 121.

on the verge of being lost to the low- and moderate-income market, as subsidies were expiring and mortgage loan prepayment privileges were vesting.[123]

Perhaps the best known CLT established during that period was created by the Dudley Street Neighborhood Initiative (DSNI), an organization of residents in the Dudley Street area of the Boston neighborhood of Roxbury that was delegated the power of eminent domain to enable it to assemble large tracts of land that then could be sold to private developers who would agree to follow a community plan developed by DSNI through an intensive, resident-driven, planning process.[124] As David Abromowitz notes, DSNI made the critical decision to retain control of the land in order to preserve the ability to ensure that housing developed on that land would remain affordable.[125] This was accomplished by implementing the CLT ground lease technique through an affiliated entity, Dudley Neighbors Incorporated (DNI).[126] According to Abromowitz, "[t]he DSNI/DNI experience is illuminating because of the explicit dedication of community members to the goal of not just separating ownership, but of allocating value as well."[127]

CLTs function on the principle that a major portion of land value is attributable to the efforts of the community or neighborhood in which the land is located:

---

123 Abromowitz, *supra* note 122; Curtin & Bocarsly, *supra* note 120, at 371. Federal efforts to encourage preservation of assisted housing included the Emergency Low-Income Preservation Act of 1987 (ELIHPA), 12 U.S.C. § 1715l, and the Low Income Housing Preservation and Resident Homeownership Act of 1990 (LIHPRHA), 12 U.S.C. §§ 4101–4125, offering incentives to preserve affordability and restricting prepayment privileges.

The Housing and Community Development Act of 1992 recognized CLTs with the following definition:

> (f) the term "community land trust" means a community housing development organization … (1) that is not sponsored by a for-profit corporation; (2) that is established to carry out activities under paragraph (3); (3) that it: (a) acquires parcels of land, held in perpetuity, primarily for conveyance under long-term ground leases; (b) transfers ownership of any structural improvements located on such leased parcels to the lessees; and (c) retains a preemptive option to purchase any such structural improvement at a price determined by a formula that is designed to ensure that the improvement remains affordable to low- and moderate-income families in perpetuity; (4) whose corporate membership that is open to any adult resident of a geographic area specified by the by-laws of the organization; and (5) whose board of directors includes a majority of members who are elected by the corporation membership; and is composed of equal numbers of (i) lessee pursuant to paragraph(3)(B), (ii) corporate members who are not lessees, and (iii) any other category of persons described in the by-laws of the organization.

42 U.S.C. § 12773(f), as quoted in Abromowitz, *supra* note 122, at 229, n. 17.

124 Abromowitz, *supra* note 122, at 222.

125 *Id.* at 223.

126 *Id.*

127 *Id.*

> DSNI views much of [a sale price greater than the purchase price] as primarily a recognition of the increased community value. The portion that the individual adds on after purchase, such as through "sweat equity" or paid-for improvements, remains with the individual, but the portion flowing from the overall increase in the area's desirability stays with the land.[128]

With this technique, CLT's are able to sell long-term leasehold interests and title to housing located on the leasehold land, while retaining the right to preserve the affordability of the housing by exercising "a long-term option to repurchase the homes at a formula-driven price when homeowners later decide to move."[129]

Owners of CLT housing include individual families, members of condominiums, cooperative housing corporations, and rental housing developers, both non-profit and for-profit.[130] For example, the Champlain Housing Trust (CHT), created in 2006 through the merger of the Burlington, VT, Community Land Trust and the Lake Champlain Housing Development Corporation, owns over 1600 apartment units and the land on which over 500 homeowners and condo owners live.[131] Under the terms of the CHT ground lease, ground rent is minimal ($25 per month) and home sellers get no part of any increase in land value and only 25 percent of the increase in home value.[132] With CHT owners and tenants sitting on the corporate board along with city officials, architects, planners, and other city residents, CHT is "an experiment in democratic self-governance as well as an affordable housing program."[133]

Community Land Trusts as a Vehicle for Linking Housing Trust Funds with Community Preservation Funds

An example of the possible use of Housing Trust Fund and Capital Magnet Fund monies for home ownership and/or rental housing is a program underway in University City, Missouri (U. City), a first line suburb of St Louis with a population of approximately 37,500, a vibrant commercial core,[134] part of the campus of Washington University of St Louis, and a variety of residential neighborhoods

---

128 *Id.* The principle of a community increment of value was recognized by the Court of Appeals of New York in Penn. Cent. Transp. Co. v. City of New York, 366 N.E. 2d 1271, 1275–1276 (1977) ("a fair return is to be accorded the owner, but society is to receive its due for its share in the making of a once great railroad"), *affirmed on other grounds*, 438 U.S. 104 (1978).

129 Davis & Jacobus, *supra* note 121, at 4.

130 *Id.* at 5.

131 Fireside, *supra* note 121.

132 *Id.*

133 *Id.*

134 The Delmar Loop was named one of "Ten Great Streets in America" by the American Planning Association in 2007. Ruth Knack, *Great Streets: What Makes Them Special?* 74 PLANNING 1, at 12, 17 (January 2008).

ranging from very high quality to deteriorating quality.[135] The Sutter Heights neighborhood, located in the northeast quadrant of U. City adjacent the City of St Louis and another first line suburb, the City of Wellston, contains a variety of small houses, including "folk ('shotgun'), bungalow and (Dutch) Colonial Revival (with gambrel roofs)" styles. Most were built in the early 1900s on 30 feet by 146 feet lots, with 900–1000 square feet of living space.[136]

Sutter Heights is part of a larger neighborhood whose center, the intersection of Kingsland and Vernon/Olive, is the site of an effort spearheaded by U. City to create a "small town" that would be "at the forefront of sustainable development that helps reduce auto-dependency."[137] When the area was studied in 2002 by the U. City Planning Department,[138] the consensus was that the lots were too small to support homes suitable to a twenty-first century lifestyle and thus a strategy of "donat[ing] or sell[ing] city-owned vacant land to adjacent landowners was adopted" to encourage the merging of lots and the construction of larger homes. However, the 2008 surge in oil prices and the impact that surge had on gas prices and utility costs has led U. City to re-think its strategy and to seek proposals for the design and construction of "smaller, energy efficient green homes."[139]

While U. City understandably may wish to attract higher income families, some portion of the planned development could well be dedicated as affordable housing for families whose incomes fall in the \$15–\$20,000 range eligible for assistance through programs funded by the NHTF. A CLT composed of representatives of the U. City target area, citizens of other neighborhoods in U. City, and educational and business leaders, could serve as the mechanism for linking NHTF monies with funds from the Missouri State Housing Trust Fund administered by the Missouri Housing Development Commission,[140] St Louis County housing funds, and private sources, to "ensure permanent affordability"[141] of the houses the city wishes to have developed, as well as apartments designated for ELI households.

135 The description of University City and its infill development project is taken from University City's Request for Proposals, *Five LEED® Certified Homes In a Key Residential Area* (August 2008) (copy on file with author).

136 *Id.*

137 *Id.*

138 University City, Missouri, Department of Planning & Development, The Northeast Neighborhood Plan Progress Report 2002, *available at* http://www.ucitymo.org/index.asp?NID=389.

139 Request for Proposals, *supra* note 135.

140 Mo. Rev. Stat. §§ 215.034–215.038 (2000).

141 The quote is from the website of CityFirst Enterprises, a non-profit organization in Washington, D.C. that is launching a city-wide CLT with the goal of providing 10,000 units of permanently affordable housing for working families, *available at* www.cfenterprises.org/cityfirst.html (last visited November 6, 2008).

A CPF could serve as the vehicle for acquiring and holding abandoned properties and vacant lots until housing and credit markets rebound.[142]

Conclusion

The NHTF legislation, enacted as the worst housing crisis in generations was nearing a climax, provides an opportunity to rethink the myriad approaches the nation and its states and municipalities have taken to the problem of affordable housing. The subprime mortgage foreclosure crisis has dramatized the point that, while homeownership is a treasured value and an important policy goal, it cannot be conferred successfully on households who do not have the resources or the skills to manage its responsibilities, nor can it be sustained if buyers, lenders, and service-providers lose sight of the economic realities of the home-buying transaction.

A balanced policy that shows respect and support for households who need or desire to rent, while supporting homeownership for whomever that prospect is reasonable, is long overdue.[143] Passage of the NHTF legislation presents just that opportunity. The long delay before full implementation of the NHTF in 2012, occasioned by the need to use prospective resources to respond to the foreclosure crisis, provides the luxury of time for thoughtful planning and analysis of implementation issues not available to Louisiana authorities responding to Katrina.

This analysis should include recognition of the long experience state governments have had in developing and testing housing approaches through their administration of state housing bond programs and the LIHTC, as well as the myriad ideas and programs local housing trust funds have implemented. The growing recognition of the potential offered by community land trusts and community preservation trusts to serve as vehicles for acquiring land and preserving affordability of residential units built on that land also should be noted. Above all, implementation analysis and planning should take place in an atmosphere of trust and respect for the persons intended to be benefited by the NHTF legislation.

---

142 CLTs and CPFs can serve the valuable function of absorbing the cost of land and thereby reducing the total cost of housing built on that land to the homeowner or renter. Curtin & Bocarsly, *supra* note 120, at 373. For an argument that the cost of assembling land in suitably sized (small)lots is a major barrier to the production of affordable housing, *see* Witold Rybczynski, *Why Can't We Build an Affordable House?*, The Wilson Quarterly (Summer 2008), *available at* http://www.wilsoncenter.org/index.cfm?fuseaction=wq.essay&essay.

143 The point is made forcefully by the Joint Center for Housing Studies of Harvard University, *supra* note 109.

Finally, people desire competency from all levels of government. Implementation of programmatic initiatives provides an excellent opportunity for competency to be demonstrated.

Acknowledgements

I appreciate the comments and suggestions given to me by John Ammann, Roger Goldman, Kerry Ryan, Nic Terry, Anders Walker, Nancy Walsh, and other participants in a faculty workshop at Saint Louis University School of Law. Research librarians Lynn Hartke, David Kullman, and Peggy McDermott were indispensable. Laura Schwarz, 3L, Saint Louis University School of Law and Jessica Tietjen, 2L, Saint Louis University School of Law, provided excellent research assistance. Special thanks to University of Colorado Law Professor Nestor Davidson, whose invitation, and patience, gave me the necessary push to write this chapter.

Chapter 6

Putting Community Equity in Community Development: Resident Equity Participation in Urban Redevelopment

Barbara Bezdek

> Property is more accurately described as being inextricably part of a network of relationships that is neither limited to, nor usefully defined by, the property boundaries with which the legal system is accustomed to dealing.[1]

Property is inextricably bound up in a network of economic and social relationships. Regulating the negative externalities of land use that traverse legal boundaries and impose social costs on neighbors lies at the heart of much of our land use law.[2] Cities are comprised of neighborhoods, within which communities sharing a geographic space over time establish that "small-scale, everyday public life" and learn to manage themselves through working relationships and voluntary association. Jane Jacobs called this the "irreplaceable social capital" that gave cities their life, as she railed against modern urban planning for destroying that cooperative condition and thus the trust and social control necessary to viable neighborhoods within big cities.[3]

The loss of communities is the predictable result of local government policies to deploy land use powers and sink public subsidy into for-profit redevelopments that disperse low-wealth residents, re-title the land, and reallocate urban blocks to remake inner city neighborhoods. In effect these redevelopment practices specially

---

1 Joseph L. Sax, *Takings, Private Property and Public Rights*, 81 Yale L. J. 149, 152 (1971).

2 Euclid v. Ambler Realty Co., 272 U.S. 365, 391 (1926) (upholding early zoning code in urban areas for the purpose of separating "noxious" and incompatible uses of neighboring properties); Joseph Sax argued 35 years ago that because certain uses of property could have adverse effects on wetlands, forests, streams, and similar natural features, members of the public seeking to preserve such resources on privately owned land sought to vindicate a public interest in common resources which was rooted in part in the "maintenance of those resources found necessary to sustain the well being of the community." Sax, *supra* note 1, at 157–9. The environmental land use movement that followed is recounted in Patricia E. Salkin, *From Euclid to Growing Smart: The Transformation of the American Local Land Use Ethic into Local Land Use and Environmental Controls*, 20 Pace Envtl. L. Rev. 109, 113 (2002).

3 Jane Jacobs, The Death and Life of Great American Cities 146–83 (1961).

tax existing communities in the path of development, sweeping aside their tangible and intangible capital and connections, while they cater generously to wealthier in-movers. The special concern of this chapter is to recalibrate the benefits of private–public partnerships to remake inner city neighborhoods, by braking the rate at which urban land is being reclaimed from low-wealth residents by local governments, whether as blight clearance or for economic revitalization post-*Kelo*.[4] Public oversight requirements have not kept pace with the dispossession, yet the costs that these development decisions impose on the social fabric of communities rend the shared networks necessary to residents' abilities to meet basic social needs, like raising children or earning a living.[5] Jacobs warned that once the web of this "social capital" is destroyed, accumulating new social capital in the re-made place is a slow and chancy proposition.[6]

Today many critics seek to limit the authority of government to use eminent domain for urban redevelopment, to shrink the opportunity for monied interests to leverage government power for their own projects. Alternatively, others argue for improving the procedures required before the exercise of eminent domain, or for changing the meaning of "just compensation."[7]

This chapter explores the creation of community equity shareholding in public–private redevelopment projects. Community equity shares (CES) embody three principles. First, community equity shareholding recognizes limited rights in an existing community, akin to land ownership, as the basis for both *participation* in the decision-making about the character of the redevelopment, and *profit participation* in the redevelopment projects that displace long-term residents.[8]

4 Kelo v. City of New London, 545 U.S. 469 (2005). Suzette Kelo's pro bono counsel, The Institute for Justice, maintains detailed accounts of municipal exercises of eminent domain for private, economic development-related land assembly, at Castle Coalition, http://castlecoalition.org. The Institute for Justice reports that following *Kelo*, the use of eminent domain for private development disproportionately affects residents who are ethnic or racial minorities, live at or below the federal poverty line, and have completed significantly less education, compared to people in the surrounding communities. Dick M. Carpenter & John K. Ross, *Victimizing the Vulnerable, The Demographics of Eminent Domain Abuse 2* (June 2007), *available at* http://www.ij.org/images/pdf_folder/other_pubs/Victimizing_the_Vulnerable.pdf.

5 Mindy Thompson Fullilove, Root Shock: How Tearing Up City Neighborhoods Hurts America, and What We Can Do About It (2004) [hereinafter Fullilove, Root Shock].

6 Jacobs, *supra* note 3, at 180.

7 James J. Kelly, Jr., *Taming Eminent Domain*, Shelterforce, March 22, 2008, *available at* http://ssrn.com/abstract=1271223; J. Peter Byrne, *Condemnation of Low Income Residential Communities under the Takings Clause*, 23 UCLA J. Envtl. L. & Pol'y 131 (2005).

8 See Barbara L. Bezdek, *To Attain "The Just Rewards of So Much Struggle": Local-Resident Equity Participation In Urban Revitalization*, 36 Hofstra L. Rev. 37 (2006) [hereinafter, Bezdek, *Local-Resident Equity Participation*].

Second, by instantiating social and geographic community as ownership in the calculus of land use, it is possible for residents in the district of a proposed redevelopment to parlay those shares for two purposes: for participation in the decision-making about proposed redevelopment, and for participation in the profits from the displacing redevelopment project. A third principle is to add a player, the special-purpose community equity corporation comprised of all the community equity shareholders and wielding their limited powers in common, to the redevelopment deal-making that, unchecked, would impose undue burdens including displacement upon the long-term residents of the targeted district. Community equity shareholding can be effectuated by changes in local governments' redevelopment and procurement procedures, which can assist to change the governmental calculus when it uses or threatens to use its land use powers to displace low income communities as it re-engineers urban environs in concert with private developers.

Status Quo Development by Dealmaking

The principal legal form for remaking city neighborhoods is the public–private partnership (PPP) by which local government agencies trade essential infrastructure at low or no cost in exchange for a profit-sharing stake or other anticipated return on the city's investment.[9] Cities have been dealmaking in this way since the 1970s,[10] yet the scale, pace, complexity, and bilateral character of today's

9 About 30 states have legislation authorizing local governments to negotiate disposition and development agreements, express contracts with private partners. The arrangement can be successful for municipalities and their private partners. "The bundle of sticks associated with land ownership has been deliberately broken apart and replaced with a pattern of contractual responsibilities that, given the nature of the deal, allocates to the respective public and private parties the specific elements of assembly, clearance, construction, maintenance, and control they are best equipped to perform." Marc B. Mihaly, *Public-Private Redevelopment Partnerships and the Supreme Court*, 7 VT. J. OF ENVTL. LAW 41 (2006).

10 City officials became dealmakers during the 1970s in order to complete projects begun under federal urban policies, and used their funds to adapt the lessons learned following the withdrawal of federal funds in the 1980s—urban fiscal distress's peak. EDWARD J. BLAKELY, PLANNING LOCAL ECONOMIC DEVELOPMENT: THEORY AND PRACTICE 153–4 (2d ed. 1994). The avowed purpose is typically to enhance the city's tax base, *see, e.g.*, Andrew Cannarsa, *Study Criticizes City's Redevelopment, Says Practices have Created "Two Cities"*, THE EXAMINER, June 24, 2008, *available at* http://www.examiner.com/a-1455745~Study_criticizes_city_s_redevelopment__says_practices_have_created__two_cities_.html (Baltimore developer Bill Stuever praises the "public–private partnerships" in an effort to build the city's tax base)

municipal reliance upon PPPs[11] evades the ability of the locality's people to assure that their government is acting for the general welfare, rather than for select other segments of the populace. A more particular application of this principle can be stated in the context of intensive redevelopment of deteriorated neighborhoods: local government should not callously jettison urban residents and scatter them for the gain of private developers and wealthier in-movers, without enabling the resident community members also to gain from the renewal of their neighborhood. In a well-functioning democracy, government's role is to responsibly assess the social welfare costs and benefits of its powers, without illegitimate favoritism or unjustifiable disparate impacts. Particularly in land use law, the central problem is to regulate the imposition of social costs onto others arising from a specific use of land. The law governing urban redevelopment is overdue for a corrective that will force the internalization of its true social costs.

The private contract model of development agreements and public–private partnerships renders invisible the inequitable allocation of the benefits and burdens of the deals that redistribute urban territories. The disfavored occupants of areas targeted for redevelopment garner no demonstrable share in the supposed gain to the general welfare which is the doctrinal justification for the city's exercise of governmental powers to condemn and re-title the residents' neighborhoods. In reality of course, courts referee very few of these clashes between the interests of low income residents for affordable housing and the social capital accrued in their neighborhood, and the interests of higher-earning and -spending denizens that cities aim to attract to the newly developed urban territories. Low-wealth communities are replaced by new upscale housing and shops and a brighter urban image. The displaced bear burdens which their compatriots do not: the destruction of their long-time neighborhoods and the social capital they have built up there. All gone in a Diaspora: the old neighborhood destroyed.[12]

11 Lynne Sagalyn recently observed that we are now in a third generation of PPP types: in the 1970s, municipalities and private developers learned by doing; in the 1980s, large specialized development companies emerged with comparative national expertise, and several cities have established special purpose corporations, project-specific entities. The third wave PPPs are commonly initiated by developers seeking public-sector involvement, which some have called "private–public" development to signal the enthusiasm for private investment in urban neighborhoods among equity investment firms. These projects pose new challenges, since government does not own the development sites in many developer-initiated projects, giving public officials less bargaining power than when they hold legal title. Lynne B. Sagalyn, *Public Private Development: Lessons from History, Research and Practice,* 73 J. of the American Planning Association 7, 17 (2007).

12 Forced displacement by development is a global problem of enormous dimensions and dire consequences for millions. Accordingly, in international development, numerous scholars track that displacement to distill knowledge of displacement's social costs for the displacees into patterns of predictable, cumulative dimensions of impoverishment, in order to devise successful resettlement practices for people involuntarily displaced by development. *See, e.g.*, Michael M. Cernea, *Impoverishment Risks, Risk Management, and*

Local governments participating in the urban real estate market in this way are often frank about their purpose to engineer new urban territories and repopulate them with the wealthier classes.[13] In the U.S. this urban social engineering is sometimes characterized as a modern version of the pioneering that peopled the American plains with striving Europeans.[14] The public policy to restructure the territories of the central city unfairly allocates the costs of revitalization to the current residents and distributes the benefits to others. Increasingly, it is the developer, not the government, who initiates the redevelopment project and dictates the deal.[15] This is the antithesis of governance for the general welfare. This is not new, but its familiarity should engender sharper scrutiny, and new thinking to correct for its inequities.

Reconstruction: A Model for Population Displacement and Resettlement, http://www.un.org/esa/sustdev/sdissues/energy/op/hydro_cernea_population_resettlement_backgroundpaper.pdf (last visited October 20, 2008).

13 Roberto G. Quercia & George C. Galster, *Threshold Effects and the Expected Benefits of Attracting Middle-Income Households to the Central City*, 8 Housing Pol'y Debate 409, 412–13 (1997) (anticipating fiscal and social benefits of revitalization). Robin Paul Malloy, *The Political Economy Of Co-Financing America's Urban Renaissance*, 40 Vand. L. Rev. 67, 101–4 (1987) (analyzing complex cross-subsidy and co-financing model of urban redevelopment and concluding that key constituents most likely to benefit are "politicians and business people ... real estate professionals—lawyers, brokers and bankers ... local union workers such as construction workers who find work at the new projects, and local workers employed to clean and service the new buildings."). See also Audrey G. McFarlane, *The New Inner City: Class Transformation, Concentrated Affluence and the Obligations of the Police Power*, 8 U. Pa. J. Const. L. 1, 6–12 (2006) (citing numerous cities' development policies to encourage upper-middle class residential occupancy).

14 *See, e.g.*, McFarlane, *supra* note 13, at 5 (documenting the territorial reclamation of city centers worldwide for the affluent). Urban places that were once racialized as Black and classified as poor, dangerous, and off-limits to anyone of affluence and with choices, have taken on new meaning today. These places are now suppliers of housing that is relatively cheap, centrally located, and often architecturally rich. They are open territories for investment speculators, redevelopment agencies, and affluent professionals who reject the suburban form of living, but demand, and can easily pay for, luxury residential, commercial retail, entertainment, and other intangible spatial amenities. The nineteenth-century federal statutory regime to expand westward and push out American Indians, An Act to Secure Homesteads to Actual Settlers on the Public Domain, 12 Stat. 392 (1862) (43 USC 161), was repealed in 1976. *See generally* Mark E. Brandon, *Home on the Range: Family and Constitutionalism in American Continental Settlement,* 52 Emory L. J. 645, 671–7 (2003) (discussing political and economic understandings of "settlers" and "speculators" at that time).

15 *See, e.g.*, City of Norwood v. Horney, 830 N.E.2d 381, 383–85 (Ohio Ct. App. 2005); Gideon Kanner, *The Public Use Clause: Constitutional Mandate or "Hortatory Fluff"?*, 33 Pepp. L. Rev. 335, 336 (2006) (arguing that cities which stand to gain financially from joint development deals have an inherent conflict of interest in the exercise of the police power for the general welfare).

Taking the Community, Inflicting "New Poverty"

Targeted redevelopment projects in central city neighborhoods cause more harm to low-wealth urban neighborhoods than the physical insertion of unaffordable amenities and the physical displacement of longstanding residents and businesses. Investigations into displacement reveal risks that deeply threaten displaced households' chances of relocating "well": these include joblessness, homelessness, marginalization, loss of commonly enjoyed spaces and social resources, increased health risks, social disarticulation, the disruption of formal educational activities, and impairments of civil rights in voting and fair housing rights. Failure to recognize and avoid these risks may generate "new poverty," as opposed to the "old poverty" that people suffered before displacement.[16]

Exclusionary Displacement

Compulsory displacements that occur for development reasons raise major questions of social justice because they inequitably distribute the losses and benefits of the redevelopment. In the paradigmatic context for the exercise of eminent domain power for true public uses, forced displacement results from the need to build infrastructure—highways, hospitals, schools, and airports. Such programs improve many people's lives, deliver indisputably important services, and proffer employment. Nonetheless, the interests of residents facing displacement differ in kind and quality from the general public's—possessory and economic—many of which do not figure in the official costs of land assembly despite their complete extinguishment. While local governments claim to advance the general welfare as they funnel public resources into the redesign of urban spaces, it is hard to avoid the unvarnished truth that municipalities are terminating the residency of some in order to construct shiny, new, private residences and shops for affluent in-movers. This presents us with ineluctable issues of social justice and equity. Outside the condemnation regime, it is low income tenants who bear the greatest burden as cities court an increased tax base through gentrification.

Displacement by Destruction of Affordable Housing

Cities' public–private redevelopment projects continue to use eminent domain powers to displace low income households and raze their homes, but not to build more affordable housing.[17] This effect was achieved on a grand scale in the Urban

---

16 *See* Theodore E. Downing, *Avoiding New Poverty: Mining Induced Displacement and Resettlement*, Mining, Minerals and Sustainable Development (MMSD) (International Institute for Environment and Development), April 2002, http://www.iied.org/mmsd/mmsd_pdfs/058_downing.pdf.

17 Matthew J. Parlow, *Unintended Consequences: Eminent Domain and Affordable Housing*, 46 Santa Clara L. Rev. 841, 856–7 (2006) ("By taking such affordable housing

Renewal Era of the 1950s–1970s,[18] and in the successive forms of redevelopment since then[19] as local governments have actively courted gentrification in inter-jurisdictional competitions for tax base. Animating the legislative responsiveness to condo conversion was the powerful appeal of the security of "home."

The specter of being forced from one's home is one of the paradigms of autocratic government (as well as ruthless creditors). Protection against such uprooting by government inheres in our concept of liberty, and has always been protected to some degree by our Constitution, for example, in the Fourth Amendment as well as in the Takings Clause.

The contemporary crisis in housing affordability, which plagues millions of Americans caught in the crosshairs of disappearing low-cost housing, rising rents, and flat wages, raises the further fear among tenants of repeated relocation. Involuntary relocation discourages displaced persons from the exercise of a key organizational interest necessary in a democratic state.[20]

Even before the current foreclosure crisis, which has caused a substantial number of renters as well as homeowners to lose their homes, the number of households experiencing housing problems was increasing. From 2000 to 2006, the number of low income renter households whose housing costs exceed 50 percent of their income (a group the Department of Housing and Urban Development categorizes as having "severe housing cost burdens") increased by two million, or 34 percent. More than 12 million low income households receive no federal housing assistance

---

units off the market by their exercise of eminent domain power, cities reduce the available housing stock for low-income residents as such units are usually replaced by new high-end commercial, residential, and mixed-use projects").

18 Colin Gordon, *Blighting the Way: Urban Renewal, Economic Development, and the Elusive Definition of Blight*, 31 Fordham Urb. L.J. 305, 311–12 (2004); Wendell E. Pritchett, *The "Public Menace" of Blight: Urban Renewal and the Private Uses of Eminent Domain*, 21 Yale L. & Pol'y Rev. 1, 49 (2003); Chester W. Hartman, *Relocation: Illusory Promises and No Relief*, 57 Va. L. Rev. 745 (1971) (describing extensive uncompensated losses suffered by victims of urban renewal condemnations).

19 George Lefcoe, *Redevelopment Takings after Kelo: What's Blight Got to Do with It?*, 17 S. Cal. Rev. L. & Soc. Just. 803, 815 (2008); Lynn E. Blais, *Urban Revitalization in the Post-Kelo Era*, 34 Fordham Urb. L.J. 657, 674 (2007) (noting that, of the 34 states that enacted post-Kelo limitations on their eminent domain powers, two thirds of these retained exceptions for areas that could be shown to be blighted).

20 John Ely, Democracy and Distrust 86–88 (1980); Frank Michelman, *Property as a Constitutional Right*, 38 Wash & Lee L. Rev. 1097, 1112 (1981) (articulating the view that rights, including property rights, under a political constitution such as that of the U.S., are first to be regarded as political rights); Lawrence H. Tribe, *Forward: Toward a Model of Roles in the Due Process of Life and Law*, 87 Harv. L. Rev. 1, 9 (1973) (rights between associational rights and rights of personhood).

and face housing problems that public housing (or other housing assistance) would alleviate, if there were a sufficient stock of assisted housing.[21]

Studies of urban renewal reveal that the typical residents displaced by urban renewal paid 20 percent more rent after being relocated;[22] from one-fourth to one-half of displaced families lived in substandard housing despite a substantial rent increase.[23] In 1970 Congress enacted the Uniform Relocation Act (URA) to compel federal agencies, as well as state and local agencies receiving federal funds, to provide relocation assistance to "displaced persons," including payments to secure "comparable replacement housing." The most extensive study conducted since the URA was enacted is U.S. Department of Transportation Relocation Retrospective Study in 1995. Nearly 90 percent of the homeowners surveyed indicated that they were "able to significantly upgrade" their housing, but over 50 percent of those surveyed were no longer living in their replacement housing a year after receiving the payment.[24] As reported recently by the United States General Accounting Office,

> When private property is taken by eminent domain, hardship often follows. Neighborhoods may be disassembled, businesses may be forced to close. At an absolute minimum, individuals and businesses may be uprooted against their will. The "just compensation" mandated by the Fifth Amendment often does not and cannot provide adequate redress. For example, a tenant renting a house

21 Barbara Sard & Will Fischer, Preserving Safe, High Quality Public Housing Should be a Priority of Federal Housing Policy 5 (Center on Budget and Policy Priorities, September 18, 2008). The nation retains 1.2 million public housing units, in 14,000 projects spread throughout 3,500 communities. These house 2.3 million Americans who are among the poorest and most vulnerable, due chiefly to age and disability. Two thirds of the households include an elderly person; and 41 percent include children. *Id.* at 3. Most public housing residents are extremely poor; the typical (or median) household in public housing had annual income of just $8,788 in 2006. *Id.* at 4. Seventy-three percent of the households living in public housing have incomes of 30 percent or less of the area median income for their household size. *Id.* at 5. A family must be "low-income"—meaning that its income may not exceed 80 percent of the local median income—in order to move into public housing. At least 40 percent of the new families an agency admits each year must be "extremely low income," with incomes at or below 30 percent of the local median. Generally, agencies exceed this 40 percent requirement by a wide margin. Most tenants are required to pay 30 percent of their income (after certain deductions are taken out) for rent and utilities. *Id.*

22 Bernard J. Frieden & Lynne B. Sagalyn, Downtown, Inc.: How America Rebuilds Cities 34–5 (1997).

23 Hartman, *Relocation*, *supra* note 18, 781–817.

24 Fed. Highway Admin., U.S. Dep't of Transp., Relocation Retrospective Study 2 (1996).

or apartment from month to month would most likely get nothing except an eviction notice.[25]

Gentrification for Some

Disputes about whether gentrification causes displacement, and if so, whether that is a good thing for the poor among the public, have been at the heart of heated analytic and political debates over urban change for the last 40 years.[26] There can be no serious disagreement that the U.S. has seen 20 years of intense gentrification and sweeping public policy changes that impact the shape of our cities. These operate in contemporary housing market dynamics at the national, regional, and city levels, and can be expected to create a variety of displacement pressures, intersecting in locally contingent ways on neighborhoods occupying desired redevelopment locales.

Residents may be displaced directly as a result of housing demolition, owners' conversion of rental units to condominiums, increased housing costs in the form of rent or taxes, landlord pressure, and eviction. Residents who manage to avoid these direct displacement pressures may nonetheless be displaced by rising housing expenses associated with gentrification. As affordable housing becomes scarce in gentrifying areas, neighborhoods become too pricey, requiring lower-income residents to search elsewhere for housing.[27]

Where earlier research accepted displacement as a part of the gentrification process, some recent studies raised doubt, finding that disadvantaged renters in New York City were somewhat less likely to move out of gentrifying neighborhoods than out of non-gentrified neighborhoods.[28] Even so, this evidence, while new

---

25 U.S. GAO, *Relocation Assistance*, IV Principles of Federal Appropriations Law, 16 GAO RB pt C, s. 1 (2d. ed. 2001). Whereas payments made to "displaced persons" under the URA are not to be considered as income for purposes of federal income taxation or social security, they are deemed income for low income housing assistance. *Id.* at 3 (citing 42 USC § 4636).

26 *See* Kathe Newman & Elvin K. Wyly, *The Right to Stay Put, Revisited: Gentrification and Resistance to Displacement in New York City*, 43 Urb. Studies 23–57 (2006) (reviewing that literature, and presenting quantitative and qualitative analysis; concluding that while not all low income residents are displaced by gentrification, those who manage to stay do so because of New York City's "historically specific web of housing supports that developed … from the 1920s to the 1970s." *Id.* at 51–2.

27 Interim housing strategies for some include doubling or tripling up with family and friends; becoming homeless or moving to city shelters; or moving out of the city. Newman & Wyly, *supra* note 26 at 45–6 (reporting study results in Central Harlem, Lower Park Slope).

28 L. Freeman & F. Braconi, *Displacement or Succession? Residential Mobility in Gentrifying Neighborhoods*, 40 Urb. Aff. 463 (2004); L. Freeman & F. Braconi, *Gentrification and Displacement*, 8 The Urban Prospect 1 (2002); J. Vigdor, *Does Gentrification Harm the Poor?*, 2002 Brookings-Wharton Papers on Urban Affairs 134.

and useful, fails to reach far enough, for example, to address the effects of rapid gentrification in hot neighborhoods to accelerate rent hikes and price out even those lower-income residents who managed to remain during initial economic transition.[29]

The restructuring of urban space as cities experience economic and policy change impacts the ability of low income residents to stay put. This narrow new evidence, suggesting displacement may not always be dramatic, can be overused to dismiss concerns about the exclusionary effect of contemporary market-oriented urban strategies, featuring homeownership, mixed income and social-dispersal strategies, and affluent-attractant downtown destinations, which have been widely embraced as curatives for the disinvested inner city.[30]

Taking Social Capital

Invasive redevelopment projects destroy vital social and cultural ties crucial to residents' ability to meet their basic social and economic needs.[31] Displacement specialists working in international development call this "the resettlement effect," defined as the loss of physical and non-physical assets, including homes, communities, land, income-earning assets and sources, cultural sites, social structures, networks and ties, cultural identity, and mutual help mechanisms.[32] In the U.S., numerous studies document the significant economic and social

---

See also Andres Duany, *Three Cheers for Gentrification*, AMERICAN ENTERPRISE MAGAZINE, April/May 2001, at 36–9; J. Peter Byrne, *Two Cheers for Gentrification*, 46 HOW. L. J. 405 (2003).

29 Newman & Wyly, *supra* note 26.

30 *Id.* at 25.

31 Bezdek, *Local-Resident Equity Participation*, *supra* note 8, at 80–83; Fullilove, ROOT SHOCK, *supra* note 5. Sheila Foster documents and discusses the concentration of hazardous land uses in certain neighborhoods that impair physical health and entrench discriminatory land use patterns that fragment urban space by race and class, in Sheila Foster, *Justice From the Ground Up: Distributive Inequities, Grassroots Resistance, and the Transformative Politics of the Environmental Justice Movement*, 86 CAL. L. REV. 775, 779–807 (1998).

32 Cernea, *supra* note 12, at 14. DOLORES KOENIG, TOWARD LOCAL DEVELOPMENT MITIGATING IMPOVERISHMENT IN DEVELOPMENT-INDUCED DISPLACEMENT AND RESETTLEMENT, RESEARCH PROGRAMME ON DEVELOPMENT-INDUCED DISPLACEMENT AND SETTLEMENT (Refugee Studies Centre, Oxford University 2003) (reviewing the literature of more than 30 years' study of the impoverishment problem, critiquing the field's dominant model for mitigating risks and reconstruction developed by Cernea for the World Bank, as unduly dependent upon the state planning function, and recommending the democratization of planning by employing participation rather than by involving people in a project whose lines have already been dictated by higher levels), *available at* http://www.rsc.ox.ac.uk/PDFs/rrtowardlocal01.pdf.

welfare gains enjoyed by communities with strong social networks.[33] William Julius Wilson has described the social organization needed to realize and maintain common neighborhood goals, and has argued that communities unable to sustain the social networks that enable collective action are made vulnerable to a range of urban problems, preventing the types of collaboration essential to community-building.[34]

Scholarly investigations of social capital feature its collective dimensions, and identify the forms of social capital within viable communities.[35] Social capital is what persons draw on when they enlist the aid of others to solve problems, seize opportunities, or accomplish objectives—or seek just to cope.[36] Social capital is formed by informal networks of people (family, friends, neighbors) who can collaborate to address shared problems and gain access to city political power.[37] One form, *coping capital*, is especially important for people who are chronically poor because it takes the place of services that money otherwise would buy.[38] Two other forms include *social support*—which may come in myriad forms such as help with a flat tire, a ride, a small loan—and *social leverage* that helps one get ahead or improve one's opportunities, as through access to job information or scholarship recommendation.[39]

The legal framework offered by property law recognizes numerous rights of persons residing in the path of municipality-assisted redevelopment, which currently are destroyed, without acknowledgement or compensation, in the exercise of urban redevelopment powers.[40] Important community interests of persons and communities are similarly destroyed. Lee Ann Fennell has argued recently that spatial association should be treated as a distinct property entitlement, at least where patterns of exclusion combine to produce persistent spatial concentrations

---

33 For an extended review of the history, conceptualization, and debates over social capital, *see* David Halpern, Social Capital 1–19 (2005). Several studies are reviewed by Sheila Foster in *The City as an Ecological Space: Social Capital and Urban Land Use*, 82 Notre Dame L. Rev. 527, 543–7 (2006). Commentators have long lamented the loss of social capital in American communities. More recently scholars have begun to offer methods by which to measure the presence and amount of social capital, and while quantitative assessment is complicated, a significant body of literature across many academic disciplines examines the empirical consequences of social capital and demonstrates an array of effects. *Id.*

34 William Julius Wilson, When Work Disappears: The World of the New Urban Poor (1997).

35 Elise M. Bright, Reviving America's Forgotten Neighborhoods: An Investigation of Inner City Revitalization Efforts 13 (2000).

36 *Id.*; Xavier de Souza Briggs, *Brown Kids in White Suburbs: Housing Mobility and the Many Faces of Social Capital*, 9 Housing Pol'y Debate 177, 178 (1998).

37 Bright, *supra* note 36 at 8.

38 *Id.*

39 *Id.*

40 *See* Bezdek, *supra* note 8, at 70–73.

of poverty in urban areas, because of its character as a common resource that is vulnerable to problems of collective action.[41]

Neighborhood is a necessity for urban living.[42] Urban renewal and gentrification, which clear out the old residents of stable yet poor neighborhoods, deprive poor residents of a vital support structure.[43]

In its physical aspect, a community provides benefits to persons that they otherwise could not enjoy alone: amenities such as schools, stores, transit, and other public goods or privately provided services are only available because of the sufficient demand in the area.[44] Social interactions are another set of important benefits—friendships and interpersonal networks of all kinds that are possible because of physical proximity and common experiences of place and connection that endure over time.[45] Particularly for people living at the lowest levels of income and material goods, the concern and support of neighbors is critical to physical survival, as well as to psychic well-being. "When this milieu is destroyed and its members scattered, it is irretrievably lost."[46]

---

41 Lee Anne Fennell, *Properties of Concentration*, 73 U. CHI. L. REV. 1227 (2006).

42 *See* Peter L. Berger & Richard John Neuhaus, *Neighborhood*, *in* TO EMPOWER PEOPLE: FROM STATE TO CIVIL SOCIETY 165, 165–76 (Michael Novak ed., 2d ed., 1996); *see also, e.g.*, Jack L. Nasar & David A. Julian, *The Psychological Sense of Community in the Neighborhood*, 61 J. AM. PLAN. ASS'N 178, 181 (1995); *see also* David M. Chavis & Abraham Wandersman, *Sense of Community in the Urban Environment: A Catalyst for Participation and Community Development*, 14 AM. J. COMMUNITY PSYCHOL. 55, 55–61 (1990); Thomas J. Glynn, *Neighborhood and a Sense of Community*, 14 J. COMMUNITY PSYCHOL. 341, 349, 351 (1986) (discussing the values of length of residency, knowing people by name, and ability to have community action such as electing caring officials); Thomas J. Glynn, *Psychological Sense of Community: Measurement and Application*, 34 HUM. REL. 789, 790, 793 (1981); David W. McMillan & David M. Chavis, *Sense of Community: Definition and Theory*, 14 J. COMMUNITY PSYCHOL. 6 (1986) (measuring neighborhood sense of community).

43 *See* William Michelson, *Residential Mobility and Urban Policy: Some Sociological Considerations*, *in* RESIDENTIAL MOBILITY AND PUBLIC POLICY 79, 83–5 (W.A.V. Clark & Eric G. Moore eds., 1980); *see also* Stephanie Riger & Paul J. Lavrakas, *Community Ties: Patterns of Attachment and Social Interaction in Urban Neighborhoods*, 9 AM. J. COMMUNITY PSYCHOL. 55, 55–7 (1981). *See also* AMITAI ETZIONI, THE SPIRIT OF COMMUNITY; RIGHTS, RESPONSIBILITIES, AND THE COMMUNITARIAN AGENDA passim (1993); Oddvar Skjaeveland, Tommy Garling & John Gunnar Maeland, *A Multidimensional Measure of Neighboring*, 24 AM. J. COMMUNITY PSYCHOL. 413, 422–5 (1996).

44 Michelson, *Residential Mobility*, *supra* note 43 at 113. This concept can be viewed as the "joint defrayal of fixed costs in providing essential amenities." *Id.* at 116.

45 *Id.* at 114; *see also* Edward Glaeser, *The Future of Urban Research: Nonmarket Interactions*, 1 BROOKINGS-WHARTON PAPERS ON URB. AFF. 101, 101–4 (2000), *available at* http://muse.jhu.edu/demo/brookings-whartonpapersonurbanaffairs/v2000/2000.1glaeser.pdf.

46 "The poor must often depend on a web of mutual support … with each individual contributing to the others whatever … special talents he might have. [Such] exchanges … reinforce [each other], creating a milieu the value of which far exceeds what the physical

Community-inclusive Capital Formation

Community equity shareholding recognizes the meaningful claims of residents who will be displaced by changes in urban land use patterns, by allocating to each adult an equity stake in the wealth generated by such city-supported urban redevelopment. Absent a meaningful role for residents, local government in effect conveys their existing social place and relationships, at discount, in order to re-engineer urban environs for the mutual gain of private developers and the city. Community shareholding brokers the long experience of community residence as a basis for participation in the decision-making about redevelopment, and for profit participation as a form of material benefit from redevelopment projects that displace long-term residents.[47]

Conceptually, the collective action of those slated to be displaced by revitalization projects is a means to change the governmental calculus when it uses (or threatens to use) its land use powers to displace low income communities.[48] One form for such collective action is community legal control of the land use and redevelopment decisions accorded by the City of Boston to the Dudley Street Neighborhood Initiative—a model which is much admired but never replicated. Jim Kelly has recently proposed the creation of a federal right to "renew and remain" through amendment of the Uniform Relocation Act of 1970.[49]

The creation of community equity shareholding in public–private redevelopment projects more precisely facilitates collective action by the affected residents.

Community members ought not lose their substantial investments in their place, nor have their residency terminated by local government land use practices that transfer public resources into largely private redevelopment of residences for others, *unless and until* residents have approved the redevelopment. Such approval might be accompanied by an agreement to exchange their community residency interests for an equity stake in the benefits generated by the new development. Such an equity stake could take the form of an alienable right to comparable replacement housing in the new development, or to shares in the increased

reality might suggest." Denis J. Brion, *The Meaning of the City: Urban Redevelopment and the Loss of Community*, 25 Ind. L. Rev. 685, 702 (1992). Personal recollections of such webs of mutual support are related by Dr Fullilove in Root Shock, *supra* note 5.

47 Bezdek, *Local-Resident Equity Participation*, supra note 8.

48 This practice and the recurring outcomes motif might well be altered by raising the cost to local officials of trading away low income housing located in neighborhoods or localities eyed for redevelopment. Low income residents would benefit from policies that would provide meaningful incentive to create substitute low income housing in the same neighborhood, and configure new development so as to leave such housing in place.

49 Kelly, *Taming Eminent Domain, supra* note 7. The Uniform Relocation and Real Estate Acquisition Policies Act (URA) requires the governmental agency involved in any project using federal funds to provide relocation benefits to homeowners, tenants, businesses, and non-profits who are "displaced persons" as defined in the Act.

economic value justifying the public participation in the project and generated by it over time, or both.

This set of property interests can be recognized through reforms of the redevelopment planning requirements of state enabling statutes, to create community equity shares held by residents of the properties whose area is targeted for redevelopment. The result is a process that invests residents with rights to consent to development beforehand, and to a share in the benefits of the deal in which the locality partnered.[50]

Building Wealth: Models of Inclusive Capital Analysis

Poor people and racial minorities have for generations gotten the disproportionate share of the burdens of land expropriation for urban redevelopment; and eminent domain doctrine is insufficient to reach their reality. "Property" forms a crucial nexus between the struggle for well-being and the capacity to accumulate some predicate quantity of the material aspects that aid persons to be well, secure, and autonomous.

Assets and opportunities for enhanced well-being

The critical assets of poor households in our cities tend to be largely undocumented, and not readily parlayed into formal recognition in the legal processes that structure land transfer and land use decision-making.[51] When Hernando de Soto, seeking to document the asset accumulation capacity of deeply impoverished people in developing nations, estimated their undocumented property holdings to exceed

50 *See generally* Daphna Lewinsohn-Zamir, *The Objectivity of Well-being and the Objectives of Property Law*, 78 N.Y.U. L. Rev. 1669 (2003) (arguing for an objective theory of well-being for legal theory and developing an objective approach to property law). Applying a new economic 'happiness' literature in the context of corporate governance, James McConvill has proposed that shareholder participation should be seen as an end in itself, rather than simply a means to a corporate-oriented end. James McConvill, *Shareholder Empowerment as an End in Itself: A New Perspective on Allocation of Power in the Modern Corporation*, 33 Ohio Northern U. L. Rev. 1013, 1015 (2007). *Cf.* Harry G. Hutchison & R. Sean Alley, *The High Costs of Shareholder Participation*, http://ssrn.com/abstract=1112885 (last visited February 25, 2009).

51 The disparity in assets between the poor, middle class, and wealthy, is even greater than the gap in income, according to pioneers in the emerging field of asset-building as a poverty-alleviation strategy. The assets essential to economic security and opportunity include quality jobs, human capital, savings, and investments—which at times have been aided by public policies such as 401k retirement savings vehicles and the GI Bill—but also include small-scale items of consumption required to get or keep employment, such as having a telephone, transportation, a uniform. See Michael Sherraden, Assets and the Poor: A New American Welfare Policy (1991).

$9 trillion, he also argued that the absence of legal recognition of their property presented a near-complete impediment to turning their assets into useful capital.[52]

Significant movement toward this recognition is perhaps underway. Anti-poverty advocates and policymakers have embraced asset-building strategies, prompted by the influential work of Michael Sherraden and colleagues who, since 1991, have argued that modern welfare policy fails in its singular emphasis on income rather than a recognition of assets as a measure of economic well-being.[53] Assets, argues Sherraden, properly understood, encompass less tangible resources including human capital, cultural capital, political capital, and social capital,[54] as well as tangible money savings, real property, stocks, and bonds.[55] The meaningful assets in the lives of many working yet poor urban residents in the U.S. consist of items far removed from our ordinary understandings of real property, or of "place," or of capital, but pivotal nonetheless in individuals' capacity to function—a car, a ladder, one's uniform.[56]

This is an important shift in attention to the wealth-building opportunities for low income urban dwellers. For most of U.S. history, land was the ultimate asset and primary root of wealth. It was durable financially as well as physically, in the sense that land retained its value, it was legally secured by "property rules" and by due process, and it could generate wealth. Land in the Homesteading Acts era[57] was the most highly generative asset: the source of political power in the early republic, and of self-sufficiency for households and economic development for communities.[58] But in today's economy, corporate capital has eclipsed land as the

---

52 Hernando De Soto, The Mystery of Capital: Why Capitalism Triumphs in the West and Fails Everywhere Else (1st ed. 2000).

53 Sherraden, *supra* note 51. Sherraden argues that public policies prevent welfare recipients from accumulating assets under the rules of the income-transfer programs, *Id.* at 6; while enabling the non-poor to build wealth and well-being through tax subsidies for homeownership, and for corporate and individual retirement pensions. *Id.* at 68.

54 *Id.* at 101–5.

55 Kathryn Edin recounts the decision by one woman who resigned her job as a nurse's aid just months shy of earning her certificate, in order to work in retail at Wal-Mart where she would have the opportunity, after three years, to vest in a pension. Kathryn Edin, *More Than Money: The Role of Assets in the Survival Strategies and Material Well Being of the Poor, in* Assets for the Poor: The Benefits of Spreading Asset Ownership ch. 6 at 206 (Thomas M. Shapiro & Edward N. Wolff, eds., 2001).

56 *Id.* at 217–19.

57 *See generally* Homestead Act of 1862, ch. 75, 12 Stat. 392 (1862), *repealed by* Act of October 21, 1976 Pub. L. No. 94-579, 90 Stat. 2787 (1976).

58 Robert Hockett, *A Jeffersonian Republic by Hamiltonian Means: Values, Constraints, and Finance in the Design of a Comprehensive and Contemporary "Ownership Society,"* 79 S. Cal. L. Rev. 45, 99–104 (parsing early American land laws, from the Land Act of 1796 through the Homestead Acts of the nineteenth and early twentieth centuries, for their wealth-building import).

asset that confers autonomy, given its characteristics as highly generative,[59] highly liquid, and thus more disposable than real estate. Arguably it is even more legally secure than land, because business capital is not generally subject to comparable restrictions on alienability or specific use, or to eminent domain.

Imagine that instead of the fiscal illusion of public benefit from the proliferation of public–private redevelopments that deplete the jurisdiction's affordable housing stock, it were possible to make those who bear the burdens of dislocation direct beneficiaries of the new project.[60] Imagine that local law directs or incentives the PPP to offer equity shares in the value-adding redevelopment to all the residents in the project impact area. This approach would provide much-needed modernization to the public comment practices of land use planning, and offer direct benefits to the affected city residents. Community equity shareholding as I describe it here would allow public–private redevelopment of urban community space to be bargained for and approved by the affected city residents, so that the community may benefit as a whole, and the members of the displaced population receive meaningful equity shares in the value added redevelopment. This approach would modernize resident participation strategies in urban land use planning and regulation extant now for nearly 60 years, by recognizing with market value the legitimate interests of residents in the space they co-inhabit.

Bargaining for beneficiary status: Community benefit agreements

Existing law has partially recognized aspects of these interests and the ineffective remedies offered for prospective displacees in the path of urban redevelopment.

Recognition of community interests in land use decisions comes chiefly in the form of nominal public participation rights by residents in the path of prospective redevelopment projects.[61] Public notice and hearing processes, or consultation via charette, offer a veneer of inclusive deliberation yet exclude residents as stakeholders in the decision about community destruction.[62] These processes

---

59 *Id.* at 140 ("[H]istoric average annual returns on equity cluster around 6.6%–7.2%." (citing Jeremy J. Siegel, Stocks for the Long Run 11 (2d ed., 1998)).

60 Such a project could sensibly entail requirements for the production of affordable housing elsewhere: a trade of one occupancy right for another comparable one, akin to the rule undergirding the Uniform Relocation Act.

61 *See generally* Alejandro E. Camacho, *Mustering the Missing Voices: A Collaborative Model for Fostering Equality, Community Involvement and Adaptive Planning in Land Use Decisions, Installment Two*, 24 Stan. Envtl. L.J. 269 (2005); Audrey G. McFarlane, *When Inclusion Leads to Exclusion: The Uncharted Terrain of Community Participation in Economic Development*, 66 Brook. L. Rev 861, 868–91 (2001) (reviewing resident participation requirements under various government programs for urban redevelopment from 1949 to the present).

62 *Id.* An array of successful resident-controlled redevelopment is discussed in, *e.g.*, Heather McCulloch with Lisa Robinson, Sharing the Wealth: Resident Ownership Mechanisms, A PolicyLink Report (2001), *available at* http://www.policylink.org/pdfs/ROMS.pdf; Benjamin B. Quinones, *Redevelopment Redefined: Revitalizing the City*

offer no avenue to shift the burden allocation.[63] Public hearings occur too late and address too little for the incorporation of the community's interests into the project.

In recent years, community benefits agreements (CBAs) have garnered significant interest among communities and their advocates, precisely because they redress this procedural insufficiency, and produce community-inclusive modifications to proposed redevelopment projects. Typically a community benefits agreement is a private contract negotiated between a prospective developer and representatives of affected communities.[64] Several agreements have been reached whose terms and process show promise for this as one strategy to ameliorate many of the inequitable results of public–private redevelopments. Under a CBA, community parties gain promises modifying original development concepts, including affordable housing, employment participation, open space or other amenities, monitoring provisions, and potential remedies for breach. Practically speaking, it is a device limited in availability to those communities already served by established organizations that can muster resources and make their way to the bargaining table, either before local officials and private developers have made the deal, or in sufficiently muscular coalition to effect

---

with Resident Control, 27 U. MICH. J. L. REFORM 689, 753–8, 767 (discussing the Dudley Street Neighborhood Initiative in Boston and other examples of resident-controlled redevelopment).

63 Jon C. Teaford, *Urban Renewal and its Aftermath*, 11 HOUSING POL'Y DEBATE 443, 446 (2000) (relating the evisceration of: an Italian enclave in Boston's West End; a Croatian-American community in the Vaughan Street area in Portland, Oregon; displacement of the residents of Philadelphia's Eastwick project; the inhabitants of New York's West Village; the Mexican American residents of Los Angeles' Bunker Hill; and the inhabitants of San Francisco's Western Addition). *Id.* at 446–9. The Atlantic Yards project began after its targeted site had begun to gentrify, but it appears to have encompassed a substantial number of low income households and minority households in 2000. *See* JUNG KIM & GUSTAV PEEBLES, ESTIMATED FISCAL IMPACT OF FOREST CITY RATNER'S BROOKLYN ARENA AND 17 HIGH RISE DEVELOPMENT ON NYC AND NYS TREASURIES 14–15 (2004), *available at* www.nolandgrab.org/report/EconReport.pdf, and Develop Don't Destroy Brooklyn, www.dddb.net/times/; Develop Don't Destroy Brooklyn, Response to the Atlantic Yards Arena and Redevelopment Project Blight Study Contained within the General Project Plan, at 3 (September 26, 2006), *available at* http://www.dddb.net/documents/environmental/DEIS/testimony/DDDBBlightResponse.pdf. Tenants have gotten "the hardest hit," losing rent-stabilized apartments with no guarantee of relocation assistance and no real option but to leave their community. Deborah Kolben, *Nets Site Renters Left Out in Eminent Domain Payouts,* THE BROOKLYN PAPER, February 3, 2006; *see also* Deborah Kolben, *Market for Sellers, Not Renters,* THE BROOKLYN PAPER, February 3, 2006 (reporting tenants' complaints regarding impending dislocation and the absence of assured relocation assistance).

64 JULIAN GROSS WITH GREG LEROY & MADELINE JANIS-APARICIO, COMMUNITY BENEFITS AGREEMENTS: MAKING DEVELOPMENT PROJECTS ACCOUNTABLE 9–10 (Good Jobs First & the California Partnership for Working Families 2005), *available at* www.goodjobsfirst.org/pdf.

modifications. In practice, a CBA may have particular utility in relation to very large projects affecting multiple neighborhoods, faith groups, and unions; and conversely, require significant delegation by residents to community agents to navigate the coalition, negotiate and monitor the CBA. More worrisome, a few case studies of CBAs caution that some of those organizations that can muster themselves to the table may be insufficiently representative of the community facing displacement.[65]

CBAs suffer from two significant drawbacks then. The first is uncertainty as to enforceability as contract. Commentators have raised questions whether the community members have standing to enforce the terms in the event of breach. Doctrinally and factually the issue is one of actual consideration. If the community signatories assent, courts may treat CBAs as a bilateral agreement with beneficial promises to third parties. The CBA does not alter the legal structure of the public–private arrangement; it remains fundamentally contractual. It seeks to involve additional community parties who otherwise would be excluded from crafting the character and benefit of the proposed development, thus the bilateral negotiation becomes multi-lateral.

A second difficulty is that the CBA's hallmark—its community-representativeness—may modify the political bargaining essence of the public–private partnership by degree, but not in kind. This raises a political economy caution, because community benefits agreements do not necessarily assure an inclusive or transparent process for neighborhood residents. Several recent CBAs have come under stinging criticism for insufficiently inclusive representation. For example, the Bronx Terminal Market CBA, negotiated in 2006, involved no grass roots community organizations.[66] Instead, 18 community groups were handpicked by the borough president, and then were given just 30 days to draft an agreement. They received no technical assistance in a process that, in cities around the U.S., would include enforceable developer commitments to incorporate affordable housing, local and minority hiring, job training, and living wage provisions, and often, community facilities such as day care centers and parks.[67] In the Bronx, however, the organizations did not see the completed CBA until the morning of the city council's vote to approve the development plans. At that point, seven of

65 Patricia Salkin & Amy Lavine, *Negotiating for Social Justice and the Promise of Community Benefits Agreements: Case Studies of Current and Developing Agreements*, 17 J. Aff. Housing & Comm. Dev. 113 (2008).

66 Heather Haddon, *Terminal Market Deal Criticized*, 19 Norwood News 4, February 23, 2006–March 8, 2006, *available at* http://www.bronxmall.com/norwoodnews/past/022306/news/N60223page1.html; Jimmy Vielkind, *How to Mediate Manhattanville: A New Negotiating Partner is Born*, City Limits Weekly, December 4 2006, *available at* http://citylimits.org/content/articlees/viewarticle,cfm?article_id=3223.

67 Gross et al., *supra* note 64; Harold Meyerson, *No Justice, No Growth: How Los Angeles is Making Big-Time Developers Create Decent Jobs*, The American Prospect, October 22, 2006.

the organizations refused to sign,[68] but the plan was approved nonetheless. The Yankee Stadium CBA lacked any pretense of being negotiated or signed by any community groups. Instead, it expressed the agreement between the Yankees, the Bronx borough president, and the Bronx delegation of the New York City Council.[69] Critics worry about the true representativeness of groups who step forward to participate.[70]

To achieve equitable resident benefit from redevelopment, communities need a device that will transform association and democratic participation into ownership-spreading through equity participations. Real resident benefit from urban redevelopment requires three things: (1) recognition of the significant investments of the residents of poor communities which stake them in their collectively inhabited neighborhood space;[71] (2) expression of residents' stakes in the form of a correlative claim on the public resources committed to the redevelopment; and (3) a pragmatic means for crediting residents' claims within the relevant time frames of decision and benefit as to the land use planning, public funding, and decision-making of the redevelopment project. Shares in joint economic undertakings can fit this bill.

Community-based joint ventures

Joint ventures in ownership

If corporate capital vehicles are useful for upper income folks to build assets, then surely that can be true for low-wealth communities as well. Community enterprises that engage poor people as stakeholders can formulate cooperative relationships in ways that extend the social capital of the collective undertaking. Chronically poor people in the United States living in starkly segregated enclaves are not likely to know people with the kind of social leverage that can help them gain freedom from poverty. The sister who provides grey-market child care may permit one to attend school, but not to assist in gaining admission to a school on a higher rung

68 Haddon, *supra* note 66.

69 Patricia E. Salkin, *Community Benefits Agreements: Opportunities and Traps for Developers, Municipalities and Community Organizations*, 59 Planning & Env. Law 3 (2007).

70 "'Groups pop up and you're not sure who they represent,' said Patricia A. Jones, the co-chairwoman of the Manhattan Community Board 9 task force on Columbia University's expansion in Manhattanville." Terry Pristin, *In Major Projects Agreeing Not to Disagree*, N.Y. Times, June 14, 2006, *available at* http://www.nytimes.com/2006/06/14/realestate/commercial/14agree.html. A potentially related concern by some observers is the capacity of community coalitions to participate constructively. Good Jobs First and Policy Link, two non-profit think tanks in the forefront of promoting community benefit and equitable development, each advocate significant technical assistance as a necessary predicate to the effective bargaining position of community parties to CBAs. *See* Gross et al., *supra* note 64 at 25–6; McCulloch with Robinson, *supra* note 62.

71 Bezdek, *Local-Resident Equity Participation*, *supra* note 8, at 86–90.

in the opportunity structure. That kind of leverage may not be within the kin and friendship networks of the poorest urban communities. In the United States, a chronically poor person's chances of securing such leverage from social capital are greater where one's community includes some people not like him or her.[72]

Community development corporations (CDCs) have been an important engine of community-based self-help for 30 years.[73] CDCs have been criticized as no longer accountable to the communities where they engage in revitalization, dependent on a mix of public and foundation contracts, grants and loans, and consequently more responsive to funders' views than to their purported community base.[74] Despite occasional critiques, numerous CDCs have managed to scrap their way further into market-based practices in service of their community stakeholders. Some CDCs are contemplating issuing shares—to enable their stakeholders to be shareholders.

One particularly important path is the creation of enterprises formed with equity interests. Examples include the New Community CDC of Newark, New Jersey, which developed a supermarket;[75] the Kansas City CDC that owns a cement block factory; child care centers, health care facilities.[76] Preliminary results from the Market Creek Plaza "People's IPO" demonstrate the capacity of community enterprises to engage poor people as shareholders in successful enterprises.

The People's IPO: Market Creek Plaza

The most robust model thus far for community equity shareholding is illustrated by Market Creek Plaza, an enterprise to revitalize a 20-acre industrial site in southeastern San Diego. The Market Creek Plaza enterprise was formed by a non-profit organization and designed for the express purpose of engaging residents of

---

72 Briggs, *supra* note 36, at 179.

73 *See generally* Michael H. Schill, *Assessing the Role of Community Development Corporations in Inner City Economic Development*, 22 N.Y.U. Rev. L. & Soc. Change 753, 766–72 (1997) (giving a brief history and overview of CDCs' involvement in community-based economic development); Norman J. Glickman & Lisa J. Servon, *More than Bricks and Sticks: Five Components of Community Development Corporation Capacity*, 9 Housing Pol'y Debate 497, 504–12 (1998).

74 Randy Stoecker, *The CDC Model of Urban Redevelopment: A Critique and an Alternative*, 19 J. Urban Aff. 1, 1–4 (1997); cf. Rachel G. Bratt, *CDCs: Contributions Outweigh Contradictions, a Reply to Randy Stoecker*, 19 J. Urban Aff. 23, 23–8 (1997).

75 Schill, *supra* note 73 at 771–2. (The CDC leases the land and provided a share of the capital; day-to-day management of the company is by a separate supermarket corporation, with the CDC providing support services to augment hiring, product selection, and security. Members of the CDC sit on the board of the store corporation.)

76 *See, e.g.*, Peter Pitegoff, *Child Care Enterprise, Community Development, and Work*, 81 Geo L. J. 1897 (1993); Anne Inserra, Maureen Conway & John Rodat, Cooperative Home Care Associates: A Case Study of a Sectoral Employment Development Approach (The Aspen Institute 2002); McCulloch with Robinson, *supra* note 62.

the low-wealth Diamond Neighborhoods in the process and benefits of the project.[77] In July 2006, Market Creek Partners offered 50,000 shares to local community residents at $10 a share, with a minimum investment of $200. At the time of the offering, Diamond Neighborhood residents had a median income of $32,800, and nearly one third of the households earned less than $20,000 each year.[78] Market Creek is now a thriving, $45 million commercial enterprise, making distributions to its investors. Its anchor tenant is a full service supermarket—the first major grocer to locate in the area in 30 years.[79] The revitalization now includes a library and performing arts center, an elementary science center, a state-of-the-art high school, ethnic restaurants, and a conference center. In the next phase, more than 800 affordable housing units will be built on the site.[80]

Purchasers become Diamond Community Investors and members of Market Creek Partners, LLC. As members, each purchaser is entitled to cast one vote, regardless of the number of units purchased, in the election of the company's advisory board.[81] The minimum offering amount was $250,000, and the maximum offering amount was $500,000.[82] These terms enabled local residents to own up to a 20 percent interest in the venture, while the Jacobs Center for Neighborhood Innovation (JCNI) retained a 60 percent interest, and the Neighborhood Unity

---

77 The project was spearheaded by the Jacobs Center for Neighborhood Innovation (JCNI), a California non-profit established in 1995 by the Jacobs Family Foundation. Urban Land Institute, Market Creek Plaza, http://www.commerce.uli.org/AM/Template.cfm?Section=Home&CONTENTID=109950&TEMPLATE=/CM/ContentDisplay.cfm (last visited May 8, 2009).

78 *Id.*

79 Lisa Robinson, *Market Creek Plaza: Toward Resident Ownership of Neighborhood Change*, PolicyLink Case Study 12 (2005).

80 Lori Weisberg, *Affordability by Design*, San Diego Union-Trib., June 10, 2007, at D1.

81 Market Creek Partners, LLC is managed by Diamond Management, Inc., and it is composed of the following members: Jacobs Center for Neighborhood Innovation (JCNI), the Neighborhood Unity Foundation (NUF), and Diamond Community Investors. Diamond Management was incorporated for the purpose of managing Market Creek Partners, LLC, and it is entirely owned by JCNI. JCNI is a non-profit public benefit corporation organized in California that engages in public–private partnerships intended to promote sustainable communities by transferring ownership interests in community development projects to local residents. NUF is also a non-profit public benefit corporation in California that was organized to benefit the Diamond Neighborhoods. Diamond Community Investors are the shareholders from the local community. Market Creek Partners, LLC, Offering Circular, at 2 (2005).

82 The offering achieved its maximum offering amount of $500,000. Doug Sherwin, *Community Members Purchase Shares of Market Creek IPO*, San Diego Daily Transcript, November 13, 2006.

Foundation (NUF), retained the remaining 20 percent interest.[83] The project is intended to transfer complete ownership to local residents within 12 years.

Shareholder qualification Market Creek Partners established strict eligibility criteria for all purchasers.[84] Most importantly, each purchaser was required to be a resident of the revitalization district as well as a state resident.[85] The purchaser had either to reside currently or previously to have resided in one of eight designated "Diamond Neighborhoods."[86] Shares' initial purchase and resale were limited to "Diamond Neighborhood Stakeholders" as defined by residency and investment intention.[87]

To educate its prospective investors to make informed investment decisions in a commercial real estate venture, Market Creek Partners transformed its 200-page prospectus into a 20-page executive summary that included pictures and graphs to answer the investors' most frequently asked questions. The company's business model entailed involving Diamond Community residents to determine the types of businesses and services the residents hoped would be developed at Market Creek Plaza.[88]

---

83 Market Creek's operating agreement provided for an allocation of income to members/shareholders in the following order of priority: (1) DCI units—a 10 percent return, (2) NUF—a 10 percent return, and (3) JCNI and DMI units—a 7 percent return. Following this order of allocation, any remaining balance of income was to be distributed to the company's members in proportion to the total outstanding units. A distribution to Diamond Community Investors was subject to the manager's discretion to withhold up to 5 percent of any distribution for a repurchase reserve. Market Creek Partners, LLC, Offering Circular, at 38 (2005).

84 Both to direct the benefits of the offering to the local community, as well as to ensure compliance with the requirements of an exempt intrastate offering.

85 Market Creek Plaza was designed to qualify for the federal intrastate exemption. State residence is thus essential to qualify for the transaction exemption from Section 5's registration requirement for intrastate security offerings. 15 U.S.C.A. § 77c(a)(11). Rule 147 further requires the issuer, offerors, and purchasers all to be residents of the state of offer. 17 C.F.R. § 230.147 (2008).

86 In addition, certain others with a demonstrated commitment to the Diamond Neighborhoods were also eligible to purchase DCI units, including owners of businesses within the eight neighborhoods and certain other entities and individuals. Market Creek Partners, LLC, Offering Circular, at iv (2005).

87 *Id.* at 39. The offering's subscription agreement included "Sustainability Standards," which required a prospective investor to make certain declarations regarding her state of residency, to affirm her intent to hold the securities for investment purposes for a period of no less than nine months, and to acknowledge that the securities were subject to resale restrictions. *Id.* at iii.

88 Anne Stuhldreher, *The People's IPO*, Stan. Soc. Innovation Rev. (2007), *available at* http://www.newamerica.net/publications/articles/2007/the_people_s_ipo_4486; Market Creek Plaza website, Community Teams, *available at* http://www.marketcreek.com/mcp_teams_co.html.

Community benefit The employment-related local-resident benefits of this joint venture model are similar to those sought under many CBAs: local hiring and minority contracting. Over 90 percent of the initial employees at the supermarket were hired from the community. These jobs are unionized and include living wages, health care, and pension plans. Some 69 percent of the construction contracts for Market Creek Plaza were awarded to local minority-owned enterprises, totaling \$7.1 million.[89]

Additional benefits are potentially still more transformative. As a catalyst for civic participation, the project involved 2,000 adults and over 1,000 youth, who have participated in land planning, leasing, marketing, research, advocacy, and ownership design. Extensive use of cross-cultural community teams has been a consistent feature of project implementation.[90] In addition, the project provides for future neighborhood reinvestment, through the residents' locally controlled foundation, chartered to grant a portion of the profits from the development back into the neighborhood.[91]

It is time to activate a stage of cooperative capitalism beyond the familiar examples that include community development corporations (CDCs), microlending, community development financial institutions (CDFIs).[92] A community enterprise whose shareholders include the residents when the development project is seeking municipal approvals, and may grow to include incoming residents, is potentially an economic collaboration in which shareholders enjoy equal political and economic rights in the entity, more concretely and manageably than in the wider city polity.

From Stakeholders to Shareholders: Community Equity Shares

The fundamental premise of community equity shareholding is that community members not lose their substantial investments in their place, nor have their residency terminated by local government land use practices that transfer public resources into largely private redevelopment of residences for others, *unless and until* residents have approved the redevelopment; and unless and until residents receive shares in the economic value of the project. Such approval might be accompanied by an agreement to exchange their community residency interests

---

89 PolicyLink, Market Creek Plaza: Overview, http://www.policylink.org/Projects/MarketCreek/ (last visited October 21, 2008).

90 *Id.*

91 *Id.*

92 Instances of many of these models are described in SHARING THE WEALTH: RESIDENT OWNERSHIP MECHANISMS, 2001, prepared by PolicyLink in collaboration with FNMA and HUD, *available at* http://www.policylink.org/pdfs/ROMs.pdf. Community-rooted corporations, formed as non-profits, are importantly not as nimble nor its capital quite so mobile, due to CDC corporate missions and internal governance procedures. In this way they may be distinguished from private companies.

for an equity stake in the benefits generated by the new development. Such an equity stake could take the form of an alienable right to comparable replacement housing in the new development, or to shares in the increased economic value justifying the public participation in the project and generated by it over time, or both.

This set of property interests can be recognized through reforms of the redevelopment planning requirements of state enabling statutes. The result is a process that invests residents with rights to consent to development beforehand, and to a share in the benefits of the deal in which the locality partnered.

Community equity shares make use of a familiar capital vehicle to render visible the residents' stakes in the community. Residents receive shares in the real estate venture—in effect, becoming members of the joint venture in urban redevelopment.

A Responsive Framework

The community equity shares concept offers a responsive framework to the inequitable allocations inherent in redevelopment theory and practice. It embodies three crucial principles missing from contemporary PPP practice: the principles of fair share—fair and inclusive shares in the wealth-creation facilitated by public investment; governance—a right of residents of the targeted development zone to vote on the character of the planned redevelopment; and collective action—a framework to facilitate the recognition of the collective social capital of the community, and intentionality about exchanging it for the development sought by the public–private partnership.

Fair share

Most analyses of the inequitable development problem perpetuate the invisibility of community stakes, proposing to tweak eminent domain doctrine, but limiting redress to title owners of affected properties. One straightforward approach is to increase the payments made to displaced homeowners by monetizing the subjective value of property taken by eminent domain ("homeowner surplus") to deal with the obvious problem that forced sales at fair market value in severely disinvested neighborhoods fail to compensate displaced long-term owners for "the subjective element." While legal determinations of just compensation almost universally reject paying for the subjective value attributed by the owner, in some circumstances this seems particularly unjust. Some legal scholars have developed proposals for the award of supplemental damages to long-term owners according to a legislated schedule reflecting length of tenure;[93] and programs for self-assessed

93 Robert C. Ellickson, *Alternatives to Zoning: Covenants, Nuisance Rules, and Fines as Land Use Controls*, 40 U. Chi. L. Rev. 681, 736 (1973).

valuation.[94] These analytic developments are important for the subset of residents in disinvested/development-targeted neighborhoods whom they reach.

Yet the continued exclusion of non-title owners provides no remedy for substantial numbers of persons, households, and their communal interests, which will be destroyed by redevelopment projects that uproot them.

Governance

The second element is the incorporation of a governance principle, to effect community consent and control regarding redevelopment decisions in their backyards.[95] Recently, Michael Heller and Rick Hills proposed to make land assembly the proper subject of the consent of the residents whose neighborhoods were in need of redevelopment, through land assembly districts (LADs).[96] The model of governance they envision is direct control by referendum. Pursuant to local legislation, the local government would construct consent to the land assembly by declaring a proposed land assembly district, and putting the detailed purchase proposal to a referendum of the intended condemnees.[97]

Collective action

Collective action and community consent could be fostered through voluntary land assembly, particularly if practiced by communities as a strategy to coordinate with, and benefit from, market-based redevelopment that threatens to overtake severely deteriorated, underinvested neighborhoods.[98] Such an approach would go a long way to reconnect disinvested communities to thriving realty markets,

---

94 Lee Anne Fennell, *Taking Eminent Domain Apart*, 2004 MICH. ST. L. REV. 957, 995-1002. Fennell limits her proposal for such landowner protection to instances of public taking for private transfer where the public use is unclear. *Id.* at 995.

95 Quinones, *supra* note 62, at 698 (advocating supermajority resident representation on the board). For a related discussion of two case studies of "community-sponsored" planning in New York City, *see* Amy Widman, *Replacing Politics with Democracy: A Proposal for Community Planning in New York City and Beyond*, 11 J.L. & POL'Y 135, 150–73 (2002) (proposing legislative change to equalize the necessary resources and negotiating power among communities and to encourage inclusive processes).

96 Michael Heller & Rick Hills, *Land Assembly Districts*, 121 HARV. L. REV. 1465 (2008).

97 *Id.* at 1490. While this process could be imposed upon the residents who may not have sought this particular redevelopment, the collective decision-making is similar to that within condominium associations and labor unions. Heller and Hills are not entirely clear as to whether they would limit the procedure to landowners, homeowners, or "neighbors"; and in the event the LADs were rejected, since the rest of the eminent domain process would still be available, they structure a procedural opportunity that could be very important to communities that avail themselves of it, but not an absolute bar to redevelopment. *Id.* at 1491–2.

98 James Kelly, *"We Shall Not Be Moved": Urban Communities, Eminent Domain and the Socioeconomics of Just Compensation*, 80 ST. JOHNS L. REV. 923 (2006).

by addressing the interrelated problems of land assembly and cost posed to development-seeking cities by fragmented and diversely held titles.

Nonetheless, many communities targeted by PPPs do not have the political organization or technical support to see the development coming and to act in time. Where communities lack the leverage to negotiate meaningful promises from developers, their stakes in the urban space they share should be protected from expropriation.

Separately these principles are important advances for instantiating the equities of long-time residents of the islands of disinvestment in our comeback cities. Yet alone, each is insufficient to protect community residents' interests from destruction by public–private redevelopment projects.

Residents' Community Capital Stakes Expressed as Limited Property Right

Residents' stakes in their community ought to be protected from expropriation by public agencies when the urban space the community occupies is taken for public–private redevelopment. Legal security is essential within our system of rights over the control of resources.[99] Protection of residents' interests by property rules, rather than the liability rules of contract or tort, is appropriate to afford residents the necessary sphere of choice not to be dispossessed and disentitled to the community they have made in their shared location.[100] Applying these principles to the contested urban neighborhood, the "social capital" that entwines viable neighborhoods can be rendered cognizable in these respects by allocating shares in the targeted redevelopment enterprise.

This is not a set of interests to be limited by eminent domain doctrine. Eminent domain rules would be unaffected: for residents in the targeted redevelopment site who own homes or businesses, ordinary condemnation and compensation principles and procedures would continue to apply. Community equity shares run to residents. Limiting CESs to natural persons with established residency would not include absentee owners of rental or commercial properties, nor entities. While the local ordinance would need to establish an appropriate residency requirement of sufficient length to predate rumors of redevelopment and thus speculative in-

99 Bezdek, *supra* note 8, at 74–9. A resource or material opportunity may be viewed in more specific legal or fiscal terms as an "asset" to the degree that it possesses asset-like qualities. Is it generative of more resources? How readily can it be exchanged or converted into money? Greater liquidity and generative capability confer greater choice and autonomy on the asset's holder. Resources are more like assets to the extent they are durable and foster reliance: that is, to the extent they are secure in a physical or legal sense.

100 Property rules confer upon the holder of a property right the power to determine whether to transfer the protected asset and at what price. By contrast, liability rules do not give the holder injunctive relief, but only the remedy of damages for a non-consensual transfer, typically at a price set by a third party such as a court or legislature. *See* Guido Calabresi & A. Douglas Melamed, *Property Rules, Liability Rules, and Inalienability: One View of the Cathedral*, 85 HARV. L. REV. 1089, 1092 (1972).

moving, there is no conceptual reason to limit proof of residency to leaseholders: each adult in a household would be entitled to his or her own CES; and so should neighborhood residents who occupy transitional housing or patronize homeless shelters, or can otherwise demonstrate sufficient tenure in non-traditional abodes.[101]

Accordingly, the allocation of homestead stakes would recognize the interests of lessees, commensurate with their common-law entitlement to property. Consider the tenant who has rented the same apartment for many years, and built up friendships and networks of support unrelated to the economic value of her year-to-year lease. Land assembly will eliminate the apartment building and dispossess the tenant of her neighborhood. There is no compelling or obvious reason why the lessee should not have an equal vote in a decision so fundamentally affecting her interest.

Operational details: Resident homestead stakes and community equity shares

The elements of fair share, governance, and collective action can be unified and reinvigorated in the form of two new interests: the homestead stake, and the community equity share. Shares could be held either in an autonomous community equity company (CEC), or in the project development entity itself. Direct shareholding reflects community residents' steadfastness in their home space.

At the core of the CEC would be the community homestead stake, created by reforms to existing statutory structures. The homestead stake, embodying the governance principle, would assure that persons who hold legally recognizable interests in their community should decide collectively whether the land ought to be assembled into a larger parcel for redevelopment and put to the proposed uses.

Each resident of the geographic area identified for the redevelopment project would receive one share in the CEC, the homestead stake. The homestead stake would give its owner specific rights to participate in the development decision-making; most importantly, to vote on the constitutive question of the proposed redevelopment plan. State and local redevelopment statutes would require the redevelopment agency to submit the proposed redevelopment for a vote by the affected community homestead stake holders—effectively conducting a localized referendum on redevelopment proposals, initiated either by the government agency or the subject of an application by private developers. Property law ought to be available to retrofit community interests into a shared-ownership vehicle. One rough analogy would be to a condominium conversion.

---

101 In many urban communities, this group will include individuals who are homeless—who must sleep in shelters or on the streets within the targeted area—and street people—those who spend most of their time on the streets because of inadequate private space or who work in the informal economy on the streets, see MARGARET KAHN, BRAVE NEW NEIGHBORHOOD: THE PRIVATIZATION OF PUBLIC SPACE (2004); Jeremy Waldron, *Homelessness and Community*, 2000 U. TORONTO L. J. 50.

The legal right to vote on the question would likely enhance opportunities for the community to bargain with the public–private development partners for particular community benefits. Efforts to forge agreements between affected residents and developers or public development agencies have been undertaken from Seattle to New York in order to mitigate the harmful effects of aggressive developments and secure specific concessions.[102] However, many communities are unable to muster in time to get to the bargaining table. The homestead stake would correct this inequity. Similarly, such facilitated collective action may promote residents' self-protection from speculators in advance of redevelopment activity.

The rules for allocation of homestead stakes and the operation of the community equity corporation are designed to ensure that the people most affected by the project's need for land assembly, the residents, have a collective veto over whether the project should proceed upon the larger parcel that their displacement will allow. The justice of this quid pro quo is especially apparent where the proffered rationale for the redevelopment is to improve the neighborhood—to remove "blight" or replace aging infrastructure. The governance rule accompanies the 'fair share' principle, so that those who will bear the direct costs of the project can decide for themselves whether they want the proffered improvement.

Allocation of homestead stakes should instantiate the interests of lessees as well and commensurate with their common-law entitlement to property, since leaseholds are property interests as time-honored as the fee simple absolute. Land assembly that eliminates the apartment building will dispossess the tenant of her neighborhood, and for this reason the lessee merits an equal vote in a decision so fundamentally affecting her interest.[103]

---

102 *See* Sheila Muto, *Residents Have Their Say on LAX Expansion Plans*, Wall St. J., December 15, 2004 (discussing the community benefit agreement with the Los Angeles airport which provides for environmental mitigation, noise reduction, and airport-related work; negotiations in Seattle between a public-interest coalition, city officials, and a company planning the downtown development of a biotechnology hub over affordable housing, employment, and environmental issues; and the pressure on Columbia University in New York by neighborhood, business, and civic leaders to "help create low-income housing in the West Harlem area where [it] has proposed to expand"). Community benefits campaigns are currently underway in Denver, Miami, Milwaukee, San Diego, San Jose, and New Haven. *See also* Gross et al., *supra* note 64.

103 The same may well be true for transient and homeless people, who while having no abode, nonetheless have legal residency for voting purposes. *See, e.g.*, Coalition for the Homeless v. Jensen, 187 A.D.2d 582 (N.Y. App. Div. 1992) (holding that a state requirement that people live in a traditional dwelling in order to vote placed an unconstitutional constraint on the voting rights of homeless persons); Fischer v. Stout, 741 P.2d 217 (Alaska 1987) (ruling that when registering to vote, homeless people may designate a shelter, park, or street corner as their residence); Collier v. Menzel, 221 Cal. Rptr. 110 (Ct. App. 1985) (finding that denying voter registration because applicants listed a city park as their residence violated the Equal Protection Clause of the Fourteenth Amendment).

Recognizing the stakes of tenants addresses the 'Tyranny of the majority' concern of Federalist 10 that, as one shrinks the size of a jurisdiction, one increases the danger that the majority will enact rules solely benefiting itself at the expense of a minority for no better reason than that the majority can. This is exactly the situation when the only players in the land assembly and use decisions are title holders, many whose connections to the neighborhood are economic only.

By facilitating the collective action of all the residents, not just real property owners, the community equity shares provide ballast to the largest landowners in the community, likely to be institutions such as real estate investment trusts, corporate landowners, and speculators, who hold land primarily as an investment.[104]

In articulating rules of land use law, courts have been skeptical of neighborhood control over zoning regulations, precisely out of concern to protect the minority against a majority of neighbors willing to unite around the goal of restricting a nearby parcel's uses and so enhance the value of their own land at the expense of the burdened parcel owner.[105]

The narrowness of the homestead stake avoids the doctrinal categories by which courts have sought to limit the power of neighborhoods to impose new zoning restrictions on parcels for selfish reasons. Generally, neighbors can approve a variance from preexisting restrictions on a parcel—but they cannot impose a new restriction.[106] By limiting the vote associated with the homestead stake to the up-or-down question on the project, any bargaining as to the substantive provisions of

---

104 An individual owner within the targeted area who would calculate her interests differently and object to neighborhood decision to approve a deal would have to choose between the fair market value or the compensation forthcoming as part of that deal. An individual owner who would consent where the neighborhood refused to endorse a proposed project would be in no worse position than if developers had never eyed the community. Compared to their entitlement under eminent domain compensation principles, institutional owners of real property are not disadvantaged by this allocation of voting rights, by virtue of the likelihood that they derive relatively little producer or consumer surplus from their holdings in the neighborhood above the land's fair market value. Heller and Hills argue that a landowner whose subjective value of her parcel is higher is nonetheless better protected by the neighborhood control than by the municipality, deeming "remote" the risks that a particular land assembly district would ignore the interests of any subset of participants. *See* Heller & Hills, *supra* note 96, at 1500–1503.

105 *See generally* Donald J. Kochan, *"Public Use" and the Independent Judiciary: Condemnation in an Interest-Group Perspective*, 3 Tex. Rev. L. & Pol. 49 (1998) (describing special interest politics in the context of eminent domain). *See* Eubank v. City of Richmond, 226 U.S. 137, 143–45 (1912) (striking down an ordinance allowing a two-thirds vote of neighbors to draw a building line because the ordinance "enables the convenience or purpose of one set of property owners to control the property right of others").

106 Under the non-delegation doctrine, the local legislature cannot delegate its zoning power to the neighbors, because this power is essentially legislative in character. *Id.*; *see also* Asmara Tekle Johnson, *Privatizing Eminent Domain: The Delegation of a Very Public Power to Private, Non-Profit and Charitable Corporations*, 56 Am. U. L. Rev. 455, 460–67 (2007) (describing the private non-delegation doctrine in the context of eminent domain).

the project that provide community benefits—some of which might be viewed as new use restrictions—remain collateral to the neighbors' decision to waive extent zoning rules.

This structure simplifies the decision to the narrow question, for or against the use of land use and assembly powers *vis-à-vis* a parcel, or not. This segregates the up-or-down vote from the several differences in interest and position that might divide a community into antagonistic factions as to land tenure and other established economic networks, as well as service provision and potential employment or housing opportunities in the proposed new development.

In comparison, other community-level devices, such as business improvement districts (BIDs) having broader functions, can more readily create risks of majoritarian exploitation. BIDs, for example, provide a range of services from security, street cleaning, parking facilities, signage, and public relations, to the owners of land within their boundaries. Owners may be affected in divergent ways that foster contention in the community and difficulty with BID governance.[107]

The community equity corporation: A vehicle for collective exercise of resident homestead stakes

This proposal would also facilitate the residents' ability to overcome barriers to collective action, and thereby avoid selling their neighborhood for an inequitable return. Local jurisdictions would recognize rights of residents facing redevelopment displacement, in effect permitting them to exchange their legitimate interests in the community for shares in the equity and profit from the redevelopment deal that displaces them. This new right would be created by statute, authorizing the formation of a CEC, establishing minimum requirements for shares, and identifying the terms of residence that qualify householders within the area targeted for redevelopment as community equity shareholders.

Upon formation and assignment of shares, each shareholder would become a member of the community equity corporation (CEC), a special entity with the power by majority vote to approve, or to veto, the proposed land assembly if the PPP does not offer an adequate value to the CEC.

This up-or-down vote would combine the residents' fragmented individual interests into a whole of sufficient value, economically and politically, that the neighbors have a means to bargain collectively over the surrender value of the space they occupy collectively. Generations of experience with PPPs show us what "bargaining" in isolation looks like: to developers, it is assembly value, but to the residents, it is home, community.[108]

107 Heller and Hill give the example of merchants who may want to increase the number of parking spaces for customers, while residential owners might want to cut down on traffic. Heller & Hill, *supra* note 96, at 1500.

108 Title holders in the area could be permitted to opt out of the CEC and receive their constitutional due.

The CEC would provide a community-controlled vehicle to create and hold residents' equity shares in the value generated by the physical and economic redevelopment of their community, and provide the voting rights that accompany ownership in business entities. The CEC would reconfigure the "community interest corporation" demonstration program introduced in the Housing and Urban-Rural Recovery Act of 1983 modeled on employee stock ownership corporations;[109] and retooled in the 1992 federal housing legislation to foster "indigenous community-based financial institutions."[110]

The community equity shares are conceptually distinct from rights in real property or condemnation awards that owners of businesses or others in the neighborhood may have. While this right may be conceptualized as individual in the way that shares in corporations are personal property, the essential interest it expresses is the joint interest to determination and benefit in the collectively inhabited geographic space.

The share would give its owner specific rights to participate in the development decision-making, and in distributions of profits, just as the other equity owners. Its holder would have the right, with all others holding similar community equity shares, to participate as a class in the increased value generated as equity shareholders in the development owner entity. Redevelopment of the site would be contingent upon an exchange of equity shares in the increased values being brought to market.

Formation and operation

To promote transparency of the redevelopment project plan and resulting PPP, it is necessary to plug the CEC into the city's power source: its planning process.

---

109 Pub. L. No. 98-181, 97 Stat. 1153, 1172 (1983) (codified as amended at 42 U.S.C. § 5318 (2000)) (creating the Neighborhood Development Demonstration, requiring the Secretary of Housing and Urban Development to "provid[e] Federal matching funds . . . to [local] organizations on the basis of the monetary support such organizations have received" from neighborhood sources); *see also* Harold A. McDougall, *Affordable Housing for the 1990's*, 20 U. Mich. J. L. Reform 785-86 (1987).

110 Housing and Community Development Act of 1992, Pub. L. No. 102-550, 106 Stat. 3672, 3859 (1992) (codified at 42 U.S.C. § 5305 (2000)). The aim of the demonstration program was to replicate the success of community development capital intermediaries such as South Shore Bank in Chicago and the Center for Community Self-Help in Durham, North Carolina, to "improve access to capital for initiatives which benefit residents and businesses in targeted geographic areas." *Id.* § 853(b)(2) at 106 Stat. 3860. "Community investment corporations" were entities organized either as a depository institution of a non-profit organization affiliated with a non-depository lending institution or regulated financial institution, whose primary mission was to revitalize a targeted geographic area, maintain "accountability to community residents" "through significant representation on its governing board and otherwise." *Id.* § 853(b)(3)(D). The board would engage in development services, and have principals "who possess[ed] significant experience in lending and … development …" *Id.*

Whatever the initial or ultimate project plan, the development will require some zoning change.

Who initiates the CEC? Formation of a community equity corporation could be instigated by existing residents, by a local non-profit organization mobilizing to seek redevelopment partnerships. Its formation would be triggered when either city planning officials commence consideration of sites for public–private projects, or a developer proposes plans to the city and begins to negotiate for assistance with land assembly and related approvals.

How is it initiated? The preliminary application for development approvals would necessarily identify the boundaries of the intended development site and the lots within it. Every adult whose residence is within the boundaries would be entitled to notice at this early stage of the development proposal the formation of the CEC, the homestead stake and community shares. Because the specific boundaries of the development and affected lots may well change as the proposal is refined, residents of properties contiguous to the proposed site should be notified as well. The statute would provide for facilitated sessions to assure that CEC resident/members are well-informed about the CEC process, the development proposal, and the voting and equity rights of shareholding.

These meetings would likely be hosted by the local planning department, but could be augmented by community-based not-for-profit organizations. More assertive dissemination of notice such as door-to-door canvassing would be appropriate rather than reliance on postal or electronic notice to organizations on the planning department's radar.

How does a CEC operate? One useful template would be the business improvement district (BID), of which there are already more than a thousand, authorized in more than 40 states. Formed pursuant to state statute, local ordinance or individual district contracts, a BID is a model of sublocal governance, a geographic subdivision within a municipality, which provides district-limited services to supplement those already provided by local government.[111] BID formation statutes generally require that local government and property owners both approve the district.[112] BIDs are usually managed by a public or private BID board that advises, or is advised by, local government officials.[113] By one count, 13 percent of BIDs are operated by public agencies, 26 percent by mixed public non-profit

111 Richard Briffault, *A Government for Our Time? Business Improvement Districts and Urban Governances*, 99 COLUM. L. REV. 365, (1999).

112 *See, e.g.*, IND. CODE ANN. § 36-9-38-8 (West, WESTLAW through 2002 1st Spec. Sess.) (allowing formation process to begin with approval of owners of 20 percent of affected property).

113 BID enabling statutes generally require that district plans include boundaries, planned expenditures, and other components of the basic operating and financial structure

partnerships, and 61 percent by not-for-profit organizations.[114] BIDs are financed primarily by assessments on local property, given their highly regulated power to tax the property owners in the district, but otherwise they have no governmental powers. The CEC enabling statute, like the typical BID statute, would require the CEC charter to state the boundaries, affected properties, and basic operating and financing structure of a CEC. CECs will need technical assistance to make informed judgments about the development proposal on which they will vote, and this essential cost should be provided for expressly in the enabling legislation. States with affordable housing trust (AHT) funds, or with local jurisdictions having municipal AHTs, may specify CECs as a categorical recipient entitled to apply for such funds as well.[115] The enabling legislation would also define the length and character of tenures entitling residents to homestead stakes; and the contents for, or model of, charter documents for the CEC.

This legislation would enable the community residents to engage in collective action, through a collective voting mechanism, to approve or disapprove the conveyance of their neighborhood to the city or its development designee seeking to assemble the community-occupied land. Formation of the CEC at the relevant time in the development dealmaking would equip the community to bargain based on the consolidated value of the many parcels to the other players in the dealmaking. Municipal facilitation of CECs is an appropriate correction to the civic, social, and economic inequities that public–private development dealmaking practices externalize onto low-wealth communities. The combined interests proposed here, of community equity corporations facilitated by city government, and community equity shares in the redevelopment when the community does indeed agree to acquisition, together require the redevelopment to internalize more of the true social costs it will produce.

Conclusion: Adapting Ownership Spreading to Community Redevelopment Practice

The provenance for the community equity shares concept derives from the policies of equitable development and social inclusion that undergird federal community development law since the 1960s. A "community interest corporation" demonstration program was introduced in the Housing and Urban-Rural Recovery Act of 1983; then reconfigured as "community investment corporations" in federal housing legislation of 1992, with the purpose to replicate successful community capital initiatives like South Shore Bank in Chicago and Community Self-Help in

---

of a BID. *E.g.*, N.Y. Gen. Mun. Law § 980-a (McKinney, WESTLAW through 2002 legislation).

114 *BIDs Fare Well*, 78 N.Y.U. L. Rev. 374, 374 n.1 (2003) (citing Mitchell study).

115 The ROM study underscores the importance of technical assistance for success. See McCulloch with Robinson, *supra* note 62.

Durham, North Carolina. The federal program promoted depository institutions[116] with the mission to revitalize a geographic area. Each local institution would be statutorily obligated to maintain "accountability to community residents" through "significant representation on its governing board and otherwise."

The issuance of equity shares also seeks to address inequities that are the aim of several models of public contracting. For example, state and local procurement statutes commonly condition the selection of private developers upon contractual commitments to work with a designated community representative. Procurement rules make engagement of the targeted community residents—through a representative at the decision table—a ranked criterion in requests for proposals, development agreements, and regulatory agreements; and are incorporated into the legal documentation of each partnership deal. Such conditions are frequently imposed ad hoc in many jurisdictions, thus legislating the practice would be the reasonable next step. Many states allow certain public contracts to be awarded based on "best value," a concept which is evolving beyond traditional concerns for low price and responsible bidder to allow public contracting agencies to consider additional factors,[117] including "negotiated procurement" and "deal local" provisions.[118]

Retooling the legal regime for urban redevelopment for the inclusionary operation of familiar capital orchestration draws upon predicates in our legal history for transforming associational and democratic participation into ownership-spreading equity-like participations. Examples in real estate contexts include financial institutions with resident ownership (community development credit unions);[119] multiple forms of home-equity cooperative ventures;[120] a long history

116 Or non-profit affiliates of non-depository lending institutions or regulated financial institutions.

117 Dean B. Thomson & Michael J. Kinzer, *Best Value in State Construction Contracting*, 19 Construction Law, April 1999, at 31. States' best value procurement rules are variously named "innovative procurement," "negotiated procurement," "performance-based procurement," and "competitive negotiation." *Id.* at 32 (quotations and citations omitted). In fact, some states specifically exclude cost as a consideration in the initial stage of the procurement's "best value" standard. *Id.*

118 A procurement rule requiring bidders to "deal local" is in some sense analogous to the familiar example of "Buy America" and "Buy In-State" preferences, which many states have enacted in their design–build procurement laws. *See id.* (noting that in some jurisdictions locality of the vendor should be a factor in the best value equation).

119 *See, e.g.*, National Federation of Community Development Credit Unions—About Us, http://www.natfed.org/i4a/pages/index.cfm?pageid=256 (last visited October 19, 2006) (describing the history and purpose of community development credit unions).

120 *See* 42 U.S.C. § 12773(f) (2000) (defining community land trusts); *see generally* Duncan Kennedy, *The Limited Equity Coop as a Vehicle for Affordable Housing in a Race and Class Divided Society*, 46 How. L.J. 85 (2002) (discussing the limited equity housing coop as an alternative form of property and comparing it to the leasing cooperative and community land trust).

of agricultural cooperatives[121] as well as producer and consumer cooperatives;[122] employee ownership in the forms of employee stock ownership plans (ESOPs)[123] and worker-owned cooperatives;[124] public mechanisms to support resident investment such as IRAs and IDAs;[125] and state recognition of the shared-holding aspect of citizens in an exhaustible natural resource.[126]

U.S. policy has been extremely successful in ownership-spreading with the important and enduring success of the federal home finance structure developed through the 1930s and 1940s.[127] That innovation has been paralleled in the case of "human capital" spreading through: public provision of primary and secondary

---

121 *See* Thomas Broden, Note, *Co-operatives—A Privileged Restraint of Trade*, 23 Notre Dame L. Rev. 110, 114–19 (1947) (describing the history of agricultural cooperatives).

122 *See* Joseph G. Knapp, The Rise of American Cooperative Enterprise: 1620–1920, at 418–30 (1969) (discussing the spread of the cooperative from agriculture into other areas, including telephone service, mutual insurance, and mutual savings banks).

123 In an ESOP, a company sets up a trust fund, into which it contributes new shares of its own stock or cash to buy existing shares. Alternatively, the ESOP can borrow money to buy shares. National Center for Employee Ownership, How an Employee Stock Option Plan (ESOP) Works, http://www.nceo.org/library/esops.html, (last visited October 16, 2006). The ESOP can make tax deductible contributions to the plan with which to repay the loan. "Shares in the trust are allocated to individual employee accounts." *Id.* Plans specify the employee categories that participate in the plan, and the formula for the allocations. "In private companies, employees must be able to vote their allocated shares on major issues, such as closing or relocating [the company]," and the company can accord voting rights on additional issues (including the board of directors). *Id.* About 10,000 companies now have employee stock ownership plans, up from 200 in 1974. Crystal Detamore-Rodman, *Branching Out: An Employee Stock Ownership Plan is More than Just a Great Way to Boost Morale*, 32 Entrepreneur, April 1, 2004, at 61.

124 *See* Louis O. Kelso & Patricia Hetter, How to Turn Eighty Million Workers into Capitalists on Borrowed Money 84 (1967); Louis O. Kelso & Patricia Hetter Kelso, Democracy and Economic Power: Extending the ESOP Revolution 52 (1986); *see also* Hockett, *supra* note 58, at 102–4; Pitegoff, *supra* note 76 (proposing the use of "[c]hild care enterprise [as] a vehicle for community-based economic development").

125 42 U.S.C. § 604(h) (2000) (defining individual development accounts); *see also* Creola Johnson, *Welfare Reform and Asset Accumulation: First We Need a Bed and a Car*, 2000 Wis. L. Rev. 1221 (discussing theoretical framework of individual development accounts and their availability, usage, and success).

126 Alaska's Permanent Fund Dividend Program pays each qualified resident of the state an annual dividend from the Alaska Permanent Fund. Alaska Admin. Code tit. 15, § 23.103-23 (2006). The fund, created by the state constitution in 1977, invests one quarter of all revenue the state receives from the sale or rental of its mineral resources. Alaska Const. art. IX, § 15. Since 1982, when the current version of the program was enacted, the dividends have averaged more than $1000. *See* Alaska Permanent Fund Corp., The Permanent Fund Dividend, http://www.apfc.org/alaska/dividendprgrm.cfm (last visited October 19, 2006).

127 Hockett, *supra* note 58, at 104–17.

education; the land grant acts of the nineteenth century by which federal land "staked" the perpetual endowments for state colleges and universities; the G.I. Bill following World War II that united in one program both loan guarantees and education as an asset; and direct and indirect loans, grants, and subsidies for higher education.[128]

The community equity corporation proposed here is premised on connecting the citizenry of a geographic place to the economic generative opportunities of that place. It corresponds to the general stock ownership corporation (GSOC) envisioned by Louis Kelso, the inventor of the now widely used employee stock ownership plan.[129] The Kelsonian GSOC was designed to be a highly adaptable device to "ownerize" on a regional or community-based scale, for example, to create community-wide ownership of local business.[130]

Community equity shareholding allows residents in the path of public–private redevelopment the opportunity to enjoy not just benefit, but also ownership in the enterprise. The voting right attached to the resident share provides a basis for collective bargaining over the character of the development, and in this way may mirror CBAs' utility for community collaborators to wrest detailed provisions for affordable housing, local hiring, job training, and amenities such as parks and school investments. Market Creek Plaza's community resident investors demonstrate that residents can successfully co-exist and co-own thriving commercial ventures. The community equity shareholding proposal suggests a means for localities to meld the two in intentionally inclusionary and equity-sharing public–private redevelopments, whose neighborhood effects will induce tremendous changes to the face, and heart, of the community.

Acknowledgment

The author would like to thank the participants in the *Workshop on Affordable Housing and Public–Partnerships*, in October 2007, for their insightful comments and inspiring work.

---

128 *Id.* at 143–53.

129 *See* JEFF GATES, THE OWNERSHIP SOLUTION: TOWARD A SHARED CAPITALISM FOR THE TWENTY-FIRST CENTURY 20 (1998).

130 *Id.* at 55–8 (1998). Gates suggests that municipalities that use buy-lease arrangements to finance large land acquisitions could readily restructure such acquisitions as GSOCs to achieve broadly diversified individual ownership by community residents. Likewise, metropolitan area transit authorities that lease commercial space associated with their rail stations could restructure these dealings as community equity corporations and achieve shared ownership by community residents. *Id.* at 76–7. Revenue Act of 1978, Pub. L. No. 95-600, 92 Stat. 2762, 2893 (1978) (adding subchapter U to the Internal Revenue Code); *see* GATES, *supra* note 129, at 76.

Chapter 7

Constructing the Social Impact Statement to Measure the Full Cost to Public Housing Tenants of Urban Renewal

Susan D. Bennett

Introduction

Sometime soon—maybe next year, maybe in two years—the public housing project at the Barry Farm Dwellings will be coming down. Sometime before then, however, many families that remain in the 423 units will have moved out, some in anticipation of the demolition, some waiting until the last day; some on their own, some with the District of Columbia's help. Under the aegis of the "New Communities" program, a locally funded adaptation of HOPE VI,[1] the residents will wait out the "transformation" of their neighborhood into a "mixed income" and mixed tenure community, with some retail and other services.[2] They have

1 There is an enormous literature, encompassing disciplines of law, history, planning, sociology, and anthropology, addressing the goals and outcomes of the Homeownership and Opportunity for People Everywhere program, or HOPE VI, the only source of significant support for renovation of public housing since the program's initial implementation in 1993 as a series of public housing homeownership, voucher, and youth employment programs. For recent overviews of the program itself and of the literature, *see* Where Are Poor People to Live?: Transforming Public Housing Communities (Larry Bennett, Janet L. Smith & Patricia A. Wright eds., 2006); Susan J. Popkin, Bruce Katz, Mary K. Cunningham, Kevin D. Brown, Jeremy Gustafson & Margery A. Turner, A Decade of HOPE VI: Research Findings and Policy Challenges (Urb. Inst./Brookings Inst. 2004) [hereinafter Popkin et al, A Decade of HOPE VI]; Ngai Pindell, *Is There Hope for HOPE VI? Community Development and Localism*, 35 Conn. L. Rev. 385 (2003).

2 For a description of the District of Columbia's "New Communities" program as a project within the "housing element" of the city's revised Comprehensive Plan, *see* 1 District of Columbia, Office of Planning, *District Elements: Housing Element*, *in* The Comprehensive Plan for the National Capital 5–18 (2006), *available at* http://planning.dc.gov/planning (follow hyperlink to "Comprehensive Plan"; then follow hyperlink to "2006 Revised Comprehensive Plan"; then follow hyperlink to "Volume 1, Citywide Elements") [hereinafter D.C. Comprehensive Plan]; *see also* Draft, Government of the District of Columbia, Office of Planning, Barry Farm/Park Chester/Wade Road Redevelopment Plan (November 2006), *available at* http://planning.dc.gov/planning (follow hyperlink to

been assured that their units will not be demolished before they have new units to move to, in a phased relocation that may take over 11 years.[3] Unlike HOPE VI, New Communities promises one-for-one replacement of low rent public housing units, some on-site, some off.[4] Like HOPE VI, forces will combine to make it unlikely that many of these residents will return.[5]

There is no point in romanticizing the lives of residents in Barry Farm. They live within one of the poorest zip codes within the poorest political subdivision of the District of Columbia.[6] Viewed solely through the macrocosmic indicators,

---

"Neighborhood and Revitalization Plans"; then follow hyperlink to "Ward 8: Barry Farm/Parkchester/Wade Road Redevelopment Plan"; then follow hyperlink to "Barry Farm/Parkchester/Wade Road Redevelopment") [hereinafter Barry Farm Plan].

3 *See* Barry Farm Plan, *supra* note 2, at 38–9.

4 2 District of Columbia, Office of Planning, *Area Elements: Far Southeast/Southwest Area Element, in* The Comprehensive Plan for the National Capital 18–21 (2006), *available at* http://planning.dc.gov/planning (follow hyperlink to "Comprehensive Plan"; then follow hyperlink to "2006 Revised Comprehensive Plan"; then follow hyperlink to "Volume 2, Area Elements"; then follow hyperlink to "Far Southeast/Southwest Area Element") (citing city's policy to redevelop Barry Farm "… in a manner which (a) Ensures one for one replacement of any public housing that is removed, along with measures to assist residents and avoid dislocation or personal hardship."). The District of Columbia Housing Authority (DCHA)'s stated commitment to replacing all public housing units demolished in the course of executing certain HOPE VI projects has been widely publicized. Erik Eckholm, *Washington's Grand Experiment to Rehouse the Poor*, N.Y. Times, March 21, 2008, at A12 (describing the redevelopment of the Arthur Capper-Carrollsburg projects as the first in the country to guarantee the one–for-one replacement of all demolished public housing units); *see also* James Krohe, Jr., *Displaced and Replaced*, 72 Planning 44, 44 (2006) (on DCHA's plans to replace 702 of 752 public housing units in the Arthur Capper-Carrollsburg complex).

5 Susan J. Popkin, *The HOPE VI Program: What Has Happened to the Residents?*, *in* Where Are Poor People to Live?, *supra* note 1, 69, 73 (noting that by the end of the first ten years of the HOPE VI program, few deeply subsidized public housing units had been rebuilt, and few residents of demolished public housing units had returned to the renovated sites); *see also* Jennifer Comey, *HOPE VI'd and On the Move, in* Metropolitan Housing and Communities Center, at 2 (Urban Institute, Brief No. 1, 2007) (reporting that, of public housing residents interviewed at five HOPE VI sites from 2001–05, 5 percent had returned to renovated units).

6 The poverty rate of the Barry Farm zip code is 33 percent, compared to a city-wide average of 20 percent. Neighborhood Info DC, Data: ZIP Codes, ZIP 20020, *available at* http://www.neighborhoodinfodc.org/zip/nbr_prof_zip18.html [hereinafter ZIP 20020]. However, data from the Office of the Deputy Mayor for Planning and Economic Development (DMPED) represented the poverty rate for the Barry Farm public housing project itself at 82 percent. *See* Nikita Stewart, *Gentrification, With a Difference*, Wash. Post, July 20, 2006, District Extra at 1. The D.C. Office of Planning's poverty figure for the planning area for Ward 8, one of the District's eight political subdivisions, is actually higher than that for zip code 20020, at 37.8 percent. *See* D.C. Comprehensive Plan, *Area Elements: Far Southeast/Southwest Area Element*, *supra* note 4, at 18-6.

this zip code is also among the most segregated and the most unemployed.[7] It is an area of "poorly"s: poorly served by public transportation, poorly served by neighborhood amenities such as grocery stores or sit-down restaurants,[8] and, compared to neighborhoods across the Anacostia River, poorly served even by non-profit organizations that exist to serve the poorly served.[9] It may seem only just that the urban renewal efforts of the present compensate, if not atone, for the urban renewal failures of the past, through which southeast D.C. first became the stopping off place for hundreds of residents displaced by urban renewal in the southwest;[10] and next became split in two by the highway built to connect Bolling Air Force Base with easy access to the Capitol.[11]

But there is no point in minimizing the lives of the residents of Barry Farm Dwellings or in underestimating the neighborhood surrounding them. Other indicators reveal greater stability of residence than the city's average; and, for good or ill, a much greater appreciation in housing prices from 2000 to 2005.[12] Viewed

---

7 The population of the Barry Farm zip code is 97 percent black non-Hispanic, as compared to a citywide average of 61 percent; its unemployment rate is 18 percent compared to the city's 11 percent. ZIP 20020, *supra* note 6. Data from the DMPED represent the unemployment rate for Barry Farm at 42 percent. Stewart, *supra* note 6, at 1.

8 Barry Farm Plan, *supra* note 2, at 20.

9 No recent qualitative studies exist of the institutions serving the Anacostia neighborhood, within which Barry Farm is located. At least two have been conducted of the Washington Highlands neighborhood, about a half mile to the southwest of Anacostia, which shares some basic demographic characteristics and is included in the D.C. Comprehensive Plan's "Far Southeast/Southwest Area Element," *supra* note 4. *See* Carol J. DeVita, Carlos Manjarrez & Eric C. Twombly, Organizations and Neighborhood Networks That Strengthen Families in the District of Columbia: Final Report to the Annie E. Casey Foundation 22 (1999) (noting that in Washington Highlands one daycare provider existed for 703 children, compared with a ratio of one provider for 46 children in the central city neighborhood of Columbia Heights; *id* at 33–6 (that most non-profit organizations in southeast D.C. were far younger, had fewer paid staff, and brought in less than half the revenue of their cohorts in the center city). *See also* Caterina Gouvis Roman & Gretchen E. Moore, Urb. Inst., Measuring Local Institutions and Organizations: The Role of Community Institutional Capacity in Social Capital 31 (2004) (tabulating the number of religious institutions, businesses, neighborhood organizations, service providers, "pro-social places" such as recreation centers, and liquor stores in Washington Highlands).

10 Brochure from Smithsonian Anacostia Community Museum, East of the River: Continuity and Change, at East of the River Transformed (2007).

11 For a description of the impact of the District's transportation and urban renewal strategies during the 1950s on the historic Anacostia neighborhood of Ward 8, *see* Brett Williams, *A River Runs Through Us*, 103 Amer. Anthropologist 409, 420 (2001); *see also* Barry Farm Plan, *supra* note 2 at 16 (noting that Interstate 295 to the north and Suitland Parkway to the east separate the Barry Farm neighborhood itself from the rest of the historic Anacostia neighborhood).

12 Fifty-eight percent of the residents of this zip code live in the same residence in which they lived five years ago, as compared to 50 percent of all District residents. Median

through an "assets-based" lens, there are churches and museums close by.[13] The buildings of Barry Farm themselves are not "distressed;" in fact, the description of the housing complex on the District of Columbia Housing Authority's (DCHA) website reads much like copy from any real estate firm that is marketing "can't miss" opportunities in townhouse-style family housing.[14] The ARC, a newly constructed arts center within a short drive of Barry Farm, houses a Boys and Girls Club, Covenant House, a branch of the downtown Corcoran Gallery of Art, the Levine School of Music, and the Washington Ballet.[15] There are programs which mentor children in elementary school and train them as youth leaders in high school.[16]

Most of all, there is also a past, a collectively felt sense of history. Barry Farm began in 1867 as 375 acres which the Freedmen's Bureau bought and sold to black families. By the early 1900s, small farms and businesses thrived in far Southeast, with scores of new communities following the construction of bridges across the Anacostia River and trolley lines joining the Navy Yard to the southern

---

sales prices for homes increased by 12 percent from 2000 to 2005, as compared to the city average of 7.6 percent. ZIP 20020, *supra* note 6.

13 For the classic manual on assessing the potential for development in poor communities from affirmative attributes rather than deficits, *see* John P. Kretzmann & John L. McKnight, Building Communities from the Inside Out: A Path Towards Finding and Mobilizing A Community's Assets (1993). *See* Barry Farm Plan, *supra* note 2 at 19 (listing the many churches and the schools in the environs of Barry Farm); for descriptions of the area's hilly topography and views of the Capitol, *see* D.C. Comprehensive Plan, *Area Elements: Far Southeast/Southwest*, *supra* note 4, at p.18-10; for other cultural and recreational amenities within the Far Southeast community, *see* East of the River Community Development Corporation, Ward 8, *available at* http://www.ercdc.org/ward8.html (noting location of the Frederick Douglass House, a National Historic Site; the Southeast Tennis Center, and the Smithsonian Anacostia Museum within Ward 8).

14 The D.C. Housing Authority's website describes the Barry Farm project as follows: "Barry Farm offers 432 spacious units with a range of 2 to 6 bedrooms. Barry Farm is located within easy access of interstate 295 and Suitland Parkway. Less than a 5 minute walk to the Anacostia Metro Rail and Metro bus on the property." District of Columbia Housing Authority, *available at* http://www.dchousing.org (follow hyperlink to "view projects").

15 D.C. Department of Housing and Community Development (DHCD), Featured Projects: The ARC, *available at* http://dhcd.dc.gov (follow hyperlink to "Information – Featured Projects"; follow hyperlink to "The ARC").

16 For example, Facilitating Leadership in Youth (FLY) began in 2003 as a volunteer program for American University undergraduates to tutor grade school children from Barry Farm. Since its inception, FLY has expanded: it rents its own multi-level office in historic Anacostia, runs a summer arts and tutoring program, and mentors children for college from first through twelfth grade. Its website is *available at* http://www.flyouth.org (last visited February 8, 2009).

neighborhood of Congress Heights.[17] When residents of Barry Farm gathered in 2006 to learn of the District's plans to demolish and rebuild their complex, they were worried about displacement. But they were also concerned about the possibility of the loss of their community's historic name.[18] In short: this is not a paradise, but this is not a wasteland.

Some self-disclosure, or at least disclosure of interest, is in order. I direct a law school clinic which provides pro bono assistance to non-profit organizations, tenants' associations, and small businesses. Though Barry Farm Dwellings and the residents who live within it are not clients of my clinic, my clinic serves non-profit organizations with their own clients within this neighborhood. Those organizational clients are concerned about whether the sturdy community capital they are building will enable their clients to withstand what is coming: the uncertainty of the diaspora away from, and the uncertainty of the return to, Barry Farm Dwellings. I am concerned that they are right.

Last year I showed the documentary film *Southwest Remembered*[19] to my first year property class. The film chronicles the urban renewal in the 1950s of the southwest section of the District of Columbia. That decimation gave rise to the rushed construction of other public housing complexes east of the river to accommodate Southwest's displaced residents; it generated the eminent domain case of *Berman v. Parker*,[20] and its progeny, *Kelo v. City of New London*.[21] *Southwest Remembered* put a face on the doctrine articulated in *Berman* that the welfare of the individual household or business must yield before the federal legislature's conception of the desirable neighborhood as "… beautiful as well as healthy, spacious as well as clean, well-balanced as well as carefully patrolled."[22]

I have seen *Southwest Remembered* many times. What stayed with me this time: towards the end there was an excerpt from an interview with Daniel Thursz, a psychologist who in 1966 had interviewed several of the residents who had been displaced from their homes some ten years before. He said that in those ten years, those residents had made no new friends.

What is the cost of loss of friends, or of the loss of ability to make friendships? Of the loss of attachment to networks, neighbors, and history? Should urban renewal

17 *See* Brochure from Smithsonian Anacostia Community Museum, *supra* note 10, at *Barry Farm/Modernization*.

18 *See* Stewart, *supra* note 6 at 9.

19 Southwest Remembered: A Story of Urban Renewal (Lamont Productions, Inc. 1990).

20 Berman v. Parker, 348 U.S. 26 (1954).

21 Kelo v. City of New London, 545 U.S. 469 (2005).

22 Berman, *supra* note 20, at 33. As the court noted tangentially in *Schneider v. District of Columbia*, the lower court decision which the Supreme Court reviewed in *Berman*, the Redevelopment Land Agency Act was created by an act of Congress, which functioned as the District of Columbia's legislature in the absence of home rule. Schneider v. District of Columbia, 117 F. Supp. 705, 720 (D.D.C.1953) ('We are of the opinion that the Congress, in legislating for the District of Columbia …").

calculate and make amends for those and other intangible costs of displacement? Right now, all that a renter displaced through the operation of federal funds can claim is the right to "a comparable replacement dwelling"[23]—but beyond unit size, what are the meaningful "comparables"? If owners of real property can claim rights to "just compensation" for governmental destruction of their property in the name of public purpose (if not public use), should not renters be able to claim the proxies for everything we associate with the physical and psychological amenities of home within and without the four walls?

I do not intend for these questions to be perceived as fanciful. Nor do I intend to romanticize the lives of poor people in resource-poor communities. In a moment of sober reckoning some 40 years ago, Congress adopted the Uniform Relocation Assistance Act (URA), passing the bill at the close of the first great period of post-war urban renewal. In passing the URA, Congress recognized that poor people lost something of value when they were displaced. The URA acknowledged that the principle underlying just compensation for takings—that government should compensate the few who were damaged to secure the welfare of the many—had failed poor renters, who suffered all of the burdens and few of the benefits of the "slum clearance" and highway construction that demolished their homes. That calculation of burden and benefit should be re-examined in light of present day urban renewal, which assumes that impoverished neighborhoods lack social cohesion, provide nothing of value to their residents, and would benefit from metamorphosis into "mixed income communities." If this justification for urban renewal—to improve the lives of poor individuals—is sincere and not pretextual, then urban renewal programs need to account both for the full cost to residents of redevelopment and relocation, and for the benefits that residents will receive in return for their sacrifice.

Critics have condemned land use decisions for failing to weigh the truly foreseeable benefits to residents against the truly foreseeable costs.[24] This lapse derives from assumptions that particularly hurt poor renters, who are doubly penalized: by perceptions that there are no costs associated with moving away

---

23 *See* Uniform Relocation Assistance and Real Property Acquisition Policies Act of 1970, Pub. L. No. 91-646, 84 Stat. 1894 (1971) (codified as amended at 42 U.S.C. §§ 4601–4638) [hereinafter the Uniform Relocation Assistance Act or URA]; *see* 42 U.S.C. § 4601(10) (2008) for the definition of "comparable replacement dwelling." For a fuller exploration of the historical and current significance of "comparable replacement dwelling" for displaced poor renters, *see* discussion *infra*, "Plumbing the Meaning of 'Comparable Replacement Dwelling'."

24 For further developments of this critique, *see* Sheila R. Foster, *The City as an Ecological Space: Social Capital and Urban Land Use*, 82 NOTRE DAME L. REV. 527, 546 (2006) (commenting that comprehensive plans, which set long-term goals for development, fail to account for or foster the formation of social capital either in theory or in implementation); Tim Iglesias, *Housing Impact Assessments: Opening New Doors for State Housing Regulation While Localism Persists*, 82 OR. L. REV. 433, 451 (2003) (criticizing land use decisions for failing to account for the loss of affordable housing).

from a poor neighborhood; and by the jurisprudence of takings, which, though it recognizes compensable losses to both owners and renters from displacement, denies compensation for "consequential," non-economic losses.[25] This position affects both owners and renters, but neglects the interests of subsidized residential renters most egregiously. Municipalities are free to assume that poor renters have nothing to lose from displacement, because they own nothing that we value: renters—particularly renters in public housing—are just one step up from "no property."[26]

Recent scholarship has focused on giving poor renters as well as real property owners both a say and a stake in any development that will displace them, whether displacement occurs directly through actual demolition of their homes and businesses, or indirectly through gentrification. That investment might be individual to the stakeholder: one proposal would advance "community equity shares" to all residents, including renters and public housing renters, in the appreciated value of their neighborhood.[27] Another would allocate "community residency entitlements," which would guarantee a right to return to the neighborhood after development and in that way recognize the investment that long-term residents make in their neighborhoods.[28] Other methods of protecting existing residents' interests would re-structure local government's processes for development, to mandate longitudinal consideration of the consequences of direct and indirect displacement. The platform for a "housing impact assessment" sets forth how and why, as a prerequisite to development, local governments should provide an accounting to constituents for any foreseeable loss of critical housing resources.[29] Another proposal for re-ordering of land use processes includes a "homestead community consent," a mandatory community approval of any development project.[30]

Another commentator has proposed that any plan for development include a "social impact statement (SIS)," the urban renewal equivalent of an environmental impact statement.[31] The SIS would operate as does the environmental impact

---

25 *See, e.g.*, Mitchell v. U.S., 267 U.S. 341, 345 (1925) (stating that the Fifth Amendment's protections to property owners against takings do not extend to compensation for the "consequential damages" from any loss of or destruction to businesses).

26 *See* Jane Baron, *Homelessness as a Property Problem*, 36 URB. LAW. 273 (2004) (defining the legal category of "no property").

27 Barbara L. Bezdek, *To Attain "The Just Rewards of So Much Struggle": Local-Resident Equity Participation in Urban Revitalization*, 35 HOFSTRA L. REV. 37, 101–3 (2006).

28 James J. Kelly, Jr., *"We Shall Not Be Moved": Urban Communities, Eminent Domain and the Socioeconomics of Just Compensation*, 80 ST. JOHN'S L. REV. 923, 982 (2006).

29 Iglesias, *Housing Impact Assessments*, *supra* note 24, at 478–9.

30 Kelly, *supra* note 28, at 980.

31 Adam P. Hellegers, *Eminent Domain as an Economic Development Tool: A Proposal to Reform HUD Displacement Policy*, 2001 LAW. REV. M. ST. U. DETROIT C.L.

statement, in that it would give residents two "hooks" to assert their interests. Hook number one is substantive: the SIS would provide an articulation of the tangible and intangible elements of losing "home." That articulation should promote acknowledgment that there is indeed some personal and collective loss in moving poor residents away from a poor community. Hook number two involves process: residents would participate in the articulation of loss, but would also receive standing to petition for suspension of the development process until they are relocated in a way that assures that their "comparable replacement dwellings" truly compensate for the physical, social, and psychological dislocation which the social impact statement illuminates.

I propose to explore how a more fully developed "social impact statement" might serve the needs of residents who face upheavals in the wake of the redevelopment of communities such as the Barry Farm Dwellings. The "social impact statement" would refine further just what the significance is of loss of housing under Iglesias's proposed "housing impact assessment." There is value in articulating and quantifying. Hellegers noted that if juries already quantify "pain and suffering," then measuring the seemingly unquantifiable loss to individuals of neighboring, of comfort, of "community" is not nearly the impossible project that it might seem.[32] Indices from domestic measures of welfare and well-being quantify further what loss of community and social networks might mean, to individuals and to the collectivity. Some instruments attempting to measure quality of life have been applied in studies of public housing residents after they have been relocated through different types of "dispersal programs." Rarely, however, have these findings been considered in advance, in relocation planning or more fundamentally in the critical decision to uproot the residents.

Although they do not approach the detail of Iglesias's "housing impact statement," structures already exist within redevelopment processes which could force accountability to the preferences and the needs of the residents who will pay the greatest price for redevelopment. I will discuss where it might be possible to incorporate the construction and adoption of a social impact statement into existing requirements for land use development in general and for public housing redevelopment in particular. Incorporation of a social impact statement would give meaning to the opportunities for participation in land use decisions which even public housing residents already have but may not use. The negotiations which precede the implementation of community benefits agreements and planned unit developments may provide arenas within which poor renters could assert the costs enumerated by a social impact statement. Perhaps most importantly, the mandate to develop a social impact statement would inject rigor into the assumptions upon which dislocations of poor people are based.

The social impact statement's value lies in its inclusiveness: it evaluates how all residents, not only those residents who hold real property, might measure

---

901, 956–60.

32 *Id.* at 955.

their investment in community. The legislative backlash from *Kelo* confronts the damage only to victims whose loss of real property can be conventionally measured in condemnation proceedings.[33] The outrage following the debacle of redevelopment efforts after Hurricane Katrina reflects more fully the sense of loss of both propertied and property-less "homes."[34] The development and application of a social impact statement should force recognition of the consequences of tearing up and re-constituting community. In measuring what residents value in their present homes and neighborhoods, the social impact statement will enable public housing authorities truly to assess "comparability:" to seek out places and resources through which residents can replicate those positive attributes of home. Fully realized, a social impact statement should compel local governments to assess the true, not imagined, utility of development projects to those who will be the most affected by them.

Is It Worth It? Assessing Two Decades of Uncertainty over the Costs and Benefits of the Second Generation of Urban Renewal

"Removal of blight" was the presumed benefit to communities of urban renewal in the 1950s and 1960s.[35] "Deconcentration of poverty" is the present day version of a presumed benefit to individuals and communities of uprooting individuals from physical community and social networks.[36] Tens of thousands of poor renters have lost their homes in service to either principle.

33 *See* Patricia E. Salkin & Amy Lavine, *Measure 37 and a Spoonful of Kelo: A Recipe for Property Rights Activists at the Ballot Box*, 38 Urb. Law. 1065, 1069 (2006) (describing the intensified pressure applied by property rights activists after the *Kelo* decision for legislation and voter initiatives to limit the use of eminent domain and to expand governmental obligations to compensate property owners for "takings").

34 See, e.g., Kalima Rose, *Struggling in the Crescent City*, 151 Shelterforce 20, 21 (Fall 2007); William P. Quigley, *Obstacles to Opportunity: Housing That Working and Poor People Can Afford in New Orleans Since Katrina*, 42 Wake Forest L. Rev. 393 (2007).

35 For overviews of the uses of the term "blight" in urban re-development policy, *see* Colin Gordon, *Blighting the Way: Urban Renewal, Economic Development, and the Elusive Definition of Blight*, 31 Fordham Urb. L.J. 305 (2004); Wendell E. Pritchett, *The "Public Menace" of Blight: Urban Renewal and the Private Uses of Eminent Domain*, 21 Yale L. & Pol'y Rev. 1 (2003).

36 Extensive as is the multi-disciplinary literature reviewing the social and housing policy underlying HOPE VI, even more extensive is the literature analyzing the shift in American housing policy to the promotion of the "deconcentration" of poor persons segregated in public housing communities by economic class as well as by race. For a small sampling and overviews, *see* Margery Austin Turner & Lynette A. Rawlings, Urb. Inst., Overcoming Concentrated Poverty and Isolation (2005) (reviewing results of three federally funded programs—Moving to Opportunity, Jobs Plus, and Bridges to Work—that addressed the disadvantages suffered by poor residents of poor neighborhoods by moving

The first step in fleshing out the elements of a social impact statement requires an assessment of the difference between the presumed and the actual benefits to renters of moving under any of the modern day "dispersal programs,"[37] efforts to move poor people out of public housing projects in order to achieve a number of goals. As one critic of these programs has stated, the high costs to cities of demolition and reconstruction of public housing projects, and to individuals of dislocation and personal loss, demand both proof of tangible benefit, and clear articulation of what the goals of urban renewal are supposed to be.[38] The "social impact" of relocation consists of the degree to which the benefits of the new placement compensate, or fail to compensate, for the costs of uprooting the renter from the old.

The Fuzzy Objectives of Dispersal Programs: "Ground-clearing Operations" or "The Direct Path to a Decent Home and a Suitable Living Environment"?[39]

In 1968, the National Commission on Urban Problems assessed the aftermath of 20 years of federally financed urban renewal and interstate highway construction.

---

residents to census tracts with lower concentrations of poverty, or by supporting residents in jobs outside their neighborhoods); John Goering, *Expanding Housing Choice and Integrating Neighborhoods: The Moving to Opportunity Experiment*, *in* The Geography of Opportunity: Race and Housing Choice in Metropolitan America 127 (Xavier de Souza Briggs ed., 2005).

37 The term "dispersal programs" denotes the collection of federal housing programs that use housing choice vouchers to move public housing tenants to neighborhoods with lower concentrations of poverty; *see, e.g.*, Edward G. Goetz, *Forced Relocation vs. Voluntary Mobility: The Effects of Dispersal Programmes on Households*, 17 Housing Stud. 107 (2002).

38 Edward G. Goetz, *Comment: Public Housing Demolition and the Benefits to Low Income Families*, 71 J. Am. Planning Ass'n 407, 409 (2005) (criticizing the conclusions from a study that found improved employment and educational outcomes for residents who were relocated from public housing in Atlanta: "… the highly intrusive and expensive process of forcible relocation, full-scale demolition, and redevelopment did not result in socioeconomic improvements greater than what occurred in the control group without any such intervention …" and summarizing results from other studies indicating that public housing residents failed to improve their individual circumstances solely as a result of moving to less disadvantaged neighborhoods).

39 National Commission on Urban Problems, Building the American City 92-3 (1968) [hereinafter National Commission]. In this quotation from its report, the Commission was paraphrasing the "Declaration of National Housing Policy" that prefaced the Housing Act of 1949: "The Congress hereby declares that the general welfare and security of the Nation and the health and living standards of its people require housing production … to remedy the serious housing shortage, … the clearance of slums and blighted areas, and the realization as soon as feasible of the goal of a decent home and a suitable living environment for every American family …" Housing Act of 1949, Pub. L. No. 81-171, § 2, 63 Stat. 413 (1949).

Its evaluation supported the argument for passage of the Uniform Relocation Assistance Act. In the conclusions to its report, the Commission questioned whether the implementation of urban renewal had furthered the goals of the Housing Act of 1949, or constituted merely a pretext for moving poor people out of the way of development. I will return to the URA later, as the principles supporting its genesis and its current formulation should weigh heavily in the construction of a social impact statement. But the question of motive or purpose for the urban renewal of the 1950s and 1960s recurs with the present day "dispersal programs."

It is impossible here to reproduce fully the history, criticism, and evaluation of the Gautreaux, Moving to Opportunity (MTO), and HOPE VI programs, the three major dispersal or mobility programs currently or recently supported in federal housing policy. It is also impossible to generalize about any policy underlying them. Even the differences in the terminology used to refer to them collectively—"dispersal" or "mobility" programs—suggest differences in underlying philosophies: "dispersal" to combat the "neighborhood effects" of concentrated poverty and racial segregation;[40] "mobility" to afford individual households a chance to escape the harms absorbed through concentrated poverty and racial segregation.[41] I will attempt to summarize, first, the theories supporting the programs; and second, the consensus of whether the dispersal/mobility programs have given residents more than what they have given up: whether the relocation of residents out of public housing has improved their lives sufficiently to warrant the disruption and the expense.

All of the dispersal or mobility programs operate out of some variation of the thesis that the life chances of poor residents will improve if they live in areas with a lower concentration of poverty; put another way, if the residents live in "mixed income communities." As there are many theories for how and why poor people suffer from the neighborhood effects of living in poor communities, there are also many theories for why poor residents should benefit from living next to people who are not poor. The hypothesis that concentrating poor people in isolated low-rent housing degrades the people, the housing, and the neighborhood has figured in local and state housing policy, as well as in housing policy for the District of Columbia, since at least the turn of the twentieth century. From the 1850s until Reconstruction, an influx of European immigrants and freed blacks changed the demographics and the housing patterns of the Capitol. The back alley tenements, or "alley dwellings," into which the newcomers crowded, contrasted dismally with the architectural vision of gleaming axial monuments as the face of the Federal City. Anxious to dispel the image of the buildings and of the residents within

---

40 Susan Clampet-Lundquist, *HOPE VI Relocation: Moving to New Neighborhoods and Building New Ties*, 15 Housing Pol'y Debate 415, 418 (2004) (summarizing findings that persons living in neighborhoods with concentrated poverty are less likely to succeed in school or to find work).

41 *See, e.g.*, Florence Wagman Roisman & Hilary Botein, *Housing Mobility and Life Opportunities*, 27 Clearinghouse Rev. 334 (1993).

them, the Senate legislated first to condemn unsanitary alley dwellings, next to prohibit further construction of them, and last to demolish them regardless of their physical condition.[42] In support of the elimination of alley dwellings throughout the city, housing reformers testified that the seclusion of alley dwellers from persons of higher income deprived them of "… the restraining influences of the daily observation of their better neighbours …,"[43] damaging both their ambition and the actual physical spaces within which they lived.

Most of the rationales for deconcentration as a housing and as an anti-poverty policy are muddied, but Mark Joseph and his co-authors have summarized them brilliantly. Richer neighbors enjoy better political connections, better schools, better amenities, and faster responses to complaints, which spill over to the advantage of their poorer neighbors; richer neighbors offer connections to information about better employment and educational opportunities; richer neighbors promote safer neighborhoods through a heightened sense of collective responsibility; and richer neighbors provide role models for success.[44] While all the "dispersal" or "mobility" programs have targeted richer, whiter suburbs as "opportunity areas,"[45] the rationales for acculturation and behavioral change have been associated most closely with HOPE VI.

The dispersal programs differ in who makes the decision concerning whether or how to move public housing residents. Public housing tenants participated voluntarily in Gautreaux and MTO, using vouchers to relocate in privately owned rental housing in less segregated neighborhoods; HOPE VI tenants are displaced involuntarily, either with vouchers into the private market or into other public housing units, so that the developments from which they move out, and to which they may or may not return, might become less segregated. Further differences arise as a result of the genesis of the three programs. As has been summarized exhaustively elsewhere, the Gautreaux Assisted-Housing Program, which used vouchers to relocate Chicago public housing residents into more integrated suburbs of lesser poverty concentration, arose from parallel civil rights cases which attacked the roles of the Chicago Housing Authority and the federal Department of Housing and Urban Development in isolating African American tenants into

---

42 Margaret E. Farrar, *Making the City Beautiful: Aesthetic Reform and the (Dis)placement of Bodies*, *in* Embodied Utopias: Gender, Social Change and the Modern Metropolis 37, 39–43 (Amy Bingaman, Lise Sanders & Rebecca Zorach eds., 2002).

43 *Id.* at 45 (citing *Inhabited Alleys in the District of Columbia: Hearing before the Subcomm. on the District of Columbia*, 63rd Cong., 2d Sess. 19 (1914)).

44 Mark L. Joseph, Robert J. Chaskin & Henry S. Webber, *The Theoretical Basis for Addressing Poverty through Mixed-Income Development*, 42 Urb. Aff. Rev. 369, 373 (2007).

45 *See* Xavier de Souza Briggs & Margery Austin Turner, *Assisted Housing Mobility and the Success of Low-Income Minority Families: Lessons for Policy, Practice, and Future Research*, 1 NW. J.L. & Soc. Pol'y 25, 36 (2006) (coining the phrase, "opportunity areas").

hyper-segregated, resource-poor housing projects. The goal of the litigation was the eradication of historic segregation, as an evil in and of itself.[46]

While the impacts of relocation upon the "Gautreaux residents" came to be extensively studied over time, the goals of Gautreaux were remediation, not research. Nothing in the design of the Gautreaux mobility program explicitly tests the thesis that residents will benefit when they escape from poverty, crime, inferior housing quality, and lack of educational or vocational opportunity—in short, from all the ills presumed to be attendant upon, if not caused by, enforced segregation into poor minority neighborhoods.[47] Similarly, nothing in the design of HOPE VI projects from their inception to the present tests any one of the "mixed income" theories from which HOPE VI derives its justification as an anti-poverty program. To the extent that HUD researches the outcomes of HOPE VI—the demolition of housing units and dispersal of tenants—at all, the research focuses on the impacts of HOPE VI revitalization on neighborhoods, not on displaced public housing residents.[48]

The Moving to Opportunity program was constructed in order to rectify this absence of experimental design. MTO was a limited longitudinal demonstration which monitored outcomes for three groups of public housing residents: residents who stayed in public housing, residents who moved from public housing with the financial assistance of vouchers, and residents who moved from public housing with the financial assistance of vouchers targeted to higher income neighborhoods

---

46 For a synopsis of the history of the Gautreaux litigation, see William P. Wilen & Wendy L. Stasell, *Gautreaux and Chicago's Public Housing Crisis: The Conflict Between Achieving Integration and Providing Decent Housing for Very Low-Income African Americans*, 34 CLEARINGHOUSE REV. 117, 123–5 (July–August 2000); see also ALEXANDER POLIKOFF, WAITING FOR GAUTREAUX: A STORY OF SEGREGATION, HOUSING, AND THE BLACK GHETTO (2006). See also Greg J. Duncan & Anita Zuberi, *Mobility Lessons from Gautreaux and Moving to Opportunity*, 1 NW. J. L. & SOC. POL'Y 110, 110–11 (2006) (distinguishing the two phases of the Gautreaux relocation program: "Gautreaux I," which ensued directly from the settlement of the Gautreaux litigation and which moved thousands of families from Chicago Housing Authority properties to the suburbs from 1976 through the late 1990s; and "Gautreaux II," which began in 2002 as a new program of relocation out of public housing complexes).

47 Goering, *supra* note 36, at 131.

48 Popkin, *supra* note 5, at 71–2; *see also* Thomas D. Boston, *The Effects of Revitalization on Public Housing Residents: A Case Study of the Atlanta Housing Authority*, 71 J. AM. PLANNING ASS'N 393, 393 (2005) (noting that little research thus far has documented the impact of HOPE VI relocations on families who have been displaced from public housing); *see also* Popkin et al., A Decade of HOPE VI, *supra* note 1, at 3, 27 (noting the incoherency of any definition of "success" for HOPE VI). For a projection of the ways in which local governments might expect to recoup expenditures on HOPE VI projects, *see also* MARGERY AUSTIN TURNER, MARK WOOLLEY, THOMAS G. KINGSLEY, SUSAN J POPKIN, DIANE LEVY & ELIZABETH COVE, ESTIMATING THE PUBLIC COSTS AND BENEFITS OF HOPE VI INVESTMENTS: METHODOLOGICAL REPORT (2007).

and the added assistance of counseling and placement services.[49] Studies of the Gautreaux and MTO demonstrations involved relatively few families over time, and those by definition constituted a particular subset of residents who were more anxious or better positioned to relocate.[50]

HOPE VI has succeeded as a "ground clearing operation:" between 2001 and 2007 its funds supported the demolition of 51,220 units and the relocation of 28,565 families.[51] It has succeeded less well if its goal is to enable displaced public housing tenants to return to their former places of residence in revitalized homes.[52] HOPE VI, Gautreaux, and MTO have all succeeded as dispersal mechanisms if "dispersal" is defined as dispersal of intensely poor public housing communities, succeeded somewhat if "dispersal" is defined as relocation of poor residents into less poor communities,[53] and failed if "dispersal" is defined as relocation of poor residents into less racially segregated communities.[54] The HOPE VI program has

49 For a description of the experimental design of the MTO program, *see* Turner & Rawlings, *supra* note 36, at 8, tbl.1; Susan J. Popkin, Laura E. Harris & Mary K. Cunningham, U.S. Dep't of Housing and Urb. Dev., Families in Transition: A Qualitative Analysis of the MTO Experience: Final Report ii (2002).

50 Popkin, *supra* note 5, at 70–71; Briggs & Turner, *supra* note 45, at 32 (noting that the most successful movers in the MTO demonstration were those who wished to relocate, had access to automobiles, and had fewer children).

51 U.S. Office of Management and Budget, Detailed Information on the HOPE VI (Severely Distressed Public Housing) Assessment, *available at* http://www.whitehouse.gov/omb/expectmore.

52 *See* Comey, *supra* note 5.

53 Two thirds of the residents relocated under "Gautreaux I," as well as their children, have maintained residence in neighborhoods of lower poverty and less racial segregation. Duncan & Zuberi, *supra* note 46, at 113–14. Residents who have been tracked through HOPE VI moved from public housing complexes that were so segregated by race and class that almost any move to any other neighborhood would result in less segregated surroundings. *See* Popkin et al., A Decade of HOPE VI, *supra* note 1, at 8 (describing the public housing complexes designated in the 1990s as "severely distressed" and thus eligible for demolition as 85 percent black in neighborhoods that were 69 percent black). *See also* Turner & Rawlings, *supra* note 36, at 29 (that of the two thirds of the MTO families who moved after their first placements in low poverty neighborhoods, 82 percent moved to neighborhoods of higher poverty concentration). *See* Larry Buron, Diane K. Levy & Megan Gallagher, Urb. Inst., Housing Choice Vouchers: How HOPE VI Families Fared in the Private Market 3–4 (2007) (that 47 percent of public housing residents who used HOPE VI relocation vouchers had moved into neighborhoods with poverty rates below 20 percent).

54 Comey, *supra* note 5, at 4–5 (a "vast majority" of public housing residents who were relocated under HOPE VI and monitored in a five-year panel study moved to predominantly minority neighborhoods). Most movers from the MTO and HOPE VI programs have ended up in tracts that were less poor, but still significantly segregated. Popkin et al., A Decade of HOPE VI, *supra* note 1, at 47; *see also* Clampet-Lundquist, *supra* note 40, at 433 (finding that residents who used vouchers to move from the W.E.B. DuBois Tower public housing

been criticized for its lack of attention to the fair housing implications of its goals for relocation.[55]

All three programs strove to provide "a decent home and a suitable living environment" for public housing residents by moving them away from public housing. As I will discuss below, for some residents, they succeeded. But the programs claimed heavy freight for the deconcentration or mixed income thesis by predicting that relocation into richer, whiter neighborhoods would improve the quality of life and of functioning for those who were relocated. I will also review evaluations of the success of that claim, as well as the related but distinct claim for benefits from relocation next to richer, whiter neighbors, below.

Articulating the Costs and Benefits of Relocation

The most striking gains for families who have used vouchers to move from public housing to richer neighborhoods have come through the experience of safer streets.[56] Recent HOPE VI studies have affirmed that former residents of public housing who moved to less poor neighborhoods with the assistance of vouchers felt significantly safer. Those residents have reported both the immediate and the extended benefits of freedom from drug trafficking and gun violence: the pleasures of sitting outside on a summer evening, of not worrying about letting their children play outdoors, and of walking through their neighborhoods without fear of personal threat.[57] MTO moves preceded decreases in obesity and improvements in mental health for adults and young girls.[58] Residents also experienced higher quality housing situated within neighborhoods that showed fewer signs of vandalism or physical decay.[59]

Other benefits from relocation are less evident. It is unclear whether any of the rationales supporting the "mixed income" strategy is borne out by the results of the three dispersal programs. What *is* clear is that there is rarely much "mixing" in "mixed income." Little social interchange occurs between neighbors of

---

complex in Philadelphia found housing in neighborhoods that were more racially integrated and affluent than did other residents who chose to move into other public housing).

55 *See* Henry Korman, *HOPE VI Reauthorization and Racial Segregation*, 17 J. AFFORDABLE HOUSING & COMM. DEV. L. 353, 356 (2008) (commenting that current HOPE VI policy perpetuates racial segregation of public housing communities by allowing housing authorities to build HOPE VI replacement public housing units on hyper-segregated existing sites); *see also* Pindell, *supra* note 1, at 422–3.

56 Briggs & Turner, *supra* note 45, at 45 (summarizing findings that those participants in MTO who moved to lower poverty neighborhoods perceived significant improvement in safety).

57 SUSAN J. POPKIN & ELIZABETH COVE, URB. INST., SAFETY IS THE MOST IMPORTANT THING: HOW HOPE VI HELPED FAMILIES 6 (2007).

58 Turner & Rawlings, *supra* note 36, at 14, 30.

59 *Id.* at 14–15.

different economic backgrounds.[60] Research does not bear out the "moral uplift" justification—one that was tenuous at best and insulting to public housing residents at worst.[61] Exposure to "middle class" behaviors through living next door, even during the rare occasions when such exposures occur, provides no intrinsic benefit: no modeling, no creation of beneficial loose ties that might lead to enhanced job opportunities.[62] It is more likely that movers benefit from the correlation between a lower concentration of poverty in their new communities and lower crime rates and better housing conditions—not from a correlation (if any) between more well-connected neighbors and their own success.

We must complicate the "is it worth it?" question by asking, "is it worth it for whom?" It is clear that more recent research on outcomes for HOPE VI residents has suggested more impressive gains than had previous findings, even for those residents who were compelled to move. Those benefits are measurable (increased physical safety and improved housing conditions) and intangible (increased sense of security and of well-being). As for the costs, studies have not borne out the "mixed income" assumption that a higher income environment would ameliorate all social problems. Results of research from the MTO program, the most deliberately designed and executed of the three dispersal programs, indicate that even well-intentioned social interventions cannot be expected to achieve wide-ranging social goals unless they include specific plans to do so. Even MTO failed to design programs with sufficient supports to achieve specific outcomes. For instance, MTO counselors were not directed to focus their clients on choosing neighborhoods with better schools as part of their relocation strategy. Subsequently, those children who relocated under MTO did not enroll in appreciably better schools.[63] Other findings from the Gautreaux program and from MTO confirm that while gains from safety were significant for all participants, residents experienced little or no improvement

60 Popkin et al., A Decade of HOPE VI, *supra* note 1, at 23.

61 *See* James E. Rosenbaum, Linda K. Stroh & Cathy A. Flynn, *Lake Parc Place: A Study of Mixed Income Housing*, 9 Housing Pol'y Debate 703, 732–3 (1998) (reporting the negative comments of very poor public housing residents to questions about their reactions to their less poor neighbors, all of whom had moved to a mixed income development under a Chicago Housing Authority demonstration program); *see also* Alastair Smith, Jt. Ctr. Housing Stud. Harv. U., Mixed-Income Housing Developments: Promise and Reality 24–6 (2002) (based on a review of studies of interactions among residents with different household incomes living in mixed income developments, concluding that interactions among tenants of different income levels was inconsistent, and that these interactions rarely produced enhanced employment opportunities for the poorer tenants).

62 Joseph et al., *supra* note 44, at 385–6.

63 Turner & Rawlings, *supra* note 36, at 15; Xavier de Souza Briggs, Kadija S. Ferryman, Susan J. Popkin & María Rendón, *Why Did the Moving to Opportunity Experiment Not Get Young People into Better Schools?*, 19 Housing Pol'y Debate 53, 57–8 (2008) (describing lapses in experimental design that compromised plans to relocate public housing residents with vouchers in neighborhoods of lower poverty concentration).

in income or in employment prospects.[64] While girls whose families moved under MTO seemed to engage in fewer behavioral outbursts in their new neighborhoods, boys behaved more disruptively.[65]

Similarly, the significant gains realized by some HOPE VI residents from the perception and reality of safer neighborhoods did not manifest in more tangible improvements in the residents' physical health or employment.[66] Nor is psychic security enough to produce housing security. Forty percent of voucher holders interviewed in a HOPE VI five-year panel study had moved since their first relocation into private sector housing, with 9 percent having moved three or more times.[67] Theoretically, vouchers enable poor renters to exercise control in the private housing market—they can leave their present neighborhoods to seek better housing conditions. But the choice of housing may force other "choices," such as deciding whether to cut back on other necessities in order to pay increasing utility costs. Rather than enhancing control, renting in the private market may also subject poor renters to complete loss of it: if the owner decides to withdraw from the voucher program, or if the owner loses its building through foreclosure, the housing is gone.[68]

As some researchers who have studied residents relocated through HOPE VI have noted, it may be too soon for residents to take advantage of their newly found psychic breathing space. Other, more subtle stresses may have replaced the worries for their own and their children's physical safety: the stress of being at the mercy of the housing market, or of the choice to heat or eat.[69] Families who have been dislodged from their former networks of support may have trouble in forming new ties. I will turn now to discussing the question with which I began: what is the cost of loss of friends, of ability to make friends, and of loss of attachment to networks, neighbors, and history? As those who have interviewed relocated public housing residents have noted, these losses are observable, and have a real impact on the abilities of relocated residents to adjust and thrive. However dysfunctional policymakers may deem the former neighborhoods of poor public housing residents to be, in some instances they provided social resources, which translated into tangible economic resources, that their new mixed income neighborhoods do not seem to offer. Those losses are as important—and as possible—to quantify in a social impact statement as are gains or losses in health, education, employment opportunity, or income. To the extent that displacement eliminates critical

64 Duncan & Zuberi, *supra* note 46, at 119–20.

65 Turner & Rawlings, *supra* note 36, at 14–15.

66 Carlos A. Manjarrez, Susan J. Popkin & Elizabeth Guernsey, Urb. Inst., Poor Health: Adding Insult to Injury for HOPE VI Families 3 (2007) (noting that despite striking improvements in safety and in housing quality, public housing residents who used vouchers to move to private housing experienced no change in health).

67 Buron et al., *supra* note 53, at 5.

68 *Id.*

69 Popkin & Cove, *supra* note 57, at 6–7.

supports that nothing else supplies, or for which nothing else can substitute, those particular costs constitute a legitimate subject of a social impact statement and of compensation.

Accounting for the Value of "Place Attachment," Social Networks, and Social Capital in the Communities that Public Housing Residents Leave Behind

Anyone who lives anywhere develops both "place attachment," the emotional bonds built over time with physical and social features of a locale, and "place dependence," a more concrete assessment of how a place fulfills a range of needs.[70] "Place attachment" need not be connected with "home:" a neighborhood gathering place may provide the same sense of stability or serve as a marker for positive or negative life-forming events.[71] "Place dependence" draws from every resource that an individual has put into place to supply needs that income alone may not supply, resources that public housing residents have cited as influencing their decisions on whether to stay in place or leave in advance of involuntary relocation: proximity to neighbors, families, church, persons who speak the same language, the welfare office, day care or school, transportation, grocery stores, the safety of the neighborhood or the diversity of the neighborhood.[72]

HOPE VI and its predecessor urban renewal programs are motivated at least in part and are justified by the perception that public housing environments offer nothing to which residents could form attachments, and no resources upon which residents can depend.[73] Yet some residents of public housing do develop deep "place attachments" to their homes, to the degree that moving from public housing prompts incapacitating depression and feelings of uprootedness.[74] Whether as a

70 Rachel Garshick Kleit & Lynne Manzo, *To Move or Not to Move: Relationships to Place and Relocation Choices in HOPE VI*, 17 Housing Pol'y Debate 271, 276–7 (2006) (distinguishing between "place attachment" and "place dependence").

71 Lynne C. Manzo, *For Better or Worse: Exploring Multiple Dimensions of Place Meaning*, 25 J. Env. Psych. 67, 70 (2005).

72 Kleit & Manzo, *supra* note 70, at 293, tbl.5 (listing factors that influenced the relocation decisions of residents from the High Point, Seattle public housing projects).

73 See Lynne C. Manzo, Rachel G. Kleit & Dawn Couch, *"Moving Three Times Is Like Having Your House on Fire Once": The Experience of Place and Impending Displacement among Public Housing Residents*, 45 Urb. Stud. 1855, 1873 (2008) (commenting on the generalization to all public housing of the discourse of "severe distress," which was generated from a limited sample of public housing reviewed by the National Commission on Severely Distressed Public Housing in 1992); Susan D. Bennett, *"The Possibility of a Beloved Place": Residents and Placemaking in Public Housing Communities*, 19 St. Louis U. Pub L. Rev. 259, 270–72 (2000) (describing the predominance of negative images of public housing in popular culture and ultimately in public policy).

74 Cheryl Rodriguez, *Invoking Fannie Lou Hamer: Research, Ethnography and Activism in Low-Income Communities*, 32 Urb. Anthropology 231, 236 (2003) (interviewing residents who had used vouchers to move from their public housing communities in Tampa,

result of the social and linguistic support that public housing provides to new immigrants, or as a result of the stability of affordable shelter that public housing provides to poor residents of all ethnic backgrounds, residents' tenures in public housing tend to be stable and long-term.[75] Some residents find cohesion and mutual support in public housing communities, sharing food, lending small household items, and watching each others' children.[76]

To generalize that all public housing residents enjoy and come to depend on similar social supports would be as short-sighted as to generalize that all public housing residents have access to none. What is key to remember is that these relationships exist among public housing residents across a broad spectrum of public housing communities,[77] and moving to mixed income communities disrupts these relationships without necessarily replacing the lost resources with anything better. Some residents continue to rely on their previous places of residence for social contacts and social services, either because they do not wish to seek out new resources or because they have received no guidance as to where they might find them.[78] The failure of relocated public housing residents to improve their financial prospects even after they have lived in their new, more affluent neighborhoods for several years may result from the absence of meaningful exchange with residents of their new neighborhoods.[79] Without that exchange, the hoped-for benefits of deconcentration of poor residents into more affluent communities cannot occur.[80]

Florida, and who felt uprooted and disorganized after they moved); Clampet-Lundquist, *supra* note 40, at 436 (stating that several relocated public housing residents volunteered that they suffered from depression after they moved).

75 Manzo et al., *supra* note 73, at 1865–8 (nearly half the residents had lived in this public housing complex for at least ten years); Clampet-Lundquist, *supra* note 40, at 424 (residents had lived an average of 18 years in a Philadelphia public housing complex before their relocation).

76 Manzo et al., *supra* note 73, at 1867.

77 *See, e.g.*, Manzo et al., *supra* note 73 (summarizing interviews with former residents of a mid-size public housing complex in the Pacific Northwest); Clampet-Lundquist, *supra* note 40 (interviews with former residents of a large public housing complex in Philadelphia); Rodriguez, *supra* note 74 (residents from public housing in Florida).

78 Sudhir Venkatesh & Isil Celimli, *Tearing Down the Community*, 138 SHELTERFORCE ONLINE (November/December 2004) (summarizing results from the Robert Taylor Homes Relocation Study, which showed that over half of the relocated residents of a Chicago public housing complex returned weekly to the neighborhood to socialize, that 76 percent retained social networks composed exclusively of public housing residents, and that many still needed links to church's free food and job counseling and free medications from drugstores).

79 Clampet-Lundquist, *supra* note 40, at 434 (noting that most HOPE VI movers whom she interviewed had made none or few acquaintances in their new neighborhood); *id.* at 442 (summarizing results of studies of MTO residents who had made no contacts in their new neighborhoods some four to seven years out).

80 *Id.* at 440–41.

More than the related concepts of place attachment or place dependence, "social capital" describes the collective efficacy of members of a community.[81] Despite the perception that social disorganization prevails in poor communities,[82] social capital does develop in public housing. Charting the growth of social capital in poor and in more affluent communities is an inexact science at best.[83] But the supports, the social "chits" of reciprocity that public housing residents build up in the course of scores of exchanges with neighbors, accumulate to generate social capital. Public housing residents form social networks and organize to promote common goals.[84]

Briggs and Turner have decried as "folk wisdom" the generalization derived from modern day qualitative research that public housing tenants enjoy strong and beneficial social networks from which relocation forcibly extracts them.[85] Yet the "mixed income" hypothesis for public housing transformation fails to the extent that tenants continue to rely on their old neighborhoods for whatever resources they cannot find in the new. Some public housing authorities have adopted strategies that acknowledge residents' social networks and social capital in their previous places of residence. They create new communities of "supportive housing" by relocating small groups of public housing residents into "mini-enclaves," clusters of other relocated residents from their previous housing complex or neighborhood, or they rely on newly relocated residents to organize orientation sessions for other

---

81 The uses of the concept of "social capital" in the social sciences have been extensively reviewed in the literature. For a symposium that provides a useful overview of the development and use of the concept, *see* Robert Putnam, *Preface to Symposium: Using Social Capital to Help Integrate Planning Theory, Research and Practice*, 70 J. Am. Planning Ass'n 142 (2004); for an influential application of social capital theory to housing mobility programs, *see* Xavier de Souza Briggs, *Brown Kids in White Suburbs: Housing Mobility and the Many Faces of Social Capital*, 9 Housing Pol'y Debate 177 (1998).

82 Robert J. Sampson & Stephen W. Raudenbush, *Seeing Disorder: Neighborhood Stigma and the Social Construction of "Broken Windows"*, 67 Soc. Psych. Q. 319, 336 (2004) (finding that racial, ethnic, and class composition of neighborhoods conditions observers' perceptions of disorder in a neighborhood beyond any actual indicators of disorder).

83 Judy Hutchinson, *Social Capital and Community Building in the Inner City*, 70 J. Am. Planning Ass'n 168, 172 (2004) (survey measuring community attachment, acquaintances, trust, reciprocity, and community involvement in a poor neighborhood in L.A. found that longest lasting trusting relationships were built through long-term affirmative communal interactions, rather than through one-shot defenses against threat; that poorer residents avoided creating reciprocal obligations; and that inverse relationship existed between income and number of acquaintances known by name).

84 Brian P. Conway & David S. Hachen, Jr., *Attachments, Grievances, Resources and Efficacy: The Determinants of Tenant Association Participation among Public Housing Tenants*, 27 J. Urb. Aff. 25, 48 (2005) (noting that social disorganization in public housing projects is overstated, and that poverty does not curtail residents' participation in civic activities).

85 Briggs & Turner, *supra* note 45, at 37.

residents who are about to move or who have recently moved.[86] The availability of familiar networks influences the decisions of heads of household as to whether they stay in their new neighborhoods.[87] If stability of residence can contribute to taking advantage of the opportunities that mixed income communities are intended to provide, then residents need something to "tide them over" until they can make the transition—assuming that it is even possible for them to do so.

Mindy Fullilove, a psychiatrist who has studied the psychological impact of displacement on individuals and communities, has warned that displaced persons suffer insults to their physical and emotional health from a range of factors: from loss of control, from loss of connection, and ultimately from disintegration of community.[88] She has enumerated what a "reconstitution of order" in these injured lives would require: relocation into conditions of basic physical decency and safety; achievement of emotional connection to the new home and neighborhood; adoption of responsibility for the quality of home and neighborhood; and the ability to collaborate with neighbors to achieve common goals.[89] Fullilove recommends a process of "empowered collaboration" to achieve these four constitutive parts of life-sustaining communities. That process entails a collective assessment of what in the new environment exists and of what is lacking, and a mobilization to secure the resources that the reconstitution of order will require.[90]

Fullilove's findings and recommendations confirm the wisdom of the efforts of these public housing authorities to "reconstitute" the supportive aspects of poor communities without recreating the destructive ones. Those efforts acknowledge, as Fullilove does, that successful relocations must regenerate feelings of place attachment; in order to do so, relocations must draw on public housing residents' reserves of social capital.

Accounting for the Value of Voluntariness

Poverty frustrates choice; it also subjects poor tenants to the choices of others. It is difficult to know whether individuals who choose to relocate in order to further a vision of a better life do better than individuals who are forced to move. Poor women who chose to participate in home-building programs through Habitat for Humanity experienced significant improvement in their sense of control, confidence, and "coherence," even when their new homes were located

---

86 *Id.* at 38.

87 Melody L. Boyd, *The Role of Social Networks in Making Housing Choices: The Experience of the Gautreaux Two Residential Mobility Program*, 10 CITYSCAPE 41 (2008).

88 Mindy Thompson Fullilove, *Psychiatric Implications of Displacement: Contributions from the Psychology of Place*, 153 AM. J. PSYCHIATRY 1516, 1520–21 (1996).

89 *Id.* at 1521.

90 *Id.*

in neighborhoods offering little improvement in safety.[91] These renters, some of whom lived in public housing, enjoyed higher incomes and greater economic independence than did many public housing residents. They began their moves with already greater opportunities and security. But their sense of accomplishment and well-being derived as significantly from the control they exercised over their new situations as from the prospects of holding equity through homeownership.

We know that forced removal was devastating for the survivors of the urban renewal displacements of the 1950s and 1960s, a dislocation from which some did not recover.[92] We do not know whether the loss of control itself over the initial decision to relocate is more damaging to public housing residents than is the resulting loss of contacts and of place. Residents who moved voluntarily with the support of the first Gautreaux program adjusted productively to their new communities over time. But we have seen that public housing residents who volunteered to move under the MTO program have not necessarily found greater satisfaction in their new placements than have the residents who have been forced to move under HOPE VI. The indignity of involuntary displacement must still sting. But it may hurt less if the process assesses and honors every sacrifice that displaced persons make for what may be someone else's vision of a healthy community, and leaves those persons not merely as well off, but far better off, than before.

Assuring the "Reconstitution of Order:" What Relocation Can Achieve and What a Social Impact Statement Might Measure

Fullilove's prescription for a "reconstitution of order" and the overview in this section of the impact of the housing dispersal programs suggest several factors for consideration in the construction of a social impact statement for the displacement of public housing residents. We know that, of Fullilove's conditions for successful relocation, housing dispersal programs most predictably have been able to achieve the first: an improvement in the physical quality and safety of the basic housing environment. With care, housing authorities have also established the second, the foundation for a re-attachment to place. As we have seen, the third condition—interaction with neighbors—has proven elusive in mixed income communities and mainly unmet in multiracial communities. As I will describe later, in achievement of the fourth element—leaving residents in a position to accomplish shared goals through collective action—the public housing dispersal process has promised the most and accomplished the least.

---

91 Nancy M. Wells, *Our Housing, Our Selves: A Longitudinal Investigation of Low-Income Women's Participatory Housing Experiences*, 25 J. Envtl. Psychol. 189, 200 (2005).

92 For a summary of studies which examined the profound psychological distress affecting residents who were dispersed from their communities as a result of urban renewal in the 1950s and 1960s, *see* Marc Fried, *Continuities and Discontinuities of Place*, 20 J. Envtl. Psychol. 193, 196 (2000).

Fullilove's framework is not dispositive. But it distills many other findings concerning what is necessary to flourish in a place. A public housing authority should incorporate into a social impact statement an assessment of affective and tangible elements such as social, familial, and institutional ties that research and experience have documented as contributing to good functioning in the old place and to an easier transition to functioning in the new. That assessment can then form the baseline for calculating the likelihood of replication of those affirmative elements. The primary function of the social impact statement will be to enable housing authorities and residents, planning together, to weigh the dependably foreseeable advantages of relocation against the known advantages of remaining.

Even the most predictable benefits of relocation, those of the experience of physical safety and improved quality of housing, will only be achieved if residents receive guidance in relocating to more affluent neighborhoods. The foreseeable advantages of remaining in place include stability of an affordable housing placement, and continued access to known networks of friends, income, and social supports. The effects of relocation upon education, physical health, and income seem to be neutral. Comparing the foreseeable disadvantages of relocation with the foreseeable disadvantages of staying in place, we have seen that relocation may cause physical and emotional isolation, and increased risks of housing insecurity. The disadvantages of staying in public housing include continued exposure to deteriorating physical plant, and continued reliance on networks that serve only as valiantly engineered substitutes for meaningful access to better opportunities. With these comparisons in mind, we should look to how residents may use the guarantee of a "comparable replacement dwelling" as leverage for access to benefits that can justify the costs of destabilization.

Plumbing the Meaning of "Comparable Replacement Dwelling"

The Uniform Relocation Assistance Act expresses the first and only acknowledgment of a national obligation to compensate displaced renters for suffering the unequal burdens of urban renewal. The URA provides the only metric that residential tenants can invoke for recognition of the value of "home," one that any unit of government must acknowledge when it draws on federal financial assistance for displacement. That metric, "comparable replacement dwelling," denotes the qualities of the new home to which government assistance must enable the displaced renter to move. "Comparable" comprises both tangible and intangible elements. Its limitations and opportunities provide a benchmark for any construction of a social impact statement.

Patching Up the Fifth Amendment to Make Displaced Persons Whole

As Lorna Fox has noted, in settings of legal discourse, "... *home* is reduced to *house*."[93] Nowhere is that compression of all the meanings of lived space into the quantifiable value of a physical structure more evident than in the assessment of damages for eminent domain. For real property owners, recompense comes in the form of "just compensation" to recover some monetary estimate of fair market value for the loss of physical plant to condemnation.[94] Leaseholders share in that remedy, hammered out primarily in the context of the rights of holders of long-term, commercial leases.[95] Renters and owners end up in the same place if they seek to recover for the inevitable but "incidental" costs of displacement. Rarely may business leaseholders or owners claim compensation for the loss of "good will," for the real but doctrinally incalculable costs of drumming up a new base of customers in a new location.[96] Even for those losses that are quantifiable, and clearly not all are, the jurisprudence of the Takings Clause has excluded from eligibility for compensation virtually all costs other than payment for the "fair market value" of the owned physical property or of the unexpired leasehold, that the government actually takes.[97]

To gain a sense of how public housing residents—or, for that matter, any residential renters—would fare in claims for compensation for the loss of their leases to condemnation, one must extrapolate from the generally inhospitable treatment given to their commercial counterparts. It seems clear that neither residential owners nor renters, whether they be affluent or poor, occupying private market or government owned or subsidized housing, may expect much from the

93 Lorna Fox, Conceptualising Home: Theories, Laws and Policies 139 (2007).

94 For a summary written shortly after the passage of the URA of cases establishing the "fair market value" standard for compensation under the Takings Clause, *see* Fairfax Leary, Jr. & Eric D. Turner, *The Injustice of "Just Compensation" to Fixed Income Recipients – Does Recent Relocation Legislation Fill the Void?*, 48 Temp. L. Q. 1, 8–9 (1974).

95 *See, e.g.*, Almota Farmers Elevator & Warehouse, Inc. v. United States, 409 U.S. 470 (1972) (compensation claims arising from the 50-year leasehold of a grain elevator); United States v. 0.28 Acres of Land, 347 F.Supp.2d 273 (W.D.Va.2004) (commercial lessee held an initial lease for ten years); Harco Drug Inc. v. Notsla, Inc., 382 So.2d 1 (Ala.1980) (addressing lessee's share of owner's compensation under the multi-year holdover and renewal of an initial five-year lease).

96 For an example of rejection of commercial leaseholders' claims to compensation for damages resulting from loss to businesses over and above the loss of physical plant, *see* Detroit v. Whalings, Inc., 202 N.W.2d 816, 821 (Mich.1972) (rejecting claims of clothing store owners, who had rented storefronts on the same street for over 100 years, for compensation for projected losses in business from the forced move away from their historic customer base and location). I am indebted to Nestor Davidson for steering me to this example.

97 *Id.* at 7.

Takings Clause to meet the expenses of moving, of higher rental or ownership costs, or of the increased cost or difficulty in commuting to work. Nor will "just compensation" cushion the adjustment to new and perhaps inferior schools, or the loss of attachments to friends, relatives, and institutions.

The forced removal of poor renters is an arena in which "non-economic" damages have loomed large. In the context of the present day dispersal programs, we have seen those "incidental" or "consequential" damages become "economic" when they result in expensive and disappointing experiments in relocation. As I will describe below, the first faltering attempts 40 years ago to remedy the identical problem—the failure to compensate for the devastating consequences of inconsequential damages—resulted in potentially wide-reaching remedies, to which today's public housing residents have only limited access.

The Historical Beginnings of Compensating for the Uncompensatable

A core value of "takings" jurisprudence is the balancing of burdens: when the many benefit from appropriating the property of a few, then the many must compensate those losses.[98] The human cost incurred from 1949 to 1968 of the loss of hundreds of thousands of homes to eminent domain forced Congress to address the inadequacy of "just compensation" to effectuate this core value. Swathes of urban neighborhoods and rural landscapes were plowed under as a result of federal highway construction, "slum clearance," local code enforcement, and public housing demolition. In 1968, the National Commission on Urban Problems estimated that the loss of rental and owned housing units from 1949 to 1967 reached 1,054,000. The devastation outpaced the administrative capacity or the will to keep track of it—the calculation was conservative, hampered by the failure of the Federal Bureau of Highways to collect data on the number of demolitions resulting from urban highway construction.[99] As demolitions of low rent and public housing increased, the commitment to production of low to middle income housing promised in the National Housing Act failed.[100] The Commission assessed the bulk of the dislocation to have occurred in neighborhoods that were "poor, near poor, and lower middle class," neighborhoods that offered cheaper land and less resistance than more affluent areas. Indeed, the Commission characterized the federal highway program as a "back-door slum clearance device," for which residents received no compensation.[101]

98 *See* Monongahela Navigation Company v. United States, 148 U.S. 312, 325(1893) (stating that the right to compensation "... prevents the public from loading upon one individual more than his just share of the burdens of government ...").

99 National Commission, *supra* note 39, at 81–2.

100 *Id.* at 83 (stating that while the National Housing Act had authorized the construction of 810,000 affordable housing units, at a rate of 135,000 a year for six years, actual production from 1949 to 1968 had amounted to 460,000 units).

101 *Id.* at 81–2.

Agitation accelerated during the 1960s for a uniform national approach to compensation for the victims of urban renewal and highway construction. Two considerations drove this movement: the acknowledgment that the constitutional calculation of burden and benefit damaged the inner city residents who would bear all of the hardship and enjoy none of the rewards of *Berman*'s "beautiful as well as healthy" city;[102] and speculation that a connection existed between the unfairness and urban unrest.[103] Numerous congressional hearings amassed data and testimony about the volume and impact of displacement and of the increasingly chaotic patchwork of federal, state, and local schemes to compensate the displaced.[104]

The URA resulted from these dual concerns over incoherency and inequity. The House Report accompanying the URA acknowledged the unsatisfactory results of applying "just compensation" to the modern context of urban renewal:

> As the thrust of Federal and federally assisted programs have [sic] shifted from rural to urban situations, it became increasingly apparent that the application of traditional concepts of valuation and eminent domain resulted in inequitable treatment for large numbers of people displaced by public action. When applied to densely populated urban areas, with already limited housing, the result can be catastrophic. The result far too often has been that a few citizens have been called upon to bear the burden of meeting public needs.[105]

In an article that appeared contemporaneously with the report of the National Commission on Urban Problems, Frank Michelman gave the name "demoralization costs" to the price of inequitable development: the compensation that displacing authorities should expect to pay as they contemplated "... quieting people's unease about the possibility of being strategically exploited," and redressing disproportionate injuries suffered by those who had been in no position to bargain for better.[106] He questioned the utility of conventional compensation

---

102 H.R. Rep. No. 91-1656, at 2 (1970).

103 National Commission, supra note 39, at 87; see also Ernest N. Tooby, *The Interest in Rootedness: Family Relocation and an Approach to Full Indemnity*, 21 Stan. L. Rev. 801, 818 (1969).

104 For a summary of congressional hearings on the extent of displacement, the unequal treatment and compensation of displaced persons, and proposals for a coherent federal policy for compensation and relocation assistance, *see* H.R. Rep. No. 91-1656, at 2–3 (1970); for a listing of the state code sections in effect before the passage of the URA that covered compensation to displaced persons for moving expenses, *see* Tooby, *supra* note 103, at 821–3.

105 H.R. Rep. No. 91-1656, at 2 (1970).

106 Frank I. Michelman, *Property, Utility and Fairness: Comments on the Ethical Foundations of "Just Compensation" Law*, 80 Harv. L. Rev. 1165, 1214 (1967) (proposing demoralization costs as a factor in assessing just compensation for loss of property); *id.* at 1217–18 (singling out as a factor in assessing compensation the ability of one disproportionately burdened group to have negotiated effectively for its interests).

formulae in ameliorating the incalculable price of relocation—"the shock of changing neighborhoods and the damnable inconvenience of moving" or "… the educational damage inflicted by midstream changes in schools …"—and noted the absence of any bargaining power for the urban poor: "Altogether, the spectacle of uncompensated dislocations under these circumstances is an oppressive one."[107]

Michelman's closing hypothetical described a choice which a fictional municipality might make in deciding where to locate a highway: through a university campus, engendering significant opposition and high compensation costs; through an underground tunnel, engendering significant construction costs; or through a block of modest houses occupied by low income owners and renters, engendering little opposition and low or no compensation costs. Another choice would be to refrain from building the highway. Michelman warned that any city that chose the third building option was morally obligated to pay high "demoralization costs" to defray the sense of injustice that such a decision would stimulate in those who had been powerless to oppose it.[108]

"Comparable Replacement Dwelling:" The Linchpin of Efforts to Make Displaced Renters Whole

The URA provided several major sources of relief for displaced renters, forms of compensation for displacement which remain substantially unchanged to this day. First, the URA filled in the most obvious hole left by the real property-centered jurisprudence of takings: the failure to compensate for expenses incidental to forced relocation as a result of a taking of property. In its original and current forms, the URA requires the displacing agency either to pay for actual relocation expenses, or, if the displaced renter chooses, to offer both a fixed relocation payment and a

107 *Id.* at 1255–6.
108 *Id.* at 1257.

fixed expenses payment.[109] The URA also requires non-monetary assistance in the form of counseling for relocation.[110]

Most important in the effort to correct the historical inequity between displaced renters and owners is the assistance which the URA offers to all to move to a "comparable replacement dwelling." The URA entitles displaced renters to receive payments up to $5250, to be dispersed over as long as a 42-month period, to enable them to rent a "comparable replacement dwelling"[111] which residents should have a "reasonable opportunity" to locate.[112] Payments are formulated to cover increases in rent and the cost of utilities, with explicit adjustments and income exclusions to accommodate the difference between market rents and how rent is calculated for subsidized tenants.[113] The term "comparable replacement dwelling" means at least as good as, if not better than, the home which the renter left behind: one that is "functionally equivalent to the displacement dwelling,"

---

109 *See* 42 U.S.C. § 4622(a)(1–4) (2008) (requiring the "displacing agency" to pay actual reasonable expenses for moving, for actual losses of personal property up to the amount necessary to relocate the property, expenses incurred in searching for a replacement business or form, and for re-establishment of a farm, small business or non-profit organization up to $10,000). In 1987, Congress amended the URA to designate the Department of Transportation (DOT) as the "lead agency" from which other federal agencies would take direction in drafting regulations, Uniform Relocation Act, P. L. 91-646, § 418 (codified at 42 U.S.C. § 4621(a)(5) (2008)); 42 U.S.C. § 4601(12) (2008) (defining the "lead agency" as the Department of Transportation). As a result, agencies will defer or refer to the DOT's regulations for implementation of the URA; some agencies, such as HUD, allow applicants a choice of benefits under either the DOT's regulations for the URA or under HUD's regulations, such as those described at 24 C.F.R. § 42.350 (2008) (addressing eligibility for assistance under Section 104(d) of the Housing and Community Development Act of 1974, Pub.L. 93-383, Title I, Section 104(d), 88 Stat.638 (1974), for persons displaced as a result of development activities).

110 42 U.S.C. § 4625(b–c) (2008).

111 *See* 42 U.S.C. § 4624(a) (2008) (requiring rental supplements to support relocation into a "comparable replacement dwelling" for displaced persons who were not previously homeowners entitled to compensation under § 4623). A renter may apply funds issued under this section towards a down payment to the purchase of a home. *Id.* at § 4624(b). One should note that this amount has remained unchanged since the amendment of the URA in 1987.

112 42 U.S.C. § 4625(c)(3) (2008); 49 C.F.R. § 24.204(a) (2008) (prohibiting displacement of a resident until "at least one comparable replacement dwelling," and, if possible, three or more, has been made available).

113 49 C.F.R. § 24.402(b)(1–2) (2008) (calculating monthly relocation assistance payments as the difference between the rents and utilities for the displaced tenant's former and prospective apartments). For subsidized or public housing tenants who paid little or no rent, their base rent for their former apartment is calculated at the fair market value. *Id.* at § 24.402(b)(2)(i). *See also* 49 C.F.R. Part 24, Appendix A, § 24.2(a)(14), Household income (exclusions) (exempting program benefits from calculation of household income for calculation of subsidized rent).

meaning that it "performs the same function, and provides the same utility."[114] The definition of "comparable" relies on local, tangible indicia of housing quality, such as housing and building codes, to set a baseline for relocation that in fact may improve on housing conditions which renters experienced in their previous homes.[115] "Comparable" may mean an area that is safer and cleaner—"not subject to unreasonable adverse environmental conditions;"[116] it means an apartment that is "decent, safe and sanitary"[117] and not overcrowded.[118] In short, "comparable" expresses one of the core historic purposes of the URA: not merely to provide for a coherent system of relocation under federally financed eminent domain, but also to assure that relocation advanced broader social goals: "(This legislation) provides a humanitarian program of relocation payments, advisory assistance, assurance that comparable, decent, safe and sanitary replacement housing will be available for displaced persons prior to displacement …"[119]

"Comparable" also requires replication of less tangible but also enumerable qualities of a displaced person's original housing. The URA specifies that the location of the replacement dwelling be "generally not less desirable" as was the previous residence "with respect to public utilities, facilities, services and the displaced person's place of employment."[120] For residents displaced as a result of projects funded through Community Development Block Grant (CDBG) funds, that preferred location *is* the displaced person's previous residence—or, at least, the displaced person's previous neighborhood. The Housing and Community Development Act of 1974 requires that local government recipients of federal funds locate the "comparable replacement dwellings" "… within the same community …," and that they build sufficient numbers of those units so that all who lose their low and moderate income dwelling units can return.[121] When put to the test, this "right of return" to the same neighborhood has fallen before governmental claims of impracticability.[122]

114 49 C.F.R. § 24.2(a)(6)(ii) (2008), 49 C.F.R Part 24, Appendix A (2008).

115 *See* 49 C.F.R. § 24.2(a)(8) (2008) (defining "Decent, safe and sanitary dwelling" as one which meets either local codes or a list of basic functional criteria for wiring, heating, bathroom and kitchen plumbing and other basic kitchen facilities, accessibility, and number and size of rooms).

116 42 U.S.C. § 4601(10)(E) (2007).

117 42 U.S.C. § 4601(10)(A) (2007), 49 C.F.R. § 24.2(a)(8).

118 42 U.S.C. § 4601(10)(B) (2007) ("The term 'comparable replacement dwelling' means any dwelling that is … (B) adequate in size to accommodate the occupants …").

119 H.R. Rep. No. 91-1656, at 3 (1970).

120 42 U.S.C. § 4601(10)(F) (2007).

121 42 U.S.C. § 5304(d)(2)(A)(i) (2008); *see also* 24 C.F.R. § 42.375(b)(1) (2007) ("To the extent feasible and consistent with other statutory priorities, the units shall be located within the same neighborhood as the units replaced.")

122 *See* Mejia v. Department of Housing and Urban Development, 688 F.2d 529, 533 (7th Cir. 1982) (denying plaintiff displaced homeowners' and renters' claims that the

The Exclusion of Public Housing Residents from the URA

The residents of Barry Farm will not be able to appeal for relocation assistance under the URA. When Congress, in 1998, legislated the HOPE VI program into the U.S. Housing Act, it explicitly stripped the URA's coverage away from any demolition or disposition of public housing units.[123] Public housing residents lost the URA's direct guarantee of subsidies and its formula for compensation for increased value of a leasehold, and its guarantee of services, to an indirect guarantee of process: in order to win permission to demolish units, public housing authorities only need certify their intention to provide subsidies and services.[124] Still, if public housing authorities do provide relocation assistance, that assistance could look very much like the assistance carved out under the URA. The services will include relocation assistance and reimbursement, and placement in "comparable housing," defined as housing that meets quality standards, and is "located in an area that is generally not less desirable than the location of the displaced person's housing."[125] Unlike the URA, the statute leaves blank any specification as to the meaning of "not less desirable." However ephemeral the guarantee might be, public housing residents also lose the promise made to other residents displaced through the use of federal financial assistance of relocation in or near their old neighborhoods.

The exclusion of public housing residents from the protection of the URA revives the historic inequities that inspired passage of the statute in the first place. As were displaced public housing residents before, so are displaced public housing residents now pushed back into reliance on the meager support of the Fifth Amendment. We have seen how little that offers. One obvious remedy is to amend the Quality Housing and Work Responsibility Act of 1998 to restore the URA's protections to public housing residents who lose their leaseholds as a result of the demolition or disposition of their residences. Another remedy may be to push wide a crack in the jurisprudence of just compensation, provided by unlikely standard bearers: the operators of grain elevators leased from a Washington state railroad.

In *Almota Farmers Elevator & Warehouse, Inc. v. United States*,[126] with seven and a half years left running on the lease, the government condemned the grain elevators which the plaintiff elevator operators had leased from the railroad since

---

Uniform Relocation Act and the Housing and Community Development Act required the local government to build replacement units in the same neighborhood).

123 42 U.S.C. § 1437p(g) (2008) (removing public housing demolition and disposition activities from the coverage of the URA).

124 *See* 42 U.S.C. § 1437p(a) (2008) (setting conditions for housing authorities to meet in order to gain approval of applications for demolition or disposition conducted with or without federal financial assistance).

125 42 U.S.C. § 1437p(a)(4)(A–E) (2008).

126 Almota Farmers Elevator & Warehouse, Inc. v. United States, 409 U.S. 470 (1972).

1919. The plaintiffs claimed that the expectation of renewal of the lucrative long-term lease should enhance its fair market value. In a departure from its previous interpretations of fair market value as encompassing only present day calculated value, the Court agreed. It noted that "just compensation" should reflect what a "willing buyer would pay in cash to a willing seller."[127] In this instance, the attractiveness of the lease lay in its longevity and in the reliability of its renewal. The Court found the prospect of renewal to constitute more than a mere expectation.[128]

The expectation of a public housing resident in the long-term renewability of her lease may seem to bear little resemblance to that of a grain elevator operator. There is no "market" for that particular form of residential leasehold; even if there were, the fair market value to a homeless family for a public housing unit in a context in which waiting lists may be 50,000 families long might be truly said to be "priceless." But if there is no market, there is an expectation of renewability. As distinct from private market residential rentals, in which an owner may terminate the leasehold at the end of a term of months or at the end of the lease term, public housing rentals are subject to a version of a "good cause eviction standard:" only commission of enumerated offenses will cost the family its leasehold.[129] That potentially infinite renewability of an increasingly precious commodity expresses a value driven at least by public policy, if not by markets: the social value of providing stable housing, and all the support that stable housing provides, to those least able to secure it on their own.[130] To a degree, the value to all society of maintaining public housing residents in place is recognized formally through the Fourteenth Amendment, through the administrative hearings to which residents threatened with eviction are entitled as an extra level of process before they defend their leaseholds in state court landlord–tenant proceedings.[131] Arguably that value should be recognized through the Fifth Amendment as well.

---

127 *Id.* at 474.

128 *Id.* at 475.

129 *See* 24 C.F.R. § 966.4(a)(2)(i) (2008) (requiring automatic renewal of a public housing resident's 12-month lease, unless the tenant or family member commits one of a list of infractions).

130 *See* Megan J. Ballard, *Legal Protections for Home Dwellers: Caulking the Cracks to Preserve Occupancy*, 56 Syracuse L. Rev. 277, 299 (2006) (arguing that the federal government subsidizes poor tenants in order to provide much-needed stability of housing, from which economic self-sufficiency and greater involvement in community can grow).

131 *See* 24 C.F.R. § 966.50 (2008) (setting forth administrative grievance procedures to which a tenant is entitled whenever a public housing authority takes action affecting a tenant's lease).

The Construction and Use of the Social Impact Statement

Assessing the "Comparables" that a Social Impact Statement Might Measure: Accounting for the Affective Value of "Home"

We treat "fair market value" as though the concept incorporates observable and verifiable data, such as a house's square footage, its physical condition, its amenities, and its convenience as measured in the distance to schools, supermarkets or public transportation. Whatever the jurisprudence of fair market value asserts, we know that fair market value also draws from intangibles more expansive than a house's physical attributes. The house also draws value from the non-measurable qualities of its community.[132] Does a neighborhood "feel" edgy or homey? Does it include active community organizations? Are there "eyes on the street"[133] and "work of the street," the sharing of responsibilities for securing safety and for circulating information?[134] Some of these attributes of neighborhood grow organically; some arise from the conscious attempts of land use planning to achieve a certain dynamic. Not all are directly reflected in "fair market value," but many are in fact commodified into a house's market price or an apartment's market rent.[135] We know that there are many uncommodified values to home, elements of "place attachment" such as stability and belonging which are particular to each home dweller but whose effect is generalizable to all.[136]

As I described earlier, the standard of "comparable replacement dwelling" in the URA allows renters to demand incorporation of the intangible: of whatever the value to the displaced renter might be of a location "generally not less desirable" than that of her previous dwelling. Unlike the "fair market value" metric, the "location generally not less desirable" explicitly allows for consideration of the intangible elements extrinsic to the brick and mortar of home. Public housing residents facing displacement from their homes might assess some desirable elements of their current homes, against which any future home must compare favorably, no differently from anyone else. As I have noted, these assessments may

132 Mark Oppenheimer, *It's a Wonderful Block*, N.Y. Times Mag., October 5, 2008, at 70 (describing the effect of the "built environment" on relationships among neighbors living on two blocks of West Rock Avenue in New Haven, Connecticut).

133 Jane Jacobs, The Death and Life of Great American Cities 35 (1961) (describing the necessary orientation of sidewalks, streets, and buildings to enable the "natural proprietors of the street" to monitor strangers).

134 For a description of the functions of information exchange in a dense, diverse urban neighborhood, *see* Brett Williams, Upscaling Downtown: Stalled Gentrification in Washington, D.C. 76–9 (1988).

135 *See* Tim Iglesias, *Our Pluralist Housing Ethics and the Struggle for Affordability*, 42 Wake Forest L. Rev. 511, 570, n. 322 (2007) (commenting that, as part of the commodification of housing as an "economic good," non-housing elements become part of the calculation of the cost of a dwelling).

136 *Id.* at 530–38 (reviewing analyses of the subjective significance of "home").

include the value of attachments to friends, family, and community institutions. The loss of these attachments warrants more than sympathy for "grieving for a lost home."[137] As we have seen, public housing residents build networks of exchange, information, and support to compensate for absence of critical personal and material resources. If their new neighborhoods do not provide that support, residents will either seek out the old sources, or move again until they find the neighborhoods that do.

"Just compensation" measures the loss to the individual primarily of her investment in her physical property and only secondarily of her investment in and dependence upon the fabric of her neighborhood. "Social impact" measures both, and in doing so considers also the loss to community of the individual's contribution. Scholars concerned with calculating the intangible value of "home" have addressed both from the perspective of what the displaced renter loses and from what the community loses from the severance of that attachment.

Hellegers and others have noted just a few of the easily calculable aspects of residents' investment in community, such as length of residence and length of work in the neighborhood.[138] Others have proceeded farther to identify and then measure proxies for the intangible features of investment in and benefit from community ties. Robert Putnam has developed concrete measures of informal social involvement, such as sending greeting cards to friends or relatives or having friends over for dinner.[139] Participant observer surveys in poor neighborhoods in Los Angeles have developed measures for proxies for the constituent elements of place attachment and place dependence, as well as for social capital: community attachment, duration and number of acquaintances; trust (quantified as frequency of exchange of important personal information); and reciprocity and community involvement (quantified as the number of community meetings attended).[140] Another model for proxies for the affective costs of losing a home is the Department of Agriculture (USDA)'s annual Measurement of Food Security, which quantifies

---

137 Marc Fried's study of the psychology of involuntary relocation from attachments formed in dense urban communities informed other assessments of the 1949–1968 period of highway construction and urban renewal. *See* Marc Fried, *Grieving for a Lost Home*, *in* The Urban Condition: People and Policy in the Metropolis 151 (Leonard J. Duhl ed., 1963).

138 Hellegers, *supra* note 31, at 954–5; *see also* Iglesias, *Our Pluralist Housing Ethics*, *supra* note 135, at 537, n. 125 (suggesting that compensation for loss of rentership be pegged to length of occupancy, while cautioning that length of occupancy may not always truly capture the value of decent and welcoming shelter to, for instance, someone recently saved from homelessness).

139 Robert D. Putnam , Bowling Alone: The Collapse and Revival of American Community 93–115 (pb. ed. 2000).

140 Judy Hutchinson, *Social Capital and Community Building in the Inner City*, 70 J. Am. Planning Assoc. 168, 172 (2004) (describing a survey for measuring community attachment, acquaintances, trust, reciprocity, and community involvement in a poor neighborhood in Los Angeles).

"food insecurity" through questions about frequency of skipping meals and of running out of money for food.[141]

Scholars have argued that stable, long-term tenancies are valuable both to the poor renter and her family and to society: valuable as a defense against eviction,[142] or as part of the computation of a renter's equity stake in neighborhood development.[143] Those renters who are not the subjects of eviction, but for whom relocation is equally involuntary, should be able to demand just compensation for their displacement, based on quantifiable factors such as the monetary value of an unexpired leasehold to the tenant and the contribution that the monthly rent makes to the landlord's equity interest. The social impact statement for displacement of poor renters should also reflect what, borrowing from the USDA, I will label as "insecurity costs" for a range of factors, such as disruption of social capital. Most important among these insecurity costs is "housing insecurity," defined as the risk of loss of subsidy once the displaced tenant's affordable housing in a tangible "hard" public housing unit is replaced with the riskier option of deploying a housing choice voucher to pay for a market rate unit. Tenants at risk of displacement should receive premium payments for these insecurity costs of relocation, as do homeowners in some jurisdictions.[144] These payments should be treated as are current payments for relocation assistance, and should not affect eligibility for housing assistance or other transfer payments.

---

141 *See* Mark Nord, Margaret Andrews & Steven Carlson, U.S. Dep't of Agric., Household Food Security in the United States, 2005, *Household Food Security*, at 3 (2005) (listing questions asked to ascertain level of household food security). For an assessment of the USDA's current survey instruments and choices for measurement, *see* Committee on Nat'l Statistics, Nat'l Research Council of the Nat'l Academies, Food Insecurity and Hunger in the United States: An Assessment of the Measure (2006); *id.* at 32 (summary of questions presented in interviews conducted for the Current Population Survey to assess food insecurity: frequency within last 12 months of skipping or cutting meals; frequency of running out of money for food; frequency of stinting on adults' or children's meals to stretch the food farther; frequency of not eating despite feeling hungry).

142 *See* Ballard, *supra* note 130, at 307–10 (addressing four factors—length of tenure, the interests of any dependents, the tenant's improvements to the dwelling, and the circumstances of the tenant's conduct—that should be considered as weighing against a landlord's suit to evict a resident from a subsidized tenancy).

143 *See* notes 27–31, *supra*, and text.

144 *See* note 156 *infra*, and accompanying text.

The Use of the Social Impact Statement

Involvement in "a meaningful way:" re-inserting meaning into meaningful participation[145]

The urgency to find something to help Barry Farm arose from despair that its residents have few meaningful tools with which to control the pace or the process of development. Currently, HOPE VI[146] and the portion of the United States Housing Act that governs demolition or disposition of public housing property[147] mandate some degree of resident participation in the processes of development. That participation may entail oversight of a public housing authority's five-year plan for its entire inventory, or consultation from residents affected by development in a targeted property. While mandatory, consultation with residents' representatives on the five-year plan entails a system-wide review of targets for demolition or disposition, and not a direct vote on the particulars of specific projects. But in some instances, consultation with residents has produced demonstrable results, creating opportunity for hard-to-house families.[148]

---

145 Public housing authorities that applied for HOPE VI funds in the most recent grant cycle were required to demonstrate plans to involve "residents and the broader community" "in a meaningful way" throughout the course of the development process. *See* Dept. of Housing and Urban Development, *NOFA for the HOPE VI Revitalization Program*, 72 Fed. Reg. 41822, 41831 (July 31, 2007) [hereinafter HOPE VI NOFA]; for an overview of War on Poverty era programs which sought to empower residents through "maximum feasible participation" in decisions on development and other projects affecting their communities, *see* George Adler, *Community Action and Maximum Feasible Participation: An Opportunity Lost but Not Forgotten for Expanding Democracy at Home*, 8 NOTRE DAME J.L. ETHICS & PUB. POL'Y 547 (1994).

146 *See* HOPE VI NOFA, *supra* note 145 (describing requirements for content and scheduling of public meetings and trainings for "affected residents" and also for other actors, such as state and local agencies, developers, and service providers. Minimum requirements include three public informational meetings and one training session for residents, to be scheduled on different days and to be physically and linguistically accessible. Documentation of more extensive public involvement would contribute "... toward demonstration of continual inclusion of the residents and community." *Id.* at 41831.

147 *See* 42 U.S.C. § 1437p(b)(2) (2008) (requiring public housing authorities to consult with affected residents before the authorities apply to HUD for permission to demolish or dispose of public housing property).

148 Krohe, *supra* note 4, at 47 (describing instances in which consultation with residents in the design stages of HOPE VI projects resulted in inclusion of more units large enough to accommodate large families); U.S. GOVERNMENT ACCOUNTABILITY OFFICE, GAO-04-109, PUBLIC HOUSING HOPE VI RESIDENT ISSUES AND CHANGES IN NEIGHBORHOODS SURROUNDING GRANT SITES 17–18 (2003). *See also* 24 C.F.R. § 903.13(c) (2008) (requiring public housing authorities to review the recommendations of their Resident Advisory Boards concerning the authorities' five-year plans, which must include any designations of units for demolition).

Such outcomes emerge from good will, not from mandates. The standards for consultation of residents during the HOPE VI planning process derive from guidelines for HOPE VI applications, not from regulations. Critics have decried participation in HOPE VI processes as likely to be pallid, consisting of resident attendance at truncated pre-development planning presentations, held after the important decisions have been made.[149] There is participation, but no control, and no veto. Commentators are justifiably skeptical over whether participation alone necessarily leads to power, particularly in situations in which the likely targets of development are poor people in poor neighborhoods.[150] Even if residents do exercise real influence in the creation of plans for re-development, not all viewpoints may be represented. If local governments truly seek and are willing to be influenced by the opinions of public housing residents, they must schedule meetings at night or on weekends, on-site and not at headquarters downtown, and they must provide child care. They must conduct meetings in ways to encourage questions and comments.[151] The single training which a public housing authority must certify as a precondition to receiving a HOPE VI grant will be inadequate to enable residents to comment meaningfully on plans that will change their neighborhoods and uproot them from their homes, perhaps forever.

Other participatory processes, either structured into the processes of land use regulation or conducted outside it, do focus on a negotiation of community benefit. Community benefits agreements (CBAs) have generally resulted from concerted action taken by coalitions to force developers to grant concessions to community interests, usually in return for an agreed truce in any potentially crippling opposition to the development. Issues for CBAs include, first, the definition of the "community" and the interests that are being represented, and second, the enforceability of the agreement.[152] Closer to home (literally), during

149 *See* Susan D. Bennett, *Little Engines that Could: Community Clients, Their Lawyers, and Training in the Arts of Democracy*, 2002 Wis. L. Rev. 469, 470–71 (citing a generation's worth of critique by planners and organizers of the dangers of superficially planned public participation in development decisions).

150 Audrey G. McFarlane, *When Inclusion Leads to Exclusion: The Uncharted Terrain of Community Participation in Economic Development*, 66 Brook. L. Rev. 861, 928 (2001) (concluding that mandates for participation alone do not contribute towards community control over development).

151 Saara Greene, *Including Young Mothers: Community-Based Participation and the Continuum of Active Citizenship*, 42 Comm. Dev. J. 167, 177 (2007) (documenting how formal indices of participation in New Labour program in Edinburgh manifest class-based assumptions about civic engagement, impose material barriers to participation for poor young mothers, and fail to acknowledge the more fluid contributions of "activist mothering;" that residents' failure to participate may also reflect internalized stigma of association with public housing communities, at 175).

152 For definitions and a critique of CBAs, *see* Julian Gross, *Community Benefits Agreements: Definitions, Values, and Legal Enforceability*, 17 J. Affordable Housing & Comm. Dev. 35 (2007–08).

the administrative process of zoning approvals in the District of Columbia, residents already affect development processes through the advocacy of advisory neighborhood commissions (ANCs), ground-level units of local government. ANCs have standing as petitioner in all zoning decisions, including developers' petitions for variances and for special exceptions.[153] Of particular interest in the context of providing benefits for public housing residents in major developments, this automatic standing includes standing as a petitioner in petitions for planned unit developments (PUDs), which in the District of Columbia contain a community benefits condition. One of the many hurdles which petitioners for a PUD in D.C. must surmount is to demonstrate how the PUD will meet community needs for affordable housing, employment and training, or social services.[154] The major problem with any of these options is that only forceful advocacy would make them responsive to the interests of public housing residents; it is not obvious that those interests are necessarily represented in any articulation of the "community" that is benefitted through CBAs, or through representation in these smallest units of local government.

Giving "meaning" to "meaningful participation" will achieve the fourth of Fullilove's elements for the post-displacement "reconstitution of order:" the creation of capacity for residents to improve their environment through collective action. The scoring criteria for HOPE VI applications wanly require documentation of consultation with residents before displacement. At that point, when collective action most matters, residents need some reassurance of control rather than consultation. The social impact statement could serve as a vehicle for the "empowered collaboration" she recommends. Residents, neighbors, and housing authorities should collaborate to describe the strengths of the current order, and to assess soberly the costs in the proposed place of relocation of recreating those strengths and of improving on past deficiencies. In this way, "meaningful participation" in the old and in the reconstituted communities achieves its full value as both process and product.

Inserting Equity into the Calculation of "Just Compensation"

I return to the historical underpinnings of the Uniform Relocation Assistance Act and to the injustices it was designed to correct. In the ferment leading up to and in the assessments made after the passage of the URA, many questioned that this

---

153 Single member districts of ANCs are drawn to represent a population of approximately 2000. D.C. Code § 1-309.03(a) (2008). ANCs have the power to advise any D.C. agency concerning, among many administrative decisions, zoning changes, D.C. Code § 1-309.10(c)(1) (2008), and agencies are required to give the recommendations of the ANCs "great weight" in their deliberations, D.C. Code § 1-309.10(d)(3)(A) (2008). *See also* D.C. Mun. Regs. tit. 11, § 3115.2 (2007) (requiring the Board of Zoning Adjustment to give the recommendations of an ANC "great weight" in any decision).

154 D.C. Mun. Regs. tit. 11, § 2409.9 (2007) (enumerating the "public benefits and project amenities" which proponents of a PUD must include).

patch to the Fifth Amendment would or did make poor homeowners and renters whole.[155] Today, some states have reacted to the *Kelo* decision by legislating what essentially are place attachment and place dependence premiums into just compensation formulae for condemnation: the loss of a principal residence, or of a residence owned within a family for generations, increases the payment beyond "fair market value."[156] One state acknowledges "demoralization costs," those which residents suffer when they watch another private actor benefit from their misfortune, by ratcheting up the condemnation premium for takings that are converted to private economic development.[157] As researchers have concluded in tracing the fortunes of poor residents in their diasporas from one impoverished community to another that is slightly less so, gains are demonstrable, but "demoralization costs" are measurable and real. I join others in arguing that these costs should be incorporated into an evaluation of "just compensation" for poor renters.[158] The social impact statement will enumerate these costs.

Conclusion

Michelman's hypothetical described two demoralizations: that of the betrayed urban poor, and that of the debased majoritarian elite. The cynical decision to take the path of least resistance in development makes government less worthy of the public trust. Michelman described the costs of facing up to public anger when the injustices of urban renewal were made apparent. What is most troubling about the reactions of current public housing residents to interviewers is not their anger,

155 *See* Chester W. Hartman, *Relocation: Illusory Promises and No Relief*, 57 Va. L. Rev. 745, 771–81 (1971) (criticizing the limited capacity of the URA to require sustained support to displaced tenants or to do any more than mitigate the impact of loss of affordable housing).

156 Katrina Miriam Wyman, *The Measure of Just Compensation*, 41 U.C. Davis L. Rev. 239, 257 n. 61 (2007) (reviewing post-*Kelo* enactments such as the amendment to the Michigan Constitution to require payment of 125 percent of fair market value for condemnation of a principal residence; and the amendment in the Missouri Statutes Annotated of the definition of "just compensation" to require compensation at 125 percent of fair market value for loss of primary residences and compensation at 150 percent of fair market value for loss of property owned within a family for at least 50 years). Wyman also distinguishes between subjective valuation of intangible losses from displacement and objective valuation of subjective losses. *Id.* at 260–61. She prescribes an objective measure of compensation for takings that disrupt subjective attachments. *Id.* at 274–80.

157 *Id.* (noting that the revised Kansas Session Laws require compensation at 200 percent of fair market value if the taking occurs to further private economic development).

158 Michele Alexandre, *"Love Don't Live Here Anymore": Economic Incentive for a More Equitable Model of Urban Redevelopment*, 3 B.C. Envtl. Aff. L. Rev. 1, 5 (2008) (recommending that the formula for "just compensation" incorporate the social contributions that poor homeowners and poor renters make).

but their despondency. They seem defeated. Whether the true motive of urban renewal is ground clearance for something better, or something better for those forced to clear the ground, displaced residents will thrive, cope or fail depending on the care that is taken to locate them in suitable new communities. What is suitable, or at least "not less desirable," in the new location will consist of social networks and institutional supports, the presence of which is no less ascertainable than proximity to suitable schools, opportunities for adult education and training, safe and accessible housing stock, and real employment opportunity.

As Briggs and Turner recommend in their thoughtful summary and analysis of research findings from the MTO and Gautreaux programs, if the goal of "deconcentration of poverty" truly is to benefit residents, then housing authorities must assume the significant costs in time and money to assess the strengths and deficits of each departing resident against the resources (of all kinds) of each receiving neighborhood. Recognizing that race and class are proxies for economic opportunity, housing authorities should consult closely with residents to pick "opportunity-rich" neighborhoods with an eye to attributes explicitly mentioned by residents as important to them, such as social networks, schools, and safety.[159]

Briggs and Turner ask whether housing authorities should target those residents for relocation who are the most likely to be able to weather the stresses of it, either as a result of their own resources or of ties in destination neighborhoods.[160] That suggestion is understandable but unacceptable. If one unambiguous finding emerges from studies of a quarter century of dispersal programs, it is that even the least intentional and most poorly planned of them bestow upon public housing residents the incalculable benefit of safety. This is the minimum that any sovereign should provide for any resident; if it cannot do so on site within public housing, then it must provide for all residents who wish it that chance for respite from fear somewhere else.

Acknowledgements

My thanks to Connie Kim and Andrew Lim for their research assistance, which support from the Washington College of Law made possible; to the participants in the *Workshop on Affordable Housing and Public–Private Partnerships*; and to Nestor Davidson and Robin Malloy for their much-tried patience.

159 Briggs & Turner, *supra* note 45, at 28.

160 *Id.* at 34.

Chapter 8
Homeownership, Debt, and Default: The Affective Value of Home and the Challenge of Affordability

Lorna Fox O'Mahony

Introduction

The promotion of homeownership as a national housing strategy has been a central element of American housing policy since the National Housing Act 1949. Indeed, in recent decades, successive administrations have emphasized the role of the expanding homeownership sector, particularly for low-income and minority households, in enabling citizens to realize the "American Dream." Yet, as the recent mortgage lending crisis has highlighted the risks associated with homeownership, debt, and default, the tensions that exist between the political ideology of homeownership and the promotion of owner-occupation as the *sine qua non* of the American Dream, on the one hand, and the crisis of affordability and debtor default facing many American families on the other, are brought into sharp relief. This chapter focuses on these tensions by scrutinizing a paradox of government housing policies which promote an ideology of homeownership yet which run parallel to a legal context that does not adequately protect homeowners, particularly those who are at high risk, from foreclosure and repossession.

This chapter offers a more coherent analysis of the ways that law protects (or does not protect) the homeownership interest in the context of foreclosure, with a particular focus on the losses that are suffered by home occupiers in the event of losing their homes. In societies where homeownership has been promoted as the most desirable tenure, owning a home is heavily loaded with social and cultural meanings. Homeownership is not only associated with financial security, but is also strongly associated with personal and family security. Government policies seeking to extend homeownership often employ a rhetoric of homeownership as empowering, that it gives citizens a stake in society, that it enhances stability, security, control and so contributes to the "social fabric." Yet, alongside the potential benefits, borrowers must bear a range of risks in order to finance the purchase of their homes, and so to pursue this financial, personal, and family security. While the perilous positions of those caught up in the current subprime mortgage lending crisis has received much attention in the media—with considerable concerns particularly for the exposure of low-income households to increased risks of foreclosure—it is important that, alongside the debate on rescue schemes, responses to this crisis include reflection on the underlying legal, theoretical, and phenomenological issues associated with default and foreclosure. This chapter considers the affective values of *home* as they have been socio-culturally embedded in *homeownership*, and identifies a range of costs—both financial and non-financial—that can result when occupiers lose their homes through foreclosure proceedings or through bankruptcy, and which affect not only dispossessed occupiers (and their families) but also significantly impact other stakeholders across society.

Homeownership and the American Dream

It is difficult to overstate the importance of our homes, both in everyday life and, by extension, in law. Our homes provide the backdrop for our lives, and are often the scene or the subject of legal disputes. Recent analysis of home as a legal concept in the U.S. has described an: "ideology of home, where the protection of home and all it stands for is an American virtue."[1] This is not surprising: indeed, in this respect, the American ideology of home echoes the experiences of many other societies. As Irwin Altman and Carol Werner noted in the Introduction to their collection *Home Environments*:

> … people in every society usually have some type of residence. Although their form and permanence vary widely from one group to another, homes are more or less a universal. Second, in many societies, homes are one of the most important places. Homes offer physical amenities that sustain and support the residents, and they are often essential to the very survival of their occupants. Furthermore, homes are important centres for the development and manifestation of certain psychological meanings. Individuals develop identities and regulate privacy in homes; families establish, grow, bond themselves to a unit in homes and often bond themselves to the larger society through their homes. Thus homes are the repository of central and essential psychological and cultural processes.[2]

In fact, it is not only "home" (in the sense of a dwelling place) but home*ownership* that is revered in many post-industrial societies, and has been described as an "American obsession," such that: "… most Americans are willing to make dramatic sacrifices in order to own a home."[3] Many Americans are willing to take a second job, to give up time with their young children, placing them in childcare, to take jobs further away from their homes, and to spend a large portion (sometimes more

1 D. Benjamin Barros, *Home as a Legal Concept*, 46 Santa Clara L. Rev. 255 (2006).

2 Irwin Altman & Carol M. Werner, *Introduction* to Home Environments, at xix (Irwin Altman & Carol M. Werner eds., 1985).

3 Joan Williams, *The Rhetoric of Property*, 83 Iowa L. Rev. 277, 326 (1998).

than half) of their monthly disposable incomes on mortgage instalments alone.[4] Furthermore, as Fennell has recently noted: "Current legal arrangements make homeowners high-stakes gamblers. Homebuyers routinely take on crushing debt loads to put huge sums of money into risky, undiversified ventures that are utterly out of their personal control – local housing markets."[5] Fennell went on to add that, while these markets may *typically* deliver positive returns, this is: "… of little comfort to those caught on the downside of housing market volatility."[6]

This willingness to sacrifice time, money, effort, and energy has been linked to two different types of goals: on the one hand, to the pursuit of financial security, with homeownership regarded as the most effective form of wealth accumulation for most Americans, while on the other hand, homeownership may even be viewed as: "… a metaphor for *personal* and *family* security … owning one's home is, in essence, an empowering act, giving people a stake in society and a sense of control over their lives … homeownership strengthens the social fabric."[7] Indeed, the goal of a private, often suburban, single-family detached house has become a core element of the proverbial "American Dream." In the midst of the subprime mortgage lending crisis, a swell of legislative activity has sought to provide emergency relief for American homeowners in foreclosure or default. In the 110th Congress (2007–08), 44 Bills relating to the foreclosure crisis were introduced, for example, the Foreclosure Prevention and Homeownership Protection Act of 2007, which sought to establish the "Commission to Preserve the American Dream." Yet, the recent rush to enact legislation to "rescue" homeowners facing foreclosure captures an important paradox in the promotion of homeownership in the United States: the tension between the *promotion* of homeownership as a (strongly) preferred tenure, and the development of effective policies to *protect* homeowners in the event of default or foreclosure.

The phrase "American Dream" is, of course, emotionally loaded and resonates with several aspirations, deeply embedded in the socio-cultural fabric of America. Historically these values include individual freedom, social justice, the ability to participate in the consumer economy, the hope for a better life for one's children, "that dream of a land in which life should be better and richer and fuller for every man, with opportunity for each according to his ability or achievement."[8] It is interesting to note that in the original meaning of "American Dream," "better and richer and fuller" was not defined in terms of money (only) but encapsulated a range of meanings which were both financial and non-financial,[9] and included

4 *Id.*; *see also* Peter D. Hart & Robert Teeter, *Fannie Mae National Housing Survey*, Fannie Mae (1992).

5 Lee Anne Fennell, *Homeownership 2.0*, 102 Nw. U. L. Rev. 1047 (2008).

6 *Id.*

7 Williams, *supra* note 3 at 327.

8 James Trustow Adams, The Epic of America 404 (1931).

9 *See, e.g.*, Jim Cullen, The American Dream: A Short History of an Idea that Shaped a Nation 7 (2003).

freedom, independence, security, self-determination, and hard-work. Indeed, it is not difficult to see that for "successful" home*buyers*—those who remain in steady employment, meet their mortgage instalments as they fall due, and eventually discharge the debt, thus becoming home*owners*—owner-occupation (albeit subject to a mortgage) may provide a route by which the advantages associated with outright ownership—for example, freedom, continuity, security—can be delivered. Yet, it is also important to recognize that when an occupier faces the threat of losing their home through foreclosure, the position is inverted, as they risk losing both the property and all the meanings and values associated with its function as their home. Indeed, for homebuyers exposed to such risks, a new discourse has recently emerged to challenge the idea that homeownership, particularly for low-income, minority, and vulnerable households who are at greatest exposure to the risks associated with subprime and predatory lending, is more accurately described as an "American nightmare."[10]

While the potential rewards of homeownership are deeply ingrained in our psyches, less attention has been focused on the risks that some borrowers are willing to (or must) take in order to finance the purchase of their homes, and on the potential costs of achieving the financial, personal, and family security associated with homeownership. As the housing boom of expanding homeownership, especially amongst low-income and minority households, has given way to mounting defaults and rising foreclosure rates which will leave many more households at risk of losing their homes, considerable attention has focused on the impact of mortgage default for the American housing market, the American economy, and even the global economy. Meanwhile, concerns are also mounting about creditors who employ inappropriate lending strategies, mis-sales of debt packages to borrowers who will never be able to afford to repay the loan, predatory lending, and the growth of subprime lending, particularly to vulnerable households.[11] The

10 *See, e.g.*, Anne B. Shlay, *Low-income Homeownership: American Dream or Delusion?* 43 Urban Studies 511 (2006); Richard Lord, American Nightmare: Predatory Lending and the Foreclosure of the American Dream (2004); Gregory D. Squires, Why the Poor Pay More: How to Stop Predatory Lending (Gregory D. Squires ed., 2004); Kristopher Gerardi, Adam Hale Shapiro & Paul S. Willen, *Subprime Outcomes: Risky Mortgages, Homeownership Experiences, and Foreclosures* (Federal Reserve Bank of Boston, Working Paper No. 07-15, 2007), *available at* http://papers.ssrn.com/sol3/papers.cfm?abstract_id=1073182; for a general discussion, *see* National Community Reinvestment Coalition, *The 2005 Fair Lending Disparities: Stubborn and Persistent II*, NCRC Report (2006), *available at* http://www.ncrc.org/policy/analysis/policy/2006/2006-05-23_2005HMDAreport.pdf.

11 *See, e.g.*, Roberto G. Quercia, Michael A. Stegman & Walter R. Davis, *The Impact of Predatory Loan Terms on Subprime Foreclosures: The Special Case of Prepayment Penalties and Balloon Payments*, 18 Housing Policy Debate 311 (2005); Allen Fishbein & Harold Bunce, *Subprime Market Growth and Predatory Lending*, Housing Policy in the New Millenium: Proceedings (Susan M. Wachter and R. Leo Penne eds., 2005); Harold L. Bunce, Debbie Gruenstein, Christopher E. Herbert & Randall M. Scheessele, *Subprime*

Center for Responsible Lending has recently estimated that 15.6 percent of all subprime loans originated since 1998 either have ended or will end in foreclosure and the loss of homeownership.[12] Meanwhile, a study published by the National Community Reinvestment Coalition in 2006 indicated that minorities, women, and low- and moderate-income borrowers across the U.S. continue to receive a disproportionate amount of high-cost loans. In a sample of loans made in 2005, it emerged that women received 37.3 percent of high-cost conventional loans but just 28 percent of the market-rate conventional loans; men, in contrast, received a higher percentage of market-rate loans (66.8 percent) than high-cost loans (60.2 percent).[13] Furthermore, a study for the Center for Responsible Lending in 2006 found that for most types of subprime home loans, African-American and Latino borrowers were more than 30 percent more likely to receive higher-rate loans than white borrowers, even after controlling for legitimate differences in risk factors.[14]

Subprime loans have already led to one million American families losing their homes in the last decade;[15] statistics on foreclosures in New York alone showed an increase of 50 percent in the last year,[16] and the ripple effect of the crisis in the U.S. mortgage market is continuing to cause shock-waves across the national, and indeed the global economy.[17] Three million homeowners with subprime loans

---

Foreclosures: The Smoking Gun of Predatory Lending?, Housing Policy in the New Millenium: Proceedings (Susan M. Wachter and R. Leo Penne eds., 2005); Dan Immergluck, *Stark Differences: Explosion of the Subprime Industry and Racial Hypersegmentation in Home Equity Lending*, Housing Policy in the New Millenium: Proceedings (Susan M. Wachter and R. Leo Penne eds., 2005); Baher Azmy & David Reiss, *Modeling a Response to Predatory Lending: The New Jersey Home Ownership Security Act of 2002*, 35 Rutgers L.J. 645 (2004).

12 Center for Responsible Lending, *Subprime Lending: A Net Drain on Homeownership*, CRL Issue Paper No. 14, March 27, 2007, at 2, *available at* http://www.responsiblelending.org/pdfs/Net-Losership-3-26.pdf. *See also* Ellen Schloemer, Wei Li, Keith Ernst & Kathleen Keest, *Losing Ground: Foreclosures in the Subprime Market and Their Cost to Homeowners*, Center for Responsible Lending Publication (2006), asserting that one in five subprime mortgages originated in 2005 and 2006 will end in foreclosure, an increase of 200 percent from 2002.

13 NCRC Report, *supra* note 10.

14 *See* Debbie Gruenstein Bocian, Keith S. Ernst & Wei Li, *Unfair Lending: The Effect of Race and Ethnicity on the Price of Sub-Prime Mortgages*, Center for Responsible Lending Publication (2006), *available at* http://www.responsiblelending.org/pdfs/rr011-Unfair_Lending-0506.pdf.

15 *Supra* note 12.

16 Neighborhood Economic Development Advocacy Project, *Paying More for the American Dream: A Multi-State Analysis of Higher-Cost Home Purchase Lending*, Neighborhood Economic Development Advocacy Project Report (March 2007), *available at* http://www.nedap.org/pressroom/documents/2007_Report-2005_HMDA.pdf.

17 In the U.K., the Chancellor of the Exchequer recently intervened in an effort to restore consumer confidence in British banking institutions when the shock-waves across the credit economy that have followed the U.S. housing market crisis hit the U.K. lending

are expected to enter foreclosure during the next two years, with 2 million of these households forecasted to lose their homes.[18] Furthermore, the ripple effect of foreclosure, beyond the bilateral relationship of creditor and debtor, is emphasized by the projection that another 40 million homeowners will see their home values decline by $200 billion due to nearby subprime foreclosures.[19]

It is therefore timely to re-consider the consequences of foreclosure for occupiers who lose their homes at the hands of creditors. The second part of this chapter begins to consider how the tensions between *promotion* and *protection* of homeownership can be re-analyzed in light of the exposure of home occupiers in the ownership sector to the *risks* associated with mortgage debt, default, and foreclosures, alongside evidence relating to the *losses* that result from creditor actions against the owned home. The objective of the chapter is to offer a more coherent legal analysis of the home protections available to American homeowners, by focusing not only on the benefits—for the borrower, their household, society, and the economy—of successful expansions of homeownership, but also taking account of the countervailing costs—for the borrower, their household, society, the economy, other homeowners—when homeownership is unsuccessful.

While the perilous positions of homebuyers who are exposed to heightened risk by the subprime lending crisis, and the human costs of foreclosure, have received much attention in the media in recent months, this chapter explores the deeper legal, theoretical, and phenomenological issues underpinning this crisis in default and foreclosure, with a view to considering if, and, if so, how, law should respond to this new crisis of affordability for homeownership. The second part of the chapter sets out the framework for an emerging legal concept of home, which would facilitate a more coherent legal analysis of *home* protections that reflects the loss suffered when home occupiers experience foreclosure. One important aspect of this analysis is its focus on the *occupiers* of the home as the parties affected by the loss of home in foreclosure, rather than limiting consideration to the creditor–debtor relationship.[20] It is perhaps not surprising that the legal framework for foreclosure tends to focus on a bilateral view of the credit agreement, given the emphasis on legal structures and doctrines from contract law and real property law in this context. However, as recent events have clearly illustrated, debt, default,

---

institution Northern Rock. As customers queued to withdraw their money outside branches on high streets across the U.K., the government promised that the Bank of England would guarantee the security of all existing deposits; *see* BBC, *"Savers Return" to Northern Rock*, BBC News, September 18, 2007, *available at* http://news.bbc.co.uk/1/hi/business/7000035.stm.

18 Center for Responsible Lending, *Protect States' Rights to Prevent Foreclosures: Support Miller-LaTourette Amendment*, Center for Responsible Lending Policy Brief, May 7, 2008, *available at* http://www.responsiblelending.org/pdfs/protect-states-rights-support-miller-latourette.pdf.

19 *Id.*

20 This focus on occupiers in the context of the homeownership sector also bears useful parallels for analysis of security of tenure for occupiers in the rental sector.

and foreclosure also have significant consequential impacts beyond the contracting parties—from impacts on other occupiers (for example, children[21] and other family and household members) to neighbourhoods,[22] as well as broader social and economic impacts.[23] This analysis therefore seeks to weigh in the balance of the legal reasoning process, the range of consequential losses that flow from foreclosure actions and loss of home through bankruptcy, beyond the traditional legal focus on potential losses to the two contracting parties, creditor and debtor.

The third part of the chapter proceeds to analyze the nature and application of current legal provisions and procedures in the event of default. This section considers the limits of the (narrowly conceived, classical) law and economics discourse that often tends to dominate over other considerations (for example, social and psychological, experiential meanings of home, or behavioral or socio-cultural economic considerations) in this context. The fourth part then considers the ways in which the meanings of home have been influenced by the political ideology and promotion of ownership as an aspirational tenure and, particularly, policies promoting the expansion of homeownership to low-income and minority households. The fifth part considers the tensions that these policies create, between the *promotion* of homeownership, as constituent of the "American Dream," and the *protection* of homeowners when their ownership—and by extension their occupation—of the home becomes unsustainable as a result of challenges to affordability. Finally, the sixth part concludes the chapter by proposing a two-strand approach—around the protection of homebuyers, on the one hand, and the promotion of homeownership on the other—to address some of the underlying issues and problems associated with homeownership, debt and default.

The Emerging Legal Concept of Home

It is perhaps somewhat surprising that, despite the centrality of home in our lives, and the impact of legal regulation on the occupier's experience of home, the legal concept of home has received surprisingly little attention.[24] As laypersons we know that "there's no place like home," that "home is where the heart is," and

---

21 *See* Lorna Fox, Conceptualising Home: Theories, Laws and Policies, Chapter Nine (2007); Phillip Lovell & Julia Isaacs, *The Impact of the Mortgage Crisis on Children and Their Education*, First Focus, April 2008, *available at* http://www.brookings.edu/~/media/Files/rc/papers/2008/04_mortgage_crisis_isaacs/04_mortgage_crisis_isaacs.pdf.

22 Dan Immergluck & Geoff Smith, *The External Costs of Foreclosure: The Impact of Single-Family Mortgage Foreclosures on Property Values*, 17:1 Housing Policy Debate 57 (2006), *available at* http://www.fanniemaefoundation.org/programs/hpd/pdf/hpd_1701_immergluck.pdf.

23 *See* Fox, *supra* note 21, at 109–18 and Chapter Five.

24 *See* Fox, *supra* note 21, at 33–41.

we may even believe that the law recognizes that "a man's home is his castle."[25] However, notwithstanding some important recent work on this subject in the U.S.,[26] the development of home scholarship in legal discourse remains in its early stages. This is in marked contrast to the critical attention that the subject of "home" has attracted in other disciplines in recent decades. The blossoming of interest in home across social science disciplines has stimulated a considerable amount of research, in the form of both empirical studies and theoretical analysis, to explore experiences of home and to analyze the meanings and values that home represents to its occupiers. Drawing from these analyses it is possible to identify five sets of values associated with home: (1) home as a financial investment; (2) home as a physical structure; (3) home as territory; (4) home as identity; and (5) home (especially the owned home) as a cherished socio-cultural indicator.[27]

The idea of the home as a financial investment is probably the most readily comprehensible aspect of the *home* interest for legal scholarship. The value associated with the "home as a financial investment" is the factor that distinguishes the meaning of the owner-occupied home most clearly from the meaning of home for tenants, requires and connotes participation in the ideology of the market, and appears to be the most salient aspect of home as the fulfilment of the "American Dream" for contemporary perspectives. Indeed, the political, social, and cultural ideologies of homeownership have contributed much to the meanings and values associated with the owner-occupied home, and particularly to the idea of home as a financial investment.

Secondly, the value of the home as a physical structure is concerned with the tangible "bricks and mortar" elements of *home*. Whilst much of the scholarship concerning *home* has focused on the intangible attachments identified as the "*x* factor" meanings [if *home* = house + *x*], occupiers also place considerable value on the tangible aspects of home: that is, the house itself. Home provides physical shelter for its occupiers: "… [h]omes offer physical amenities that sustain and support the residents, and they are often essential to the very survival of their occupants."[28] There can be no doubt that, from a practical perspective, the need for physical shelter is the most immediately pressing consequence of losing one's

25 The expression "An Englishman's home is his castle" is a misquotation from the decision in *Semayne's Case* (1604) 5 Co Rep 91a at 91b, 77 ER 194 at 195, when Coke CJ commented that: "… the house of everyone is to him as his castle and fortress."

26 *See* Barros, *supra* note 1; Megan J. Ballard, *Legal Protections for Home Dwellers: Caulking the Cracks to Preserve Occupancy*, 56 Syracuse L. Rev. 277 (2006). For some recent literature in the U.K., *see* Fox, *supra* note 21; Lorna Fox, *The Meaning of Home: A Chimerical Concept or a Legal Challenge?*, 29 J.L. Soc'y 580 (2002); Lorna Fox, *The Idea of Home in Law*, 2 Home Cultures 25 (2005); Avital Margalit, *The Value of Home Ownership*, 7 Theoretical Inquiries in Law (2006).

27 *See* Fox, *supra* note 21, especially Chapter 4.

28 Altman & Werner, *supra* note 2, at Preface, xix.

home. In fact, it is the loss of this physical shelter, "*house*lessness," which is politically and popularly referred to as "homelessness."

The concept of home as a physical structure is also closely associated with the *territoriality* of home.[29] "Territoriality" has been defined as: "… the act of laying claim to a geographic area, marking it for identification, and defending it when necessary against others of the same kind."[30] Territorial behavior, in both animals and humans, is linked to the instinct for survival, to safety and security, and to protecting one's family: "… mating, safeguarding the nest, and protecting the food supply, functions that are basic to the survival of the organism and the perpetuation of the species."[31] For humans, the exercise of territorial behavior is characterized generally as: "… the relationship between an individual or group and a particular physical setting that is characterised by a feeling of possessiveness, and by attempts to control the appearance and use of space."[32] The idea that occupiers would exhibit territorial behavior in the *home* environment is evident, since the occupied home is clearly a "primary territory"—that is, a place: "… where one spends most of one's time and interacts with one's primary reference group."[33] In fact, the function of the home as territory satisfies a range of social and psychological needs: home is the sole area of control for the individual; home is the most appropriate physical framework for family and family life; home is a place of self-expression; and home provides a feeling of security.[34] These responses are generally recognized as positive for the occupier, since: "[i]n stable circumstances a deep embeddedness can be beneficial by providing a stable sense of self in connection with environment."[35]

It is important to recognize, however, that not all home occupiers will experience the positive benefits associated with territoriality, identification, security, family, privacy, autonomy, and control within the home environment. Indeed, the expectation that *home* will provide stability and security is likely to exacerbate

29 This feature is heavily emphasized by Sebba and Churchman, who argue that: "… the uniqueness of the home lies in its psychological and social meaning and in the opportunity it affords the occupants to exert control over the space and the behaviour within it"; Rachel Sebba & Arza Churchman, *The Uniqueness of Home*, 3 Architecture and Behaviour 7, 21 (1986).

30 Sidney N. Brower, *Territory in Urban Settings*, *in* Environment and Culture 179–80 (Irwin Altman, Amos Rapoport & Joachim F. Wohlwill eds., 1980).

31 *Id.* at 180.

32 *Id.*

33 *Id.* at 184–5.

34 Amos Rapoport, *A Critical Look at the Concept 'Home'*, *in* The Home: Words, Interpretations, Meanings, and Environments 30 (David Benjamin ed., 1995); *see also* Sebba & Churchman, *supra* note 29. Brown and Perkins also noted that: "[p]lace attachments clearly promote and reflect stability, signifying long term bonds between people and their homes and communities."; Barbara B. Brown & Douglas D. Perkins, *Disruptions in Place Attachment*, *in* Place Attachments 280 (Irwin Altman & Sebba M. Low eds., 1992).

35 Brown & Perkins, *supra* note 34, at 282.

the impact of disruptions to home, since: "[n]ormally homes provide a secure and private place where one's identity is protected."[36] The object of establishing a territorial space is to achieve privacy and control, to: "create predictable environments with an accompanying sense of order and security."[37] Many of the values associated with territoriality are also associated with the idea that the occupier who enjoys the home as territory has a satisfactory degree of *control* over their home territory. For this reason, the ideologies of homeownership, with their expectations of enhanced control, privacy, and security, heighten the notion of "home as territory." Yet, notwithstanding the emphasis on *ownership* in socio-political constructions of positive home meanings, it is important to note that the construction of a legal concept of home has important critical potential for analysis of debates concerning rental property, for example, around security of tenure. The extent to which homeownership in fact "delivers" on the "*x*-factor" meanings depends entirely on the legal framework that governs "home-type" interests in any particular jurisdiction. As such, Marcuse has argued that the characteristics associated with *home*—such as control, status, and privacy—are *not* inherently attributable to homeownership. Rather, the features of home allegedly enhanced by ownership—security of tenure, control, and so on—could be, if governments chose to do so as a matter of policy, factored into the law that governs rental property.[38]

It is also pertinent to consider the effectiveness of the "owned home" as a source of satisfaction for territoriality, in light of the risk of foreclosure, which has major implications for the meaning of the owner-occupied home as territory. On the one hand, the occupier's sense of territoriality at home is likely to be heightened when the home is placed under attack. When occupiers are faced with the forced loss of their homes through creditor possession actions, there is a tendency to become *more* territorial in order to counter the threats made to personal security, to self-esteem, or to self-identity. Empirical research[39] has shown that: "… as anxiety, stress, and nervousness increased there was an increased tendency for individuals to become territorial with respect to their own beds, chairs, and spaces at the table. On the other hand, as levels of stress and anxiety decreased, territorial behaviour became less evident."[40]

One particular aspect of territorial defensiveness that is interesting with reference to foreclosure is the different types of responses occupiers may have to the threat of interference with their home territory. Brower has claimed that:

---

36 *Id.* at 285.

37 Brower, *supra* note 30, at 181.

38 Peter Marcuse, *The Ideologies of Ownership and Property Rights*, *in* Housing Form and Public Policy in the U.S. 41 (Richard Plunz ed., 1980).

39 *See* Irwin Altman, Dalmas A. Taylor & Ladd Wheeler, *Ecological Aspects of Group Behaviour in Social Isolation*, 1 Journal of Applied Social Psychology 76 (1971).

40 Brower, *supra* note 30, at 182.

> As threat or the perception of threat increases, territorial behaviour tends to become more defensive ... There are several different ways of handling increased threat. One is to defend all claims more aggressively. Another is to shrink the boundaries of one's claims, falling back to the territories that are most defensible—much like retreating to one's bedroom to avoid having to face unwelcome guests in the living room. Yet another strategy is to renounce, or at least not to press, one's claims to ineffective types of occupancy ... The last two strategies may well result in the abandonment of territorial claims.[41]

Occupiers' responses to the threat of possession can be mapped onto the types of responses identified above, in relation to territorial threats: that is, they may defend claims more aggressively, shrink the boundaries of their claims, or renounce their claims to ineffective types of occupancy.

On the one hand, the occupier who willingly gives up possession of the property at the request of the creditor can be viewed as renouncing their claim to ineffective occupancy. As the threat of foreclosure sweeps across the U.S., there is indeed evidence that many occupiers have responded by relinquishing territoriality over the property. There are various systemic reasons that make it more desirable for the occupier to give up possession of the property voluntarily, including the resources which are saved, through administrative and court costs, and time, by avoiding litigation. However, abandonment of homes is also resource-wasteful, through the non-use of vacant properties, and the consequent risks of vandalism, illegal activity, and so on in such properties.

Another possibility is that the occupier's response is motivated by alternative, territorial factors: for example, research has indicated that: "[h]ouseholds with children were more likely to want to stay put, regardless of how they now viewed the house and all the associated financial problems."[42] Such households are arguably more likely to "defend all claims more aggressively," a response which may prove counter-productive from a legal perspective. While the rational argument suggests that, in the event of default, debtors should negotiate with lenders to mitigate their losses, for example, by downsizing to a cheaper property or by re-negotiating the mortgage or re-structuring payments, there is evidence to indicate that the presence of children in a home makes downward economic adjustment more difficult.[43] In addition, the presence of child occupiers exacerbates the psychological barriers to giving up the home. Thus, Warren has argued that:

> To face economic reversals for oneself may be very much easier than imposing those reversals on someone else, especially a much-loved child. To give up an

41 *Id.* at 190–91.

42 Hazel Christie, *Mortgage Arrears and Gender Inequalities*, 15 Housing Studies 877, 896 (2000).

43 Elizabeth Warren, *Bankrupt Children*, 86 Minn. L. Rev. 1003, 1022 (2002).

> expensive home may be hard enough for an adult, but when it means that a child may be forced to change schools and leave friends, resistance may deepen.[44]

Indeed, Warren has also suggested that there are practical reasons for clinging on to the home, even after default, since: "[m]oving out of a home entails high transaction costs, and families with deteriorating credit know they are unlikely to qualify for another home loan."[45]

"Home as identity" represents another significant cluster of meanings associated with the phenomenon of home, and provides the principal framework within which the emotional connotations of home are expressed. While the role of the home as a financial investment, as a physical structure providing shelter, and even as a valued territory, can all be regarded as having a "strong cognitive element," the meanings of home associated with identity are: "... primarily affective and emotional, reflecting the adage *home is where the heart is*."[46] It is important to recognize that while the idea of "home" as an emotional attachment may not easily fit within the value structures of the traditional law-and-economics approach to property law, the significance of the home as identity is undoubtedly real for occupiers. In fact, the significance of the home as a reflection of the occupier's identity is very easy to grasp from a lay perspective: for one thing, the sense of pride that dwellers take in their homes reflects the importance of the home as a symbol of identity. Empirical studies have shown that: "[p]hysical settings and artefacts both reflect and shape people's understandings of who they are as individuals and as members of groups."[47] The importance of the home as a physical setting for everyday life, combined with the significance attached to the way that the home is presented, indicates the extent to which the home is felt to reflect the occupier's identity.

There are two main constituent elements to home as identity, both of which are principally associated with the symbolic significance of home for its occupiers. On the one hand, the psycho-analytical perspective addresses the importance of home in an occupier's self-identity: that is, "home as a symbol of one's self," and suggests a deep connection between the home and the human spirit.[48] "Home as identity" is also evidenced in the socio-psychological theory that home is an integral element of the occupier's social identity. The ideologies of homeownership have also promoted the idea of the owned home as a means of achieving control, ontological security, and autonomy. Owning one's own home is significant for social identity, since it grants membership to a respected category of people—in

---

44 *Id.* at 1023.

45 *Id.* at 1023.

46 Kim Dovey, *Home and Homelessness*, *in* HOME ENVIRONMENTS 40 (Irwin Altman & Carol M. Werner eds., 1985).

47 Brown & Perkins, *supra* note 34, at 280.

48 Dovey, *supra* note 46, at 40.

part because it demonstrates one's commitment to the work ethic.[49] The owned home, the largest single expenditure most people ever make, requires many years of earning and saving, and represents a long-term commitment to the work ethic.[50] This feature of home meanings also resonates strongly with the social and cultural significance of the home—particularly the owned home—and the impact of losing one's home through foreclosure. In societies in which homeownership is culturally cherished—including the U.S., U.K., Australia, New Zealand, and Canada—the socio-cultural significance of home is intrinsically linked to *owning* one's own home, and this necessarily exacerbates the practical, emotional, and psychological impacts of losing one's home.[51] Furthermore, the expansion of homeownership, and the additional meanings and expectations associated with "owning one's own home," have played a major role in embedding these meanings, both socially and culturally.

When considering the potential for taking account of the impact of loss of home within property law, it is interesting to bear in mind that, although there is little evidence that these values have weighed heavily on the balancing scales against the creditor's claim to the capital value of the property in a foreclosure or bankruptcy contest, the possibility of focusing on a protection for the *possession* of occupiers is strongly rooted in the property law tradition. For example, Hume argued that: "[m]en generally fix their affections more on what they are possess'd of than on what they never enjoyed ... it would be greater cruelty to dispossess a man of anything than not to give it to him."[52] However, the question of *why* law would, or should, treat interests in possession as carrying some special status, rendering them worthy of particular protection, is brought into particularly sharp relief when the claim of a person in possession of land comes into conflict with a competing interest bearing a relatively superior title or ownership interest. In Pollock and Maitland's analysis of *possession* they asked: "Why should law, when it has on its hand the difficult work of protecting ownership and other rights in things, prepare puzzles for itself by undertaking to protect something that is not ownership, something that will from time to time come into sharp collision

49 *See, e.g.*, CONSTANCE PERIN, EVERYTHING IN ITS PLACE: SOCIAL ORDER AND LAND USE IN AMERICA (1977), which described homeowners as being near the top of life's ladder, and having achieved a sort of "perfected citizenship," which qualifies them for full "American social personhood."

50 See also Janet M. Fitchen, *When Toxic Chemicals Pollute Residential Environments: The Cultural Meanings of Home and Home Ownership*, 48 HUMAN ORGANISATION 313, 320 (1989).

51 *See further*, "The Meaning and Experience of 'Owning' One's Home," *infra*, discussing the losses associated with the experience of foreclosure.

52 DAVID HUME, A TREATISE OF HUMAN NATURE: BEING AN ATTEMPT TO INTRODUCE THE EXPERIMENTAL METHOD OF REASONING INTO MORAL SUBJECTS, Book III, Part II, Sect. 1 (1817).

with ownership?"[53] While one may recognize, as a matter of fact, that certain interests carry value in some intangible sense, it is another matter entirely to attribute sufficient weight to such interests to outweigh other claims, for example, proprietary interests, such as those that are vested in secured creditors.

The value conferred on *possession* in the medieval doctrine of *seisin* has been described as a reflection of a fundamental impulse to acknowledge: "… the organic element in the relationship between man and land …"[54] This focus on the relationship between the occupier and the property gives the idea of *possession* as an organizing concept considerable contemporary relevance for the conceptualization of home in law.[55] The enduring relevance of *possession* as symbolic of a significant relationship between the occupier and the land was reflected in Tay's suggestion that: "… it is because all proprietary and possessory rights ultimately stem from enjoyment that *seisin* lies at the very root of the development of the English law of property and of the Englishman's concept of freedom—of his home as his castle."[56]

Tay claimed that: "[t]he role of the underlying *seisin*-possession concept in the common law is to recognise and protect those still important areas in which men live, work and plan as users—owners …"[57] In fact, it was this recognition of the use value of land that was identified as: "… the base and shaper of the social sentiment that shrinks with distaste from the forcible eviction."[58]

This proposition is also linked to the economic theory of the "endowment effect." The endowment effect is the idea that principles of rational choice can be displaced by the fact of possession, so that the person in possession of an item of property values that property more highly than a non-possessor. Pollock and Maitland reasoned that: "[p]ossession as such deserves protection ... He who possesses has by the mere fact of his possession more right in the thing than the non-possessor has."[59] In fact, the idea that possession *ought* to be protected often seems to be derived from an instinctive awareness that the value that an item of property represents to the possessor of that property is greater than the value that the property holds for a non-possessor, *because of the fact of possession.* Consequently, the degree of harm caused to a possessor (for example, the home occupier) by losing that property would be greater than the harm suffered by

53 Sir Frederick Pollock & Frederic William Maitland, The History of the English Law Before the Time of Edward I 40 (2d ed. 1898).

54 K.J. Gray & P.D. Symes, Real Property and Real People 48–9 (1981).

55 Thus Gray & Symes wrote that: "[i]n its technical sense seisin is no longer of importance today. However the emphasis which it placed upon possession rather than title continues to influence several areas of modern law"; *Id.* at 49.

56 Alice Ehr-Soon Tay, *Law, the Citizen and the State*, *in* Law and Society: The Crisis in Legal Ideas 11 (E. Kamenka, R. Brown, and A. E-S Tay eds., 1978).

57 *Id.*

58 *Id.*

59 Pollock & Maitland, *supra* note 53, at 42–3.

depriving the non-possessor (for example, the creditor, or landlord) of the property. Tay described this impulse to preserve the status quo as a "bias in favour of the factual situation";[60] while the idea that possession is worthy of legal protection—whether or not it is supported by ownership—because it nurtures an attachment to the property, was reflected in Oliver Wendell Holmes' comment that:

> It is in the nature of a man's mind. A thing which you enjoyed or used as your own for a long time, whether property or opinion, takes root in your being and cannot be torn away without your resenting the act and trying to defend yourself, however you came by it. The law can ask no better justification than the deepest instincts of man.[61]

Evidence of the endowment effect provides a modern basis for the idea that possessors have a natural interest in retaining property, and supports the argument that possessors of property tend to *value* that property more highly than non-possessors.[62] The existence of an "endowment effect" resonates with the nature of the *value* that *home* represents for occupiers—who are in possession—as compared to the value that the property holds, as a financial asset, for creditors. It is also interesting to note that studies exploring the "endowment effect" have shown that the desire to maintain the status quo in terms of one's possessions is rooted in *loss aversion*. In fact, it has been suggested that: "… the main effect of endowment is not to enhance the appeal of the good one owns, only the pain of giving it up."[63] In the context of creditor possession or foreclosure actions, the endowment effect will therefore function to increase the loss to the possessor (occupier), compared to the loss suffered by the non-possessor (creditor, landlord). Finally, for the purposes of the debate surrounding the *promotion* of homeownership as the "American Dream," without *protection* in the event of default, it is significant to note that: "[a]n implication of the endowment effect is that people treat opportunity costs differently than 'out-of-pocket' costs. Foregone gains are less painful than perceived losses."[64] It is therefore arguable that a homeowner who suffers the loss of their home as a result of default may suffer greater loss than a tenant who never entered into the homeownership sector at all.

60 Tay, *supra* note 56, at 11.

61 Oliver Wendell Holmes, *The Path of the Law*, 10 Harv. L. Rev. 457, 477 (1897).

62 *See* Colin Camerer, *Individual Decision Making*, *in* The Handbook of Experimental Economics 665–70 (J.H. Kagel & A.E. Roth eds., 1995), for an account of empirical studies of the endowment effect, and some possible psychological explanations for such effects.

63 Daniel Kahneman, Jack L. Knetsch & Richard H. Thaler, *Anomalies: The Endowment Effect, Loss Aversion and Status Quo Bias*, 5 Journal of Economic Perspectives 193, 197 (1991); *see* George Loewenstein & Daniel Kahneman, *Explaining the Endowment Effect* (Department of Social and Decision Sciences, Carnegie Mellon University, Working Paper, 1991).

64 Kahneman et al., *supra* note 63, 203.

Until relatively recently, the idea of seeking to capture the meanings and values of home—as a financial investment, as a physical structure, as territory, as identity, and as socio-cultural unit—had not impacted significantly on legal discourse. The recent flourish of interest in this area[65] is timely in light of concerns about the impact of growing foreclosure rates in the U.S. The next section considers the balance struck between the creditor's commercial claim against the capital value of property and the occupier's interest in continuing to live in the property as a home in the contexts of foreclosure and bankruptcy. This section considers whether, and, if so, how, the meanings and values that the home represents to occupiers at risk of dispossession might be filtered into legal discourses around foreclosure and bankruptcy in the U.S.

The Creditor/Occupier Contest: U.S. Context

Creditor actions against the owner-occupied home are generally triggered by the debtor's default on repayment, leading the creditor to respond by seeking to recover the capital value of the property through foreclosure, thus forcing the eviction of the occupier and the sale of the property. The object of the foreclosure process is to ensure that secured creditors are able to exercise their proprietary rights against the property itself if the debtor goes into default. In the context of prime lending, the grant of proprietary rights over the property by a borrower may benefit both parties: the lender reduces its risk and the borrower benefits from a resultant reduction in the price of the debt.[66] However, considering the transaction from the perspective of the risk faced by the borrower, it is important to recognize that:

> [t]he point of a lender's seeking a mortgage is to reduce the risks of unsecured credit, and the primary reason why a mortgage reduces these risks is that the lender can foreclose if need be … [T]he main reason … why the mortgage reduces risk is that if the borrower defaults by failing to pay the debt or by breaking other promises, the lender has the option to do more than bring an action for breach of promise or an action on the unpaid instalments or the accelerated debt. The lender also has the option to foreclose.[67]

State law varies on the processes for foreclosures, which may take place out-of-court, either by strict foreclosure, which extinguishes the mortgagor's equity of

65 In the United States, *see* Ballard, *supra* note 26; Barros, *supra* note 1. In the United Kingdom, *see* Fox (2006), *supra* note 21; Fox (2005), *supra* note 26; and Fox (2002), *supra* note 26. In Israel, *see* Margalit, *supra* note 26.

66 *See* Robin Paul Malloy & James Charles Smith, Real Estate Transactions: Problems, Cases, and Materials 764 (2d ed. 2002).

67 *Id.*

redemption, by power-of-sale foreclosure, whereby the mortgage lenders can foreclose by selling the property without the need for a court order, or by bringing foreclosure proceedings through the court (judicial foreclosure). Yet, although the procedure for foreclosure varies from state to state, it is important to recognize that, across the board, once the borrower has defaulted on repayments, the balance of power lies firmly with the lender.

Mortgage law provides a range of protection for borrowers—from barring clogs on the equity of redemption to requiring that secured creditors follow proper foreclosure procedures. However, it is important to recognize that, once the debtor is in default, and so long as the secured creditor follows the proper procedure, a defaulting occupier who remains unable to discharge the debt and faces foreclosure will lose her home. From a law-and-economics perspective, this represents the *sine qua non* of the creditor's security: in the event of default, the borrower who cannot pay will ultimately lose their home. Indeed, this pro-creditor position can be justified on several grounds. Since the debtor owes a contractual obligation to the creditor, by facilitating foreclosure, the law is merely enforcing that contract. It is also suggested that creditors must be protected in order to ensure that they remain willing to lend money to homebuyers, thus underwriting the policy goal of expanding homeownership. Yet, while the idea that creditors must prevail in the event of default is often accepted without much question, the economic and social consequences of repossession and forced sale are not straightforward but highly complex.

The proposition that valid contracts—freely entered into—should be enforced between the parties is, at a basic level, difficult to dispute. However, it is important to bear in mind that, when balancing the interests of creditors and occupiers, the outcome will often have significant impact beyond the contracting parties themselves. Although a creditor has no direct right of action against the non-debtor occupier, the exercise of remedies against the secured property itself has obvious implications on other occupiers—either non-debtor adults or children. Non-debtor occupiers stand outside the contractual relationship between the creditor and the debtor: they stand outside the transaction, although they are clearly going to be affected by the exercise of the mortgagee's remedies. Indeed, while the costs of foreclosure are clearly most acute for the debtor and other members of her household, the financial impact beyond the debtor's household has also recently been quantified at 0.9 percent decline in value for every conventional foreclosure within an eighth of a mile of a single-family home.[68]

Another law-and-economics justification for the prioritization of the secured creditor's right to foreclose might be the possible consequences of refusing the creditor's action for economic efficiency and the availability of credit; as Karl

68 *See, e.g.*, Dan Immergluck & Geoff Smith, *The External Costs of Foreclosure: The Impact of Single-Family Mortgage Foreclosures on Property Values*, 17:1 Housing Policy Debate 57 (2006), in which the authors track the impact of foreclosures on neighboring property values.

Llewellyn cautioned in 1931: "Remove the legal sanction and men will give credit with more care."[69] Yet, Llewellyn also acknowledged that this argument was rooted in assumption rather than fact, and that: "[s]peculation is unfortunately much easier than finding out, as well as less useful … My own guess is that in the main writers, both legal and other, tend to over estimate heavily the effects of law …"[70] More recently, empirical analysis has suggested that higher borrower protections have: "… a significant, positive effect on the probability that households will be turned down for credit or discouraged from borrowing";[71] and that the effect of lowering creditor protections on credit availability is distributed disproportionately across borrower income groups. While high-income households had the most to gain from high exemptions—that is, when creditor protections are lowered—low-income households experienced greatest difficulty obtaining credit in these circumstances.[72] The consequences, for the borrower, may take various forms including higher interest rates and higher qualification requirements for loans, increased collateral requirements, more vigorous screening of loan applications. Again, these consequences are likely to create greater difficulty for low-income borrowers seeking credit.

It is interesting to note that any economic analysis underpinning the pro-creditor presumption in foreclosure necessarily focuses on the *availability* of credit over and above other measures of economic efficiency in credit markets, and regardless of the debtor's ability to repay. The prioritization of credit *availability* is rooted in the premise that: "the primary economic function of the credit market is to provide cheap funds, and that this function can only be accomplished when creditor rights are protected and sanctions on non-performing debtors are enforced."[73] This approach has been criticized on the basis that, in assessing the performance of the credit market, the availability of cheap credit has been inappropriately emphasized at the expense of other important factors—such as effective screening by the lender, insuring risk-averse entrepreneurs and protecting overconfident individuals and households.[74] These factors also resonate with the prevailing condition of the larger credit market. Thus, when funds are readily available, as they had been from the turn of the century until the recent credit crunch, the motivation to ensure the

---

69 Karl Llewellyn, *What Price Contract? – An Essay in Perspective*, 40 Yale L.J. 704, 725 (1931).

70 *Id.* at 725, footnote 47.

71 Reint Gropp, John Karl Scholz & Michelle J. White, *Personal Bankruptcy and Credit Supply and Demand*, 112 Quarterly Journal of Economics 217, 220 (1997).

72 *Id.*

73 A. Jorge Padilla & Alejandro Requejo, *The Costs and Benefits of the Strict Protection of Creditor Rights: Theory and Evidence* 5 (Washington, D.C.: Inter-American Development Bank, Research Network Working Paper #R-384, 2000).

74 *Id.* at 6. *See also* Michael Manove & A. Jorge Padilla, *Banking (Conservatively) with Optimists*, 30 Rand Journal of Economics 324 (1999); Michael Manove, A. Jorge Padilla & Marco Pagano, *Collateral versus Project Screening: A Model of Lazy Banks*, 32 Rand Journal of Economics 4, 726–44 (2001).

availability of cheap credit tends to "trump" all other considerations: however, the mortgage crisis has functioned as a cautionary reminder of the range of issues at stake, and has triggered a new wave of economic analysis seeking to unpack the connections between the inability of some borrowers to repay subprime debt, leading to high and rising delinquency rates of subprime mortgages, which in turn triggered a downturn in the housing economy and the global credit crisis that followed in 2007.[75]

The links between legal policies in the context of creditor protections and broader measures of economic efficiency were highlighted by Posner, who argued that when considering law's attitude towards creditor protections, it is important to take account of the role of creditors as effective gate-keepers. While high creditor protections may encourage creditors to lend money, particularly to low-income households, this may also result in creditors assuming unjustified risks, which in turn are linked to higher rates of bankruptcy.[76] Yet, while lower creditor protections encourage entrepreneurship, they are also linked to higher interest rates and higher rates of default. Although Posner acknowledges that the outcome of his analysis is ambiguous,[77] the complexity of economic efficiency arguments in the context of creditor protections must cast some doubt on the narrow approach that has appeared to inform legal analysis, and which has tended to prioritize the *availability* of credit over and above other measures of economic efficiency in credit markets. While the pro-creditor position can be justified by reference to the need for widely available credit to fund homeownership, a focus on lending *volume*, at the exclusion of other measures of market performance including default rates, is questionable. Indeed, some studies have suggested that an *effective judicial system* and *macroeconomic stability* are more significant as determining factors for the development and optimal performance of the credit market than high legal protections for creditors.[78]

---

75 Ben S. Bernanke, Chairman of the Federal Reserve System, Speech at the Women in Housing and Finance and Exchequer Club Joint Luncheon (January 10, 2008), *available at* http://www.federalreserve.gov/newsevents/speech/bernanke20080110a.htm.

76 "Some [U.S.] states have generous household exemptions for insolvent debtors, others chintzy ones. In the former states, the risk of entrepreneurship is reduced because the cost of failure is less, but interest rates are higher because default is more likely and the creditor's position in the event of default is weaker. And note that higher interest rates make default all the more likely. Cutting the other way, however, is the fact that in low-exemption states lenders' risk is less, which induces lenders to make more risky loans, i.e., loans likely to end in bankruptcy. It is therefore unclear whether there will be more bankruptcies in the high-exemption states or in the low-exemption states"; Richard A. Posner, The Economic Analysis of Law 440–41 (1992).

77 Similarly, Padilla and Requejo's empirical study of the costs and benefits of strict creditor protections found no conclusive evidence on the sign and magnitude of the effect of creditor rights protection on credit market efficiency; *supra* note 73.

78 Rafael La Porta, Florencio Lopez-De-Silanes, Andrei Shleifer & Robert W. Vishnay, *Legal Determinants of External Finance*, 52 Journal of Finance 1131–50 (1997);

It is also important to recognize that a policy of facilitating the widespread availability of credit—particularly for low-income households—is intrinsically linked to the political ideology of homeownership and the *expectation* that homeownership should be a legitimate aspiration for all U.S. citizens, as a central tenet of the "American Dream." Furthermore, while the ideology of homeownership is often assumed to derive from the desire to enable citizens to achieve an enhanced level of social and financial security for their own well-being, critical analyses of the ideological veneration of homeownership in the U.S. have suggested, *inter alia*, that the long-term indebtedness associated with the mortgage contract (which usually turns the homebuyer into a permanent debtor) reflects the real estate and credit industry perspective that indebtedness functions as a social good.[79] Indeed, Shlay has argued that the "real reason" for the federal government's promotion of homeownership, in the wake of the collapse of the U.S. economy in the 1920s, was as "a tool to stimulate consumption and increase production while improving American's housing conditions."[80] This view also resonates with Vincent's observation that the publication of Adams' *The Epic of America* in 1931 (which coined the phrase "American Dream"),[81] sought to revive the belief that:

> America was a land of infinite possibilities, that hard work, honesty and determination could be enough, that the surrounding economic system was not stronger than the willpower and fortitude of individuals, and that there was something left to dream about in America … at a time when it appeared to many Americans, if not to all, that the American dream had been replaced by a nightmare …[82]

Shlay has noted that homeownership, particularly low-income homeownership, is rooted in a "deterministic tradition" which promises "a wide range of social, behavioural, political, economic and neighbourhood changes …"[83] Yet, amidst rising concerns that homeownership as a "fits all" tenure has been oversold, a major body of literature has considered its impact on a range of variables,

---

Rafael La Porta, Florencio Lopez-De-Silanes, Andrei Shleifer & Robert W. Vishnay, *Law and Finance*, 106 JOURNAL OF POLITICAL ECONOMY 1113–55 (1998); Mark Meador, *The Effects of Mortgage Laws on Home Mortgage Rates*, 34 JOURNAL OF ECONOMICS AND BUSINESS 143, 147 (1982).

79 Perin, *supra* note 49.

80 Shlay, *supra* note 10, at 511.

81 Adams, *supra* note 8.

82 Bernard Vincent, *The American Dream – When was the Phrase Born?*, PRINTEMPS 81, 86 (2005).

83 Shlay, *supra* note 10, at 513.

including child outcomes,[84] economic well-being,[85] and social stability.[86] Analysis of empirical studies indicates that homeownership bears costs as well as benefits:[87] the putative advantages of owning your own home for the realization of *home* meanings (the economic, social, and personal rewards which have been associated with greater security of tenure, financial well-being, autonomy, privacy, enhanced social- and self-identity, and so on) must be tempered in the context of increased levels of risk and foreclosure. For example, McCarthy et al.'s analysis of empirical studies across a range of jurisdictions concluded that: "… homeownership may not always be a good investment, particularly for low-income … owners";[88] but that: "… while homeownership brings considerable economic benefits for families and the country, these benefits are not evenly distributed across income groups. Low- and moderate-income families are likely to gain less and risk more through homeownership."[89] Furthermore, the authors also noted that: "[m]ortgage default is costly for families and numerous other stakeholders";[90] and that low-income households are more exposed to these costs than other homebuyers. A range of factors render low-income households more vulnerable to default, including higher risk and lower, and less certain, returns on housing investment; links between housing and labor markets which increase the likelihood that local job losses will be coupled with house price declines;[91] the likelihood that low income households "will have lower cash reserves to help them weather an interruption in income or unforeseen expenses."[92] McCarthy et al. concluded that: "… affordable lending efforts might be exposing these households to higher default risk."[93]

Yet, in the event of default, and presuming that the borrower is no more able to pay the money owed by the time foreclosure proceedings are brought, the law is clearly on the side of the lender. There can be little doubt that the growth of

---

84 Donald R. Haurin, Toby L. Parcel & Ruth J. Haurin, *The Impact of Homeownership on Child Outcomes* (Joint Center for Housing Studies of Harvard University, Low-Income Homeownership Working Paper Series LIHO-01.14, 2001).

85 George McCarthy, Shannon Van Zandt & William M. Rohe, *The Economic Costs and Benefits of Home Ownership: A Critical Assessment of the Research*, Research Institute for Housing America (2001).

86 William M. Rohe, Shannon Van Zandt & George McCarthy, *The Social Benefits and Costs of Home Ownership: A Critical Assessment of the Research*, Harvard University Joint Center for Housing Studies (2001).

87 Shlay notes that: "[r]esearch does not provide uniform support for [homeownership] as a tool for asset accumulation, neighbourhood economic development or other social and political goals."; *supra* note 10, at 511.

88 McCarthy, Van Zandt & Rohe, *supra* note 85, at 18.

89 *Id.* at 1.

90 *Id.* at 32. *See also* Immergluck & Smith, *supra* note 68 and associated text, concerning the financial costs in declining property values for neighboring properties.

91 *Id.*

92 *Id.* at 31.

93 *Id.* at 32.

homeownership, particularly low-income homeownership, would not have been possible without major government interventions in the market—in the form of credit market participation and regulation, tax subsidies, and other investment—over several decades. However, when it comes to protecting those borrowers who have been exposed to the risk of losing their home, law has adopted a non-interventionist approach. Once a borrower is in default, the options available to her include seeking to renegotiate with the lender, or agree to a restructure of payments. However, it is important to recognize that where a borrower simply does not have the money owed, and the creditor is not inclined to wait, the creditor has a clear advantage as far as legal principles of foreclosure are concerned:[94] there is no opportunity, at this stage, for a court to balance the competing interests of the creditor and the debtor, and the impact of foreclosure on the debtor home-occupier (and other co-occupiers) is not considered relevant.

Of course, another option that may be open to occupiers seeking to protect their homes would be to apply for bankruptcy, with a view to invoking the homestead exemptions, which provide a special protection for the bankrupt's *home* against actions to force the sale of the property by creditors. The protection afforded to the debtor's primary residence under homestead legislation varies, but 46 out of 50 states offer some form of homestead exemption to protect equity in the home from the general reach of creditors.[95] The amount of the exemption ranges from $500 in Iowa, to $200,000 in Minnesota, with only five states[96] offering total exemption. Where a total exemption is offered, the home itself will be preserved, since creditors are barred from forcing the sale of the property. However, where only a partial exemption is available, the creditor may still force a sale if the value of the property is greater than the amount of the exemption. In these cases, if the borrower files for bankruptcy, the bankrupt may receive a share of the equity raised on sale. Nevertheless, the home itself will most likely still be sold.

The links between debtor default, bankruptcy, and forced sale of the owner-occupied home have important ramifications in a socio-cultural environment that has placed a premium on owner-occupation. Yet, against a socio-political framework that extols the advantages of homeownership (including low-income homeownership) it is important to temper the benefits and opportunities presented by homeownership with the potential costs and the risks that homebuyers are exposed to if they default on their debts. While homeownership has been promoted as enhancing the positive meanings of home for occupiers, the extent to which the benefits of homeownership are available to individual occupiers and households is determined according to their ability to sustain homeownership, and thus to

94 Malloy and Smith have noted that: "In both cases [strict foreclosure and judicial foreclosure] the mortgagor loses her equity of redemption if she does not pay by the judicial deadline"; *supra* note 66, at 768.

95 The only states offering no exemption are Delaware, New Jersey, Pennsylvania, and Rhode Island.

96 Florida, Kansas, Oklahoma, South Dakota, Texas.

avoid foreclosure or bankruptcy. Between these claims, it is reasonable to surmise that in states where total exemption is available, the importance of the home to occupiers is prioritized over and above the need to ensure that creditors can recoup their debts. Conversely, weaker homestead exemptions, or none at all, indicate that the claims of creditors to recover their debts are prioritized over the interests of occupiers in retaining the property for use and occupation *as a home*.

The Meaning and Experience of "Owning" One's Home

Although the rise in scholarly analysis of the meanings and value of home is relatively recent, the impulse to investigate the relationship between occupiers and the properties in which they reside is rooted in a long-established and largely intuitive sense that *home* is a positive phenomenon. From the philosophical foundations of home as a dwelling place that enables the occupier to become oriented in the world,[97] to the five clusters of contemporary home meanings based on empirical and theoretical research, identified by the present author in *Conceptualising Home*—home as financial asset; home as physical structure; home as territory; home as identity; and home as socio-cultural unit[98]—*home* discourse has generally presumed that the home is a source of positive meanings, attachments, and experiences for occupiers. Furthermore, the expansion of homeownership—including low-income homeownership—has been relentlessly pursued in many jurisdictions, including the U.S., on the presumption that owner-occupiers experience considerable and incontrovertible benefits compared to renters. The additional social and economic benefits that, according to political rhetoric, are associated with owning one's own home—especially for low-income

97 *See, e.g.*, Heidegger's philosophy of dwelling: Martin Heidegger, Bauen Wohnen Denken (Building Dwelling Thinking) (Albert Hofstadter trans., 1951), and the 1951 lecture, Martin Heidegger, ... *Dichterisch Wohnet Der Mensch* ... ("... *Poetically man dwells* ..."), Poetry, Language, Thought (Albert Hofstadter trans., 1951); Martin Heidegger, Sein Und Zeit (Being and Time) (John Macquarrie & Edward Robinson trans., 1927) (1962). Bachelard also described a fundamental need to take shelter from the world within the home, and highlighted the role of the home as a place of safety, security, and warmth: "[b]efore he is 'cast into the world' ... man is laid in the cradle of his house ... Life begins well, it begins enclosed, protected, all warm in the bosom of the house"; Gaston Bachelard, The Poetics of Space 7 (1964). This metaphor of home as a dwelling place also has connotations of family: references to the cradle and the bosom conjure up images of the home as a motherly body. For a philosophical perspective on the relationship between home and self-identity, *see generally*, Jeff E. Malpas, Place and Experience: A Philosophical Topography (1999); on the territoriality of home, *see* Edward S. Casey, Getting Back into Place – Toward a Renewed Understanding of the Place-World (1993).

98 Fox, *supra* note 21.

households—have been extensively analyzed in recent years.[99] For example, studies of home meanings have suggested that the significance of a person's home as a "repository of central and essential psychological and cultural processes"[100] is compounded by the additional cultural value attached to homes by owner-occupiers.[101] Culturally, homeownership has been perceived as conferring greater freedom and independence, and owner occupation has been linked, by some commentators, with a greater sense of control within the home territory, and increased ontological security.[102] The status conferred by homeownership has been linked to an occupier's self-identity.[103] Even when considering the meaning of the home as a physical structure, which may ostensibly appear to be neutral across tenures, it has been suggested that the value that the occupier puts upon the physical structure of the house is enhanced by ownership.[104]

---

99 For a detailed discussion of the promotion of low-income homeownership in the U.S., *see* Low Income Homeownership: Examining the Unexamined Goal (Nicholas P. Retsinas & Eric S. Belsky eds., 2002); and several reports published by Harvard University's Joint Center for Housing Studies as part of its Low-Income Homeownership Working Paper Series: *see*, *e.g.*, Mark Duda & Eric S. Belsky, *The Anatomy of the Low-Income Homeownership Boom in the 1990s* (Harvard University Low-Income Homeownership Working Paper Series, Working Paper No. LIHO.01-1, 2001); Michael Collins, David Crowe & Michael Carliner, *Examining the Supply-Side Constraints to Low-Income Homeownership* (Harvard University Low-Income Homeownership Working Paper Series, Working Paper No. LIHO.01.5, 2001); Haurin et al., *supra* note 84; Rohe et al., *supra* note 86; *see also* McCarthy et al., *supra* note 85. Roger Burrows & Steve Wilcox, Half the Poor: Home Owners with Low Incomes (2000) highlighted the ongoing difficulties experienced by low-income homeowners in the U.K., particularly in light of the low level of financial support currently afforded by the government for homeowning households living in poverty. For further analysis of the meanings associated with home across tenures, see Fox, *supra* note 21, especially Chapter Five.

100 Altman & Werner, *supra* note 2, at xix.

101 Fitchen, *supra* note 50, at 318.

102 *See* Sandy G. Smith, *The Essential Qualities of a Home*, 14 Journal of Environmental Psychology 31 (1994); Peter Saunders, A Nation of Home Owners (1990); Marjorie Bulos & Waheed Chaker, *Sustaining a Sense of Home and Personal Identity*, *in* The Home: Words, Interpretations, Meanings and Environments (David Benjamin ed., 1995).

103 "Owning one's own home grants membership in a respected category of people in part because it demonstrates one's commitment to the work ethic. The owned home, the largest single expenditure most people ever make, requires many years of earning and saving, and represents a long-term commitment to the work ethic."; Fitchen, *supra* note 50, at 320.

104 *See, e.g.*, Craig Gurney, *Lowering the Drawbridge: A Case Study of Analogy and Metaphor in the Social Construction of Home-Ownership*, 36 Urban Studies 1706 (1999); Craig Gurney, *Pride and Prejudice: Discourses of Normalisation in Public and Private Accounts of Home Ownership*, 14 Housing Studies 163 (1999).

Yet, one of the overriding issues to bear in mind in critical analysis of *home* is the importance of taking a real measure of the meanings and experiences of home, rather than pursuing an idealized vision of home. To this end, it is significant to recognize that, alongside the benefits of widespread homeownership, there are also potential social and economic costs to be borne by unsuccessful homebuyers.[105] The increase in risk and the potential costs associated with homeownership are brought into particularly stark relief by the rise in *unsustainable* homeownership, particularly amongst low-income households.[106] However, it is also important to bear in mind, when considering the proposition that *home* can be embraced as a universal value, the way in which households who have taken out subprime mortgages—predominately minorities, women, and low- and middle-income borrowers[107]—are exposed to rising interest rates and the risk of default and foreclosure. On the one hand, research has suggested that the meanings and values of *home* may be particularly salient for certain categories of owner-occupier, as a result of their greater need for the positive values of home (security, safety, wealth creation, privacy, identity, and so on) because of lower income levels,[108] for children,[109] for the elderly,[110] for those who are physically or mentally

105 *See, e.g.*, Rohe et al., *supra* note 86; McCarthy et al., *supra* note 85.

106 *See* discussion above, *supra* notes 15–19 and associated text.

107 NCRC Report, *supra* note 10, at 3.

108 *See, e.g.*, Lee Rainwater, *Fear and the House-as-Haven in the Lower Class*, 32 J. of the American Institute of Planners 23 (1966).

109 *See, e.g.*, Ross D. Parke, *Children's Home Environments: Social and Cognitive Effects*, *in* Children and the Environment (Irwin Altman & Joachim F. Wohlwill eds., 1978); Louise Chawla, *Childhood Place Attachments*, *in* Place Attachments (Irwin Altman & Setha M. Low eds., 1992); Louise Chawla, *Home is Where You Start From: Childhood Memory in Adult Interpretations of Home*, *in* The Meaning and Use of Housing (Ernesto G. Arias ed., 1993); Pia Christensen & Margaret O'Brien, Children in the City: Home Neighbourhood and Community (2003).

110 Pia C. Kontos, *Resisting Institutionalization: Constructing Old Age and Negotiating Home*, 12 J. of Aging Studies 167 (1998); Juliana Mansvelt, *Working at Leisure – Critical Geographies of Ageing*, 29 Area 289 (1997); Graham Mowl, Rachel Pain & Carol Talbot, *The Ageing Body and Homespace*, 32 Area 189 (2000).

disabled,[111] or for minorities.[112] Empirical studies have also suggested that when a person's economic and social resources are limited, the home and neighborhood environment play a critical role in that person's life chances and identity.[113] If, as political rhetoric has suggested, *ownership* of one's home inherently enhances the occupier's ability to experience the positive values of home, then the growth of homeownership would support these positive meanings.

However, research into the social costs of mortgage possession actions in England has also indicated the impact of loss of home on values such as the occupiers' self-identity and social-identity.[114] One consequence to emerge from this study was the impact of the change in their social status for dispossessed occupiers, and the experience of having their homes repossessed, also raised issues of stigma and shame for occupiers. Thus: "… a number of people said they had been caught short by the awful realisation that they were now 'homeless'."[115] Many respondents also emphasized the significance of the shift from "owner" to "renter" for their social identity. The researchers reported that:

> [a] number of people said that they felt they were now regarded as "second-class citizens" who were "dependent" on the state. A few respondents even said that they felt that they would now be classed as part of the "underclass" … People described how the experience had impacted on how they felt about themselves and also what they felt they could and could not do. In particular,

---

111 The issues associated with access to, and support of, homeownership for people with disabilities have attracted considerable critical attention: *see, e.g.*, Suellen Galbraith, *A Home of One's Own*, *in* THE FORGOTTEN GENERATION: THE STATUS AND CHALLENGES OF ADULTS WITH MILD COGNITIVE LIMITATIONS (Alexander J. Tymchuck, K. Charlie Lakin & Ruth Luckasson eds., 2001); E. Hepp & C. Soper, *One Family's Story of Homeownership*, 15 J. OF VOCATIONAL REHABILITATION 79 (2000); Jay Klein, *The History and Development of a National Homeownership Initiative*, 15 J. OF VOCATIONAL REHABILITATION 59 (2000); JAY KLEIN & MERRILL BLACK, EXTENDING THE AMERICAN DREAM: HOME OWNERSHIP FOR PEOPLE WITH DISABILITIES (1995); Jay Klein & Debra Nelson, *Homeownership for People with Disabilities: The State of the States in 1999*, 15 J. OF VOCATIONAL REHABILITATION 67 (2000); Jay Klein, Boyd Wilson & Debra Nelson, *Postcards on the Refrigerator: Changing the Power Dynamic in Housing and Assistance*, *in* PART OF THE COMMUNITY: STRATEGIES FOR INCLUDING EVERYONE (Jan Nisbet & David Hagner eds., 2000); John O'Brien, *Down Stairs That Are Never Your Own: Supporting People with Developmental Disabilities in Their Own Homes*, 32 MENTAL RETARDATION 1 (1994).

112 The positive relationship between home, gender, and race was explored by BELL HOOKS, YEARNING: RACE, GENDER, AND CULTURAL POLITICS (1990).

113 Susan Saegert, *The Role of Housing in the Experience of Dwelling*, *in* HOME ENVIRONMENTS (Irwin Altman & Carol M. Werner eds., 1985), *supra* note 2, at 289–90; *see also* ALVIN L. SCHORR, SLUMS AND SOCIAL INSECURITY (1964).

114 JANET FORD, ROGER BURROWS & SARAH NETTLETON, HOME OWNERSHIP IN A RISK SOCIETY: A SOCIAL ANALYSIS OF MORTGAGE ARREARS AND POSSESSIONS (2001).

115 *Id.* at 148.

> the experience had far-reaching consequences for some people's self-confidence and self-esteem.[116]

The impact of losing the home for identity was also reflected in the finding that: "... for many, social isolation was intensified by both felt and enacted stigma."[117] For some occupiers:

> ... people whom they had considered to be friends lost contact with them after the possession. For some, the experience undermined relationships with family as well as friends, especially where people had definite ideas about the "deserving and undeserving poor." One couple reported how they still felt shame and embarrassment some four and a half years after the actual possession.[118]

Children and young people who experienced repossession found it embarrassing to have to tell their friends, and found the change in social identity, from "owner" to "renter," to be difficult. In weighing the social and personal costs of foreclosure, it is important to take account of this study's claim that: "[t]he vast majority of the participants in the study felt that they had lost self-confidence and self-esteem. The majority also said they had been severely depressed, many receiving medication for it."[119]

While for the "successful" homeowner, a range of additional "benefits"—freedom, continuity, security—are associated with the security of tenure which is thought to flow from owner-occupation, for the occupier who is threatened with the loss of their home through foreclosure or bankruptcy, the converse applies, and it is low-income households—and others who are forced to rely on subprime lending—who experience the greatest risk of possession actions. It is ironic indeed if those for whom *home* is most salient are also most vulnerable to the risk of losing their homes through default and foreclosure.[120]

---

116 *Id.* at 149.

117 *Id.* at 161.

118 *Id.* at 161.

119 *Id.* at 162.

120 Low income is an obvious issue in relation to vulnerability to repossession: *see, e.g.*, Peter McCarthy & Bob Simpson, Issues in Post-Divorce Housing (1991), while the high proportion of low-income households in the owner-occupied sector emphasizes the extent of the potential for default. One study suggested that for low-income homeowners, the social and economic value of ownership was mitigated by the fact that ownership increases financial and psychological stress among families living on the economic margin: Danny Balfour & Janet Smith, *Transforming Lease-Purchase Housing Programs for Low-Income Families: Towards Empowerment and Engagement*, 18 J. of Urban Affairs 173 (1996). The experiences of children in the context of repossession actions are considered in Sarah Nettleton, *Losing a Home through Mortgage Repossession: The Views of Children*, 15 Children and Society 82 (2001). Elderly people may be rendered particularly vulnerable as occupiers for various reasons, including health problems and financial circumstances, at

The relative analytical neglect of *home* interests in legal discourse (until fairly recently), as well as the fact that—unless there is a total homestead exemption—the commercial claims of creditors will prevail in foreclosure actions, conforms to a classic market economy model of real property law as a discipline that favours: "… self-interested and rational individuals in the market place, overrid[ing] the needs of those who are different: weaker or poorer, or in a different way defined as Other."[121] In her discussion of *home* as "privilege," feminist scholar Iris Marion Young suggested that while the "privilege" of home was traditionally viewed as a *gender* privilege, it is now more likely to be linked to privileges of class and race.[122] This is substantiated by evidence that as the homeowner sector has expanded to include low-income households, these occupiers have been disproportionately exposed to the risk of losing their homes through default and foreclosure.[123] Indeed, if the financial and psychological stresses experienced by low-income homebuyers, not only by the final eventuality of losing their home in a foreclosure, but by the increased levels of risk that are clearly prevalent in the current mortgage market, are taken into account, it may be arguable that these risks and the impacts when the risks are actualized outweigh any social and economic value to be gained from having entered the homeowner sector, for dispossessed occupiers.[124]

---

a time when "home" can play a critical role in maintaining their sense of personal identity and independence: *see, e.g.*, Ann Dupuis & David C. Thorns, *Meanings of Home for Older Home Owners*, 11 Housing Studies 485 (1996); Ann Dupuis & David C. Thorns, *Home, Home Ownership and the Search for Ontological Security*, 46 The Sociological Review 24 (1998). Race also appears to have implications on the availability and sustainability of owner occupation: *see, e.g.*, John W. Frasier, Florence M. Margai & Eugene Tettley-Fio, Race and Place: Equity Issues in Urban America (2003); Dalton Conley, Being Black, Living in the Red: Race, Wealth, and Social Policy in America (1999); Wendy Webster, Imagining Home: Gender, "Race" and National Identity 1945–64 (1998).

121 Kate Green, *Being Here – What a Woman Can Say About Land Law*, *in* Feminist Perspectives on the Foundational Subjects of Law 93–4 (Anne Bottomley ed., 1996).

122 Iris Marion Young, *House and Home: Feminist Variations on a Theme*, *in* Resistance, Flight, Creation: Feminist Enactments of French Philosophy 68–70 (Dorothea Olkowski ed., 2000).

123 A range of factors render low-income households more vulnerable to default. These include higher risk and lower, and less certain, returns on housing investment; links between housing and labor markets which increase the likelihood that local job losses will be coupled with house price declines; the likelihood that low income households "will have lower cash reserves to help them weather an interruption in income or unforeseen expenses"; and the increased risk that follows from better access to credit; McCarthy et al., *supra* note 85, at 31–2.

124 Balfour & Smith, *supra* note 120; see also Rainwater, *supra* note 108.

Homeownership and Affordability

Although homeownership rates in the U.S. are currently at an all-time high, the issue of affordability is increasingly problematic across the sector, and especially for low-income households. This has important ramifications for the sustainability of homeownership for those already within the sector. In the last decade, some housing researchers have identified significant "gaps" in affordability, which undoubtedly impact on the sustainability of the owner-occupier sector. For example, Gyourko's research suggested that:

> A significant shift in home ownership affordability has occurred since the mid-1970s for less well educated and lower income households. Falling real wages have combined with rising constant quality real home prices to make lower quality homes, which were affordable in 1974, unaffordable to many comparable households in the 1990s. This problem promises to worsen in the near term as real wages of low skilled workers continue to erode in an increasingly global economy and as ever higher quality homes continue to filter down the housing stock. Virtually no new housing is being produced that is of low enough quality to be affordable to low skill households who want to own.[125]

Much of the government's attention has been focused on the consequences of affordability for *access* to homeownership: one study published by the Department of Housing and Urban Development (HUD) in 2005 indicated that while homeownership rates are currently at historically high levels for all sections of the U.S. population: "… dramatic gaps in homeownership rates have been stubbornly present over the last several decades, and even increased somewhat during the decade of the 1990s."[126] This study identified several factors accounting for the homeownership gap, including not only race and ethnicity, but also differences due to income, wealth, marital status, and age of household. Yet, while concerns about homeownership rates have triggered major policy initiatives to increase

125 Joseph Gyourko, *The Changing Strength of Socioeconomic Factors Affecting Home Ownership in the United States: 1960–1990*, 45 Scottish J. of Political Economy 466, 487 (1998).

126 Christopher E. Herbert, Donald R. Haurin, Stuart S. Rosenthal & Mark Duda, *Homeownership Gaps Among Low-Income and Minority Borrowers and Neighbourhoods* (2005), *available at* http://www.huduser.org/Publications/pdf/HomeownershipGapsAmongLow-IncomeAndMinority.pdf. The Executive Summary to this report went on to state that: "[a]s of 2004, the white homeownership rate was 76 percent while African-American and Hispanic homeownership rates remained below 50 percent, and the Asian rate was 60 percent. At the same time households with very-low income had a homeownership rate that was 37 percentage points below the rate for high-income households"; *Id.* at v.

access to homeownership,[127] it is not only access to, but the *sustainability* of, homeownership that will have a significant impact on national homeownership rates over the medium and long term.[128]

Although those who step onto the housing ladder are colloquially known as "homeowners," many are more accurately described as being in the *process* of buying their homes, subject to a mortgage: as "homebuyers" rather than "homeowners." For the vast majority of households, the purchase of a dwelling house is only possible with funding from loan capital, which is usually secured against a mortgage over the property. In a standard repayment mortgage, as the borrower makes repayments on the mortgage loan, their equity in the property increases until the mortgage is discharged and the "homebuyer" finally becomes an outright owner.[129] Yet, while the journey from initial purchase to outright ownership will usually require periodic payments over several years, in socio-cultural terms homebuyers obtain the badge of "owner occupier" as soon as the purchase is made. Yet the status associated with owner occupation, and the putative benefits of homeownership, are only as stable as the mortgagor's ability to make repayments on debts secured against the property. Successful homeownership—

127 President Clinton's policy for increasing home ownership rates was the *National Homeownership Strategy*. In a letter to Henry Cisneros (then-Secretary of HUD) dated November 3, 1994, President Clinton wrote that:

Homeownership is the American Dream. Our nation has embraced this dream since the National Housing Act of 1949 made "a decent home and a suitable living environment for every American family" a goal of national policy. The United States is the first major industrial country to make homeownership a reality for a majority of its people. Thanks to effective cooperation between industry and government, the doors of homeownership have been opened to millions of families in the past 45 years. However, since 1980, the national homeownership rate has been declining. Reversing this trend is vital to American families, to communities, and to our economy. Homeownership strengthens families and stabilizes communities. It encourages savings and investment and promotes economic and civic responsibility. Expansion of homeownership is an integral part of the Administration's economic plan. It spurs new investment, strengthening the economy and creating jobs. A stronger economy in turn enables more people to buy homes. For all these reasons, it is in our national interest to expand homeownership opportunities for all Americans.

Quoted from Marc A. Weiss, National Housing Policy in the U.S. for the 21st Century, PRAGUE INSTITUTE FOR GLOBAL URBAN DEVELOPMENT, available at http://www.globalurban.org/housing_us.htm. See Yongheng Deng & Stuart Gabriel, Risk-Based Pricing and the Enhancement of Mortgage Credit Availability among Underserved and Higher Credit-Risk Populations, 38 J. OF MONEY, CREDIT, AND BANKING 1431 (2006).

128 *See, e.g.*, Donald R. Haurin & Stuart R. Rosenthal, *The Sustainability of Homeownership: Factors Affecting the Duration of Homeownership and Rental Spells* (2004), *available at* http://www.huduser.org/publications/affhsg/homeownsustainability.html.

129 The position in relation to interest-only or endowment mortgages is obviously different, since the borrower does not accumulate equity in the property itself throughout the mortgage term, but rather accumulates payments in a fund, which may expose the borrower to additional layers of market risk.

including the benefits associated with acquiring positive *home* meanings as an owner—is clearly dependent on the ability to discharge the debt. Similarly, the negative aspects of *home* are strongly associated with financial insecurity, default, and loss of one's home at the hands of a creditor.

The sustainability of homeownership for low-income households was explored in a recent study by Haurin and Rosenthal, which found that while homeownership *was* sustainable for "typical" low-income households, a number of factors rendered some households "atypical," and: "[a]mong the demographic variables, being (and remaining) married, greater education and cognitive ability, a smaller family size, and greater age of the respondent all reduce the likelihood of terminating a spell of ownership. Race, particularly being Black, substantially increases the probability of terminating a spell of homeownership."[130] This study also noted, unsurprisingly, that low-income households experienced a higher risk of losing their homes at the hands of a creditor.[131] Haurin and Rosenthal also highlighted the significance of changes in family income as a factor in exposing households to unsustainability in relation to the repayment of debts, and, by extension, to unsustainable homeownership. Such changes can, for example, result from a change in the number of earners or the termination of marriage.[132]

The idea that owning (or buying, subject to a mortgage) one's own home enhances feelings of security, including ontological security, has been reflected in the political ideology of homeownership, as policies promoting homeownership have suggested that owner-occupation—as opposed to renting—enables occupiers to develop a stronger sense of autonomy and control in relation to their homes.[133] Yet, the argument that homeownership provides a means by which to achieve greater ontological security must be tempered in light of growing evidence of unsustainable homeownership in the U.S.[134] When considering the landscape of affordable housing, it is crucial that we recognize the costs of homeownership for those occupiers who are exposed to the risk of losing their homes in foreclosure actions alongside the potential benefits to be reaped from homeownership, as well as

---

130 Donald R. Haurin & Stuart S. Rosenthal, The Growth of Earnings of Low-Income Households and the Sensitivity of their Homeownership Choices to Economic and Socio-Demographic Shocks, Executive Summary at iv (2005).

131 The authors noted that: "[b]ecause we expect low-income respondents to have stretched their income when committing to a mortgage payment, this relationship of decreasing income and loss of ownership is not surprising"; *Id.* at 12.

132 "Of those low-income respondents terminating homeownership, twice as many ended a marriage as became married during the year of termination of homeownership"; *Id.* at 13.

133 *See, e.g.*, Robert M. Rakokff, *Ideology in Everyday Life: The Meaning of the House*, 7 Politics and Society 85 (1977); Smith, *supra* note 102; Saunders, *supra* note 102; Bulos & Chaker, *supra* note 102. *See*, however, arguments to the contrary in Marcuse, *supra* note 38; Craig Gurney, The Meaning of Home in the Decade of Owner Occupation: Towards an Experiential Perspective (1990).

134 *Supra* notes 15–19 and associated text.

the argument that these risks appear to be differentiated along fault-lines including race, ethnicity, income levels, wealth, marital status, and age, thus rendering some households particularly vulnerable to the heightened risk of foreclosure.

Although the financial and other consequences of possession actions are serious and wide-reaching, impacting on not only the debtor and the creditor, but on co-occupiers (including co-occupying children), on neighboring homeowners (who may suffer a decline in the value of their own properties as well as loss of social capital in the neighborhood), on agencies tasked with re-housing the dispossessed occupiers, and on the labor market and healthcare services where the negative effects of foreclosure lead to mental or physical ill-health, legal policy has been forged on the basis of *promoting* but not *protecting* homeownership. The rhetoric employed in policymakers' descriptions of homeownership—specifically, the use of the words independent, control, shelter, security, steady saving, and capital asset—conjures up many of the positive images associated with the home as a financial investment, home as shelter, and home as a valued territory in which the occupiers enjoy security, autonomy, and control. However, the case for taking account of the costs of unsuccessful homeownership for individuals at a general policy level is brought into sharp relief by evidence that, in the contemporary climate of homeownership, when debtors default on repayments—rendering their ownership "unsustainable"—this is often attributable to extrinsic economic factors, rather than "individual failure." As Hunter and Nixon wrote in relation to the last significant housing recession in the UK: "… the increasing propensity to arrears that arose during the late 1980s cannot simply be seen in the context of individual failures. Several structural factors are also involved, some relating directly to government policies that precipitated the individual circumstances."[135] Similarly, in a climate of high mortgage delinquency and foreclosure rates, it is arguable that regarding default by debtors, particularly subprime debtors, as a personal failure by the debtor is overly simplistic. Rather, the risks borne by those who are most vulnerable to foreclosure must be re-evaluated in light of the broader socio-economic context for mortgage borrowers (including irresponsible and predatory lending practices), and macroeconomic policies more generally.

In a study carried out in England, Ford et al.[136] pointed to a range of factors, such as labor market restructuring, demographic changes, the expansion of the homeownership sector, and the erosion of traditional safety nets for mortgagors, which have increased the levels of risk systemically associated with homeownership. Furthermore, studies in the U.S. and in other jurisdictions experiencing patterns of unsustainability in homeownership have also suggested that, putting aside these macroeconomic factors, at the micro-level, default is usually triggered by random "biological disruptions," for example, job loss, marital disruption, and

---

135 Caroline Hunter & Judy Nixon, *The Discourse of Housing Debt: The Social Construction of Landlords, Lenders, Borrowers and Tenants*, 16 Housing, Theory and Society 165, 167 (1999).

136 *See generally*, Ford, Burrows & Nettleton, *supra* note 114.

health problems.[137] The consequences of these extrinsic and somewhat "random" events for homeowners who find themselves unable to keep up repayments in their mortgage include finding the home itself and all of the meanings associated with the home vulnerable to actions by the creditor, possibly through no "fault" of their own. From this position, (property) law's instinctive assumption that debtors must bear the costs of their own default (failure) appears to favor a market framework which focuses on the opportunity to participate in home purchase transactions rather than the sustainability of the ongoing creditor/debtor relationship.

Conclusions

While the expansion of homeownership has been, and continues to be, premised on the grounds that it provides greater opportunities for occupiers to acquire positive home values, economic and non-economic—and to fulfill the "American Dream,"—it is important to remember that the positive meanings associated with *home* (and homeownership) are contingent on the (financial) ability to sustain that ownership by avoiding default on the repayment of debts secured against the property. Furthermore, mortgage default and the loss of a home through foreclosure are clearly matters of considerable personal stress and distress for the occupiers of the home. In addition to the financial costs of increased foreclosure rates, as well as the associated administrative or resource costs, empirical studies have indicated that a range of serious social, social psychological, and health costs are visited upon borrowers and other occupiers as a result of loss of their home, including the social costs of social exclusion, insecurity, and reduced standards of living; the social psychological costs include experiencing the stigma of debt as well as reported relationship difficulties, and that these factors, along with the experience of possession itself—which led to an increase in feelings of sadness, loss, and insecurity—have significant implications for mental health and well-being.[138]

In the past, it has perhaps been arguable that the impact of foreclosures, although undoubtedly serious for the individual households involved, remained relatively uncommon, that any downside should be viewed against the backdrop of a broadly

---

137 Donna Easterlow & Susan J. Smith, *Housing for Health: Can the Market Care?*, 36 Environment and Planning A 999 (2004); *see also* John Quigley & Robert Van Order, *Spatio-Temporal Measurement of House Price Appreciation in Underserved Areas*, 11 J. of Housing Research 1 (1995); Karl E. Case & Robert J. Shiller, *Mortgage Default Risk and Real Estate Prices: The Use of Index-Based Futures and Options in Real Estate*, 7 J. of Housing Research 243 (1996); Dennis R. Capozza, Dick Kazarian & Thomas A. Thomson, *Mortgage Default in Local Markets*, 25 Real Estate Economics 631 (1997); Peter J. Elmer & Steven A. Seeling, *The Rising Long-Term Trend of Single Family Mortgage Foreclosure Rates* (Federal Deposit Insurance Corporation, Working Paper Series 98-2, 1998); *see* McCarthy et al., *supra* note 85, at 29.

138 *See generally*, Ford, Burrows & Nettleton, *supra* note 114.

beneficial tenure, and that: "[i]f more people are to be given the opportunity to buy a home, then we have to accept an increased risk of default."[139] However, while on the one hand foreclosure rates, particularly for subprime borrowers, have been increasing exponentially, it is also increasingly difficult to avoid the conclusion that these foreclosures are not always attributable to individual failures on the part of the borrower, but part of a broader national crisis in mortgage lending and affordability for homeowners. It is becoming more difficult to dismiss the evidence relating to detrimental effects of default and foreclosure for both the individual debtor and across the sector, and that:

> [t]he financial benefits of [homeownership] are a double edged sword. As more and more "marginal borrowers" have taken on mortgages to pass property on to their children, or as financial investments, the negative effects of home ownership have become apparent. One thing is certain. Households facing mortgage arrears, or essential repairs they cannot afford, seem unlikely to derive the feelings of niche and belonging from home described by Saunders.[140]

Indeed, Gurney has suggested that a general rise in foreclosure rates across the sector can undermine positive *home* meanings for indebted homeowners, since: "[e]ven if a home of one's own does foster feelings of ontological security, the continual worry and struggle to avoid being 'behind with the mortgage' seems likely to deaden the effect of such a psychological boost."[141] Similarly, Harris and Pratt have claimed that: "… for many Canadians the home as a place of security and personal control is intermingled with stress, related to lack of affordability and insecurity of tenure."[142]

139 Peter Saunders & Colin Harris, *Home Ownership and Capital Gains* 18 (Urban and Regional Studies, Working Paper No. 64, 1988).

140 Gurney, *supra* note 133, at 8.

141 *Id.* at 10. Gurney claimed that:

> For many people who took out mortgages in the late 1980s the feelings of niche and belonging described by Saunders were far from their experience of home ownership. Instead, paying off a housing loan in a period when interest rates were constantly rising created profound personal anxieties, and uncertainty. The fact that people's homes are at risk if repayments on a mortgage or any other loans secured on it cannot be met has meant that fear and uncertainty of getting behind with the mortgage may have been one of the strongest emotions linked to home ownership … [suggested] links between marriage break-up, attempted suicide, child sexual abuse and the fears and uncertainty associated with mortgage arrears. Rapid increases in repossessions as a result of mortgage arrears … have meant that the threat of becoming homeless is one which more and more mortgagees now fear.

Id. at 8.

142 Richard Harris & Geraldine Pratt, *The Meaning of Home, Homeownership and Public Policy*, *in* The Changing Social Geography of Canadian Cities 297 (L.S. Bourne

The recent mortgage lending crisis provides a timely opportunity to re-consider the ideology of homeownership in the U.S., taking account of the affective value of *home* for occupiers and the struggle for affordability, particularly for low-income homebuyers. While activities associated with homeownership—such as personal investment in home and neighborhood—have been linked with improving social, psychological, emotional, and financial health,[143] and the social status and personal freedoms associated with homeownership have been linked to higher levels of self-esteem and perceived control over life,[144] it is important to recognize that the socio-psychological benefits of homeownership are also countered by the negative effects of default and possession actions. Thus, it has been suggested that:

> … homeowners, particularly lower-income homeowners, do not have as much actual control as some have claimed. Financial instability puts lower-income households at risk of losing their homes due to mortgage foreclosure. The psychological impact of homeownership could be negative if a person is unable to pay their mortgage and is forced from his or her home.[145]

The proposition that home meanings are threatened when a borrower falls into default is uncontroversial, and such events are also significant for, amongst other things, physical and psychological health. These are important factors to bear in mind when considering a range of issues relating to the meaning of the *owned home* within the legal concept of home, not least, the vigor with which the government *promotes* homeownership, welfare support for homeowners, and the degree of *legal protection* afforded to borrowers who fall into arrears and default.

This chapter therefore concludes by proposing a two-strand approach to help address some of the underlying issues and problems associated with homeownership, debt, and default. The first strand of these conclusions focuses on law's response to the debtor's default. In striking a balance between the creditor's claim to the capital asset tied up in the home and the occupier's interest in staying in possession of their home, the foreclosure procedure clearly prioritizes the enforcement of the creditor's proprietary security over and above any claim that the occupier might have in the use and occupation of the property *as a home*. The foreclosure procedure applies a strict property law approach to reach the conclusion that the creditor's superior claim must prevail. Any other outcome might arguably be rejected as an unjustifiable intervention with the market, which allows borrowers the freedom to enter into contracts, trade on their property rights, and live with the consequences in the event of default. Against this argument, however, it might alternatively be suggested that the phenomenon of widespread low-income homeownership—and with that, unsustainable homeownership—resulted from government interventions

---

& D.F. Ley eds., 1993).

143 Rohe, Van Zandt & McCarthy, *supra* note 86, at 2.

144 *Id.*

145 *Id.* at 6.

in the market through credit market participation and regulation, tax subsidies, and other incentives that set out to encourage citizens to choose homeownership over renting. If the current crisis is a result of market intervention to promote homeownership, is it still reasonable to argue that, having been exposed to risk as a result of government intervention, policymakers, including those of us who engage with legal policy, can retreat into a policy of non-intervention with respect to protecting homeowners? Furthermore, in cases where creditors have failed to act as effective gate-keepers, advanced capital to low-income borrowers in the knowledge that the debtor cannot afford to repay the loan, or adopted other abusive lending practices, should the law enforce the creditor's strict proprietary claim?

Of course, in some states the austerity of foreclosure is tempered, to varying degrees, by the possibility that the defaulting debtor can file for bankruptcy and so claim the protections of the homestead provisions. The homestead provisions provide a useful context for re-thinking law's response to the balance struck between the interests of the creditors and defaulting homebuyers. If one were to accept the argument that the meaning of the home to the occupier and the experiences of that occupier in the event of (what is increasingly likely to be viewed as systemic rather than individual failures leading to) default, and creditor possession actions should be weighed in the balance against the commercial claims of creditors to the capital value of the property, provisions in the nature of the homestead laws could potentially supply the mechanism for realizing this policy. This process could draw upon existing research into the structural factors (for example, ethnicity, low income) that expose households to risk,[146] or, alternatively, could focus on evidence relating to the differential impact of loss of home on certain groups, for example, children.[147] This approach might follow similar precepts to special protections in some states for elderly and/or disabled occupiers.[148] In addition to this, the very nature of the homestead exemption model, which usually involves exemptions for the home up to a maximum value, is equipped to distinguish between cases on the basis of property value if, for example, it were considered appropriate to focus protections on low-income households, or occupiers living in lower-value properties, rather than higher-income earners living in high-value properties.

The second strand concerns the (largely) uncritical prioritization of homeownership as the aspiration tenure for all citizens, and the *sine qua non* of the American Dream. Vincent's historical account describes the first documented use of the phrase "American Dream" in 1931 as a call to citizens to embrace the American

146 *See supra* notes 108–113 and associated text. For more detailed discussion of the income as a structural factor in debtor default, see Lorna Fox, *Re-Possessing "Home": A Re-Analysis of Gender, Home Ownership and Debtor Default for Feminist Legal Theory*, 14 Wm. & Mary J. Women & L. 423 (2008).

147 See Fox, *supra* note 21, particularly Chapter Nine.

148 *See, e.g.*, in Massachusetts, Mass. Gen. Laws ch. 188, § 1 and § 1A (for persons who are either elderly or disabled); and in Hawaii, Haw. Rev. Stat. §§ 651-91, 92 (additional homestead protection for elderly).

Dream as a means of "… get[ting] out of the current crisis and overcom[ing] the relapse of America into poverty and social disgrace."[149] Similarly, in describing the origins of U.S. government intervention in housing policy, including measures to promote homeownership, Carliner has suggested that:

> … in most cases … the principal reason they were adopted was not to facilitate or encourage homeownership [but] to stimulate construction activity and the overall economy ... to improve the physical quality of the housing stock, to bail out existing homeowners or financial institutions, or to meet other objectives, such as to reward veterans for serving the country in war-time.[150]

Nevertheless, the (unsurprisingly popular) political rhetoric of the "American Dream" continues to dominate housing policy initiatives, and it is interesting to note that recent events in the U.S. housing and mortgage market led to the establishment of the "Commission to Preserve the American Dream" through the Foreclosure Prevention and Homeownership Protection Act of 2007.[151]

There can be little doubt that homeownership has enabled many Americans to accumulate wealth (and other benefits) in ways that would not otherwise have been available to them. Yet, the expansion of homeownership appears to have gone beyond the "Dream," so that: "Homeownership policy … has not been about imagining the unattainable but about creating the expectation of owning one's own home. Ideologically, homeownership has been portrayed as a political right seemingly more popular than voting."[152] There is a real danger that the relentless promotion of homeownership functions both to deflect attention and energies from the pursuit of alternative policies for affordable housing,[153] and to encourage borrowers to take on debts that they will never be able to repay. A sustainable policy for the expansion of homeownership must be predicated not merely on *access* to homeownership but on the *affordability* of the debts undertaken in order to pursue this aspect of the "American Dream." Unsustainable homeownership generates significant losses, for both the dispossessed occupier(s) and for other stakeholders, and these costs must be properly taken into account in the formation of housing policies that enable citizens—both practically and socio-culturally—to exercise real and informed tenure choices.

---

149 Vincent, *supra* note 82, at 87.

150 Michael S. Carliner, *Development of Federal Homeownership "Policy"*, 9(2) Housing Policy Debate 299, 299 (1998).

151 *See* discussion *supra* in "Introduction."

152 Shlay, *supra* note 10, at 511.

153 *Id.*

Chapter 9
Accessible Housing and Affordability

Robin Paul Malloy

Introduction

This book addresses issues related to public and private cooperation in developing affordable housing to meet the needs of a dynamic population. In this context, accessible housing is important so that all people can actively participate in community and neighborhood activities. Unfortunately, many single-family residential homes are inaccessible to the mobility impaired. Current regulations relating to building accessibility cover public places, places of public accommodations, and publicly funded housing but they do not cover privately funded single-family residential homes. The distinction is one based on a predicate of public interest in the property, and an assumption that privately funded houses are not a matter of sufficient public concern, at least as relates to inclusive design requirements.

In contrast to this assumption, it seems relevant to take note of the public (government) support of private housing through local zoning regulations, activities in the financial markets, and inclusion of incentives in the tax code. It is also important to acknowledge the fact that private homes change hands every five to ten years, even though they remain in our national housing stock for a much longer time, perhaps 100 years or more. This means that private housing choices impact the public for many years into the future. Consequently, even development of privately funded housing includes a significant public interest, particularly with respect to affordability and the inclusion of people with disabilities.

According to the 2000 census, there were approximately 72.3 million families in the United States, and of this number approximately 21 million families had at least one member with a disability.[1] Out of the 21 million families with a member having a disability, 12 million of those families had at least one member with a *physical* disability.[2] And many of these physical disabilities involve mobility impairments that make it difficult or impossible to navigate most residential properties. Thus, even as public buildings and public spaces become increasingly accessible, most privately funded single-family residential homes remain inaccessible or unsafe

---

1 Qi Wang, *Disability and American Families: 2000*, CENSR-23 Census 2000 Special Reports (U.S. Census Bureau, Washington, D.C.), 2005, *available at* http://www.census.gov/prod/2005 pubs/censr-23.pdf.

2 *Id.*

for the mobility impaired because of exclusionary design features. As a result, many people with mobility impairment cannot visit the homes of family, friends, or colleagues because the homes have barriers to entry and are not safely or easily navigated once inside. The mobility impaired are therefore cut off from important social networks in their own neighborhoods.

While the percentage of people using wheelchairs is small, the percentage of people affected by mobility impairment is much greater. The full impact of mobility impairment is more readily understood when one considers the family context in which disability is experienced. If looked at in terms of families affected by issues associated with mobility impairment, some 17 percent of families in the United States include a member with mobility impairment.[3] And significantly, as our population ages over the next few decades, the number of affected individuals and families will be increasing dramatically since mobility impairment becomes more pronounced with age. This raises serious questions with regard to our ability to provide safe and accessible housing designs for a dynamic and aging population.

In the context of this book we must consider our ability to make affordable housing physically accessible. We need housing that can be safely lived in and easily visited by people with mobility impairment. Thus, we must consider new and inclusive designs for residential housing while seeking to assure the affordability of our overall national housing stock.

For people with mobility impairment, especially those using wheelchairs, scooters, and walkers, the typical American home is exclusionary. For example, most homes are built with steps leading up to the front door that act as barriers to easy entrance into the home, and many bathrooms, hallways, and living areas are too narrow for accommodating wheelchair use, or are only navigable by those able to easily confront internal stairways. Most homes also fail to provide grab bars and hand rails in the bathroom areas where many falls take place—falls which account for numerous injuries every year.[4]

To date there is little regulation with respect to inclusive design in private residential housing, even though millions of Americans are affected by the lack of accessible design features in our homes. While there is significant regulation related to public buildings and to public housing that is subsidized by government funds, there is no requirement that privately funded single-family residential housing be fully accessible to the mobility impaired. There are several reasons

3 *Id.*

4 *See* Check for Safety: A Home Fall Prevention Checklist for Older Adults, http://www.cdc.gov/ncipc/pub-res/toolkit/checklistforsafety.htm (last visited July 10, 2006). (Note while bathrooms and stairways are a primary source of falls they are not the only ones included in these numbers). *See Falls in the Home*, AEX-691.1-92 Ohio State University Extension (Department of Health and Human Services, Centers for Disease Control & Prevention, National Institute for Occupational Health and Safety, Washington, D.C.), http://www.cdc.gov/nasd/docs/d00010-d000300/d000131/d000131.pdf (last visited July 10, 2008).

for this regulatory failure, including the belief that residential housing design is a private market choice, and a fear that making private homes more accessible will be costly and make housing that much less affordable.

This chapter discusses the cost of making homes more accessible to the mobility impaired, and suggests that inclusive design is affordable. In discussing this matter the chapter proceeds in several steps. First, it discusses two approaches to inclusive housing design: *universal design* and *visitability*. Second, it presents evidence as to the cost of achieving certain types of accessibility in private housing design. It concludes by suggesting that inclusive housing can be affordable, especially if done in new housing rather than relying on after the fact retrofitting of housing that was originally built with exclusionary features.

Approaches to Inclusive Housing Design

Two generally referenced standards of inclusionary design, particularly in the residential housing area, are those of *universal design* and *visitability*.[5]

Universal design standards are generally quite pervasive and applied throughout an entire structure.[6] One way to quickly grasp the basic idea of universal design is that everything within a structure is designed to be readily accessible to a person in a wheelchair.[7] Thus, doorways and hallways are wider (32" minimum to 36"

---

5 The primary objective of accessible design is to provide the same opportunities for people with disabilities as are available to every citizen. Accessible design helps shift the "blame" for limitations in function from the person to the environment and allows the creation of responsive environments "… in which disabled people can display competence and, by extension, overcome much of the dependency and stigma that stems from being environmentally incompetent." Jordana L. Maisel, Center for Inclusive Design and Environmental Access (IDeA), Visitability as an Approach to Inclusive Housing Design and Community Development: A Look at its Emergence, Growth, and Challenges 9 (2005).

6 *See* Maisel, *supra* note 5, at 10–12; Wendy A. Jordan, Universal Design for the Home: Great Looking, Great Living Design for all Ages, Abilities, and Circumstances (2008); Selwyn Goldsmith, Universal Design (2001). Broadly, universal design means that the products which designers design are universally accommodating, that they cater conveniently for all users. On the route toward this goal a product that was initially designed primarily for the mass market of normal able-bodied people could have been subsequently … modified—the effect … being that it would suit all its other potential users as well, including people with disabilities.

Jordan, id. at 1. See also Information from the Universal Design Alliance, http://www.universaldesign.org/ (last visited September 22, 2008); AARP.org, Home Design, http://www.aarp.org/families/home_design/ (last visited September 22, 2008).

7 *See generally supra* note 6, and *infra* note 8. (These sources provide guidelines and standards which are briefly stated in a simplified form in this paragraph of the text.)

width recommendation), and have entrances that are barrier-free.[8] Bathrooms include appropriate grab bars, are bigger in size to accommodate the turning radius of a wheelchair, and include showers designed for easy roll in and out with a wheelchair. Throughout the home light switches are placed lower, and traditional round doorknobs give way to lower positioned levers. Storage shelves and cabinets are lower, and counter tops are lower with "cut outs" so that a wheelchair user can push close enough to have the chair frame fit under the counter, thus permitting the user to be positioned to make full use of the counter space. In addition, the residential living unit is generally designed on a single level layout, and provides appropriate means for ready access to the entire unit and to any common property. These universal accessibility design criteria are applied to every room, and every element throughout the home.

The visitability standard is much less pervasive.[9] The general idea behind this standard, as applied to residential housing, is one of making it possible for every home to be easily and safely visited by anyone in the community.[10] In other words, if I am hosting a neighborhood party at my house, it should be possible for all of my neighbors to be included and to feel that they are full participants in the social life of the neighborhood, without regard to mobility impairment. In order for this to readily happen my home would have to meet some minimal inclusive design standards. The entrance to my home would have to have a zero step elevation through the doorway and appropriate grade of incline from street level to the entrance. And my entrance doorway, hallway, and first floor doors would have to have at least 32 inches of clearance (32"–36" in width to be consistent with that

8 The minimum requirement for door width is 32". ADA Accessibility Guidelines for Buildings and Facilities (ADAAG), http://www.access-board.gov/adaag/html/adaag.htm#4.13 (last visited September 22, 2008); AARP, Home Design, http://www.aarp.org/families/home_design/ (last visited September 22, 2008). On the other hand some recommendations are for going beyond the minimum and using 34"–36" wide doors. *See* The Center for Universal Design, North Carolina State University: College of Design, *Universal Design In Housing*, UD Features in Housing (rev. 9/2003). The entrance way to a home should also have a minimum 5' X 5' clear space inside and outside of the entry door. *Id.* at 4.

9 *See* Maisel, *supra* note 5. *See also* Visitability, http://www.visitability.org (last visited September 22, 2008). There are three minimal standards for visitability: (1) a zero step entrance, (2) wider doorways on the main floor (32" minimum clearance), and (3) a half bath on main floor with space enough to handle a wheelchair. These three minimum guidelines ensure that everyone, without regard to mobility impairment, will at least be able to visit someone else's home, be able to use the bathroom, and safely enter and exit the property. *See also* Canadian Centre on Disability Studies, Visitability Canada, http://www.visitablehousingcanada.com/ (last visited September 22, 2008); The Center For An Accessible Society, http://www.accessiblesociety.org/topics/housing (last visited September 22, 2008).

10 The text in this paragraph explains the basic ideas of visitability as reflected in the sources identified *supra* note 9.

of universal design). The main portions of my entertainment area would need to be on one level floor, no drop living rooms or raised dining rooms, for instance. In addition, for all of my guests to feel equally comfortable, I would have to have a bathroom on the main floor of the home and it would need to be sized to permit entrance and appropriate turning radius for a wheelchair. Ideally, the bathroom would also have light switches and a sink at appropriate levels (slightly lower than the traditional non-accessible levels). Round doorknobs would be replaced with lever style door openers placed at the appropriate height (these are easier to open). This would be a minimal visitability standard imposing very little cost on the design requirements of a housing unit. I refer to this standard as a Level I Visitability Standard.

Going a step further than the Level I standard would involve the need for at least one bedroom to be located on the main floor of the home (could be a bedroom/den) and a bathroom on the main floor which would have a roll-in shower and grab bars. These additional features would make the home visitable by anyone, such as a close friend or family member with mobility impairment, who is staying for a day or more as a house guest. I refer to this standard as a Level II Visitability Standard.[11]

From an aesthetic perspective, issues sometimes arise concerning the "look" of inclusionary housing. Young people sometimes feel that a home with grab bars in the bathroom, for instance, signifies that they are living in an "old person's home." Consequently, they often react by removing such devices in an effort to make the premises signify that a cooler and more hip younger resident has moved in to occupy the space. There are two logical responses to this concern. First, as more and more homes incorporate these accessibility features, we can expect them to be manufactured in styles and colors that go beyond the typical cold steel ones often found in today's housing structures. Second, as the presence of these features becomes pervasive, they will lose their signification of old age and will disappear into the realm of the "ordinary." For example, in years gone by it was odd or unusual to have a toilet inside one's home rather than out, but now the toilet, like the soap dish and toothbrush holder, have all become ordinary fixtures in the current customary bathroom. No one even notices or thinks twice about their presence, and in fact it is their absence that is likely to be of note today. Moreover, the accessibility standard might be met by simply building the home with the necessary reinforced bathroom walls needed as a prerequisite to affixing grab bars.[12] With the walls properly reinforced to bear the weight, grab bars might

---

11 Level II Visitability is a standard that I suggest in this chapter as a design standard going beyond minimal visitability goals and being short of universal design. I use this category as a way of identifying a desirable middle standard of inclusionary design.

12 Grab bars are part of the requirements of universal design and make getting in and out of the tub or shower easier and safer for all users. *See* Center For Universal design, *Universal Design in Housing* 1–7 (2006); Maisel, *supra* note 5, at 19. Since grab bars are meant to carry weight as a person grabs on to them, they must be fastened to a wall structure

be installed at a later date or made removable so that they can be put on and taken off as desired.

A second set of aesthetic concerns relates to the front view of the home; the "curb appeal" of the property, as some real estate sales people might say. The inclusionary design standard that requires a zero elevation entranceway to permit an easy roll in on a wheelchair constrains some designs for front porches and patios. Again, these design features are in large part influenced by expectations of what is perceived as a norm in the housing market. Design norms can be changed and inclusive housing design can be made pleasing to the eye. Acceptability depends not so much on the entrance door itself but on the planning that goes into integrating other home design features and landscaping with the view of the accessible point of entry. In new construction housing this issue can be readily addressed with good inclusive design work done up front.

With remodeling of existing structures and with properties designated with historical significance, some compromises may be needed.[13] There are ways to design residential housing changes to provide aesthetically pleasing front views of the entrance while providing a side riser to the porch or patio. In addition to creative use of landscaping to eliminate a need for steps, a raised front patio might include a side ramp permitting access to the same front door but without being positioned as the primary focal point of the front yard. In the alternative, for situations in which remodeling and rehab work is cost prohibitive, it is often possible to construct a reasonably equal alternative point of access to the premises. This less desirable approach of using an alternative entranceway for accessibility might be a reasonable accommodation (or a permitted variance in zoning terminology) in cases where it can be demonstrated that historic preservation needs or remodeling costs make it prohibitive to properly rebuild a particular front entrance.[14]

Estimated Cost of Inclusive Housing Design

One point to keep in mind when considering the cost of inclusive housing is that in some respects private housing may be private space, yet at the same time the unit itself is a quasi-public place. This arises from the fact that most Americans move

capable of bearing the anticipated weight. Even if one has never seen grab bars in a private residence, they can be seen in hotel and motel rooms across the country.

13 Historic district and landmark zoning to protect buildings and areas is constitutional and has been upheld under the power to zone for aesthetic purposes. Daniel R. Mandelker, Land Use Law § 1.05 (LexisNexis 5th ed. 2003 & Supp. 2007); Julian Conrad Juergensmeyer & Thomas E. Roberts, Land Use Planning and Development Regulation Law 798–814 (West 2d ed. 2007). Historic district and landmark zoning typically prohibit any changes in the exterior of such a property. *See* Mandelker, *id.*; Juergensmeyer and Roberts, *id.*

14 For general discussion on variances in zoning *see* Mandelker, *supra* note 13, at §§ 6.39–6.52; Juergensmeyer and Roberts, *supra* note 13, at 260–80.

every five to ten years and yet the housing units they occupied stay in our national housing stock for many more years.[15] Some 25 percent of current national housing stock was built before the 1920s, and the median age of our national housing stock is 30 years.[16] This means that the social cost of having houses with poor accessibility is higher than initially thought since these units impose exclusionary costs on generations of homeowners, and not simply the first occupants. Likewise, the individuals bargaining for particular housing designs do not fully account for the actual cost of an exclusionary design since the buyer uses a cost and benefit comparison related to a shorter time horizon than that of the durability of the unit. In other words, with respect to the decision to build a home with exclusionary features, the marginal private costs and marginal private benefits do not equal marginal public costs and marginal public benefits. This leads to suboptimal consumer choices in housing design selection.

The recognition of this cost and benefit disequilibrium with respect to relying on private choice to optimize public benefits is important. It demonstrates the structural problem with relying only on private markets bargaining to properly produce an adequate stock of inclusive housing units.

Given that we can expect suboptimal public outcomes from a consumer-driven market approach, there is a need to require the market to account for the normative goal of inclusion. A design criterion for inclusive housing needs to be set and the issue then becomes one of determining the cost of such requirements. Stated differently, we need to know how much it will cost, if anything, to make houses more accessible to the mobility impaired, and to what extent these costs reduce the affordability of housing to those otherwise capable of acquiring a private residential unit.

As to what I identify above as Level I and Level II Visitability design standards, the cost of meeting these design features is estimated in one study to be as low as $0 to $1500.[17] Keeping costs low is generally a matter of up front planning and design. Another study reports that the typical cost of making a home visitable is $100 for homes on concrete slabs, and $300–$600 for homes with crawl spaces or basements.[18] These numbers are based on experience with building 30 homes in Atlanta with crawl spaces, and 800 homes elsewhere in Georgia on sites varying

15 Summary, *How We Are Housed: Results from the 1999 American Housing Survey*, U.S. Housing Market Conditions (U.S. Department of Housing and Urban Development, Office of Policy Development and Research, Washington, D.C.), 3rd Quarter 2000, *available at* http://www.huduser.org/periodicals/ushmc/fall00/summary-2.html; Barbara T. Williams, *These Old Houses: 2001*, Current Housing Reports, H121/04-1 (U.S. Department of Housing and Urban Development: Office of Policy Development and Research, U.S. Department of Commerce: Economics and Statistics Administration, U.S. Census Bureau, Washington, D.C.), February 2004. This accounts for about 10 million housing units. *Id.*

16 *See How We Are Housed*, *supra* note 15.

17 *See* Maisel, *supra* note 5, at 14.

18 *See* Eleanor Smith, *Builder Executive Affirms Low Cost of Visitability*, Concrete Change, February 22, 2004, http://concretechange.org/construction_affirmed.aspx.

from flat and sandy, to hard clay on steep slopes, for houses ranging in price from $80,000 to over $600,000.[19]

A recent study in Canada indicates a potentially higher cost.[20] The study took several actual housing designs and worked up the cost to make them visitable.[21] The costing included charges for design, labor, and 25 percent mark up on all items.[22] The home designs included special grading work to eliminate the need for steps into the home sitting on a lot positioned with a three-foot rise in grade from the road.[23] This was basically a retrofit to a pre-deigned house. Based on the house designs studied, the cost was $3000–$5000 Canadian.[24] The cost estimate report found that interior adjustments were negligible in cost, and that cost would be lower if visitable housing units could be built in groups rather than as isolated units (such that community-wide standards would lower the cost compared to doing isolated units in a scattered or random order of placement). Most of the cost involved design work, and addressing elevation and landscaping to produce the zero step entry on the lots. In particular, the design work addressed an approximate three-foot elevation rise up to the level of the main entrance door, and a great deal of the cost was related to the concrete sidewalk to be installed at a 2 percent grade leading up to the entry to the house (approximately one third or more of the cost). Assuming a template design of a visitable house to begin with, we should be able to assume lower costs over a large volume of production. Likewise, we have to carefully consider the lot and drainage issues. Some lots will need less work than those in the study, others perhaps more. Also, costs could be shaved down if ramping is used rather than addressing the zero step entry simply by land elevation adjustments. Even using cost numbers from 1999, a $3000 increase in cost of a home amounts to a 1.2–1.3 percent addition to the average cost of a residential unit in the U.S.[25] And, note that when this amount is financed over 30 years in a

---

19 *Id.*

20 Progressive Accessibility Re-Form Associates (PARA), *Visitable Housing: Cost Estimate Summary 2007*, 2007 Canadian Center on Disability Studies Report, http://www.visitablehousingcanada.com/documents/costanalysisreport/VisitableCosts_Report_MHRC_forwebsite.pdf.

21 *Id.*

22 *Id.*

23 *Id.*

24 Based on the 2007 exchange rates when this report came out, the Canadian dollar was worth 15 percent less than the U.S. dollar in the first quarter of 2007. The U.S. Consulate General Toronto, Exchange Rates for 2007, http://toronto.usconsulate.gov/content/uscitizens/pdfs/exchangeRates2007.pdf (last visited July 10, 2008).

25 Robin Paul Malloy & John Charles Smith, Real Estate Transactions: Problems, Cases and Materials 506 (2d ed. 2002) (1.3 percent based on a 1999 value of $220,000); or a 1.2 percent increase to the average price of a home based on 2004 prices (average cost of a home reported as $244,000 in 2004), U.S. Department of Housing and Urban Development, *Are Subdivision Requirements Excessive?*, 5:4 Research Works (April 2008), *available at* http://www.huduser.org/periodicals/ResearchWorks/april_08/RW_vol5num4t1.html.

typical mortgage situation, its actual impact on affordability amounts to only a few dollars per month.

It is also important to note that money can be saved by making housing units slightly smaller, a move that makes sense in light of the smaller size of families in the twenty-first century as opposed to the size in the 1950–60s. For example, the typical new single-family home in 1950 had about 1200 square feet of living room and a one-car garage; by 1990 the typical new home had 1700 square feet and a two-car garage;[26] and by 2005 the median square footage of an owner-occupied single-family home was 1858 square feet (for two-person occupancy the median is 1862 square feet).[27] Thus, a cost of as much as $3000 could be absorbed by simply reducing the size of a home by 15 square feet (making a reasonable assumption of a $200 per square foot cost of construction for new housing).

And costs should decline as inclusive standards become the norm rather than the exception in building design, because normalizing certain design features permits mass production and economies of scale. This can apply, for example, to a change in the "standard size" door, or in moving from round doorknobs to lever style door openers. Thus, special order cost considerations for many accessible design features disappear once the accessibility feature is implemented as the new norm.

Finally, let us conclude by considering a likely assertion to be made by some people opposing a national inclusive design standard. Some will suggest that even if inclusive design imposes relatively small costs on new housing units, it nonetheless adds to costs and therefore raises a conflict between competing goals of housing accessibility and housing affordability. In response, it should be acknowledged that exclusionary housing design is not cost-free; to the contrary it is expensive and imposes costs in ways not readily captured by economic models because of the market imperfections discussed above. Large costs are imposed on the people with mobility impairment who have a difficult time navigating our neighborhoods, who are marginalized and isolated by our existing housing policy, and who have important social networks truncated as a result of being excluded from the vast majority of residential units existing in this country. And these costs continue to mount as we add increasing numbers of exclusionary units to our housing stock every day. Likewise, we have added health costs from falling injuries in the home, and we have added costs from having to relocate or institutionalize older Americans who are unable to age in place because of the

---

26 *See* Robin Paul Malloy & John Charles Smith, Real Estate Transactions 601 (1st ed. 1998) (citing Bureau of the Census – Statistical Brief, "Home Sweet Home", SB/95-18, July 1995).

27 See *American Housing Survey 2005, Square Footage by Household and Unit Size, Income, and Costs – Owner Occupied Units*, 2005 U.S. Census Bureau tbl.3-18, http://www.census.gov/hhes/www/housing/ahs/ahs05/tab3-18.pdf.

design of their homes, or who are prematurely in need of institutional support as a result of falling and injury.[28]

Building accessible housing in the first instance is cheaper than having to do the more costly rehab work at a later date.[29] In reality, therefore, it is clear that cost and affordability issues run both ways.

Conclusion

There are currently no national regulations requiring new privately funded single-family residential housing units to have inclusive design features for the mobility impaired. The result is that very few homes are safely and easily accessible to this group of people. This makes it difficult for a significant part of our population to interact with each other in ways in which the non-impaired population takes for granted. It is difficult to visit the homes of family and friends, for instance, when there are barriers to entry and to safe and easy navigation within the home.

Part of the problem arises from market structures that fail to internalize the full cost of current exclusionary housing designs. Thus, steps must be taken to ensure that we have an adequate supply of inclusive units in our national housing stock. This is particularly important as our population ages since the incidence of mobility impairment increases with age.

Given the need for inclusive housing design, the question shifts to one of determining the cost of requiring greater accessibility to residential housing units. As pointed out herein, the cost is not unreasonable. Moreover, it is not as if there is no cost associated with a policy of continuing to build exclusionary housing. The quest, therefore, involves the search for a cost-effective way to make housing both accessible and affordable.

Acknowledgements

Copyright © 2008 by Robin Paul Malloy, all rights reserved. E.I. White Chair and Distinguished Professor of Law, College of Law, Syracuse University. Series Editor (with Peter Blanck), DISABILITY LAW AND POLICY BOOK SERIES (Cambridge University Press); Series Editor, LAW, PROPERTY, AND SOCIETY (Ashgate Publishing); Author of LAW IN A MARKET CONTEXT: AN INTRODUCTION TO MARKET CONCEPTS IN LEGAL REASONING (Cambridge 2004); LAW AND MARKET ECONOMY: REINTERPRETING THE VALUES OF LAW AND ECONOMICS (Cambridge 2000) (now translated into Chinese and Spanish); REAL ESTATE TRANSACTIONS (Aspen 3d ed. 2007) (authored with

---

28 *See* Check for Safety, *supra* note 4. (Note, while bathrooms and stairways are a primary source of falls they are not the only ones included in these numbers). *Falls in the Home*, *supra* note 4.

29 MAISEL, *supra* note 5, at 14; Smith, *Low Cost of Visitability*, *supra* note 18.

James Charles Smith); LAW AND ECONOMICS: A COMPARATIVE PERSPECTIVE (West 1990) (now translated into Japanese); PLANNING FOR SERFDOM: LEGAL ECONOMIC DISCOURSE AND DOWNTOWN DEVELOPMENT (Penn. 1991); and numerous other books and articles. This chapter is part of a larger project including an article titled, *Inclusion By Design: Accessible Housing and Mobility Impairment*, 60 HASTINGS L.J. 699 (2009) (the article expands on all of the ideas identified in this chapter and elaborates on the public aspects of privately funded housing).

Chapter 10
Managing the Risks of Natural Disasters in Public Housing

James Charles Smith

The devastation wrought by major natural disasters often includes substantial damage to, and loss of, housing stock. Hurricane Katrina, the most recent large-scale U.S. exemplar, gave rise to an immediate and severe housing crisis. Hundreds of thousands of residents became homeless, with many of them transported far away from the affected coastal areas. For some of the displaced, the dislocation was temporary, and they returned home within weeks or months, striving to repair their residences and their lives. Thousands of others, however, encountered long-term housing displacement, which has lingered on far longer than many people had expected at the time of the storm's wake. For many affected persons, displacement appears likely to be permanent, as they assimilate to new lives in different communities. Katrina inflicted overwhelming physical damage on the housing stock in New Orleans and in other Gulf Coast communities. Thousands of multi-family buildings and single-family homes incurred substantial damage from flooding and wind, rendering many properties total losses, being incapable of repair at a reasonable economic cost. The storm destroyed or made unlivable an estimated 300,000 homes, several times more than any previous natural disaster.[1]

Many of the Katrina-displaced persons were residents of public housing in New Orleans and nearby communities. In many respects, the impacts of Katrina on public housing residents and public housing were much the same as they were for private-sector residents and housing stock. Not surprisingly, as the storm devastated housing units it paid no attention to their form of ownership or the tenure of their occupants. The tragedies stemming from Katrina are widely, and properly, perceived not as the unavoidable consequences of a major storm, but rather as significantly exacerbated by human error. The term "natural disaster" is commonly said to be an oxymoron; the atypical environmental event is seen as disastrous only due to human proximity and thus there are only "human disasters,"

1 Daniel A. Farber & Jim Chen, Disasters and the Law: Katrina and Beyond 3 (2006). Hurricane Andrew destroyed or damaged approximately 80,000 homes in 1992. *Id.*

not "natural disasters."[2] There is already a large literature that attempts to analyze what went wrong with respect to decisions made before, during, and after Katrina, by a multitude of actors, including federal, state, and local governmental agencies, non-profit organizations, architects and engineers, mortgage lenders, landlords, and insurance companies.

One key part of the aftermath of Katrina is a new emphasis on disaster planning, given the dismal failures of disaster plans in the New Orleans community. Before and after Katrina, many organizations have developed disaster plans, sometimes known as a "disaster response plan," a "disaster preparedness plan," or an "emergency preparedness plan." This chapter focuses on one discrete planning issue associated with disasters: the status and prospects for pre-disaster planning in the public housing industry. The major decision-makers are the federal Department of Housing and Urban Development (HUD), which regulates public housing, and all of the individual public housing authorities (PHAs), which own, manage, and operate all of the nation's public housing units. I also consider several issues related to the rehabilitation, conversion, or abandonment of public housing properties damaged or impacted by a disaster, as illustrated by decisions made by the Housing Authority of New Orleans (HANO) before and after Katrina.

Disaster planning for PHAs should be seen in the larger context of long-term asset management, which includes not only risk management focused on other types of perils, but also insurance policies, reserves for the replacement of capital assets, and other considerations bearing on the objective to preserve PHA assets for the long run.

The Legal Framework for Public Housing Authorities

All planning by PHAs, including disaster planning, must fit within the character and structure of the institution of public housing. For disaster planning in general (that is, planning by actors outside of the public housing sector), significant concerns of federalism emerge, as demonstrated by the immense problems presented by Katrina, when federal and state entities attempted to coordinate their efforts within the confines of their respective spheres of authority. Critics of the

---

2 The idea is at least as old as Rousseau, who observed:

> [T]he majority of our physical misfortunes are also our work. Without leaving your Lisbon subject, concede, for example, that it was hardly nature that there brought together twenty-thousand houses of six or seven stories. If the residents of this large city had been more evenly dispersed and less densely housed, the losses would have been fewer or perhaps none at all.

Rousseau's Letter to Voltaire Regarding the Poem on the Lisbon Earthquake, August 18, 1756, reprinted in 3 The Collected Writings of Rousseau 110 (Roger D. Masters & Christopher Kelly eds., 1992). See There is No Such Thing as a Natural Disaster: Race, Class, and Hurricane Katrina (Chester Hartman & Gregory D. Squires eds., 2006).

woefully inadequate governmental response to Katrina identify as an underlying cause the division of efforts from multiple federal agencies—in particular, the Federal Emergency Management Agency (FEMA) and Homeland Security—and from State of Louisiana agencies as well as local governments. The overriding questions for all disaster planning are: "Who is to plan?" and "How do we coordinate among a number of entities?"

The Nature of Public Housing

For public housing, the same general issues of identifying the planner and coordinating among multiple entities are presented. But public housing raises special considerations due to its distinctive character. Each public housing authority (PHA) is a separate legal entity, chartered under the law of the State where the authority is located. Thus, their powers and responsibilities are determined by state statutes, which vary to some extent from state to state. Although PHAs are state-chartered, in almost all jurisdictions they are not units of state or local government. Typically, they are independent public authorities, governed by an appointed board of commissioners. PHAs receive no state funding, and for this reason are not within the regulatory jurisdiction of any state agency.[3] Instead, PHAs receive federal funding, which subjects them to federal oversight administered by HUD. Notwithstanding the lack of a strong tether to state government, PHAs are unavoidably members of distinct local communities, necessitating that they forge and maintain relationships with local governments. Thus, each PHA has a long-term contractual relationship with the local government within whose boundaries it operates.[4]

Public housing has a clear and simple mission: to house the poor.[5] The Housing Act of 1937 aimed to house a particular tranche—the working poor who could afford rents sufficient to pay PHA operating costs[6]—and that targeted population has changed over time, but the overall mission (to provide decent housing for lower-income Americans) has remained stable.[7] The goal is "soft," or precatory, in the sense that no individual, no matter how poor or needy, has a legal right to

---

3 PHAs must comply with a number of state and local laws that are generally applicable to housing and their properties, such as local building codes.

4 Typically the relationship is based on a contract known as a "cooperation agreement." *See* CAL. HEALTH & SAFETY CODE § 34518 (West 1999) (authorizing cooperation agreements between state public bodies and housing authorities); GA. CODE § 8-3-153 (2004) (same).

5 *See* 42 U.S.C. § 1437a (2000) (public housing units "shall be rented only to families who are low-income families at the time of their initial occupancy").

6 *See* LAWRENCE M. FRIEDMAN, GOVERNMENT AND SLUM HOUSING: A CENTURY OF FRUSTRATION 108–13 (1968).

7 Federal housing began in the 1930s as a New Deal initiative. At first during the Depression, the primary group served was working-class families, who had an employed head of the household. During the 1970s, a change in federal law resulted in PHAs accepting an increasing percentage of residents with income in the bottom two deciles. Nevertheless,

have public housing, or for that matter to other forms of housing assistance, such as Section 8 vouchers. Because public housing cannot accommodate all families who need and ask for housing assistance, access to public housing is rationed by local PHAs. Each PHA maintains a waiting list, which is managed by the PHA staff. Priority on a waiting list is not simply "first come, first served." A list of criteria determines when a person on a PHA waiting list is offered a housing unit. Federal law supplies a framework for PHA waiting lists; in other words, every PHA must follow certain procedures, and there are certain criteria that a PHA may not employ.[8] Within that federal framework, each local PHA has the discretion to select criteria and to define "preferences" that allow one family to obtain housing before other families who are on the PHA's waiting list.[9]

Each PHA resident must pay a minimum rental amount,[10] but most residents pay more than the minimum, based on the resident's income.[11] Since a series of statutory reforms beginning in 1969, tenant rents have not been sufficient to pay for the operating expenses of a PHA,[12] and therefore each PHA receives an operating subsidy from the federal government to make up the difference between costs and rents.[13] Congress appropriates money for the Public Housing Operating Fund, which HUD allocates among all PHAs. HUD determines each PHA's subsidy pursuant to a statutory mandate that HUD "establish a formula for determining the amount of assistance."[14] Pursuant to negotiated rulemaking, in 2005 HUD established a formula that compares the PHA's projected rents and other income with the PHA's

---

a constant has remained: only persons with insufficient income to obtain decent standard housing are eligible to become public housing tenants.

8 For example, a PHA may not apply a preference for working families to the disadvantage of an elderly applicant.

9 *See* 42 U.S.C. § 1437d(c)(5)(A) (Supp. 2005) (a PHA "may establish a system for making dwelling units available that provides preference for such occupancy to families having certain characteristics; each system of preferences established pursuant to this subparagraph shall be based upon local housing needs and priorities, as determined by the public housing agency using generally accepted data sources …")

10 Presently, the highest allowable minimum rent is $50 per month. 42 U.S.C. § 1437a(a)(3) (2000).

11 The formulas for income-based rents are set forth in 42 U.S.C. § 1437a(a) (2000).

12 The acts were known as the Brooke amendments for their sponsor, Senator Edward Brooke of Massachusetts. The first act limited tenant rents to 25 percent of a family's income. Pub. L. No. 90-448, 82 Stat. 476 (1969). Prior to the Brooke amendments, PHAs set rents at a level sufficient to pay the authority's entire operating costs. The federal subsidy was limited to the construction cost of the properties. *See* Alex F. Schwartz, Housing Policy in the United States: An Introduction 113 (2006).

13 *See* 42 U.S.C. § 1437g(c)(1)(B) (2000) and 42 U.S.C. § 1437g(e)(1) (2000) (requiring HUD to establish a formula for Operating Fund to be allocated to each housing authority).

14 42 U.S.C. § 1437g(e)(2)(A) (2000).

projected reasonable costs for operations, maintenance, and management. The expense side of the equation consists of a "project expense level" (PEL), a utility expense level (UEL), and other "add-on" expenses.[15]

The Budget Crisis

Beginning in 1996, Congress has failed to appropriate sufficient funds for public housing to allow PHAs to receive their full operating subsidies.[16] The cumulative deficit for 1996 through 2006 is $1.684 billion.[17] The shortfall was less than 10 percent of HUD's projected needs each year until 2005, when the proration percentage fell to 89 percent. For fiscal year 2008, PHAs received only 80 percent of the needed operating funds, the lowest ever, and for fiscal year 2009, the President's proposed budget requests $4.3 billion, which constitutes 81 percent of HUD's projection of the $5.3 billion subsidy that it should cost to run the nation's stock of approximately 1.2 million housing units.

The repeated shortfalls for the Public Housing Operating Fund are only one part of a bigger picture of diminished federal funding for public housing. PHAs also receive capital improvement funding from the federal government, which, like the operating funds, have fallen short of projected needs for capital repairs and replacements. More generally, HUD's funding has been slashed dramatically since the late 1970s.[18] For fiscal year 2007, its budget was $35.36 billion. For 1978, the high water mark, HUD's budget was $109.29 billion (in dollars adjusted to 2007).[19] This is the biggest cut of any federal agency over this time period.[20]

---

15 24 C.F.R. § 990.160 (2008) (overview of calculating formula expenses).

16 *See* a chart for fiscal years 1996–2006 at Council of Large Public Housing Authorities (CLPHA), http://www.clpha.org/page.cfm?pageID=659 (last visited November 11, 2008).

17 *Id.*

18 HUD operates many programs in addition to public housing, including the Section 8 housing voucher program. Congress has also reduced funding for other subsidies for low-income housing. Housing assistance as a share of total non-defense discretionary spending fell from 10.2 percent in 1998 to 7.7 percent in 2006. Joint Center for Housing Studies of Harvard University, The State of the Nation's Housing 2007, http://www.jchs.harvard.edu/publications/markets/son2007 (last visited November 11, 2008).

19 Budget of the United States Government, Fiscal Year 2009, Historical Tables, Table 5.2 – Budget Authority by Agency: 1976–2013, http://www.gpoaccess.gov/usbudget/fy09/ hist.html (last visited November 11, 2008); *Id.* at Table 1.3 – Summary of Receipts, Outlays, and Surpluses or Deficits in Current Dollars, Constant (FY 2000) Dollars, and as Percentages of GDP: 1940–2013, http://www.gpoaccess.gov/usbudget/fy09/ hist.html (last visited November 11, 2008).

20 *Id.* at Table 5.3 – Percentage Distribution of Budget Authority by Agency: 1976-2013, http://www.gpoaccess.gov/usbudget/fy09/ hist.html (last visited November 11, 2008).

The chronic underfunding for public housing operations and for capital expenditures has caused many PHAs to scramble to remain solvent. Many have delayed ordinary maintenance and diverted capital funds away from needed capital repairs, replacements, and improvements to pay for operations. They have been forced to maintain properties at a lower level and to curtail social service programs for their residents. The budget crisis for public housing is severe, and within the next few years many PHAs will have to make further, substantial reductions in their programs unless they are able to obtain additional funding from the federal government or from other sources.

The budget crunch for public housing is disheartening because, on balance, this sector has displayed a strong record of performance, notwithstanding charges leveled by its many critics. Public housing is generally an effective mechanism for providing housing assistance for poor people. Unlike other major affordable housing programs, including the Section 8 housing voucher program and the Low Income Housing Tax Credit, public housing provides housing units that are permanently affordable because they are publicly owned. The major competing affordable housing programs all incorporate private-sector ownership or finance, whose participants seek profits from their investments. In contrast, public housing is not owned and operated for profit and cannot be sold for speculative gain. Revenues and expenses are matched, with no profit being withdrawn. Because a profit factor need not be supplied to private capital, public housing is inherently more efficient and less expensive than Section 8 housing, low-income tax credit projects, and other affordable housing initiatives that marry profit-seeking private actors to government entities or non-profit organizations. If a PHA is well run, it can provide affordable housing at a lower cost than the private sector.

The Changing Management Philosophy: The Harvard Cost Study (2003)

There is great tension in the public housing industry today as to direction and purpose. One aspect of tension comes from the budget crisis described above, but another goes to the core and the very meaning of the enterprise. When one examines the federal statutes that govern public housing, one and only one "constant" emerges—the statutes are subject to constant amendments, many of them relatively minor but some major. The Quality Housing and Work Responsibility Act of 1998[21] triggered the modern debate over the meaning of, and management philosophy for, public housing, although that consequence probably was not intended by the Act's authors. The Act established an Operating Fund and a Capital Fund program to replace and consolidate previous funding programs, which were splintered and multiply funded. The statute called for the Secretary of HUD to "establish a formula for determining the amount of assistance provided to" all PHAs, setting

21 Quality Housing and Work Responsibility Act of 1998, Pub. L. No. 105-276, § 501, 112 Stat. 2518 (1999) (codified at 42 U.S.C. § 1437g (2000)).

forth a non-exclusive list of six criteria that "[t]he formula may take into account."[22] Congress then directed HUD to initiate negotiated rulemaking with public housing constituencies to arrive at an Operating Fund formula. A rulemaking committee met, with its charge being to determine the level of funding necessary to run a "well-managed public housing project."[23] HUD had data covering PHA spending going back almost three decades, but the data was not organized in a manner that could inform judgments as to proper funding levels. The underlying problem was the absence of a frame of reference: PHAs historically had spent whatever the federal government gave them through appropriations. Some PHAs were better funded than others, but "well-managed" PHAs simply spent all their available resources, as did PHAs that were not so well managed. This presented a problem of circular logic.[24] The rulemaking committee failed to achieve consensus on a new formula due to the lack of objective data and the circularity problem.[25]

As a consequence of the failure of negotiated rulemaking, Congress, as part of the 1999 HUD Appropriations bill, instructed HUD to contract with the Harvard University Graduate School of Design to conduct a study to determine what it should cost to operate good-quality public housing. The School assembled a staff, collected data, and held public meetings. This culminated in release of the Public Housing Operating Cost Study,[26] popularly known as the "Harvard Cost Study." True to its charge, the study framed the basic question as, "What should it cost to administer good quality public housing?"[27] To do this, the study compared public housing costs and organizational structure to private rental properties, using data from a benchmark database consisting of multifamily rental housing whose mortgages were insured by the Federal Housing Administration (FHA). The implicit assumption underlying the study was that private-sector landlords manage their assets efficiently, and for that reason a cost analysis comparing PHAs to private-sector landlords would yield useful information. The study's final report strayed far beyond the charge that it analyze the costs of operating public housing. The study advocated for a drastic change in organizational structure for PHAs, calling for HUD to "require property-based budgeting, accounting and

---

22 42 U.S.C. § 1437g(e)(2)(A) (2000).

23 *Id.* § 1437g(e)(2)(A)(i) (2000).

24 That is to say, *PHA A*, an agency that by objective criteria has succeeded in providing decent housing to its residents, spent $ x dollars. Spending $ x dollars has enabled *PHA A* to be "well managed." Or *PHA A*'s being "well managed" has enabled it to succeed with $ x dollars.

25 Interview with J. Richard Parker II, Executive Director, Athens Housing Authority, in Athens, Georgia (October 14, 2008).

26 Harvard University Graduate School of Design, *Public Housing Operating Cost Study, Final Report* (June 6, 2003), *available at* http://www.gsd.harvard.edu/research/research_centers/phocs/documents/Final%206.12.pdf (last visited November 11, 2008).

27 Closing Message from James Stockard, *Public Housing Operating Cost Study*, *supra* note 26.

management, consistent with practices in private industry."[28] Based on the FHA benchmark, the study called for a 5 percent increase in the aggregate level of public housing operating expenses (other than utilities).[29] In a subsequent paper the authors of the study elaborated:

> Our work on the Public Housing Operating Cost Study suggests that the operating funding currently made available for public housing, in the aggregate, is just about right, if one assumes a cost structure essentially similar to non-profit operators of assisted housing. In the aggregate, we estimated that today's formula expense levels for public housing were some 5% lower than other federally assisted housing, after controlling for such factors as building type, location, number of bedrooms per unit, etc. If one were to include certain investment and other income that PHAs are currently allowed to keep (without an offset in subsidy), however, total funding is roughly equal to estimated needs.[30]

Since the Harvard Cost Study, the federal government's perspective has been to push the industry toward private-sector models of doing things. This is an application of a general philosophy—the perspective that private enterprise can do

---

28 *Public Housing Operating Cost Study*, *supra* note 26. The report strongly criticized the public housing sector for not following private-sector norms:

> Public housing has existed since its inception in isolation from the rest of the housing development and management world. This isolation has led to an unhealthy reliance on HUD as its measure of performance (please the funder) instead of reliance on consumer preference and market value (please the client, maximize return). Case studies call attention to the organizational distortions, with major cost implications, of years of a system that has been immune to market forces and administered from HUD with an agency performance focus rather than a property performance focus. PHAs operate like public agencies and not like real estate businesses, managing under extremely centralized arrangements that run counter to good business practice. Resources are not being used effectively because this condition is not addressed …

Id.

29 *Id.* at iii. The recommended modest increase would not be evenly distributed among PHAs. The study concluded that some PHAs were currently overfunded and others underfunded:

> 38% of PHAs would remain within +/- 10% of current formula amounts. Only 6% would have their expense levels reduced by more than 10% while 28% would have their formula amounts increased by more than 20%. These estimates presume a cost structure for public housing that is substantially equivalent to non-profit operators of assisted housing.

Id.

30 Gregory A. Byrne, Kevin Day & James Stockard, *Taking Stock of Public Housing* 4–5 (September 16, 2003) (unpublished study presented to the Public Housing Authority Directors Association, *available at* http://www.gsd.harvard.edu/research/research_centers/phocs/study_results.html (last visited May 13, 2009)).

many things better than government, and that when government provides goods or services, it must do so as efficiently as the private market.

The latest manifestation of this private-sector orientation, following the Harvard Cost Study, is a HUD mandated shift to a business model known as "asset management," which embraces the three components of property-based accounting, property-based budgeting, and property-based management (also called "project-based" accounting, budgeting, and management). Most PHAs own multiple projects or properties. Traditionally, for operations and for budgeting, a PHA managed all of its housing stock on a unitary basis. The conversion to property-based management and accounting has resulted in a mandate that PHAs manage and account for properties individually, following private-sector norms. Practically, this means that PHAs of a medium or large size must adopt a new organizational structure. Rather than have a unitary, centralized structure, PHAs must adopt a hierarchical structure, dividing its properties into individual units or small groups and assigning its employees to these units or groups.

Property-based management and accounting has also had important consequences for PHA managerial staff. All PHA costs must be allocated either to a specific property (such as the cost of painting housing units) or to the central office, where management resides (such as the salary of the PHA's executive director). The central office has its own budget, which is independent of the budgets for the individual properties, and HUD regulations limit the central office budget. A central office is allowed to collect asset management fees from its properties, similar to what a private management firm would charge for managing a private residential apartment complex, but those fees are limited to a HUD-determined reasonable maximum.

The asset management model includes two domains, which could have been kept separate. Financial planning on a property-by-property basis depends upon property-based budgeting and property-based accounting. These two tools together give a PHA a more accurate picture of what it is spending to operate the various properties within its portfolio. With unitary budgeting and accounting (portfolio-wide), a PHA may have had a general sense of which communities were more expensive to run, but it lacked hard data. The shift to mandatory property-based budgeting and accounting creates much greater transparency, and encourages a PHA in its planning processes to consider the advisability of measures, such as building modernization or the retirement of dwelling units, directed to high-cost properties.

The second domain of asset management, property-based management, could have been severed. Property-based management reflects a norm that each property (or group of properties) should have its own staff of managers and other employees, with each property generally having its own equipment and supplies. Depending upon the size of the PHA properties, such decentralization is often not economically efficient. The Harvard Cost Study, nonetheless, called for property-based management, not fully appreciating that in private-sector housing the dynamics are different and that larger private-sector owners and management firms often employ centralized staff for some services.

The mandatory transition of all PHAs to the private-sector asset management model during an era of pervasive funding shortfalls has caused additional stress. The transaction costs of transition are significant. With adequate funding, all well-run PHAs could have accommodated the major change in business model, but federal imposition of the change during a time of drastic federal budgetary underfunding has caused at least some PHAs to divert resources away from regular programmatic needs.

Casualty Insurance for PHA Properties

In the private rental housing sector, owners almost always obtain casualty insurance to protect buildings and other improvements from loss due to fire, flooding, explosion, and similar risks. Most policies cover a broad range of perils, and although many owners may not obtain insurance with dollar limits equal to the full replacement cost of buildings, in general policy limits represent a high percentage of property value. The norm that private owners obtain and maintain insurance is almost certainly not solely attributable to the property owners' decision-making. Third parties—mortgage lenders—have a decisive impact. A prudent lender will not make a mortgage loan on residential housing unless the borrower carries casualty insurance, in an amount and covering perils satisfactory to the lender. The insurance policy is made payable to the lender, or payable to both parties with the lender in control of insurance proceeds under the terms of the mortgage loan documentation. Not surprisingly, mortgage underwriting standards require that lenders make sure that the collateral for their loans is insured. In the absence of mortgage loan requirements, many owners of residential real estate would probably attempt to save money (or augment profits) by going without insurance or "underinsuring," betting that fire or other casualty would not strike their property.

PHAs traditionally operate in a very different regime. Their capital improvements are not mortgaged, and thus PHAs are not forced to insure physical assets by institutional lenders. When federal public housing first began in the 1930s and 1940s, the federal government paid the entire construction cost for buildings and related improvements. Governments traditionally have followed casualty insurance practices that are very different from those employed in the private sector. The federal government does not usually insure the buildings and other facilities it owns. For an entity as large as the federal government, such a decision to "self-insure" (as it is often called) is very probably prudent. Casualty insurance, like other forms of insurance, is risk spreading. Spreading risk by insurance is not costless. Private insurers must make a profit after paying claims and the transactions costs that are associated with issuing insurance. For an entity as large as the federal government, over the long run government purchases of casualty insurance would result in a net loss of funds.

No federal statute directly requires that PHAs insure their assets, but HUD requires certain insurance coverage under the Annual Contributions Contract (ACC) that it enters into with each PHA.[31] With respect to property insurance, a HUD notice advises that coverage is mandatory and that "each policy must be written with a blanket limit, on a replacement cost basis, and with an agreed value clause eliminating any coinsurance provision."[32] Nothing is stated with respect to the nature of the perils that must be covered, policy exclusions, or the amount of deductibles. The notice allows a PHA to request a waiver or to establish "self insurance," subject to HUD approval if the PHA provides "a justification as to why the request should be approved."[33]

An individual PHA, unlike the federal government, generally will not be acting prudently if it seeks to forgo casualty insurance or to "underinsure" by obtaining a weak policy (such as one with low dollar limits or exclusions for perils that are in fact possible to insure). A PHA may hope that, if it suffers an uninsured casualty, it will receive federal funds to pay the costs of reconstruction. But a PHA should realize that there is no such federal promise, whether the disaster is a garden-variety fire or a large-scale federally declared disaster. The recent history of federal appropriations demonstrates the uncertainty of federal disaster funding. In 1998, when Congress reworked the overall funding plan for public housing, it added Section 9(k) to the National Housing Act.[34] The provision authorized the Secretary of HUD to establish a reserve for "emergencies and other disasters," with the Secretary having discretion to determine the amount, subject to a cap of 2 percent of the capital and operating fund budget. The provision then allowed the Secretary to allocate emergency reserve funds to PHAs who made appropriate requests for such funds. Shortly thereafter, an important question arose: What should be the relationship between the HUD emergency reserve fund and FEMA disaster assistance funds? In 2001, HUD and FEMA entered into a Memorandum of Understanding to coordinate "disaster assistance to PHAs for properties damaged by major disasters declared by the President." FEMA agreed it would evaluate PHA requests "for essential assistance [to] include debris removal, demolition of unsafe structures, and any actions necessary to reduce an immediate threat to life, property, and public health and safety."[35] In return, HUD agreed to provide funding for "PHAs' disaster recovery costs not covered by insurance and essential assistance from FEMA" from the Section 9(k) emergency reserve, "subject to the availability of appropriations." In 2003, HUD and FEMA amended the Memorandum of Understanding to recognize that some forms of

31 24 C.F.R. § 965.201(a) (2008).

32 HUD Form 53012B (7/95).

33 *Id.* § 4.

34 Pub. L. No. 105-276, § 519(a), 112 Stat. 2461, 2551 (1998).

35 Such "essential assistance" grants are authorized by the Robert T. Stafford Disaster Relief and Emergency Assistance Act, Pub. L. 100-707, § 403, 102 Stat. 4689, 4697 (1988) (codified at 42 U.S.C. § 5170b (2000)).

federally subsidized housing, such as Section 8 housing and housing built with FHA mortgage insurance, were not eligible to receive HUD "emergency reserve" funds. In the 2003 amendment FEMA thus agreed to accept funding requests for permanent repairs and reconstruction necessitated by disaster damage to such other types of subsidized housing. Subsequently, federal appropriations for the HUD "emergency reserve" funds dried up. In fiscal year 2005, the reserve obtained only $29 million; in fiscal year 2008, only $18.5 million; and for fiscal year 2009 HUD requested zero. This provoked an outcry from public housing advocates, who adopted the strategy of calling for a repeal of the enabling legislation (Section 9(k)), the rationale being that FEMA would no longer have a basis for refusing to entertain PHA requests to apply for FEMA funds to be used for permanent repairs and reconstruction. Congress assented, repealing the "emergency reserve" provision in July 2008.[36]

What the latest Congressional action means with respect to PHA requests for funds to rebuild disaster-damaged housing is by no means clear. The 2008 repeal leaves open a window—some PHAs might receive FEMA funds to rebuild dwelling units, but only if the disaster is presidentially declared, and FEMA has available funds, and FEMA exercises its discretion to allocate those funds to the particular requesting PHA. This "solution," if it is one at all, is probably temporary, and what might replace it is uncertain. The present push for PHAs to emulate private-sector management decision-making suggests that Congressional appropriations for PHA disaster rebuilding are misguided. PHAs would be better off, and would have clearer instructions from the federal government, if they were simply told that they should obtain appropriate casualty insurance for all types of disasters, natural and artificial; and that they are on their own if disaster impacts their capital improvements. Such an abdication of direct federal responsibility, of course, is only fair and rational if the federal government makes it possible for PHAs in fact to pay the going rate for insurance premiums to fully insure their properties. In other words, HUD appropriations must be sufficient in funds for PHAs to purchase insurance policies from private insurers.

Katrina's Impact on Public Housing in New Orleans

The Housing Authority of New Orleans (HANO) before Katrina

The Housing Authority of New Orleans (HANO) was a troubled authority for more than a decade prior to Katrina's assault.[37] In January 2002, HUD placed HANO under federal receivership. One thing federal receivership has not accomplished for

36 Pub. L. No. 110-289, § 2804, 122 Stat 2654 (2008).

37 A "troubled public housing agency" is "an agency that fails on a widespread basis to provide acceptable basic housing conditions for its residents." 42 U.S.C. § 1437d(j)(2)(A)(i) (2000). HUD designates agencies as troubled based on the "identification

HANO is continuity of leadership. In the short time period since the receivership began, HUD has appointed five separate persons to serve as executive director of HANO, the most recent being Karen Cato-Turner, who began in October 2007.[38] Federal receivership could be organized a number of ways, but in the case of HANO, receivership has had the effect, presumably intended, of eliminating local political control of HANO. From April 2006 until May 2008, the sole member of the HANO Board of Commissioners was C. Donald Babers, a long-term deputy regional director assigned to the HUD office in Fort Worth, Texas.[39] In May 2008, HUD appointed a new Chair for the Board of Commissioners, also an outsider.[40] Ms Cato-Turner is chief of HUD's Miami, Florida office, and her two predecessors, Jeffrey Riddel and William Thorson—each of whom served less than one year as HANO executive director—were both long-time employees of HUD's Washington, D.C. office.[41]

Prior to Katrina, New Orleans public housing was undergoing drastic change. In the 1980s, HANO had an inventory of approximately 14,000 public housing units, sheltering approximately 60,000 people. In 2005, prior to Katrina, the number of public housing units in the city had fallen to 7,379, and only about 5,000 of those units were occupied. In the years prior to Katrina, HANO had experienced, or caused, what executor director William Thorson called a "fundamental breakdown in maintenance."[42]

Part of the shrinkage before Katrina was due to the HOPE VI program, which provides federal money for large construction projects.[43] HOPE VI targeted "severely distressed" housing projects, which generally consisted of high-density communities built decades ago in inner-city neighborhoods, where residents often suffered from a host of social-economic problems, including high rates of crime. The vast majority of HOPE VI grants awarded by HUD do not provide

---

of serious and substantial failure to perform as measured by … performance indicators … and such other factors as the Secretary may deem to be appropriate." *Id.*

38 Gwen Filosa, *HANO Will Pursue Rebuilding Grants: Agency Takes Heat for Housing Management*, New Orleans Times Picayune, October 18, 2007.

39 Interview with William Thorson, Executive Director, Housing Authority of New Orleans, in New Orleans, Louisiana (June 9, 2006); Donna White, Homes & Communities, U.S. Department of Housing and Urban Development, *HUD Appoints New HANO Board Chair as Major Public Housing Redevelopment Advances*, HUD News Release, May 7, 2008, http://www.hud.gov/news/release.cfm?content=pr08-063.cfm.

40 Donna White, Homes & Communities, U.S. Department of Housing and Urban Development, *New HANO Board Chair Introduced at Board Meeting*, HUD News Release, May 21, 2008, http://www.hud.gov/news/release.cfm?content=pr08-071.cfm (announcing appointment of Diane Johnson, director of HUD's field office in Newark, New Jersey).

41 Mr Thorson fulfilled his duties as executive director by commuting to New Orleans.

42 Interview with William Thorson, *supra* note 39.

43 The Affordable Housing Act of 1990 inaugurated the program, known as Homeownership Opportunities for People Everywhere (HOPE).

for the rehabilitation of existing properties. Instead, large-scale demolition of one or more housing projects takes place, resulting in a bare site where new design and construction takes place. HOPE VI plans generally reduce site density significantly, perceiving high-density as a contributor to social distress. Moreover, HOPE VI plans seek to combat the income homogeneity of the old community, which housed only public housing families, by building mixed-income residential communities. Such plans incorporate a range of public housing units, market rate dwelling units, and affordable housing units with shallower subsidies than those available for public housing units, financed by a variety of mechanisms in addition to the federal HOPE VI grant. As a consequence of these planning objectives, new HOPE VI construction almost always includes far fewer public housing units than the number destroyed. HOPE VI projects, at least in principle, seek to protect existing residents who are not rehoused in the new communities, by providing such residents with Section 8 vouchers. Thus, the HOPE VI program is designed not to lead to the immediate displacement of families from the overall affordable housing sector, but studies of several completed redevelopments indicate vouchers in fact are insufficient to satisfy the housing needs of substantial numbers of former PHA resident families.

This has served as the model for HOPE VI, followed nationally; in this respect, New Orleans is not unique. In New Orleans, an exemplar of the HOPE VI model is the redevelopment of the St Thomas housing project. Built in 1941 and demolished in 2000, St Thomas contained 1510 units on 64 acres of valuable land in the city's Lower Garden District. HANO replaced St Thomas with a new development called River Garden, which is mixed-use, with new homes occupied by residents of mixed income. The St Thomas property was a large island, not integrated with the city's street grid. River Garden opened new streets, re-establishing the street grid through the site better to integrate the new housing with the surrounding neighborhood. As of 2007, River Garden had 296 dwelling units, with only 122 earmarked as affordable with subsidies. Very few of the original public housing tenants were able to remain: approximately 100 of the former St Thomas families reoccupied these apartments.[44] The remaining units are market rate, some rental and some owner-occupied. After the city passed a request for rezoning, a new Wal-Mart Supercenter opened on the site. A number of local community leaders opposed the River Garden development. Several lawsuits filed to stop the development before it proceeded failed to realize that objective, but one resulted in a settlement, with the developer committing to set aside 125 units for HANO clients out of the 310 apartments to be built in River Garden's next phase, to be completed in 2009.[45]

---

44 Deon Roberts, *River Garden Proves Problematic for Developers*, New Orleans City Business, January 22, 2007.

45 Susan Finch, *Plan for Resettling Public Housing Residents OK'd*, New Orleans Times Picayune, July 10, 2007. Federal district judge Peter Beer called the settlement "even-handed, impartial and essentially equitable," but his opinion criticized the developer for leasing River Garden units meant for St Thomas residents to HANO management

Some of the prior St Thomas tenants were given Section 8 housing vouchers, which enabled them to seek assisted housing elsewhere (this phenomenon is what is called being "vouchered out" of public housing).

Reconstruction of New Orleans Public Housing

Katrina inflicted massive damage on New Orleans' public housing communities. Damage from flooding, rain, and wind was highly visible, but many units also became uninhabitable due to mold contamination. Ten months after Katrina's devastation, in June 2006, HANO had about 1000 dwelling units occupied.[46] Almost two years later, in May 2008, the number of families housed by HANO had risen to close to 2000.[47] Thus, the post-Katrina shrinkage in public housing units stands at more than 5300 units (7379 occupied in August 2005). In June 2006, HANO's executive director Thorson stated that finances precluded any possibility of short- or immediate-term replacement of all of the pre-Katrina units. He gave the following arithmetic: The average cost of repair or rebuilding for HANO's damaged units is $100,000 (this varies according to a number of factors, including the unit size). Multiply this cost by 7000 units; the product is $700 million. "This amount of money isn't there."[48]

Katrina had the effect of drastically accelerating the downsizing of public housing in New Orleans, a process well underway pre-Katrina as illustrated by the elimination of St Thomas and the huge numbers of unoccupied units in other properties. Despite substantial opposition from former HANO residents and housing activists, HANO decided to take down four of its largest communities. Demolition of the Saint Bernard, C.J. Peete, and B.W. Cooper communities are nearly complete, with construction of new improvements on those sites slated to begin in late 2008.[49] Demolition of the fourth property, Lafitte, has begun, with

employees at below-market rates. "The scorn and incompetence visited upon those citizens in such perilous need set a new low for federally supported agencies, whose very reason for existence was to provide decent low-income housing. … all the while playing bureaucratic games with those whose lack of education or understanding left them essentially without an avenue of relief." *Id.*

46 Interview with William Thorson, *supra* note 39.

47 White, *supra* note 40. At the same time, New Orleans had approximately 5700 families with Section 8 vouchers and 885 families using HUD's disaster voucher program. *Id.*

48 Interview with William Thorson, *supra* note 39. If HANO had obtained casualty and flood insurance on its properties, the estimated costs of repair to HANO and the government of course would have been drastically less.

49 Destruction of Saint Bernard attracted the strongest criticism. Built in the 1940s, Saint Bernard was a huge project with 963 units arranged in barracks-style architecture. The surrounding neighborhood was heavily distressed by the time of Katrina. Yet former Saint Bernard residents protested HANO's decision not to repair Saint Bernard. They organized public protests, seeking to have property fixed and reopened. Gwen Filosa,

redevelopment to take place later. Another old, large community in the Upper Ninth Ward, Desire, is being redeveloped with the new name "Abundance Square."[50]

River Garden serves as a template for the new development: mixed-income residential units, designed to reduce the scale of public housing and to deconcentrate poverty. The New Orleans City Council approved HANO's plans for radically remaking its public housing. HANO's redevelopment plans naturally reflect HUD's vision of the future of public housing; HANO in effect has operated as a federal agency—a division of HUD—since its receivership began. In a speech in New Orleans only three months after Katrina's blow, HUD Secretary Alphonso Jackson announced a promise to build $1.8 billion worth of public housing along the Gulf Coast. Jackson also emphasized that "We're not going to build traditional public housing anymore."[51]

Criticism of New Orleans' downsizing of its public housing communities became a hot topic for international news in March 2008, when a United Nations committee, the Committee on the Elimination of Racial Discrimination (CERD), admonished the United States for "the disparate impact that this natural disaster [Katrina] continues to have on low-income African American residents, many of whom continue to be displaced after more than two years after the hurricane." The committee called for the government to provide displaced residents with "adequate and affordable housing, where possible in their place of habitual residence," and to facilitate the "genuine consultation and participation of persons displaced by Hurricane Katrina in the design and implementation of all decisions affecting them."[52]

HANO's Disaster Planning

Any disaster plan worth having must include two overarching elements: protection of people and protection of property. HANO had a written evacuation plan in place when Katrina stuck, and considering the circumstances—the overall profound chaos involved in the evacuation of the greater New Orleans area—neither the plan nor its execution was terrible. The authorities insisted upon evacuation of

HANO Protest Becomes Scuffle: St. Bernard Residents Want to Come Home, New Orleans Times Picayune, April 5, 2006; Kate Moran, *Public Housing Advocates Protest St. Bernard's Closure: Marchers Demand HUD Reopen Units*, New Orleans Times Picayune, July 5, 2006. In January 2007, protesters occupied a number of Saint Bernard units, despite the lack of utilities, until law enforcement removed them. David Hammer, *Housing Agencies Sue to Remove Protesters: Group is Occupying St. Bernard Complex*, New Orleans Times Picayune, January 23, 2007; Gwen Filosa, *2 Swept from St. Bernard Complex: Police Say Activists were Living There*, New Orleans Times Picayune, February 1, 2007.

50 White, *supra* note 40.

51 Gwen Filosa, *Brick Housing Biting the Dust: New Homes Planned for Poor, HUD Says*, New Orleans Times Picayune, November 3, 2005.

52 David Hammer, *HUD Rebuked over Katrina Response: U.N. Panel Sees Race Disparity in Housing*, New Orleans Times Picayune, March 8, 2008.

the public housing units and compelled evacuation, thereby generally avoiding the problems incident to residents who decide, for a variety of reasons including fear of looting, to disobey evacuation orders. Many public housing residents ended up in the New Orleans Superdome and the Convention Center, where as displayed by the national media, they suffered along with other members of the community. However, once public housing residents are transported to emergency places designated by local and state governmental authorities, the failure of those authorities to provide adequate care and support can hardly be blamed on the housing authority.

When it came to HANO's property, protection of buildings was impossible due to the overwhelming magnitude of the disaster. Records do not indicate whether HANO lost significant personal property, including equipment, that could have been moved or protected prior to HANO employees leaving duty. Part of disaster planning should include consideration of property insurance, which HANO did not have. Whether insurance was available, prior to Katrina, at reasonable rates is unknown. HANO, a troubled agency, did not have the reputation of making prudent decisions with respect to its assets, and when federal receivership began, HUD apparently followed a policy that is common for the federal government—to "self insure" (that is, leave uninsured) its physical assets.

Pre-disaster planning, and post-disaster response and recovery, are two different things. It is not possible before a disaster to predict with any degree of precision what measures may have to be taken after a particular disaster impacts a public housing community. From the Katrina experience, we can learn a number of things. First, when the destruction is community-wide and near total, it is not possible to rebuild damaged public housing properties until other actors repair or reconstruct basic infrastructure. In June 2006, HANO's executive director observed: "The City's infrastructure is in terrible shape. HANO cannot make decisions on particular properties without working with city and other entities to determine availability of water, sewer, transportation, and other infrastructure components."[53] Second, when large numbers of public housing residents are evacuated far outside the metropolitan area, including thousands in other states, there are significant hurdles to overcome to remain in communication with those people. To maintain contact, HANO's Client Services department did significant work to locate their residents. This is made easier by use of the FEMA database, which contained much of the needed information. Client Services communicated regularly with former residents who were relocated. Many former residents expressed a desire to return to HANO public housing whenever possible, but many who were living elsewhere decided not to return to New Orleans. The nature of the public housing population made communication harder and, for many residents, stressful. A number of evacuated residents had never lived anywhere except New

53 Interview with William Thorson, *supra* note 39.

Orleans, and some had never travelled anywhere outside New Orleans before the evacuation.[54]

HANO has a waiting list for prospective tenants, and understandably gives priority to former residents who wish to return to HANO housing. Since Katrina, no potential new customers have been allowed to apply for public housing. For repaired and new housing units, HANO has focused exclusively on re-housing evacuated former residents. After that is accomplished, HANO will give priority to applicants placed on the waiting list before Katrina hit. It is not clear when HANO will begin to accept new residents.[55]

Housing Evacuees Outside the Disaster Area

One of the most significant problems stemming from Katrina was the need to arrange temporary housing for hundreds of thousands of evacuees who left the Gulf Coast. The efforts spearheaded by FEMA received most of the media attention, not only due to their large scale, but also due to the inappropriateness and fiscal irresponsibility of long-term rentals of hotel rooms and the environmental flaws of the now infamous FEMA trailers. Public housing also played a role, but not a major role, in providing housing for persons who were displaced by Katrina and the other major hurricanes of 2005. The role was limited because of the nature of what public housing does. PHAs usually own and manage units for long-term occupancy, not emergency shelters or other dwelling units that are earmarked for short-term needs, such as a homeless shelter.

The experience of the Athens (Georgia) Housing Authority is representative of the efforts of many PHAs located outside of, but not extremely distant from, the Katrina disaster area. The Athens Housing Authority does not have any units that are designated for short-term occupancy. The Board of Commissioners took action to modify the Authority's waiting list rules to give preference to Katrina-displaced persons. The preference lasted for a period of almost six months, from September 6, 2005 to February 28, 2006, putting Katrina victims at the top of the waiting list. This decision (as is true for every waiting-list preference rule) had the disadvantage of extending the wait times for local residents who applied for housing with the Authority earlier. The justification was that Katrina evacuees generally had a greater need in the sense that their present housing situation was less stable or suitable than the typical local applicant on the waiting list. The Athens Housing Authority, which has a stock of 1255 dwelling units, housed a total of 37 families

---

54 *Id.*

55 As of June 2008, HANO's public housing waiting list consisted of 6572 families. HANO, Annual Plan for Fiscal Year Beginning 10/2008, at 6 (Draft), http://www.hano.org/Documents/ (last visited June 18, 2008). The Annual Plan does not indicate how many of these families were formerly housed by HANO and how many were pre-Katrina applicants. The Section 8 waiting list has 10,873 families. *Id.* at 7. For both lists the Plan states: "Updates will be provided once the pre-Katrina waiting list is purged." *Id.* at 6, 7.

(a total of 66 persons) from Hurricanes Katrina and Rita over the six-month time period. As of the end of 2006, more than one-half of those families chose to leave their new homes, at least some of them returning to the Gulf Coast.

Even though the measures taken by the Athens Housing Authority were relatively modest and short-term, HUD involvement was necessary. Federal law allows PHAs to develop and implement preferences for waiting lists, and thus HUD approval was not necessary to give preference to hurricane evacuees. HUD, however, requires mandatory screening procedures for all families admitted to public housing to ascertain facts such as social security numbers, family income, employer identification numbers, immigration or residency status, prior history of residing in assisted housing, and criminal background checks. A PHA's verification of such matters, which necessarily involves contacting a number of third parties, can often take weeks. For Katrina evacuees, speedy verification was especially difficult because many of the third parties were located in the disaster area, subject to its chaos, and could not readily respond to information requests. HUD responded to the crisis in stages, first notifying PHAs on September 2 that HUD had relaxed the admissions requirements for existing public housing residents and Section 8 voucher recipients, but not for other displaced persons. On September 27, 2005, HUD issued a notice providing for the issuance of Regulatory and Administrative Waivers for all displaced persons who, based on their income, qualified for public housing. The waivers were not automatically granted, on a blanket basis. The Athens Housing Authority applied for the waivers by email, which HUD quickly approved. The HUD waivers enabled the Authority to house Katrina families immediately, before it was possible to complete normal verifications. The interagency cooperation between HUD and local PHAs led to a positive outcome, and demonstrates that it is sometimes possible to make appropriate decisions in a reasonable timeframe after a disaster strikes, notwithstanding the involvement of a massive federal bureaucracy. A cautionary note, however, is appropriate for two reasons. First, a short-term suspension of the verification of resident credentials is a minor issue, and the need for federal approval in advance is questionable. Second, Katrina came ashore on August 29, and HUD's issuance of the notice almost one full month later, on September 27, does not represent prompt action under the circumstances.

The Present State of Public Housing Disaster Planning

Reasons Why PHAs Should Engage in Disaster Planning

Federal law does not require that PHAs adopt pre-disaster plans, and at the present time few PHAs have detailed disaster plans. Nevertheless, they should do so for several reasons. First, the nature of the typical PHA resident population makes disaster planning advisable. Most, if not all, PHAs house significant numbers of persons with special needs, including elderly residents. This makes long-term planning particularly critical, especially with respect to disaster risk, but also with respect to other risks associated with the disruption of normal services to dwelling units (for example, the interruption of electric power to a unit will often be only an inconvenience for healthy residents, but for a person who relies on medical equipment, such as equipment supplying continuous oxygen to manage lung disease, a lengthy power interruption poses significant risk).

Second, public housing properties are substantial assets, which should be protected from loss and damage. In the planning process, there should be consideration for the protection of physical assets from damage from storms and other perils. Advance preparation is essential, especially if the properties are located in communities where evacuation is a foreseeable risk. If a PHA must evacuate residents due to a community-wide peril, many of the PHA employees who facilitate evacuation are likely to evacuate their own homes as soon as possible. Thus, consideration of how to protect equipment and structures has to be accomplished before the crisis hits.

A third possible reason why PHAs may desire to adopt disaster plans is the risk of legal liability. There are no reported cases in which plaintiffs have asserted tort claims against PHAs for the failure to protect persons or property from the consequences of natural disaster, but there is no reason to conclude that such claims are highly implausible.[56] In many states, the shield of sovereign immunity does not shelter PHAs from negligence claims brought by residents or other persons who suffer an injury due to a PHA's conduct. Thus, the risk of tort liability for the failure to have a disaster plan may motivate plan adoption. In any disaster-related lawsuit against a PHA, the authority's adoption of a reasonable disaster plan, coupled hopefully with the PHA's good faith attempt to implement the plan, should go a long way toward a judicial resolution in favor of the authority.

Contents of a Disaster Plan

How should PHA disaster planning be accomplished? It is important to recognize that PHAs are highly diverse, not only with respect to their different geographical settings but also in terms of size of operation and the demographics of their resident population. A housing authority in south Florida obviously need not concern itself with how to respond to a snow and ice blizzard, just as a Montana authority will not spend time on a hurricane evacuation plan.

The contents of a disaster plan for a PHA could vary widely. The main points to address are resident safety and property protection. With respect to resident safety, a system for notifying residents of emergencies or possible emergencies is of critical importance. An evacuation plan when the vacation of homes is necessary

56 *See* Denis Binder, *Emergency Action Plans: A Legal and Practical Blueprint "Failing To Plan Is Planning To Fail"*, 63 U. Pitt. L. Rev. 791 (2002) (contending that a general standard of reasonable care should apply to (1) the absence of an emergency action plan, (2) the inadequacy of the plan, and (3) failure to follow the plan).

is also an essential component. Some PHAs should have a large-scale evacuation plan that covers the PHA's entire inventory of dwelling units, but such an element is not always needed. Depending upon the risks that are foreseeable in the local community, a smaller scale evacuation plan may be all that is necessary.

It is also important to realize that a large part of pre-disaster planning involves the coordination of efforts among various entities. The different levels of government have different responsibilities, and a disaster plan cannot envision that PHA employees will do everything if and when a disaster hits. In planning for a disaster, a PHA must coordinate with city and state planners, and during a disaster many necessary measures will be taken by other actors. For example, in evacuation settings, if buses are to transport PHA residents outside of the metropolitan area to safe locations, it will seldom make sense for the PHA to hire its own buses or vans. Rather, it is far more likely that the PHA's role will be to assist its residents to access transportation provided by the city or a larger entity that has evacuation responsibilities.

HUD Initiatives for Disaster Planning by PHAs

Federal law has never required, and does not presently require, PHAs to have written disaster plans of any kind.[57] Conceivably, HUD has the authority to enact a regulation requiring PHAs to adopt disaster plans, even though there is no express statutory authorization for such a requirement. In August 2006, HUD conducted what it entitled an "Emergency Preparedness Plan Survey," asking all PHAs to submit information as to their plans. The public notice for the survey, sent to the Office of Management and Budget for approval, described the purpose thus:

> The Emergency Preparedness Plan Survey will be used by HUD to determine the degree of readiness for public housing agencies (PHAs) and Tribe/Tribally Designated Housing Entities (TDHEs) in the case of a natural disaster. HUD will provide pertinent information and technical assistance to establish viable and executable Emergency Preparedness Plans to PHAs and Tribes/TDHEs.[58]

On July 21, 2006, HUD sent the survey instrument to the PHAs, with the letter of transmittal explaining:

---

57 HUD, like other federal agencies, engages in its own disaster planning, which is designed in part to allow HUD to continue to operate despite the impact of a severe disaster. HUD also has disaster policies that affect its programs other than public housing. For example, HUD offers advice for operators of multi-family housing in the event of a presidentially declared disaster, and requires the submission of reports to HUD when multi-family housing insured or assisted by HUD incurs disaster damage. *See* Multifamily Housing Guidance for Disaster Recovery, http://www.hud.gov/offices/hsg/mfh/disasterguide.cfm (last visited February 11, 2009).

58 71 Fed. Reg. 32997 (June 7, 2006).

> The purpose of this survey is to determine your baseline level of preparedness in case of any type of an emergency. Information derived from the survey will enable the Department to provide pertinent information and technical assistance to PHAs so you may establish viable and executable Emergency Preparedness Plans. Improved Emergency Preparedness Plans will help ensure that PHAs are adequately prepared for an emergency situation and will facilitate the efficient and effective evacuation of residents, thereby reducing additional costs to disaster impacted locations.[59]

HUD never published the results of its 2006 survey, but it addressed the topic in its Annual Performance Plan for 2008, which, as a goal under the topic heading "Promote Decent Affordable Housing," stated:

> B2.12: Ensure 10 percent of PHAs have realistic emergency preparedness plans in place.
>
> *Background and context.* As demonstrated during the 2005 hurricane season, it is imperative that public housing agencies have viable emergency preparedness plans. The Department learned that, while reviewing the shortcomings in reaction to these disasters, many communities lacked any comprehensive plan to deal with the evacuation of a large number of families. An adequate plan should address continuity of operations as well as how the housing authority will handle both evacuees from their area or the receipt of evacuees from other disaster impacted areas. These emergency preparedness plans will support HUD's strategic goal of strengthening communities through the goal of assisting in disaster recovery in the Gulf Coast region.
>
> During FY 2007, HUD appointed six regional disaster coordinators who will survey their regions to determine whether their respective PHAs have emergency preparedness plans, as well as to serve as technical advisors to help the PHAs develop or improve such plans. During FY 2008, 10 percent of the PHAs will have realistic emergency preparedness plans.
>
> *Data Source.* HUD's disaster coordinators will survey their regions to determine which PHAs have a plan and assist those that do not in developing a comprehensive plan. The disaster coordinators will forward the status of all PHAs in their region to the Housing Choice Voucher Operations and Management division for APP reporting. PHA plans will be collected and reviewed in each of the six regions by the appropriate disaster coordinator.

59 Office of Public Housing, *News-to-Use* (July 2006), *available at* http://www.fhasecure.gov/local/shared/working/r8/ph/newsletters0706.pdf.

> *Limitation/advantages of the data.* Because HUD has neither mandated the requirement for PHA disaster plans nor established a template of required data, the plans may vary by PHA.
>
> *Validation and verification.* The review of the PHA plans by the disaster coordinator will verify whether an acceptable plan exists.[60]

One infers from the "Data Source" field of Goal B2.12 that the response rate by PHAs to the 2006 survey was disappointingly low; therefore, HUD's disaster coordinators were instructed to survey PHAs in their individual regions to determine which ones had disaster plans.

Goal B2.12 may have had some merits as a step in the right direction toward PHA disaster planning, but we will never know. In the Annual Performance Plan for 2009, released only months later in February 2008, HUD announced an abandonment of the target of "realistic emergency preparedness plans" for at least 10 percent of the PHAs. HUD's explanation was that this was part of an overall strategy of providing less detail for its annual plan: "This indicator [the percentage of PHAs with emergency preparedness plans] will no longer be reported in the FY 2008 APP. The Department streamlined the content of the report to emphasize departmental indicators that will best capture the significant efforts and results for each major program area."[61]

In summary, HUD has made efforts to survey PHAs to ascertain the extent to which they have engaged in disaster planning and to attempt to assess their degree of emergency preparedness, but these initiatives have apparently ground to a halt. HUD could draft templates for written disaster plans, or provide other technical assistance to PHAs who desire outside assistance, but this has not happened. Despite the planning failures evinced by Katrina, HUD has made no serious effort to address disaster preparedness at a national level.

Challenges for PHAs that Want to Engage in Pre-Disaster Planning

The recent developments in public housing described above in "The Legal Framework for Public Housing Authorities" have implications for disaster planning. They represent constraints. At the present time and for the foreseeable future, PHAs operate in a climate of reduced federal funding and limited financial resources. Federal policy, epitomized by the Harvard Cost Study, pushes PHAs to behave like private-sector landlords. When PHAs contemplate the risk of a disaster, what can they do? PHA decision-makers realize that their neighborhoods may be severely impacted by a disaster. Yet meaningful disaster planning

---

60 U.S. Department of Housing and Urban Development, *Annual Performance Plan Fiscal Year 2008*, at 121–2 (September 2007).

61 U.S. Department of Housing and Urban Development, *Annual Performance Plan Fiscal Year 2009*, at 119 (February 2008).

consumes resources, and the modern thrust of public housing reform is to compel or induce PHAs to behave the same as actors in the private-sector rental market. Presently the vast majority of private providers of housing do not prepare plans on how to assist their residents in an emergency, whether the emergency necessitates resident evacuation or other measures. Typically, the only "disaster plan" a private apartment complex has consists of: "In Case of Fire, Do Not Use Elevator." The dearth of private-sector disaster planning means that the PHAs can only afford disaster planning if they obtain new funding or divert funds from other activities, such as normal maintenance, capital repairs, or resident services. Is a good disaster plan worth more than replacing a roof that will leak soon or painting dwelling units to make them suitable for occupancy?

The reform movement sends a strong message. There should be synchronization between what the public sector and the private sector provide when it comes to disaster planning and other key areas that bear on housing quality. PHAs should not provide services that the private sector does not. A level playing field between the sectors is appropriate. If private providers of housing do not prepare plans on how to assist their residents in evacuation in an emergency, then PHAs will not have the resources to do so.

Whether this situation is appropriate depends upon how one views the mission of public housing. Presently, many public housing residents have special needs. Many are elderly. Many do not own cars; or the cars they own are often old and unreliable; and they may not have the same financial resources to use to survive a disaster, as do many families who own homes or rent in the private sector. Some public housing residents are less independently sufficient than private-sector residents in that they rely on public housing staff for maintenance and other services to an extent seldom seen in the typical private-sector housing development.

Public housing residents tend to differ from private-sector tenants in another important respect—duration of tenure. In many public housing communities, residents remain in public housing for longer periods, on average, than private-sector tenants. This is probably due, at least partially, to the difficulty of obtaining public housing. In many communities, there are long waiting lists for applicants. Departing from public housing, when the family is still income-eligible to occupy the dwelling unit, represents the relinquishment of a valuable asset, which will not be easy to reacquire, either from the same PHA or in a different community served by another PHA. Moreover, the relative immobility of the PHA population also contributes to longer tenure. It is physically harder for the many PHA residents who are elderly or disabled to navigate the steps required to relocate a household.

Should the Government Mandate PHA Disaster Planning?

Might the recent HUD initiatives with respect to PHA disaster planning (the 2006 Survey of disaster plans and the 2008 10 percent goal, since withdrawn) be a precursor to a federal mandate requiring that PHAs develop disaster plans? Should the federal government (Congress by statute, or HUD by regulation) mandate such planning? Or should this be left to the discretion of each PHA (its board of commissioners)? A federal mandate would raise significant problems. There is tremendous diversity among PHAs in terms of size, types of properties, and disaster risk profiles. There are approximated to be 1.3 million dwelling units in the United States managed by over 3300 PHAs. For a disaster plan to be meaningful, it must be tailored to the particular circumstances of each PHA, taking into account many factors, including the nature of its resident population, the condition and situation of its properties, and the nature of potential disasters in the particular region of the country and community. Thus, a useful disaster plan cannot be an "off the shelf" document, which is downloaded and enacted by a resolution of the PHA board of commissioners. Significant attention must be paid to the matter, and for many PHAs a consultant may be necessary or helpful.

If disaster planning by PHAs will have a real price tag, a key question—which comes up for so many modern issues of public policy—emerges: Who will pay for the task of public planning? In recent years, state and local governments have sometimes deflected the imposition of new federal requirements using the mantra of "unfunded federal mandates." Heretofore that defensive strategy has had little or no vigor in forestalling new federal requirements for PHAs, and so a federal disaster planning mandate, with no provision for federal reimbursement of the cost, would not be surprising. However, it would be highly inadvisable from a policy standpoint. A federal mandate that PHAs do more to protect their residents and properties from disaster risk runs directly contrary to the general thrust of modern federal policy—to move public housing to a private-sector model with respect to management and costs.

Conclusion: Is Public Housing Still "Social Housing"?

The issues concerning whether PHAs should engage in disaster planning, although important, are narrow. In seeking answers to the key questions (for example, which PHAs should have disaster plans? What should be the content of disaster plans? What role should HUD play? Should there be a federal mandate and federal funding for plans?), it is useful to ask ourselves more fundamental questions about the purpose of public housing. The core question, stated with the highest degree of generality, is whether public housing is still "social housing." The answer implicit in most recent federal reforms is "no"—public housing should operate on a private-sector model, with the only significant difference between public and private-sector housing providers being that the residents of public housing are low-income people who require rent subsidization. This approach ignores the fact that public housing residents often have special needs, which PHAs traditionally have sought to serve by a number of mechanisms, including the direct provision of social services.

The ascending private-sector model, which is being applied to public housing, has these implications for disaster planning. PHAs are pushed to ask an empirical question: Do the private-sector housing providers in their community have disaster preparedness plans? If not, then why not? The private-sector model implies that PHAs should not undertake to develop a disaster plan, but should the PHA have such a plan nonetheless? In most U.S. communities, the private sector norm, when it comes to natural disasters, is "Every man for himself." In other words, residential landlords, no matter how large their communities or sophisticated their management operations, do not have plans. Rather, they assume that their residents will take care of themselves, and if they are to have assistance, it will come from the government (local, state, or federal), not from the landlord. This norm seems unlikely to change anytime soon. Even post-Katrina, no one argues that private landlords (or mortgage lenders) should have primary responsibility for their residents' well-being if confronted by natural disaster.

There is, however, another private-sector housing market to consider. Assisted-living communities (including nursing homes) are privately owned, but they are special cases, in which management usually undertakes a significant role in protecting or evacuating residents when disaster strikes. Should PHAs engage in disaster planning and emergency preparedness because assisted-living communities do so? Even though many PHA residents are elderly or have limitations in their ability to care for themselves, public housing serves a general population. Very few PHAs operate assisted-living communities, and thus the appropriate analogy for disaster plans is not assisted-living private communities.

Neither analogy—general private residential communities or assisted-living communities—comes close enough to the typical PHA community to offer useful guidance with respect to the proper nature and type of planning. Public housing has embraced the mission to serve as the housing of last resort for underprivileged populations, supported by a web of PHA-provided social services. It carries a broader safety net than private, non-assisted communities, and that safety net should not evaporate when natural disaster threatens the community. Responsible PHA management should include the preparation of disaster plans addressed to reasonably foreseeable risks, with sufficient resources devoted to the enterprise to ensure that the plan is more than a plan "on paper." In other words, training must be sufficient so that PHA staff, with the help of other community resources, will be able to implement the adopted plan should disaster strike.

Acknowledgements

I have served as a member of the Board of Commissioners of the Athens (Georgia) Housing Authority since 2003, and several of my observations are based on that service. The views expressed in this chapter are mine alone, and do not reflect positions or policies of the Authority. For many helpful comments on an earlier draft of this chapter, I thank Professor Nestor Davidson and Mr Richard Parker, executive director of the Athens Housing Authority.

Table of Cases

Almota Farmers Elevator & Warehouse, Inc. v. United States, 409 U.S. 470 (1972).
Berman v. Parker, 348 U.S. 26 (1954).
City of Norwood v. Horney, 830 N.E.2d 381, 383-85 (Ohio Ct. App. 2005).
Coalition for the Homeless v. Jensen, 187 A.D.2d 582 (N.Y. App. Div. 1992).
Collier v. Menzel, 221 Cal. Rptr. 110 (Ct. App. 1985).
Detroit v. Whalings, Inc., 202 N.W.2d 816 (Mich.1972).
Eubank v. City of Richmond, 226 U.S. 137, 143-45 (1912).
Euclid v. Ambler Realty Co., 272 U.S. 365, 391 (1926).
Fischer v. Stout, 741 P.2d 217 (Alaska 1987).
Harco Drug Inc. v. Notsla, Inc., 382 So.2d 1 (Ala.1980).
Home Builders Ass'n of Northern California v. City of Napa, 108 Cal. Rptr. 2d 60 (Ct. App. 2001).
Home Builders Association of Northern California v. City of Napa, 90 Cal. App. 4th 188 (1st Dist. 2001), *cert. denied*, 535 U.S. 954 (March 25, 2002).
Kelo v. City of New London, Conn. et al., 125 S. Ct. 2655, 2665 (2005).
Kelo v. City of New London, 545 U.S. 469 (2005).
Lindsey v. Normet, 405 U.S. 56 (1972).
Mejia v. Department of Housing and Urban Development, 688 F.2d 529 (7th Cir. 1982).
Mitchell v. U.S., 267 U.S. 341 (1925).
Monongahela Navigation Company v. United States, 148 U.S. 312 (1893).
Penn. Cent. Transp. Co. v. City of New York, 366 N.E. 2d 1271, 1275-1276 (1977), *affirmed on other grounds*, 438 U.S. 104 (1978).
Schneider v. District of Columbia, 117 F. Supp. 705 (D.D.C.1953).
Semayne's Case (1604) 5 Co Rep 91a at 91b, 77 ER 194 at 195.
State v. Hutchinson, 624 P. 2d 1116, 1121 (Utah 1980).
United States v. 0.28 Acres of Land, 347 F.Supp.2d 273 (W.D.Va.2004).
Utah Housing Finance Agency v. Smart, 561 P.2d 1052 (1977).

Bibliography

Abromowitz, David M., *An Essay on Community Land Trusts: Toward Permanently Affordable Housing*, *in* PROPERTY AND VALUES: ALTERNATIVES TO PUBLIC AND PRIVATE OWNERSHIP 213 (Charles Geisler & Gail Daneker eds., 2000).

Abromowitz, David M., *Community Land Trusts and Ground Leases,* 1 J. OF AFFORDABLE HOUSING & COMMUNITY DEVELOPMENT LAW 2 (1992).

ADAMS, JAMES TRUSTOW, THE EPIC OF AMERICA (1931).

Adler, George, *Community Action and Maximum Feasible Participation: An Opportunity Lost but Not Forgotten for Expanding Democracy at Home*, 8 NOTRE DAME J.L. ETHICS & PUB. POL'Y 547 (1994).

THE AFFORDABLE CITY: TOWARD A THIRD SECTOR HOUSING POLICY (JOHN EMMEUS DAVIS ED., 1994).

Affordable Housing Needs: A Report to Congress on the Significant Need for Housing, 2005 UNITED STATES DEPARTMENT OF HOUSING AND URBAN DEVELOPMENT, OFFICE OF POLICY DEVELOPMENT AND RESEARCH 14.

Affordable Housing Needs 2005: Report to Congress, 2007 U.S. DEPARTMENT OF HOUSING AND URBAN DEVELOPMENT, OFFICE OF POLICY DEVELOPMENT AND RESEARCH 23.

Affordable Housing Needs: A Report to Congress on the Significant Need for Housing, 2007 UNITED STATES DEPARTMENT OF HOUSING AND URBAN DEVELOPMENT, OFFICE OF POLICY DEVELOPMENT AND RESEARCH 14.

Alexandre, Michele, *"Love Don't Live Here Anymore": Economic Incentive for a More Equitable Model of Urban Redevelopment*, 3 B.C. ENVTL. AFF. L. REV. 1 (2008).

Alpert, Norman, *Property Tax Abatement: An Incentive for Low Income Housing*, 11 HARV. J. ON LEGIS. 1 (1973).

Altman, Irwin, Taylor, Dalmas A. & Wheeler, Ladd, *Ecological Aspects of Group Behaviour in Social Isolation*, 1 JOURNAL OF APPLIED SOCIAL PSYCHOLOGY 76 (1971).

Altman, Irwin & Werner, Carol M., *Introduction* to HOME ENVIRONMENTS, at Preface (Irwin Altman & Carol M. Werner eds., 1985).

American Housing Survey 2005, Square Footage by Household and Unit Size, Income, and Costs – Owner Occupied Units, 2005 U.S. CENSUS BUREAU tbl.3-18, http://www.census.gov/hhes/www/housing/ahs/ahs05/tab3-18.pdf.

Anderson, Scott, *Building Partnerships for a Better Tomorrow*, 3(5) THE CAMPAIGN FOR AFFORDABLE HOUSING NEWSLETTER (The Campaign for Affordable Housing, Los Angeles, CA), September 10, 2007.

Andrews, Edmund L., *Vast Bailout Plan is Proposed in Bid to Stem Economic Crisis*, N.Y. Times, September 19, 2008, at A1.

Augusta, Brian, Comment, *Building Housing from the Ground Up: Strengthening California Law to Ensure Adequate Locations for Affordable Housing*, 39 Santa Clara L. Rev. 503 (1999).

Axel-Lute, Miriam, *A Meeting of Movements*, 103 Shelterforce Magazine, January/February 1999.

Azmy, Baher & Reiss, David, *Modeling a Response to Predatory Lending: The New Jersey Home Ownership Security Act of 2002*, 35 Rutgers L.J. 645 (2004).

Bachelard, Gaston, The Poetics of Space (1964).

Balfour, Danny & Smith, Janet, *Transforming Lease-Purchase Housing Programs for Low-Income Families: Towards Empowerment and Engagement*, 18 J. of Urban Affairs 173 (1996).

Ballard, Megan J., *Legal Protections for Home Dwellers: Caulking the Cracks to Preserve Occupancy*, 56 Syracuse L. Rev. 277 (2006).

Baron, Jane, *Homelessness as a Property Problem*, 36 Urb. Law. 273 (2004).

Barros, D. Benjamin, *Home as a Legal Concept*, 46 Santa Clara L. Rev. 255 (2006).

Basolo, Victoria, *Explaining the Support for Homeownership Policy in US Cities: A Political Economy Perspective*, 22 Housing Studies 99 (2007).

BBC, *"Savers Return" to Northern Rock*, BBC News, September 18, 2007, *available at* http://news.bbc.co.uk/1/hi/business/7000035.stm.

Beerman, Nick, *Comment: Legal Mechanisms of Public-Private Partnerships: Promoting Economic Development or Benefiting Corporate Welfare*, 23 Seattle U. L. Rev. 175 (1999).

Bell, Carol A., *Workforce Housing: The New Economic Imperative?*, 4(2) Fannie Mae Housing Facts & Findings, *available at* http://www.fanniemaefoundation.org/programs/hff/v4i2-workforce.shtml.

Bengtsson, Bo, *Housing as a Social Right: Implications for Welfare State Theory*, 24(4) Scandinavian Political Studies 255 (2001).

Bennett, Susan D., *Little Engines that Could: Community Clients, Their Lawyers, and Training in the Arts of Democracy*, 2002 Wis. L. Rev. 469.

Bennett, Susan D., *"The Possibility of a Beloved Place": Residents and Placemaking in Public Housing Communities*, 19 St. Louis U. Pub L. Rev. 259 (2000).

Berger, Peter L. & Neuhaus, Richard John, *Neighborhood*, *in* To Empower People: From State to Civil Society 165 (Michael Novak ed., 2d ed., 1996).

Bernanke, Ben S., Chairman of the Federal Reserve System, Speech at the Women in Housing and Finance and Exchequer Club Joint Luncheon (January 10, 2008), *available at* http://www. federalreserve.gov/newsevents/speech/bernanke20080110a.htm.

Bernstein, Edward A., *Law & Economics and the Structure of Value Adding Contracts: A Contract Lawyer's View of the Law & Economics Literature*, 74 OR. L. REV. 189 (1995).

Bernstine, Nancy & Saraf, Irene Basloe, *New Rental Production and the National Housing Trust Fund Campaign*, 12 J. OF AFFORDABLE HOUSING AND COMMUNITY DEVELOPMENT LAW 389 (2003).

Bezdek, Barbara L., *To Attain "The Just Rewards of So Much Struggle": Local-Resident Equity Participation in Urban Revitalization*, 36 HOFSTRA L. REV. 37 (2006).

BIDs Fare Well, 78 N.Y.U. L. REV. 374 (2003).

Binder, Denis, *Emergency Action Plans: A Legal and Practical Blueprint "Failing To Plan Is Planning To Fail"*, 63 U. PITT. L. REV. 791 (2002).

Bishaw, Alemayehu & Semega, Jessica, *Income, Earnings, and Poverty Data from the 2007 American Community Survey* 3, U.S. CENSUS BUREAU (August 2008).

Blais, Lynn E., *Urban Revitalization in the Post-Kelo Era*, 34 FORDHAM URB. L.J. 657 (2007).

BLAKELY, EDWARD J., PLANNING LOCAL ECONOMIC DEVELOPMENT: THEORY AND PRACTICE (2d ed. 1994).

BLAKELY, EDWARD J. & SNYDER, MARY GAIL, FORTRESS AMERICA: GATED COMMUNITIES IN THE UNITED STATES (1997).

Block, Fred, *Reframing the Political Battle: Market Fundamentalism vs. Moral Economy*, http://www.longviewinstitute.org/projects/moral/sorcerersapprentice (last visited January 12, 2008).

Bocian, Debbie Gruenstein, Ernst, Keith S. & Li, Wei, *Unfair Lending: The Effect of Race and Ethnicity on the Price of Sub-Prime Mortgages*, CENTER FOR RESPONSIBLE LENDING PUBLICATION (2006), *available at* http://www.responsiblelending.org/pdfs/rr011-Unfair_Lending-0506.pdf.

Bosselman, Fred, *Four Land Ethics: Order, Reform, Responsibility, Opportunity*, 24 ENVTL. L. 1439 (1994).

Boston, Thomas D., *The Effects of Revitalization on Public Housing Residents: A Case Study of the Atlanta Housing Authority*, 71 J. AM. PLANNING ASS'N 393 (2005).

Boyd, Melody L., *The Role of Social Networks in Making Housing Choices: The Experience of the Gautreaux Two Residential Mobility Program*, 10 CITYSCAPE 41 (2008).

Brandon, Mark E., *Home on the Range: Family and Constitutionalism in American Continental Settlement*, 52 EMORY L. J. 645 (2003).

Bratt, Rachel G., *Nonprofit Developers and Managers: The Evolution of their Role in U.S. Housing Policy*, *in* SHELTER AND SOCIETY: THEORY, RESEARCH, AND POLICY FOR NONPROFIT HOUSING (C. Theodore Koebel ed., 1998).

Bratt, Rachel G., *A Withering Commitment*, SHELTERFORCE MAGAZINE, July/August 1997.

Bratt, Rachel G., *CDCs: Contributions Outweigh Contradictions, a Reply to Randy Stoecker*, 19 J. URBAN AFF. 23, 23–8 (1997).

Briffault, Richard, *A Government for Our Time? Business Improvement Districts and Urban Governances*, 99 COLUM. L. REV. 365, (1999).

Briggs, Xavier de Souza, Ferryman, Kadija S., Popkin, Susan J. & Rendón, Maria, *Why Did the Moving to Opportunity Experiment Not Get Young People into Better Schools?*, 19 HOUSING POL'Y DEBATE 53 (2008).

Briggs, Xavier de Souza & Turner, Margery Austin, *Assisted Housing Mobility and the Success of Low-Income Minority Families: Lessons for Policy, Practice, and Future Research*, 1 NW. J.L. & SOC. POL'Y 25 (2006).

Briggs, Xavier de Souza, *Brown Kids in White Suburbs: Housing Mobility and the Many Faces of Social Capital*, 9 HOUSING POL'Y DEBATE 177 (1998).

BRIGHT, ELISE M., REVIVING AMERICA'S FORGOTTEN NEIGHBORHOODS: AN INVESTIGATION OF INNER CITY REVITALIZATION EFFORTS (2000).

Brion, Denis J., *The Meaning of the City: Urban Redevelopment and the Loss of Community*, 25 IND. L. REV. 685, 702 (1992).

Brochure from Smithsonian Anacostia Community Museum, East of the River: Continuity and Change, at East of the River Transformed (2007).

Broden, Thomas, Note, *Co-operatives – A Privileged Restraint of Trade*, 23 NOTRE DAME L. REV. 110 (1947).

Brooks, Mary, Director of the Housing Trust Fund Project, Centre for Community Change, http://www.communitychange.org/housing-trust-funds/ (last visited June 9, 2008).

Brooks, Rich & Ford, Constance Mitchell, *The United States of Subprime; Data Show Bad Loans Permeate the Nation; Pain Could Last Years*, WALL ST. J., October 11, 2007, at A1.

Brower, Sidney N., *Territory in Urban Settings*, *in* ENVIRONMENT AND CULTURE (Irwin Altman, Amos Rapoport & Joachim F. Wohlwill eds., 1980).

Brown, Barbara B. & Perkins, Douglas D., *Disruptions in Place Attachment*, *in* PLACE ATTACHMENTS (Irwin Altman & Sebba M. Low eds., 1992).

Budget of the United States Government, Fiscal Year 2009, Historical Tables, Table 1.3 – Summary of Receipts, Outlays, and Surpluses or Deficits in Current Dollars, Constant (FY 2000) Dollars, and as Percentages of GDP: 1940–2013, http://www.gpoaccess.gov/usbudget/fy09/hist.html (last visited November 11, 2008).

Budget of the United States Government, Fiscal Year 2009, Historical Tables, Table 5.2 – Budget Authority by Agency: 1976–2013, http://www.gpoaccess.gov/usbudget/fy09/hist.html (last visited November 11, 2008).

Budget of the United States Government, Fiscal Year 2009, Historical Tables, Table 5.3 – Percentage Distribution of Budget Authority by Agency: 1976–2013, http://www.gpoaccess.gov/usbudget/fy09/hist.html (last visited November 11, 2008).

Bulos, Marjorie & Chaker, Waheed, *Sustaining a Sense of Home and Personal Identity*, *in* THE HOME: WORDS, INTERPRETATIONS, MEANINGS AND ENVIRONMENTS (David Benjamin ed., 1995).

Bunce, Harold L., Gruenstein, Debbie, Herbert, Christopher E. & Scheessele, Randall M., *Subprime Foreclosures: The Smoking Gun of Predatory Lending?*, HOUSING POLICY IN THE NEW MILLENIUM: PROCEEDINGS (Susan M. Wachter and R. Leo Penne eds., 2005).

BURON, LARRY, LEVY, DIANE K. & GALLAGHER, MEGAN, URB. INST., HOUSING CHOICE VOUCHERS: HOW HOPE VI FAMILIES FARED IN THE PRIVATE MARKET (2007).

BURROWS, ROGER & WILCOX, STEVE, HALF THE POOR: HOME OWNERS WITH LOW INCOMES (2000).

Byrne, Gregory A., Day, Kevin & Stockard, James, *Taking Stock of Public Housing* (September 16, 2003) (unpublished study presented to the Public Housing Authority Directors Association, *available at* http://www.gsd.harvard.edu/research/research_centers/phocs/study_results.html (last visited May 13, 2009)).

Byrne, J. Peter & Diamond, Michael, *Affordable Housing, Land Tenure, and Urban Policy: The Matrix Revealed*, 34 FORDHAM URB. L.J. 527 (2007).

Byrne, J. Peter, *Condemnation of Low Income Residential Communities under the Takings Clause*, 23 UCLA J. ENVTL. L. & POL'Y 131 (2005).

Byrne, J. Peter, *Two Cheers for Gentrification*, 46 HOW. L.J. 405 (2003).

Calabresi, Guido & Melamed, A. Douglas, *Property Rules, Liability Rules, and Inalienability: One View of the Cathedral*, 85 HARV. L. REV. 1089 (1972).

Calavita, Nico, Grimes, Kenneth & Mallach, Allan, *Inclusionary Housing in California and New Jersey: A Comparative Analysis*, 8 HOUSING POL'Y DEBATE 109 (1997).

Camacho, Alejandro E., *Mustering the Missing Voices: A Collaborative Model for Fostering Equality, Community Involvement and Adaptive Planning in Land Use Decisions, Installment Two*, 24 STAN. ENVTL. L.J. 269 (2005).

Camerer, Colin, *Individual Decision Making*, *in* THE HANDBOOK OF EXPERIMENTAL ECONOMICS (J.H. Kagel & A.E. Roth eds., 1995).

THE CANDIDATE (Warner Bros. 1972).

Cannarsa, Andrew, *Study Criticizes City's Redevelopment, Says Practices have Created "Two Cities"*, THE EXAMINER, June 24, 2008, *available at* http://www.examiner.com/a-1455745~Study_criticizes_city_s_redevelopment__says_practices_have_created__two_cities_.html (last visited November 7, 2008).

Capozza, Dennis R., Kazarian, Dick & Thomson, Thomas A., *Mortgage Default in Local Markets*, 25 REAL ESTATE ECONOMICS 631 (1997).

Carliner, Michael S., *Development of Federal Homeownership "Policy"*, 9(2) HOUSING POLICY DEBATE 299 (1998).

CARLSON, PAUL H., THE PLAINS INDIANS (1998).

Carpenter, Dick M. & Ross, John K., Victimizing the Vulnerable, The Demographics of Eminent Domain Abuse 2 (June 2007), *available at* http://www.ij.org/images/pdf_folder/other_pubs/Victimizing_the_Vulnerable.pdf.

Case, Karl E. & Shiller, Robert J., *Mortgage Default Risk and Real Estate Prices: The Use of Index-Based Futures and Options in Real Estate*, 7 J. of Housing Research 243 (1996).

Casey, Edward S., Getting Back into Place – Toward a Renewed Understanding of the Place-World (1993).

Center for Community Change, Housing Trust Fund Progress Report (2007) *available at* http://www.communitychange.org/our-projects/htf.

Center for Responsible Lending, *Protect States' Rights to Prevent Foreclosures: Support Miller-LaTourette Amendment*, Center for Responsible Lending Policy Brief, May 7, 2008, *available at* http://www.responsiblelending.org/pdfs/protect-states-rights-support-miller-latourette.pdf.

Center for Responsible Lending, *Subprime Lending: A Net Drain on Homeownership*, CRL Issue Paper No. 14, March 27, 2007, at 2, *available at* http://www.responsiblelending.org/pdfs/Net-Losership-3-26.pdf.

Center for Universal Design, North Carolina State University: College of Design, *Universal Design In Housing*, UD Features in Housing (rev. 9/2003).

Cernea, Michael M., *Impoverishment Risks, Risk Management, and Reconstruction: A Model for Population Displacement and Resettlement*, http://www.un.org/esa/sustdev/sdissues/energy/op/hydro_cernea_population_resettlement_backgroundpaper.pdf (last visited October 20, 2008).

Champlin, Dell, *The Privatization of Community: Implications for Urban Policy*, 32 J. Econ. Issues 595 (1998).

Chavis, David M. & Wandersman , Abraham, *Sense of Community in the Urban Environment: A Catalyst for Participation and Community Development*, 14 Am. J. Community Psychol. 55, 55–61 (1990).

Chawla, Louise, *Home is Where You Start From: Childhood Memory in Adult Interpretations of Home*, *in* The Meaning and Use of Housing (Ernesto G. Arias ed., 1993).

Chawla, Louise, *Childhood Place Attachments*, *in* Place Attachments (Irwin Altman & Setha M. Low eds., 1992).

Christensen, Pia & O'Brien, Margaret, Children in the City: Home Neighbourhood and Community (2003).

Christie, Hazel, *Mortgage Arrears and Gender Inequalities*, 15 Housing Studies 877 (2000).

Christy, Angela M., *Revitalizing Public-Private Partnerships (Chair's Message)*, 9 J. of Affordable Housing and Community Development Law 207 (2007).

Clampet-Lundquist, Susan, *HOPE VI Relocation: Moving to New Neighborhoods and Building New Ties*, 15 Housing Pol'y Debate 415 (2004).

Closing Message from James Stockard, *Public Housing Operating Cost Study, Final Report* (June 6, 2003), *available at* http://www.gsd.harvard.edu/research/research_centers/phocs/documents/Final%206.12.pdf.

Collins, Michael, Crowe, David & Carliner, Michael, *Examining the Supply-Side Constraints to Low-Income Homeownership* (Harvard University Low-Income Homeownership Working Paper Series, Working Paper No. LIHO.01.5, 2001).

Colton, Kent W., Housing in the Twenty-First Century: Achieving Common Ground (2003).

Colton, Kent W., *Housing Finance in the United States: The Transformation of the U.S. Housing Finance System*, Joint Center for Housing Studies at Harvard University (2002), *available at* http://www.jchs.harvard.edu/publications/finance/W02-5_Colton.pdf.

Comey, Jennifer, *HOPE VI'd and On the Move*, *in* Metropolitan Housing and Communities Center (Urban Institute, Brief No. 1, 2007).

Community Assn's Inst., An Introduction to Community Association Living (2003), *available at* http://www.regenesis.net/community_association_living.pdf (last visited May 6, 2008).

Committee on Nat'l Statistics, Nat'l Research Council of the Nat'l Academies, Food Insecurity and Hunger in the United States: An Assessment of the Measure (2006).

Conley, Dalton, Being Black, Living in the Red: Race, Wealth, and Social Policy in America (1999).

Conway, Brian P. & Hachen Jr., David S., *Attachments, Grievances, Resources and Efficacy: The Determinants of Tenant Association Participation among Public Housing Tenants*, 27 J. Urb. Aff. 25 (2005).

Creswell, Julie, *Long Protected by Washington, Fannie and Freddie Ballooned*, N.Y. Times, July 12, 2008, at A1.

Cullen, Jim, The American Dream: A Short History of an Idea that Shaped a Nation (2003).

Cummings, Scott L., *Community Economic Development as Progressive Politics: Toward a Grassroots Movement for Economic Justice*, 54 Stan. L. Rev. 399 (2001).

Curtin, Julie Farrell & Bocarsly, Lance, *CLTs: A Growing Trend in Affordable Home Ownership*, 17 J. of Affordable Housing & Community Development Law 367 (2008).

Dana, David, *Environmental Lawyers and the Public Service Model of Lawyering*, 74 Or. L. Rev. 57 (1995).

Danziger, Sheldon & Gottschalk, Peter, America Unequal (1995).

Davidson, Nestor M., *Values and Value Creation in Public-Private Transactions*, 94 Iowa L. Rev. (2009).

Davidson, Nestor, *Relational Contracts in the Privatization of Social Welfare: The Case of Housing*, 24 Yale L. & Pol'y Rev. 263 (2006).

Davis, John Emmeus & Jacobus, Rick, The City-CLT Partnership: Municipal Support for Community Land Trusts (Lincoln Institute of Land Policy 2008).

D.C. Department of Housing and Community Development (DHCD), Featured Projects: The ARC, *available at* http://dhcd.dc.gov (follow hyperlink to "Information – Featured Projects"; follow hyperlink to "The ARC").

Deng, Yongheng & Gabriel, Stuart, *Risk-Based Pricing and the Enhancement of Mortgage Credit Availability among Underserved and Higher Credit-Risk Populations*, 38 J. of Money, Credit, and Banking 1431 (2006).

Department of Housing and Urban Development, *NOFA for the HOPE VI Revitalization Program*, 72 Fed. Reg. 41822, 41831 (July 31, 2007).

De Soto, Hernando, The Mystery of Capital: Why Capitalism Triumphs in the West and Fails Everywhere Else (1st ed. 2000).

Detamore-Rodman, Crystal, *Branching Out: An Employee Stock Ownership Plan is More than Just a Great Way to Boost Morale*, 32 Entrepreneur, April 1, 2004, at 61.

DeVita, Carol J., Manjarrez, Carlos & Twombly, Eric C., Organizations and Neighborhood Networks That Strengthen Families in the District of Columbia: Final Report to the Annie E. Casey Foundation (1999).

Diamond, Michael, *Community Economic Development: A Reflection on Community, Power and the Law*, 8 J. Small & Emerging Bus. L. 151 (2004).

Diamond, Michael & O'Toole, Aaron, *Leaders, Followers and Free Riders: The Community Lawyer's Dilemma When Representing Non-Democratic Client Organizations*, 31 Fordham Urb. L.J. 481 (2004).

1 District of Columbia, Office of Planning, *District Elements: Housing Element*, *in* The Comprehensive Plan for the National Capital 5-18 (2006), *available at* http://planning.dc.gov/planning (follow hyperlink to "Comprehensive Plan"; then follow hyperlink to "2006 Revised Comprehensive Plan"; then follow hyperlink to "Volume 1, Citywide Elements").

2 District of Columbia, Office of Planning, *Area Elements: Far Southeast/Southwest Area Element*, *in* The Comprehensive Plan for the National Capital 18-10, 18-21 (2006), *available at* http://planning.dc.gov/planning (follow hyperlink to "Comprehensive Plan"; then follow hyperlink to "2006 Revised Comprehensive Plan"; then follow hyperlink to "Volume 2, Area Elements"; then follow hyperlink to "Far Southeast/Southwest Area Element").

Dovey, Kim, *Home and Homelessness*, *in* Home Environments (Irwin Altman & Carol M. Werner eds., 1985).

Downing, Theodore E., *Avoiding New Poverty: Mining Induced Displacement and Resettlement*, Mining, Minerals and Sustainable Development (MMSD) (International Institute for Environment and Development), April 2002, http://www.iied.org/mmsd/mmsd_pdfs/058_downing.pdf.

Draft, Government of the District of Columbia, Office of Planning, Barry Farm/Park Chester/Wade Road Redevelopment Plan (November 2006), *available at* http://planning.dc.gov/planning (follow hyperlink to "Neighborhood and Revitalization Plans"; then follow hyperlink to "Ward 8: Barry Farm/Parkchester/Wade Road Redevelopment Plan"; then follow hyperlink to "Barry Farm/Parkchester/Wade Road Redevelopment").

Drier, Peter, *The New Politics of Housing*, 63 J. of the American Planning Association 5 (1997).

Driesen, David M. & Ghosh, Shubha, *The Functions of Transaction Costs: Rethinking Transaction Cost Minimization in a World of Friction*, 47 Ariz. L. Rev. 61 (2005).

Duany, Andres, *Three Cheers for Gentrification*, American Enterprise Magazine, April/May 2001.

Duda, Mark & Belsky, Eric S., *The Anatomy of the Low-Income Homeownership Boom in the 1990s* (Harvard University Low-Income Homeownership Working Paper Series, Working Paper No. LIHO.01-1, 2001).

Duncan, Greg J. & Zuberi, Anita, *Mobility Lessons from Gautreaux and Moving to Opportunity*, 1 Nw. J. L. & Soc. Pol'y 110 (2006).

Dupuis, Ann & Thorns, David C., *Home, Home Ownership and the Search for Ontological Security*, 46 The Sociological Review 24 (1998).

Dupuis, Ann & Thorns, David C., *Meanings of Home for Older Home Owners*, 11 Housing Studies 485 (1996).

Durchslag, Melvyn R., *Property Tax Abatement for Low-Income Housing: An Idea Whose Time May Never Arrive*, 30 Harv. J. On Legis. 367 (1993).

Easterlow, Donna & Smith, Susan J., *Housing for Health: Can the Market Care?*, 36 Environment and Planning A 999 (2004).

Eckholm, Erik, *Washington's Grand Experiment to Rehouse the Poor*, N.Y. Times, March 21, 2008, at A12.

Eden, Rick & Boren, Patricia, Timely Assistance: Evaluating the Speed of Road Home Grantmaking (2008).

Edin, Kathryn, *More Than Money: The Role of Assets in the Survival Strategies and Material Well Being of the Poor*, *in* Assets for the Poor: The Benefits of Spreading Asset Ownership ch. 6 at 206 (Thomas M. Shapiro & Edward N. Wolff, eds., 2001).

Ellickson, Robert C., *Alternatives to Zoning: Covenants, Nuisance Rules, and Fines as Land Use Controls*, 40 U. Chi. L. Rev. 681 (1973).

Elmer, Peter J. & Seeling, Steven A., *The Rising Long-Term Trend of Single Family Mortgage Foreclosure Rates* (Federal Deposit Insurance Corporation, Working Paper Series 98-2, 1998).

Ely, John, Democracy and Distrust (1980).

Email from John Ammann, Director, Saint Louis University Law Clinic, to Peter Salsich (October 13, 2008).

The Encyclopedia of Housing (Willem Van Vliet ed., 1998).

Etzioni, Amitai, The Spirit of Community: Rights, Responsibilities, and the Communitarian Agenda (1993).

Executive Office of the President, Office of Management and Budget, *Department of Housing and Urban Development*, *in* Analytical Perspectives tbl. 19-2 (2008).

EXECUTIVE OFFICE OF THE PRESIDENT, OFFICE OF MANAGEMENT AND BUDGET, *Department of Housing and Urban Development*, *in* Budget of the United States Government: Fiscal Year 2009 (2008).

Falls in the Home, AEX-691.1-92 OHIO STATE UNIVERSITY EXTENSION (Department of Health and Human Services, Centers for Disease Control & Prevention, National Institute for Occupational Health and Safety, Washington, D.C.), *available at* http://www.cdc.gov/nasd/docs/d00010-d000300/d000131/d000131.pdf (last visited July 10, 2008).

FARBER, DANIEL A. & CHEN, JIM, DISASTERS AND THE LAW: KATRINA AND BEYOND (2006).

Farrar, Margaret E., *Making the City Beautiful: Aesthetic Reform and the (Dis)placement of Bodies*, *in* EMBODIED UTOPIAS: GENDER, SOCIAL CHANGE AND THE MODERN METROPOLIS (Amy Bingaman, Lise Sanders & Rebecca Zorach eds., 2002).

FED. HIGHWAY ADMIN., U.S. DEP'T OF TRANSP., RELOCATION RETROSPECTIVE STUDY (1996).

Fennell, Lee Anne, *Homeownership 2.0*, 102 NW. U. L. REV. 1047 (2008).

Fennell, Lee Anne, *Properties of Concentration*, 73 U. CHI. L. REV. 1227 (2006).

Fennell, Lee Anne, *Taking Eminent Domain Apart*, 2004 MICH. ST. L. REV. 957.

Fernandes, Deepa, *Three Years After Hurricane Katrina, Homelessness Looms*, MOTHER JONES, August 28, 2008, *available at* www.motherjones.com/cgi-bin/print_article.pl?url.

Field, Ben, *Why Our Fair Share Housing Laws Fail*, 34 SANTA CLARA L. REV. 35 (1993).

Filosa, Gwen, *HANO Will Pursue Rebuilding Grants: Agency Takes Heat for Housing Management*, NEW ORLEANS TIMES PICAYUNE, October 18, 2007.

Filosa, Gwen, *2 Swept from St. Bernard Complex: Police Say Activists were Living There*, NEW ORLEANS TIMES PICAYUNE, February 1, 2007.

Filosa, Gwen, *HANO Protest Becomes Scuffle: St. Bernard Residents Want to Come Home*, NEW ORLEANS TIMES PICAYUNE, April 5, 2006.

Filosa, Gwen, *Brick Housing Biting the Dust: New Homes Planned for Poor, HUD Says*, NEW ORLEANS TIMES PICAYUNE, November 3, 2005.

Finch, Susan, *Plan for Resettling Public Housing Residents OK'd*, NEW ORLEANS TIMES PICAYUNE, July 10, 2007.

Fireside, Daniel, *Community Land Trust Keeps Prices Affordable – For Now and Forever*, YES! MAGAZINE, Fall 2008, *available at* www.yesmagazine.org/article.asp?ID=2834.

Fishbein, Allen & Bunce, Harold, *Subprime Market Growth and Predatory Lending*, HOUSING POLICY IN THE NEW MILLENIUM: PROCEEDINGS (Susan M. Wachter and R. Leo Penne eds., 2005).

Fitchen, Janet M., *When Toxic Chemicals Pollute Residential Environments: The Cultural Meanings of Home and Home Ownership*, 48 HUMAN ORGANISATION 313 (1989).

Fleischer, Victor, *The MasterCard IPO: Protecting the Priceless Brand*, 12 Harv. Neg. L. Rev. 137 (2007).

Ford, Janet, Burrows, Roger & Nettleton, Sarah, Home Ownership in a Risk Society: A Social Analysis of Mortgage Arrears and Possessions (2001).

Foster, Sheila, *The City as an Ecological Space: Social Capital and Urban Land Use*, 82 Notre Dame L. Rev. 527 (2006).

Foster, Sheila, *Justice From the Ground Up: Distributive Inequities, Grassroots Resistance, and the Transformative Politics of the Environmental Justice Movement*, 86 Cal. L. Rev. 775 (1998).

Fox, Lorna, *Re-Possessing "Home": A Re-Analysis of Gender, Home Ownership and Debtor Default for Feminist Legal Theory*, 14 Wm. & Mary J. Women & L. 423 (2008).

Fox, Lorna, Conceptualising Home: Theories, Laws and Policies (2007).

Fox, Lorna, *The Idea of Home in Law*, 2 Home Cultures 25 (2005).

Fox, Lorna, *The Meaning of Home: A Chimerical Concept or a Legal Challenge?*, 29 J.L. Soc'y 580 (2002).

Frasier, John W., Margai, Florence M. & Tettley-Fio, Eugene, Race and Place: Equity Issues in Urban America (2003).

Freeman, L. & Braconi, F., *Displacement or Succession? Residential Mobility in Gentrifying Neighborhoods*, 40 Urb. Aff. 463 (2004).

Freeman, L. & Braconi, F., *Gentrification and Displacement*, 8 The Urban Prospect 1 (2002).

Fried, Marc, *Continuities and Discontinuities of Place*, 20 J. Envtl. Psychol. 193 (2000).

Fried, Marc, *Grieving for a Lost Home*, *in* The Urban Condition: People and Policy in the Metropolis (Leonard J. Duhl ed., 1963).

Frieden, Bernard J. & Sagalyn, Lynne B., Downtown, Inc.: How America Rebuilds Cities (1997).

Friedman, Lawrence M., Government and Slum Housing: A Century of Frustration (1968).

Fullilove, Mindy Thompson, *Psychiatric Implications of Displacement: Contributions from the Psychology of Place*, 153 Am. J. Psychiatry 1516 (1996).

Fullilove, Mindy Thompson, Root Shock: How Tearing Up City Neighborhoods Hurts America, and What We Can Do About It (2004).

Galbraith, Suellen, *A Home of One's Own*, *in* The Forgotten Generation: The Status and Challenges of Adults with Mild Cognitive Limitations (Alexander J. Tymchuck, K. Charlie Lakin & Ruth Luckasson eds., 2001).

Gates, Jeff, The Ownership Solution: Toward a Shared Capitalism for the Twenty-first Century (1998).

Geniella, Mike, *Ruling Favors Housing Lawsuit: Mendocino County Must Pay $70,000 in Legal Fees*, Santa Rosa Press Democrat, September 28, 2005.

Gerardi, Kristopher, Shapiro, Adam Hale & Willen, Paul S., *Subprime Outcomes: Risky Mortgages, Homeownership Experiences, and Foreclosures* (Federal

Reserve Bank of Boston, Working Paper No. 07-15, 2007), *available at* http://papers.ssrn.com/sol3/papers.cfm?abstract_id=1073182.

Gilson, Ronald J., Value Creation by Business Lawyers: Legal Skills and Asset Pricing, 94 YALE L.J. 239 (1984).

Gilson, Ronald J. & Robert H. Mnookin, *Foreword: Business Lawyers and Value Creation for Clients*, 74 OR. L. REV. 1 (1995).

Glaeser, Edward, *The Future of Urban Research: Nonmarket Interactions*, 1 BROOKINGS-WHARTON PAPERS ON URB. AFF. 101 (2000), *available at* http://muse.jhu.edu/demo/brookings-whartonpapersonurbanaffairs/v2000/2000.1glaeser.pdf.

Glickman, Norman J. & Servon, Lisa J., *More than Bricks and Sticks: Five Components of Community Development Corporation Capacity*, 9 HOUSING POL'Y DEBATE 497, 504–12 (1998).

Glynn, Thomas J., *Neighborhood and a Sense of Community*, 14 J. COMMUNITY PSYCHOL. 341, 349, 351 (1986).

Glynn,Thomas J., *Psychological Sense of Community: Measurement and Application*, 34 HUM. REL. 789, 790, 793 (1981).

Goering, John, *Expanding Housing Choice and Integrating Neighborhoods: The Moving to Opportunity Experiment*, *in* THE GEOGRAPHY OF OPPORTUNITY: RACE AND HOUSING CHOICE IN METROPOLITAN AMERICA (Xavier de Souza Briggs ed., 2005).

Goetz, Edward G., *Comment: Public Housing Demolition and the Benefits to Low Income Families*, 71 J. AM. PLANNING ASS'N 407 (2005).

Goetz, Edward G., *Forced Relocation vs. Voluntary Mobility: The Effects of Dispersal Programmes on Households*, 17 HOUSING STUD. 107 (2002).

GOLDSMITH, SELWYN, UNIVERSAL DESIGN (2001).

GOOD NEIGHBORS: THE DESIGN OF AFFORDABLE FAMILY HOUSING (Michael Pyatok, Tom Jones & William Pettus eds., 1995).

Gordon, Colin, *Blighting the Way: Urban Renewal, Economic Development, and the Elusive Definition of Blight*, 31 FORDHAM URB. L.J. 305 (2004).

Gottfried, Keith E., General Counsel, United States Department of Housing and Urban Development, Remarks at the National Settlement Services Summit (June 14, 2006).

GRAY, K.J. & SYMES, P.D., REAL PROPERTY AND REAL PEOPLE (1981).

Green, Kate, *Being Here – What a Woman Can Say About Land Law*, *in* FEMINIST PERSPECTIVES ON THE FOUNDATIONAL SUBJECTS OF LAW (Anne Bottomley ed., 1996).

Greene, Saara, *Including Young Mothers: Community-Based Participation and the Continuum of Active Citizenship*, 42 COMM. DEV. J. 167 (2007).

Gropp, Reint, Scholz, John Karl & White, Michelle J., *Personal Bankruptcy and Credit Supply and Demand*, 112 QUARTERLY JOURNAL OF ECONOMICS 217 (1997).

Gross, Julian, *Community Benefits Agreements: Definitions, Values, and Legal Enforceability*, 17 J. AFFORDABLE HOUSING & COMM. DEV. 35 (2007–08).

GROSS, JULIAN WITH LEROY, GREG & JANIS-APARICIO, MADELINE, COMMUNITY BENEFITS AGREEMENTS: MAKING DEVELOPMENT PROJECTS ACCOUNTABLE (Good Jobs First & the California Partnership for Working Families 2005), *available at* www.goodjobsfirst.org/pdf.

Gurney, Craig, *Lowering the Drawbridge: A Case Study of Analogy and Metaphor in the Social Construction of Home-Ownership*, 36 URBAN STUDIES 1706 (1999).

Gurney, Craig, *Pride and Prejudice: Discourses of Normalisation in Public and Private Accounts of Home Ownership*, 14 HOUSING STUDIES 163 (1999).

GURNEY, CRAIG, THE MEANING OF HOME IN THE DECADE OF OWNER OCCUPATION: TOWARDS AN EXPERIENTIAL PERSPECTIVE (1990).

Gyourko, Joseph, *The Changing Strength of Socioeconomic Factors Affecting Home Ownership in the United States: 1960–1990*, 45 SCOTTISH J. OF POLITICAL ECONOMY 466 (1998).

HABERMAS, JURGEN, BETWEEN FACTS AND NORMS: CONTRIBUTIONS TO A DISCOURSE THEORY OF LAW AND DEMOCRACY (1998).

Haddon, Heather, *Terminal Market Deal Criticized*, 19 NORWOOD NEWS 4, February 23, 2006–March 8, 2006, *available at* http://www.bronxmall.com/norwoodnews/past/022306/news/N60223page1.html.

HALPERN, DAVID, SOCIAL CAPITAL (2005).

Hammer, David, *Road Home Deadlines Are Rescinded; Thousands of Applicants Have Encountered Technical Obstacles*, NEW ORLEANS TIMES-PICAYUNE, August 28, 2008, at 1.

Hammer, David, *HUD Rebuked over Katrina Response: U.N. Panel Sees Race Disparity in Housing*, NEW ORLEANS TIMES PICAYUNE, March 8, 2008.

Hammer, David, *Housing Agencies Sue to Remove Protesters: Group is Occupying St. Bernard Complex*, NEW ORLEANS TIMES PICAYUNE, January 23, 2007.

HANO, Annual Plan for Fiscal Year Beginning 10/2008, at 6 (Draft), *available at* http://www.hano.org/ Documents/ (last visited June 18, 2008).

Hardin, Garrett, *The Tragedy of the Commons*, SCIENCE, December 13, 1968, at 1243.

Harris, Richard & Pratt, Geraldine, *The Meaning of Home, Homeownership and Public Policy*, *in* THE CHANGING SOCIAL GEOGRAPHY OF CANADIAN CITIES (L.S. Bourne & D.F. Ley eds., 1993).

Hart, Peter D. & Teeter, Robert, *Fannie Mae National Housing Survey*, FANNIE MAE (1992).

Hartman, Chester, *The Case for a Right to Housing*, 9 HOUSING POL'Y DEBATE 223 (1998).

Hartman, Chester W., *Relocation: Illusory Promises and No Relief*, 57 VA. L. REV. 745 (1971).

HARVARD JOINT CENTER FOR HOUSING STUDIES, AMERICA'S RENTAL HOUSING: THE KEY TO A BALANCED NATIONAL POLICY (2008).

Harvard University Graduate School of Design, *Public Housing Operating Cost Study, Final Report* (June 6, 2003), *available at* http://www.gsd.harvard.edu/research/research_centers/phocs/documents/Final%206.12.pdf.

Harvey, Bart, *Building Alliances at All Levels*, 144 SHELTERFORCE MAGAZINE, November/December 2005, *available at* http://www.nhi.org/online/issues/144/buildingalliances.html (last visited January 12, 2008).

Haurin, Donald R., Parcel, Toby L. & Haurin, Ruth J., *The Impact of Homeownership on Child Outcomes* (Joint Center for Housing Studies of Harvard University, Low-Income Homeownership Working Paper Series LIHO-01.14, 2001).

HAURIN, DONALD R. & ROSENTHAL, STUART S., THE GROWTH OF EARNINGS OF LOW-INCOME HOUSEHOLDS AND THE SENSITIVITY OF THEIR HOMEOWNERSHIP CHOICES TO ECONOMIC AND SOCIO-DEMOGRAPHIC SHOCKS, Executive Summary at iv, 12–13 (2005).

Haurin, Donald R. & Rosenthal, Stuart R., *The Sustainability of Homeownership: Factors Affecting the Duration of Homeownership and Rental Spells* (2004), *available at* http://www.huduser.org/publications/affhsg/homeownsustainability.html.

Hays, R.A., *Housing America's Poor: Conflicting Values and Failed Policies*, 28 J. OF URBAN HISTORY 369 (2002).

HEATER, DEREK, WHAT IS CITIZENSHIP? (1999).

HEIDEGGER, MARTIN, BAUEN WOHNEN DENKEN (BUILDING DWELLING THINKING) (Albert Hofstadter trans., 1951).

Heidegger, Martin, ... *Dichterisch Wohnet Der Mensch* ... ("... *Poetically man dwells* ..."), POETRY, LANGUAGE, THOUGHT (Albert Hofstadter trans., 1951).

HEIDEGGER, MARTIN, SEIN UND ZEIT (BEING AND TIME) (John Macquarrie & Edward Robinson trans., 1927) (1962).

Hellegers, Adam P., *Eminent Domain as an Economic Development Tool: A Proposal to Reform HUD Displacement Policy*, 2001 LAW. REV. M. ST. U. DETROIT C.L. 901.

Heller, Michael & Hills, Rick, *Land Assembly Districts*, 121 HARV. L. REV. 1465 (2008).

Heller, Michael A. & Hills Jr., Roderick M., The Art of Land Assembly 3 (January 28, 2004) (unpublished draft), *available at* http://www.law.uchicago.edu/Lawecon/workshop-papers/Heller.pdf.

Hepp, E. & Soper, C., *One Family's Story of Homeownership*, 15 J. OF VOCATIONAL REHABILITATION 79 (2000).

Herbert, Christopher E., Haurin, Donald R., Rosenthal, Stuart S. & Duda, Mark, *Homeownership Gaps Among Low-Income and Minority Borrowers and Neighbourhoods* (2005), *available at* http://www.huduser.org/Publications/pdf/HomeownershipGapsAmongLow-IncomeAnd Minority.pdf.

Herszenhorn, David M., *Senate Gives Final Approval to Sweeping Housing Bill*, N.Y. TIMES, July 27, 2008, *available at* www.nytimes.com/2008/07/270washington/26cnd-housing.html?.

Herszenhorn, David M., *Congress Sends Housing Relief Bill to President*, N.Y. TIMES, July 27, 2008, at 12, 16.

Hockett, Robert, *A Jeffersonian Republic by Hamiltonian Means: Values, Constraints, and Finance in the Design of a Comprehensive and Contemporary "Ownership Society"*, 79 S. CAL. L. REV. 45, 99–104.

Holmes, Oliver Wendell, *The Path of the Law*, 10 HARV. L. REV. 457 (1897).

HOOKS, BELL, YEARNING: RACE, GENDER, AND CULTURAL POLITICS (1990).

HOUSING COMMISSION ON FINANCIAL SERVICES, NATIONAL AFFORDABLE HOUSING TRUST FUND ACT OF 2007, Report 110-362 (October 2, 2007).

HUD Form 53012B (7/95).

HUME, DAVID, A TREATISE OF HUMAN NATURE: BEING AN ATTEMPT TO INTRODUCE THE EXPERIMENTAL METHOD OF REASONING INTO MORAL SUBJECTS, Book III, Part II, Sect. 1 (1817).

Hunter, Caroline & Nixon, Judy, *The Discourse of Housing Debt: The Social Construction of Landlords, Lenders, Borrowers and Tenants*, 16 HOUSING, THEORY AND SOCIETY 165 (1999).

Hutchinson, Judy, *Social Capital and Community Building in the Inner City*, 70 J. AM. PLANNING ASS'N 168 (2004).

Hutchison, Harry G. & Alley, R. Sean, *The High Costs of Shareholder Participation*, *available at* http://ssrn.com/abstract=1112885 (last visited February 25, 2009).

Iglesias, Tim, *Our Pluralist Housing Ethics and the Struggle for Affordability*, 42 WAKE FOREST L. REV. 511 (2007).

Iglesias, Tim, *Housing Impact Assessments: Opening New Doors for State Housing Regulation While Localism Persists*, 82 OR. L. REV. 433 (2003).

Iglesias, Tim, *Managing Local Opposition to Affordable Housing: A New Approach to NIMBY*, 12 J. OF AFFORDABLE HOUSING & COMMUNITY DEVELOPMENT LAW 78 (2002).

Immergluck, Dan, *Stark Differences: Explosion of the Subprime Industry and Racial Hypersegmentation in Home Equity Lending*, HOUSING POLICY IN THE NEW MILLENIUM: PROCEEDINGS (Susan M. Wachter and R. Leo Penne eds., 2005).

Immergluck, Dan & Smith, Geoff, *The External Costs of Foreclosure: The Impact of Single-Family Mortgage Foreclosures on Property Values*, 17:1 HOUSING POLICY DEBATE 57 (2006), *available at* http://www.fanniemaefoundation.org/programs/hpd/pdf/hpd_1701_immergluck.pdf.

Inclusionary Zoning: The California Experience, 3(1) NHC AFFORDABLE HOUSING POLICY REVIEW (National Housing Conference, Washington, D.C.), February 2004, *available at* http://www.nhc.org/pdf/pub_ahp_02_04.pdf.

INSERRA, ANNE, CONWAY, MAUREEN & RODAT, JOHN, COOPERATIVE HOME CARE ASSOCIATES: A CASE STUDY OF A SECTORAL EMPLOYMENT DEVELOPMENT APPROACH (The Aspen Institute 2002).

Interview by Chester Hartman with Bill Apgar, Executive Director, Harvard's Joint Center for Housing Studies, *in* SHELTERFORCE MAGAZINE, July/August 1995.

Interview with J. Richard Parker II, Executive Director, Athens Housing Authority, in Athens, Georgia (October 14, 2008).

Interview with William Thorson, Executive Director, Housing Authority of New Orleans, in New Orleans, Louisiana (June 9, 2006).

Jacobs, Jane, The Death and Life of Great American Cities (1961).

Jacobus, Rick & Brown, Michael, *City Hall Steps In*, 149 Shelterforce Magazine, Spring 2007, *available at* http://www.nhi.org/online/issues/149/cityhall.html (last visited May 6, 2008).

Johnson, Asmara Tekle, *Privatizing Eminent Domain: The Delegation of a Very Public Power to Private, Non-Profit and Charitable Corporations*, 56 Am. U. L. Rev. 455 (2007).

Johnson, Creola, *Welfare Reform and Asset Accumulation: First We Need a Bed and a Car*, 2000 Wis. L. Rev. 1221.

Joint Center for Housing Studies of Harvard University & Center for Workforce Preparation of the U.S. Chamber of Commerce, *Strengthening our Workforce and our Communities Through Housing Solutions*, Report on Making the Connection ... Housing and Workforce Development: A National Leadership Forum (2006), *available at* http://www.jchs.harvard.edu/publications/markets/wh05-1_workforce_housing_report.pdf.

Jordan, Wendy A., Universal Design for the Home: Great Looking, Great Living Design for all Ages, Abilities, and Circumstances (2008).

Joseph, Mark L., Chaskin, Robert J. & Webber, Henry S., *The Theoretical Basis for Addressing Poverty through Mixed-Income Development*, 42 Urb. Aff. Rev. 369 (2007).

Judd, Rick & Kautz, Barbara E., *Local Government Financing Powers and Sources of Funding*, *in* The Legal Guide to Affordable Housing Development (Tim Iglesias & Rochelle E. Lento eds. 2005).

Juergensmeyer, Julian Conrad & Roberts, Thomas E., Land Use Planning and Development Regulation Law (West 2d ed. 2007).

Kahn, Margaret, Brave New Neighborhood: The Privatization of Public Space (2004).

Kahn, Mitch, *Paradise Lost*, 138 Shelterforce Magazine, November/December 2004 (book review of J.S. Fuerst, When Public Housing Was Paradise: Building Community in Chicago (University of Illinois Press 2004)).

Kahneman, Daniel, Knetsch, Jack L. & Thaler, Richard H., *Anomalies: The Endowment Effect, Loss Aversion and Status Quo Bias*, 5 Journal of Economic Perspectives 193 (1991).

Kanner, Gideon, *The Public Use Clause: Constitutional Mandate or "Hortatory Fluff"?*, 33 Pepp. L. Rev. 335 (2006).

Keating, W. Dennis, *Encouraging Middle-Class Homeownership in NYC*, Shelterforce Magazine, July/August 1998 Reviews (book review of Charles J. Orlebecke, New Life at Ground Zero: New York, Homeownership, and the Future of American Cities (The Rockefeller Institute Press 1997)).

Keating, W. Dennis, *The Housing Affordability Crisis: Progressive Responses*, Book Review: Edward G. Goetz, SHELTER BURDEN: LOCAL POLITICS AND PROGRESSIVE HOUSING POLICY (Temple University Press 1993), SHELTERFORCE MAGAZINE, March/April, 1994, *available at* http://www.nhi.org/online/issues/books/74.html (last visited January 12, 2008).

Kelly, James, *"We Shall Not Be Moved": Urban Communities, Eminent Domain and the Socioeconomics of Just Compensation*, 80 ST. JOHNS L. REV. 923 (2006).

Kelly Jr., James J., *Taming Eminent Domain*, SHELTERFORCE, March 22, 2008, *available at* http://ssrn.com/abstract=1271223.

Kelly Jr., James J., *Refreshing the Heart of the City: Vacant Building Receivership as a Tool for Neighborhood Revitalization and Community Empowerment*, 13 J. AFFORDABLE HOUSING & COMMUNITY DEV. L. 210 (2004).

KELSO, LOUIS O. & HETTER, PATRICIA, HOW TO TURN EIGHTY MILLION WORKERS INTO CAPITALISTS ON BORROWED MONEY (1967).

KELSO, LOUIS O. & KELSO, PATRICIA HETTER, DEMOCRACY AND ECONOMIC POWER: EXTENDING THE ESOP REVOLUTION (1986).

Kennedy, Duncan, *The Limited Equity Coop as a Vehicle for Affordable Housing in a Race and Class Divided Society*, 46 HOW. L.J. 85 (2002).

KIM, JUNG & PEEBLES, GUSTAV, ESTIMATED FISCAL IMPACT OF FOREST CITY RATNER'S BROOKLYN ARENA AND 17 HIGH RISE DEVELOPMENT ON NYC AND NYS TREASURIES (2004), *available at* www.nolandgrab.org/report/EconReport.pdf, and Develop Don't Destroy Brooklyn, www.dddb.net/times/.

Klein, Jay, *The History and Development of a National Homeownership Initiative*, 15 J. OF VOCATIONAL REHABILITATION 59 (2000).

KLEIN, JAY & BLACK, MERRILL, EXTENDING THE AMERICAN DREAM: HOME OWNERSHIP FOR PEOPLE WITH DISABILITIES (1995).

Klein, Jay & Nelson, Debra, *Homeownership for People with Disabilities: The State of the States in 1999*, 15 J. OF VOCATIONAL REHABILITATION 67 (2000).

Klein, Jay, Wilson, Boyd & Nelson, Debra, *Postcards on the Refrigerator: Changing the Power Dynamic in Housing and Assistance*, *in* PART OF THE COMMUNITY: STRATEGIES FOR INCLUDING EVERYONE (Jan Nisbet & David Hagner eds., 2000).

Kleit, Rachel Garshick & Manzo, Lynne, *To Move or Not to Move: Relationships to Place and Relocation Choices in HOPE VI*, 17 HOUSING POL'Y DEBATE 271 (2006).

Knack, Ruth, *Great Streets: What Makes Them Special?*, 74 PLANNING 1 (January 2008).

KNAPP, JOSEPH G., THE RISE OF AMERICAN COOPERATIVE ENTERPRISE: 1620–1920 (1969).

Knight, Heather, *Newsom Taking Rich on Tours of Housing for Poor: He Seeks Donations to Rebuild Projects*, SAN FRANCISCO CHRONICLE, August 29, 2007, at A1.

Kochan, Donald J., *"Public Use" and the Independent Judiciary: Condemnation in an Interest-Group Perspective*, 3 TEX. REV. L. & POL. 49 (1998).

KOENIG, DOLORES, TOWARD LOCAL DEVELOPMENT MITIGATING IMPOVERISHMENT IN DEVELOPMENT-INDUCED DISPLACEMENT AND RESETTLEMENT, RESEARCH PROGRAMME ON DEVELOPMENT-INDUCED DISPLACEMENT AND SETTLEMENT (Refugee Studies Centre, Oxford University 2003), *available at* http://www.rsc.ox.ac.uk/PDFs/rrtowardlocal01.pdf.

Kolben, Deborah, *Market for Sellers, Not Renters*, THE BROOKLYN PAPER, February 3, 2006.

Kolben, Deborah, *Nets Site Renters Left Out in Eminent Domain Payouts*, THE BROOKLYN PAPER, February 3, 2006.

Kontos, Pia C., *Resisting Institutionalization: Constructing Old Age and Negotiating Home*, 12 J. OF AGING STUDIES 167 (1998).

Korman, Henry, *HOPE VI Reauthorization and Racial Segregation*, 17 J. AFFORDABLE HOUSING & COMM. DEV. L. 353 (2008).

KRETZMANN, JOHN P. & MCKNIGHT, JOHN L., BUILDING COMMUNITIES FROM THE INSIDE OUT: A PATH TOWARDS FINDING AND MOBILIZING A COMMUNITY'S ASSETS (1993).

Krohe Jr., James, *Displaced and Replaced*, 72 PLANNING 44 (2006).

Krumholz, Norman, *The Reluctant Hand: Privatization of Public Housing in the U.S.* (criticizing the HOPE VI program), http://www.uic.edu/cuppa/cityfutures/papers/webpapers/cityfuturespapers/session1_4/1_4reluctanthand.pdf (last visited January 12, 2008).

Kushner, James, *Apartheid in America: An Historical and Legal Analysis of Contemporary Residential Segregation in the United States*, 22 HOW. L.J. 547 (1979).

Land Centre, *The Role of Public-Private Partnerships in Producing Affordable Housing: Assessment of the U.S. Experience and Lessons for Canada*, available at http://landcentre.dreamhosters.com/?q=node/4336 and http://www.cmhc.ca/publications/en/rh-pr/socio/socio047.pdf (last visited May 6, 2008).

La Porta, Rafael, Lopez-De-Silanes, Florencio, Shleifer, Andrei & Vishnay, Robert W., *Law and Finance*, 106 JOURNAL OF POLITICAL ECONOMY 1113 (1998).

La Porta, Rafael, Lopez-De-Silanes, Florencio, Shleifer, Andrei & Vishnay, Robert W., *Legal Determinants of External Finance*, 52 JOURNAL OF FINANCE 1131 (1997).

Leary, Jr., Fairfax, & Turner, Eric D., *The Injustice of "Just Compensation" to Fixed Income Recipients – Does Recent Relocation Legislation Fill the Void?*, 48 TEMP. L. Q. 1 (1974).

Lee, Matthew R., *Concentrated Poverty, Race, and Homicide*, 41(2) THE SOCIOLOGICAL QUARTERLY 189 (Spring 2000).

Lefcoe, George, *Redevelopment Takings after Kelo: What's Blight Got to Do with It?*, 17 S. CAL. REV. L. & SOC. JUST. 803 (2008).

THE LEGAL GUIDE TO AFFORDABLE HOUSING DEVELOPMENT (Tim Iglesias & Rochelle E. Lento eds., 2005).

Lento, Rochelle E., *Federal Sources of Financing, in* THE LEGAL GUIDE TO AFFORDABLE HOUSING DEVELOPMENT (Tim Iglesias & Rochelle E. Lento eds., 2005).

Lester, Margot Carmichael, *Sign of the Times – Five Cities Bringing New Life to Abandoned Sites*, DEVELOPER, August 11, 2008, *available at* www.developeronline.com/sign-of-the-times-five-cities-turning.

Letter from Sheila Crowley, President and CEO, NLIHC, to John Kerry, United States Senator from Massachusetts (June 5, 2008), *available at* www.nhtf.org.

Letters, The Myth of the Double Bottom Line, 127 SHELTERFORCE MAGAZINE, January/February 2003, *available at* http://www.nhi.org/online/issues/127/letters.html.

Leviner, Sagit, *Affordable Housing and the Role of the Low Income Housing Tax Credit Program: A Contemporary Assessment*, 57 TAX LAW. 869 (2004).

Lewinsohn-Zamir, Daphna, *The Objectivity of Well-being and the Objectives of Property Law*, 78 N.Y.U. L. REV. 1669 (2003).

Linder, Stephen H., *Coming to Terms With the Public-Private Partnership: A Grammar of Multiple Meanings*, AMERICAN BEHAVIORAL SCIENTIST (1999).

Llewellyn, Karl, *What Price Contract? – An Essay in Perspective*, 40 YALE L.J. 704 (1931).

Lockhart, James B., Director, Federal Housing Finance Agency, Statement of FHFA Director James B. Lockhart (September 7, 2008), *available at* http://www.ofheo.gov/media/statements/FHFAStatement9708.pdf.

Loewenstein, George & Kahneman, Daniel, *Explaining the Endowment Effect* (Department of Social and Decision Sciences, Carnegie Mellon University, Working Paper, 1991).

Logan, Tim, *Renters Often Become the Forgotten Victims*, ST. LOUIS POST-DISPATCH, June 20, 2008, at B1.

Lopez, Ian F. Haney, *The Social Construction of Race: Some Observations on Illusion, Fabrication and Choice*, 29 HARV. C.R.-C.L. L. REV. 1 (1994).

LORD, RICHARD, AMERICAN NIGHTMARE: PREDATORY LENDING AND THE FORECLOSURE OF THE AMERICAN DREAM (2004).

Lovell, Phillip & Isaacs, Julia, *The Impact of the Mortgage Crisis on Children and Their Education*, FIRST FOCUS, April 2008, *available at* http://www.brookings.edu/~/media/Files/rc/papers/2008/04_mortgage_crisis_isaacs/04_mortgage_crisis_isaacs.pdf.

LOW INCOME HOMEOWNERSHIP: EXAMINING THE UNEXAMINED GOAL (Nicholas P. Retsinas & Eric S. Belsky eds., 2002).

MAISEL, JORDANA L., CENTER FOR INCLUSIVE DESIGN AND ENVIRONMENTAL ACCESS (IDEA), VISITABILITY AS AN APPROACH TO INCLUSIVE HOUSING DESIGN AND COMMUNITY DEVELOPMENT: A LOOK AT ITS EMERGENCE, GROWTH, AND CHALLENGES (2005).

MALLACH, ALAN, TACKLING THE MORTGAGE CRISIS: 10 ACTION STEPS FOR STATE GOVERNMENT (2008).

Malloy, Robin Paul, *Inclusion by Design: Accessible Housing and Mobility Impairment*, 60 HASTINGS L.J. 699 (2009).

MALLOY, ROBIN PAUL, LAW IN A MARKET CONTEXT: AN INTRODUCTION TO MARKET CONCEPTS IN LEGAL REASONING (2004).

Malloy, Robin Paul, *The Political Economy Of Co-Financing America's Urban Renaissance*, 40 VAND. L. REV. 67 (1987).

MALLOY, ROBIN PAUL & SMITH, JAMES CHARLES, REAL ESTATE TRANSACTIONS: PROBLEMS, CASES, AND MATERIALS (2d ed. 2002).

MALLOY, ROBIN PAUL & SMITH, JAMES CHARLES, REAL ESTATE TRANSACTIONS (1st ed. 1998).

MALPAS, JEFF E., PLACE AND EXPERIENCE: A PHILOSOPHICAL TOPOGRAPHY (1999).

MANDELKER, DANIEL R., LAND USE LAW § 1.05 (LexisNexis 5th ed. 2003 & Supp. 2007).

MANJARREZ, CARLOS A., POPKIN, SUSAN J. & GUERNSEY, ELIZABETH, URB. INST., POOR HEALTH: ADDING INSULT TO INJURY FOR HOPE VI FAMILIES (2007).

Manove, Michael & Padilla, A. Jorge, *Banking (Conservatively) with Optimists*, 30 RAND JOURNAL OF ECONOMICS 324 (1999).

Manove, Michael, Padilla, A. Jorge & Pagano, Marco, *Collateral versus Project Screening: A Model of Lazy Banks*, 32 RAND JOURNAL OF ECONOMICS 4, 726–44 (2001).

Mansvelt, Juliana, *Working at Leisure – Critical Geographies of Ageing*, 29 AREA 289 (1997).

Manzo, Lynne C., *For Better or Worse: Exploring Multiple Dimensions of Place Meaning*, 25 J. ENV. PSYCH. 67 (2005).

Manzo, Lynne C., Kleit, Rachel G. & Couch, Dawn, *"Moving Three Times Is Like Having Your House on Fire Once": The Experience of Place and Impending Displacement among Public Housing Residents*, 45 URB. STUD. 1855 (2008).

Marcuse, Peter, *The Ideologies of Ownership and Property Rights*, *in* HOUSING FORM AND PUBLIC POLICY IN THE U.S. (Richard Plunz ed., 1980).

Margalit, Avital, *The Value of Home Ownership* (Israel), 7 THEORETICAL INQUIRIES IN LAW (2006).

Market Creek Partners, LLC, Offering Circular, at 2 (2005).

MASSEY, DOUGLAS S. & DENTON, NANCY A., AMERICAN APARTHEID (1993).

McCarthy, George, Van Zandt, Shannon & Rohe, William M., *The Economic Costs and Benefits of Home Ownership: A Critical Assessment of the Research*, RESEARCH INSTITUTE FOR HOUSING AMERICA (2001).

MCCARTHY, PETER & SIMPSON, BOB, ISSUES IN POST-DIVORCE HOUSING (1991).

McConvill, James, *Shareholder Empowerment as an End in Itself: A New Perspective on Allocation of Power in the Modern Corporation*, 33 OHIO NORTHERN U. L. REV. 1013, 1015 (2007).

MCCULLOCH, HEATHER WITH ROBINSON, LISA, SHARING THE WEALTH: RESIDENT OWNERSHIP MECHANISMS, A POLICYLINK REPORT (2001), *available at* http://www.policylink.org/pdfs/ROMS.pdf.

McDougall, Harold A., *Affordable Housing for the 1990's*, 20 U. MICH. J.L. REFORM 785 (1987).

McFarlane, Audrey G., *The New Inner City: Class Transformation, Concentrated Affluence and the Obligations of the Police Power*, 8 U. PA. J. CONST. L. 1 (2006).

McFarlane, Audrey G., *When Inclusion Leads to Exclusion: The Uncharted Terrain of Community Participation in Economic Development*, 66 BROOK. L. REV 861 (2001).

McMillan, David W. & Chavis, David M., *Sense of Community: Definition and Theory,* 14 J. COMMUNITY PSYCHOL. 6 (1986).

McNeely, Adam, *Improving Low Income Housing: Eliminating the Conflict Between Property Taxes and the LIHTC Program*, 15 J. AFFORDABLE HOUSING & COMMUNITY DEV. L. 324 (2006).

Meador, Mark, *The Effects of Mortgage Laws on Home Mortgage Rates*, 34 JOURNAL OF ECONOMICS AND BUSINESS 143 (1982).

Meyerson, Harold, *No Justice, No Growth: How Los Angeles is Making Big-Time Developers Create Decent Jobs*, THE AMERICAN PROSPECT, October 22, 2006.

Michelman, Frank, *Property as a Constitutional Right*, 38 WASH & LEE L REV. 1097 (1981).

Michelman, Frank I., *Property, Utility and Fairness: Comments on the Ethical Foundations of "Just Compensation" Law*, 80 HARV. L. REV. 1165 (1967).

Michelson, William, *Residential Mobility and Urban Policy: Some Sociological Considerations*, *in* RESIDENTIAL MOBILITY AND PUBLIC POLICY 79, 83–5 (W.A.V. Clark & Eric G. Moore eds., 1980).

Mihaly, Marc B., *Public-Private Redevelopment Partnerships and the Supreme Court: Kelo v. City of New London*, 7 VT. J. ENVTL. L. 41 (2005/2006).

Minton, Jeffrey James, *Rent Control: Can and Should It Be Used to Combat Gentrification?*, 23 OHIO N.U. L. REV. 823 (1997).

MNOOKIN, ROBERT H., PEPPET, SCOTT R. & TULUMELLO, ANDREW S., BEYOND WINNING: NEGOTIATING TO CREATE VALUE IN DEALS AND DISPUTES (2000).

Montgomery, Lori & Kane, Paul, *Housing Bill Won't "Perform Miracles"*, WASHINGTON POST, July 27, 2008, at A1.

Moran, Kate, *Public Housing Advocates Protest St. Bernard's Closure: Marchers Demand HUD Reopen Units*, NEW ORLEANS TIMES PICAYUNE, July 5, 2006.

Mowl, Graham, Pain, Rachel & Talbot, Carol, *The Ageing Body and Homespace*, 32 AREA 189 (2000).

Muto, Sheila, *Residents Have Their Say on LAX Expansion Plans*, WALL ST. J., December 15, 2004.

Nasar, Jack L. & Julian, David A., *The Psychological Sense of Community in the Neighborhood*, 61 J. AM. PLAN. ASS'N 178, 181 (1995).

NATIONAL COMMISSION ON URBAN PROBLEMS, BUILDING THE AMERICAN CITY (1968).

National Community Reinvestment Coalition, *The 2005 Fair Lending Disparities: Stubborn and Persistent II*, NCRC REPORT (2006), *available at* http://www.ncrc.org/policy/analysis/policy/2006/2006-05-23_2005HMDAreport.pdf.

National Housing Institute, *Our Housing Markets Don't Work*, Shelterforce Magazine, May/June 2001.

National Housing Institute, Shelterforce Online, *Saving Affordable Housing: Introduction, available at* http://www.nhi.org/online/issues/90/intro.html (last visited January 12, 2008).

National Housing Trust Fund, *NHTF Falsely Characterized in Debate on Bail-Out Bill*, 13 Nat'l Low Income Housing Coalition 39 (October 3, 2008).

National Housing Trust Fund, *What Fannie and Freddie Crisis Means for NHTF*, 13 Nat'l Low Income Housing Coalition 35 (September 5, 2008).

National Housing Trust Fund, Memo to Members, *Victory: House Passes Housing Trust Fund Act*, 12 Nat'l Low Income Housing Coalition. 40 (October 12, 2007).

Neighborhood Economic Development Advocacy Project, *Paying More for the American Dream: A Multi-State Analysis of Higher-Cost Home Purchase Lending*, Neighborhood Economic Development Advocacy Project Report (March 2007), *available at* http://www.nedap.org/pressroom/documents/2007_Report-2005_HMDA.pdf.

NeighborWorks America, *National Community Stabilization Trust to be Established by NeighborWorks America and Other Nonprofit Organizations*, August NeighborWorks Alert, available at www.nw.org.

Nelson, Robert H., *Pro-Choice Living Arrangements*, Forbes, June 14, 1999, at 222.

Nettleton, Sarah, *Losing a Home through Mortgage Repossession: The Views of Children*, 15 Children and Society 82 (2001).

Newman, Kathe & Wyly, Elvin K., *The Right to Stay Put, Revisited: Gentrification and Resistance to Displacement in New York City*, 43 Urb. Studies 23 (2006).

Nord, Mark, Andrews, Margaret & Carlson, Steven, U.S. Dep't of Agric., Household Food Security in the United States, 2005, *Household Food Security* (2005).

Nossiter, Adam, *After Fanfare, Hurricane Grants Leave Little Mark*, N.Y. Times, August 31, 2008, at 15.

NPR Morning Edition: Wilbur Ross: Finding His Calling (NPR radio broadcast September 15, 2008), available at www.npr.org.

O'Brien, John, *Down Stairs That Are Never Your Own: Supporting People with Developmental Disabilities in Their Own Homes*, 32 Mental Retardation 1 (1994).

Office of Policy Development and Research, U.S. Department of Housing and Urban Development, Affordable Housing Needs 2005: A Report to Congress 23 (2007).

Office of Public Housing, *News-to-Use* (July 2006), *available at* http://www.fhasecure.gov/local/shared/working/r8/ph/newsletters0706.pdf.

Office of the Surgeon General, Healthy People: The Surgeon General's Report on Health Promotion and Disease Prevention (United States Public Health Service 1979).

OIG Finds Eligibility Problems in Louisiana's Road Home Program, 36 HOUSING & DEVELOPMENT RPTR. No. CD-17 [Current Dev.] (September 1, 2008), *available at* www.hud.gov/offices/oig.

Oppenheimer, Mark, *It's a Wonderful Block*, N.Y. TIMES MAGAZINE, October 5, 2008, at 70.

Ouroussoff, Nicolai, *Reflections: New Orleans and China*, N.Y. TIMES, September 14, 2008, at WK 1.

Our View: Trust the People, ST LOUIS POST-DISPATCH, September 15, 2008, at A16.

Padilla, A. Jorge & Requejo, Alejandro, *The Costs and Benefits of the Strict Protection of Creditor Rights: Theory and Evidence* (Washington, D.C.: Inter-American Development Bank, Research Network Working Paper #R-384, 2000).

Paletta, Damien, *Housing Bill Relies On Banks to Take Loan Losses*, WALL ST. J., July 28, 2008, at A3.

Parke, Ross D., *Children's Home Environments: Social and Cognitive Effects*, *in* CHILDREN AND THE ENVIRONMENT (Irwin Altman & Joachim F. Wohlwill eds., 1978).

Parlow, Matthew J., *Unintended Consequences: Eminent Domain and Affordable Housing*, 46 SANTA CLARA L. REV. 841 (2006).

Parr, Beth, Note, *Almost Home: Policy and Politics in the Campaign for a National Housing Trust Fund*, 11 GEO. J. POV. L. & POL. 321 (2004).

Paulson Jr., Henry M., Secretary, U.S. Treasury Dept., Statement on Treasury and Federal Housing Finance Agency Action to Protect Financial Markets and Taxpayers (September 7, 2008), *available at* http://www.ustreas.gov/press/releases/hp1129.htm.

Pear, Robert, *Panel Urges Sale of Public Housing*, NEW YORK TIMES, November 11, 1987, *available at* http://query.nytimes.com/gst/fullpage.html?res=9B0DE6D81F3DF932A25752C1A961948260 (last visited May 5, 2008).

PERIN, CONSTANCE, EVERYTHING IN ITS PLACE: SOCIAL ORDER AND LAND USE IN AMERICA (1977).

Pindell, Ngai, *Is There Hope for HOPE VI? Community Development and Localism*, 35 CONN. L. REV. 385 (2003).

Pitegoff, Peter, *Child Care Enterprise, Community Development, and Work*, 81 GEO. L.J. 1897 (1993).

Poindexter, Georgette C., *Who Gets the Final No? Tenant Participation in Public Housing Redevelopment*, 9 CORNELL J.L. & PUB. POL'Y 659 (2000).

POLICYLINK IN COLLABORATION WITH FNMA AND HUD, SHARING THE WEALTH: RESIDENT OWNERSHIP MECHANISMS (2001), *available at* http://www.policylink.org/pdfs/ROMs.pdf.

POLIKOFF, ALEXANDER, WAITING FOR GAUTREAUX: A STORY OF SEGREGATION, HOUSING, AND THE BLACK GHETTO (2006).

POLLOCK, SIR FREDERICK & MAITLAND, FREDERIC WILLIAM, THE HISTORY OF THE ENGLISH LAW BEFORE THE TIME OF EDWARD I (2d ed. 1898).

Popkin, Susan J., *The HOPE VI Program: What Has Happened to the Residents?*, *in* WHERE ARE POOR PEOPLE TO LIVE?: TRANSFORMING PUBLIC HOUSING COMMUNITIES (Larry Bennett, Janet L. Smith & Patricia A. Wright eds., 2006).

POPKIN, SUSAN J. & COVE, ELIZABETH, URB. INST., SAFETY IS THE MOST IMPORTANT THING: HOW HOPE VI HELPED FAMILIES (2007).

POPKIN, SUSAN J., HARRIS, LAURA E. & CUNNINGHAM, MARY K., U.S. DEP'T OF HOUSING AND URB. DEV., FAMILIES IN TRANSITION: A QUALITATIVE ANALYSIS OF THE MTO EXPERIENCE: FINAL REPORT (2002).

POPKIN, SUSAN J., KATZ, BRUCE, CUNNINGHAM, MARY K., BROWN, KEVIN D., GUSTAFSON, JEREMY & TURNER, MARGERY A., A DECADE OF HOPE VI: RESEARCH FINDINGS AND POLICY CHALLENGES (Urb. Inst./Brookings Inst. 2004).

POSNER, RICHARD A., THE ECONOMIC ANALYSIS OF LAW (1992).

Posting of Jon Seward in response to Lester (August 19, 2008, 9:05 a.m.).

Press Release, Board of Governors of the Federal Reserve System (September 16, 2008), *available at* http://www.federalreserve.gov/newsevents/press/other/20080916a.htm.

Pristin, Terry, *In Major Projects Agreeing Not to Disagree*, N.Y. TIMES, June 14, 2006, *available at* http://www.nytimes.com/2006/06/14/realestate/commercial/14agree.html.

Pritchett, Wendell E., *The "Public Menace" of Blight: Urban Renewal and the Private Uses of Eminent Domain*, 21 YALE L. & POL'Y REV. 1 (2003).

Progressive Accessibility Re-Form Associates (PARA), *Visitable Housing: Cost Estimate Summary 2007*, 2007 CANADIAN CENTER ON DISABILITY STUDIES REPORT, http://www.visitablehousingcanada.com/documents/costanalysisreport/VisitableCosts_Report_MHRC_forwebsite.pdf.

PROPERTY AND VALUES: ALTERNATIVES TO PUBLIC AND PRIVATE OWNERSHIP (Charles Geisler & Gail Daneker eds., 2000).

Public-Private Partnership Announces Loan Fund to Create Affordable Housing in Louisiana, PHILANTHROPY NEWS DIGEST, April 26, 2007, *available at* http://foundationcenter.org/pnd/news/story.jhtml?id=176500022 (last visited January 12, 2008).

Putnam, Robert, *Preface to Symposium: Using Social Capital to Help Integrate Planning Theory, Research and Practice*, 70 J. AM. PLANNING ASS'N 142 (2004).

PUTNAM, ROBERT D., BOWLING ALONE: THE COLLAPSE AND REVIVAL OF AMERICAN COMMUNITY (pb. ed. 2000).

Quercia, Roberto G. & Galster, George C., *Threshold Effects and the Expected Benefits of Attracting Middle-Income Households to the Central City*, 8 HOUSING POLICY DEBATE 409 (1997).

Quercia, Roberto G., Stegman, Michael A. & Davis, Walter R., *The Impact of Predatory Loan Terms on Subprime Foreclosures: The Special Case of Prepayment Penalties and Balloon Payments*, 18 HOUSING POLICY DEBATE 311 (2005).

Quigley, John & Van Order, Robert, *Spatio-Temporal Measurement of House Price Appreciation in Underserved Areas*, 11 J. of Housing Research 1 (1995).

Quigley, William P., *Obstacles to Opportunity: Housing That Working and Poor People Can Afford in New Orleans Since Katrina*, 42 Wake Forest L. Rev. 393 (2007).

Quinones, Benjamin B., *Redevelopment Redefined: Revitalizing the City with Resident Control*, 27 U. Mich. J. L. Reform 689, 753–8, 767.

Rainwater, Lee, *Fear and the House-as-Haven in the Lower Class*, 32 J. of the American Institute of Planners 23 (1966).

Rakokff, Robert M., *Ideology in Everyday Life: The Meaning of the House*, 7 Politics and Society 85 (1977).

Rapoport, Amos, *A Critical Look at the Concept "Home"*, *in* The Home: Words, Interpretations, Meanings, and Environments (David Benjamin ed., 1995).

Rawls, John, A Theory of Justice (1971).

Reddy, Sudeep, *Fannie, Freddie Woes Vex Experts and Leave U.S. Hard Choices*, Wall St. Journal, August 25, 2008, at A2.

Retsinas, Nicolas P. & Apgar, William, *Opinion: Homeownership Should Not be Sole Barometer of Housing Success*, Massachusetts Housing Partnership News, July 15, 2005, *available at* http://www.mhp.net/homeownership/news.php?page_function=detail&mhp_news_id=22.

Riger, Stephanie & Lavrakas, Paul J., *Community Ties: Patterns of Attachment and Social Interaction in Urban Neighborhoods*, 9 Am. J. Community Psychol. 55, 55–7 (1981).

Roberts, Deon, *River Garden Proves Problematic for Developers*, New Orleans City Business, January 22, 2007.

Robinson, Lisa, *Market Creek Plaza: Toward Resident Ownership of Neighborhood Change*, PolicyLink Case Study (2005).

Rodriguez, Cheryl, *Invoking Fannie Lou Hamer: Research, Ethnography and Activism in Low-Income Communities*, 32 Urb. Anthropology 231 (2003).

Rohe, William M., Van Zandt, Shannon & McCarthy, George, *The Social Benefits and Costs of Homeownership: A Critical Assessment of the Research* (Joint Center for Housing Studies of Harvard University, Low-Income Homeownership Working Paper Series LIHO-01.12, October 2001), *available at* http://www.jchs.harvard.edu/publications/homeownership/liho01-12.pdf.

Roisman, Florence Wagman & Botein, Hilary, *Housing Mobility and Life Opportunities*, 27 Clearinghouse Rev. 334 (1993).

Roman, Caterina Gouvis & Moore, Gretchen E., Urb. Inst., Measuring Local Institutions and Organizations: The Role of Community Institutional Capacity in Social Capital (2004).

Romer, Thomas & Rosenthal, Howard, *The Elusive Median Voter*, 12 Journal of Public Economics 143 (1979).

Rose, Kalima, *Struggling in the Crescent City*, 151 Shelterforce 20 (Fall 2007).

Rosenbaum, James E., Stroh, Linda K. & Flynn, Cathy A., *Lake Parc Place: A Study of Mixed Income Housing*, 9 Housing Policy Debate 703 (1998).

Rousseau's Letter to Voltaire Regarding the Poem on the Lisbon Earthquake, August 18, 1756, *reprinted in* 3 THE COLLECTED WRITINGS OF ROUSSEAU 110 (Roger D. Masters & Christopher Kelly eds., 1992).

Rybczynski, Witold, *Why Can't We Build an Affordable House?*, THE WILSON QUARTERLY (Summer 2008), *available at* http://www.wilsoncenter.org/index.cfm?fuseaction=wq.essay&essay.

Saegert, Susan, *The Role of Housing in the Experience of Dwelling*, *in* HOME ENVIRONMENTS (Irwin Altman & Carol M. Werner eds., 1985).

Sagalyn, Lynne B., *Public Private Development: Lessons from History, Research and Practice*, 73 J. OF THE AMERICAN PLANNING ASSOCIATION 7 (2007).

SALAMON, LESTER M., PARTNERS IN PUBLIC SERVICE: GOVERNMENT-NONPROFIT RELATIONS IN THE MODERN WELFARE STATE (1995).

Salkin, Patricia E., *Community Benefits Agreements: Opportunities and Traps for Developers, Municipalities and Community Organizations*, 59 PLANNING & ENV. LAW 3 (2007).

Salkin, Patricia E., *From Euclid to Growing Smart: The Transformation of the American Local Land Use Ethic into Local Land Use and Environmental Controls*, 20 PACE ENVTL. L. REV. 109, 113 (2002).

Salkin, Patricia & Lavine, Amy, *Negotiating for Social Justice and the Promise of Community Benefits Agreements: Case Studies of Current and Developing Agreements*, 17 J. AFF. HOUSING & COMM. DEV. 113 (2008).

Salkin, Patricia E. & Lavine, Amy, *Measure 37 and a Spoonful of Kelo: A Recipe for Property Rights Activists at the Ballot Box*, 38 URB. LAW. 1065 (2006).

Salsich, Peter, *National Affordable Housing Trust Fund Legislation: The Subprime Mortgage Crisis Also Hits Renters*, 16 GEO. J. POV. L. & POL. (forthcoming 2008).

Salsich, Peter, *State Sources of Housing Finance*, *in* THE LEGAL GUIDE TO AFFORDABLE HOUSING DEVELOPMENT (Tim Iglesias & Rochelle E. Lento eds., 2005).

Salsich Jr., Peter W., McDonnell Professor of Justice in American Society, Saint Louis University School of Law, Speech for the Faculty Workshop Series at the Saint Louis University School of Law: The National Housing Trust Fund: A Challenge and an Opportunity for Creative Public-Private Partnerships (October 1, 2008).

Sampson, Robert J. & Raudenbush, Stephen W., *Seeing Disorder: Neighborhood Stigma and the Social Construction of "Broken Windows"*, 67 SOC. PSYCH. Q. 319 (2004).

Sanyal, Bishwapriya, *Beyond the Theory of Competitive Advantage: Political Imperatives of the Government-Nonprofit Relationship*, *in* SHELTER AND SOCIETY: THEORY, RESEARCH, AND POLICY FOR NONPROFIT HOUSING (C. Theodore Koebel ed., 1998).

SARD, BARBARA & FISCHER, WILL, PRESERVING SAFE, HIGH QUALITY PUBLIC HOUSING SHOULD BE A PRIORITY OF FEDERAL HOUSING POLICY (Center on Budget and Policy Priorities September 18, 2008).

SAUNDERS, PETER, A NATION OF HOME OWNERS (1990).

Saunders, Peter & Harris, Colin, *Home Ownership and Capital Gains* (Urban and Regional Studies, Working Paper No. 64, 1988).

SAVAS, E.S., PRIVATIZATION AND PUBLIC-PRIVATE PARTNERSHIPS, *available at* http://www.cesmadrid.es/documentos/Sem200601_MD02_IN.pdf (last visited May 5, 2008).

Sax, Joseph L., *Takings, Private Property and Public Rights*, 81 Yale L. J. 149 (1971).

Schill, Michael H., *Assessing the Role of Community Development Corporations in Inner City Economic Development*, 22 N.Y.U. REV. L. & SOC. CHANGE 753, 766–72 (1997).

Schizer, David M., *Frictions as a Constraint on Tax Planning*, 101 COLUM. L. REV. 1312 (2001).

Schloemer, Ellen, Li, Wei, Ernst, Keith & Keest, Kathleen, *Losing Ground: Foreclosures in the Subprime Market and Their Cost to Homeowners*, CENTER FOR RESPONSIBLE LENDING PUBLICATION (2006).

SCHORR, ALVIN L., SLUMS AND SOCIAL INSECURITY (1964).

Schwarcz, Steven, *Explaining the Value of Transactional Lawyering*, 12 STAN. J.L. BUS. & FIN. 486 (2007).

SCHWARTZ, ALEX F., HOUSING POLICY IN THE UNITED STATES: AN INTRODUCTION (2006).

Schwartz, John, *Gustav Was No Katrina, But Next Time ...*, N.Y. TIMES, September 7, 2008, at WK 3.

Schwarx, Laura, Comment, *The 2007 National Affordable Housing Trust Fund Act: A National Fund for a National Need*, 17 J. OF AFFORDABLE HOUSING AND COMMUNITY DEVELOPMENT LAW 393 (2008).

Schwemm, Robert G., *Barriers to Accessible Housing: Enforcement Issues in "Design and Construction" Cases Under the Fair Housing Act*, 40 U. RICH. L. REV. 753 (2006).

Sebba, Rachel & Churchman, Arza, *The Uniqueness of Home*, 3 ARCHITECTURE AND BEHAVIOUR 7 (1986).

Seccombe, Karen, *Families in Poverty in the 1990s: Trends, Causes, Consequences, and Lessons Learned*, 62 JOURNAL OF MARRIAGE AND THE FAMILY 1094 (November 2000).

SHELTER AND SOCIETY: THEORY, RESEARCH, AND POLICY FOR NONPROFIT HOUSING (C. THEODORE KOEBEL ED., 1998).

SHERRADEN, MICHAEL, ASSETS AND THE POOR: A NEW AMERICAN WELFARE POLICY (1991).

Sherwin, Doug, *Community Members Purchase Shares of Market Creek IPO*, SAN DIEGO DAILY TRANSCRIPT, November 13, 2006.

Shlay, Anne B., *Low-income Homeownership: American Dream or Delusion?*, 43 URBAN STUDIES 511 (2006).

SIEGEL, JEREMY J., STOCKS FOR THE LONG RUN (2d ed., 1998).

Simon, William H., *Social-Republican Property*, 38 UCLA L. REV. 1335 (1991).

Skjaeveland, Oddvar, Garling, Tommy & Maeland, John Gunnar, *A Multidimensional Measure of Neighboring*, 24 AM. J. COMMUNITY PSYCHOL. 413, 422–5 (1996).

SMITH, ALASTAIR, JT. CTR. HOUSING STUD. HARV. U., MIXED-INCOME HOUSING DEVELOPMENTS: PROMISE AND REALITY (2002).

Smith, Eleanor, *Builder Executive Affirms Low Cost of Visitability*, CONCRETE CHANGE, February 22, 2004, *available at* http://concretechange.org/construction_affirmed.aspx.

Smith, Eric A., *Low-Income Housing Tax Credit Basics*, 3 J. FIN. PLAN. 114 (2000).

Smith, Sandy G., *The Essential Qualities of a Home*, 14 JOURNAL OF ENVIRONMENTAL PSYCHOLOGY 31 (1994).

SOUTHWEST REMEMBERED: A STORY OF URBAN RENEWAL (Lamont Productions, Inc. 1990).

Southworth, Ann, *Business Planning for the Destitute? Lawyers as Facilitators in Civil Rights and Poverty Practices*, 1996 WIS. L. REV. 1121.

SQUIRES, GREGORY D., WHY THE POOR PAY MORE: HOW TO STOP PREDATORY LENDING (Gregory D. Squires ed., 2004).

Steinberg, Richard, *The Theory of the Nonprofit Sector in Housing*, *in* SHELTER AND SOCIETY: THEORY, RESEARCH, AND POLICY FOR NONPROFIT HOUSING (C. Theodore Koebel ed., 1998).

Stewart, Nikita, *Gentrification, With a Difference*, WASHINGTON POST, July 20, 2006, District Extra at 1.

Stoecker, Randy, *The CDC Model of Urban Redevelopment: A Critique and an Alternative*, 19 J. URBAN AFF. 1, 1–4 (1997).

Streitfeld, David & Morgenson, Gretchen, *Building Flawed American Dreams: Helping Low-Income Families Buy Homes and Watching the Failures*, N.Y. TIMES, October 19, 2008, at 1.

Stuhldreher, Anne, *The People's IPO*, STAN. SOC. INNOVATION REV. (2007), *available at* http://www.newamerica.net/publications/articles/2007/the_people_s_ipo_4486.

Suchman, Mark C., *Translation Costs: A Comment on Sociology and Economics*, 74 OR. L. REV. 257 (1995).

Sullivan, Brian, *Preston Allocates Nearly $4 Billion to Stabilize Neighborhoods in States and Localities Hard-Hit by Foreclosure: HUD Plans Housing Summit to Explain New Neighborhood Stabilization Plan*, HUD NEWS RELEASE No. 08-148 (September 26, 2008), available at http://www.hud.gov/news/release.cfm?content=pr08-148.cfm.

Summary, *How We Are Housed: Results from the 1999 American Housing Survey*, U.S. HOUSING MARKET CONDITIONS (U.S. Department of Housing and Urban Development, Office of Policy Development and Research, Washington, D.C.), 3rd Quarter 2000, *available at* http://www.huduser.org/periodicals/ushmc/fall00/summary-2.html.

Susilawati, Connie & Armitage, Lynne, *Do Public Private Partnerships Facilitate Affordable Housing Outcome in Queensland?*, 2004 AUSTRALIAN PROPERTY JOURNAL 184 (2004) (Proceedings 11th European Real Estate Society Conference, Milan, Italy).

Symposium, *AALS Common Interest Communities Symposium*, 37 URB. LAW. 325 (2005).

Tarantello, Rocky, *Affordable Housing Through Non-Profit/Private-Public Partnerships*, BUSINESS NETWORK, Fall 1998, *available at* http://findarticles.com/p/articles/mi_qa3681/is_199810/ai_n8823514.

Tay, Alice Her-Soon, *Law, the Citizen and the State*, *in* LAW AND SOCIETY: THE CRISIS IN LEGAL IDEAS (E. Kamenka, R. Brown, and A. E-S Tay eds., 1978).

Teaford, Jon C., *Urban Renewal and its Aftermath*, 11 HOUSING POLICY DEBATE 443 (2000).

THERE IS NO SUCH THING AS A NATURAL DISASTER: RACE, CLASS, AND HURRICANE KATRINA (Chester Hartman & Gregory D. Squires eds., 2006).

Thomson, Dean B. & Kinzer, Michael J., *Best Value in State Construction Contracting*, 19 CONSTRUCTION LAW., April 1999.

Tooby, Ernest N., *The Interest in Rootedness: Family Relocation and an Approach to Full Indemnity*, 21 STAN. L. REV. 801 (1969).

Tribe, Lawrence H., *Forward: Toward a Model of Roles in the Due Process of Life and Law*, 87 HARV. L. REV. 1, 9 (1973).

TURNER, MARGERY AUSTIN & RAWLINGS, LYNETTE A., URB. INST., OVERCOMING CONCENTRATED POVERTY AND ISOLATION (2005).

TURNER, MARGERY AUSTIN, WOOLLEY, MARK, KINGSLEY, THOMAS G., POPKIN, SUSAN J., LEVY, DIANE & COVE, ELIZABETH, ESTIMATING THE PUBLIC COSTS AND BENEFITS OF HOPE VI INVESTMENTS: METHODOLOGICAL REPORT (2007).

UNITED STATES GENERAL ACCOUNTING OFFICE, PUBLIC-PRIVATE PARTNERSHIPS: TERMS RELATING TO BUILDING AND FACILITY PARTNERSHIPS (1999).

United States General Accounting Office, *Relocation Assistance*, IV PRINCIPLES OF FEDERAL APPROPRIATIONS LAW, 16 GAO RB pt C, s. 1 (2d. ed. 2001).

UNIVERSITY CITY, MISSOURI, DEPARTMENT OF PLANNING & DEVELOPMENT, THE NORTHEAST NEIGHBORHOOD PLAN PROGRESS REPORT 2002, *available at* http://www.ucitymo.org/index.asp ?NID=389.

University City's Request for Proposals, *Five LEED® Certified Homes In a Key Residential Area* (August 2008) (copy on file with author).

U.S. Department of Housing and Urban Development, *Annual Performance Plan Fiscal Year 2008* (September 2007).

U.S. Department of Housing and Urban Development, *Annual Performance Plan Fiscal Year 2009* (February 2008).

U.S. Department of Housing and Urban Development, *Building Public-private Partnerships to Develop Affordable Housing*, 1583 HUD COMMUNITY PLANNING AND DEVELOPMENT (May 1996), *available at* http://www.ezrc.hud.gov/offices/cpd/affordablehousing/library/modelguides/1583.cfm.

U.S. Department of Housing and Urban Development, *Are Subdivision Requirements Excessive?*, 5:4 RESEARCH WORKS (April 2008), *available at* http://www.huduser.org/periodicals/ResearchWorks/april_08/RW_vol5num4t1.html.

U.S. Department of Housing and Urban Development, *Community Building in Public Housing: Ties that Bind People and Their Communities* (1997), *available at* http://www.cpn.org/tools/manuals/Community/publichousing.html.

U.S. Department of Housing and Urban Development (HUD), *Guidebook: Building Public-private Partnerships to Develop Affordable Housing* (Hud-1583-cpd, May 1996), *available at* http://www.ezrc.hud.gov/offices/cpd/affordablehousing/library/modelguides/1583.cfm (last visited May 6, 2008).

U.S. GOVERNMENT ACCOUNTABILITY OFFICE, GAO-04-109, PUBLIC HOUSING HOPE VI RESIDENT ISSUES AND CHANGES IN NEIGHBORHOODS SURROUNDING GRANT SITES (2003).

U.S. Office of Management and Budget, Detailed Information on the HOPE VI (Severely Distressed Public Housing) Assessment, *available at* http://www.whitehouse.gov/omb/expectmore.

VALE, LAWRENCE J., RECLAIMING PUBLIC HOUSING: A HALF CENTURY OF STRUGGLE IN THREE PUBLIC NEIGHBORHOODS (2002).

VALE, LAWRENCE J., FROM THE PURITANS TO THE PROJECTS: PUBLIC HOUSING AND PUBLIC NEIGHBORS (2000).

Venkatesh, Sudhir & Celimli, Isil, *Tearing Down the Community*, 138 SHELTERFORCE ONLINE (November/December 2004).

Vielkind, Jimmy, *How to Mediate Manhattanville: A New Negotiating Partner is Born*, CITY LIMITS WEEKLY, December 4, 2006, *available at* http://citylimits.org/content/articlees/viewarticle,cfm?article_id=3223.

Vigdor, J., *Does Gentrification Harm the Poor?*, 2002 BROOKINGS-WHARTON PAPERS ON URBAN AFFAIRS 134.

Vincent, Bernard, *The American Dream – When was the Phrase Born?*, PRINTEMPS 81 (2005).

Waldron, Jeremy, *Homelessness and Community*, 2000 U. TORONTO L. J. 50.

Wang, Qi, *Disability and American Families: 2000*, CENSR-23 CENSUS 2000 SPECIAL REPORTS (U.S. Census Bureau, Washington, D.C.), 2005, *available at* http://www.census.gov/prod/2005pubs/censr-23.pdf.

Warren, Elizabeth, *Bankrupt Children*, 86 MINN. L. REV. 1003 (2002).

Wayman, Carol, *Neighborhood Assistance Programs*, SHELTERFORCE MAGAZINE, January/February 1997.

WEBSTER, WENDY, IMAGINING HOME: GENDER, "RACE" AND NATIONAL IDENTITY (1998).

Weisberg, Lori, *Affordability by Design*, SAN DIEGO UNION-TRIB., June 10, 2007, at D1.

Weiss, Marc A., *National Housing Policy in the U.S. for the 21st Century*, PRAGUE INSTITUTE FOR GLOBAL URBAN DEVELOPMENT, *available at* http://www.globalurban.org/housing_us.htm.

Wells, Nancy M., *Our Housing, Our Selves: A Longitudinal Investigation of Low-Income Women's Participatory Housing Experiences*, 25 J. ENVTL. PSYCHOL. 189 (2005).

Werwath, Peter, *Words into Action: A New Housing Delivery System for Santa Fe*, SHELTERFORCE MAGAZINE, March/April 1996, *available at* http://www.nhi.org/pdf/EnterpriseRelease1106.pdf.

WHERE ARE POOR PEOPLE TO LIVE?: TRANSFORMING PUBLIC HOUSING COMMUNITIES (Larry Bennett, Janet L. Smith & Patricia A. Wright eds., 2006).

White, Donna, Homes & Communities, U.S. Department of Housing and Urban Development, *New HANO Board Chair Introduced at Board Meeting*, HUD NEWS RELEASE, May 21, 2008, *available at* http://www.hud.gov/news/release.cfm?content=pr08-071.cfm.

White, Donna, Homes & Communities, U.S. Department of Housing and Urban Development, *HUD Appoints New HANO Board Chair as Major Public Housing Redevelopment Advances*, HUD NEWS RELEASE, May 7, 2008, *available at* http://www.hud.gov/news/release.cfm?content=pr08-063.cfm.

Widman, Amy, *Replacing Politics with Democracy: A Proposal for Community Planning in New York City and Beyond*, 11 J.L. & POL'Y 135 (2002).

Wilen, William P. & Stasell, Wendy L., *Gautreaux and Chicago's Public Housing Crisis: The Conflict Between Achieving Integration and Providing Decent Housing for Very Low-Income African Americans*, 34 CLEARINGHOUSE REV. 117 (July–August 2000).

Williams, Barbara T., *These Old Houses: 2001*, CURRENT HOUSING REPORTS, H121/04-1 (U.S. Department of Housing and Urban Development: Office of Policy Development and Research, U.S. Department of Commerce: Economics and Statistics Administration, U.S. Census Bureau, Washington, D.C.), February 2004.

Williams, Brett, *A River Runs Through Us*, 103 AMER. ANTHROPOLOGIST 409 (2001).

WILLIAMS, BRETT, UPSCALING DOWNTOWN: STALLED GENTRIFICATION IN WASHINGTON, D.C. (1988).

Williams, Joan, *The Rhetoric of Property*, 83 IOWA L. REV. 277 (1998).

WILSON, WILLIAM JULIUS, WHEN WORK DISAPPEARS: THE WORLD OF THE NEW URBAN POOR (1997).

Wyman, Katrina Miriam, *The Measure of Just Compensation*, 41 U.C. DAVIS L. REV. 239 (2007).

Young, Iris Marion, *House and Home: Feminist Variations on a Theme*, *in* RESISTANCE, FLIGHT, CREATION: FEMINIST ENACTMENTS OF FRENCH PHILOSOPHY (Dorothea Olkowski ed., 2000).

Legislative Acts and Statutes

17 C.F.R. § 230.147 (2008).

24 C.F.R. § 42.350 (2008).
24 C.F.R. § 42.375(b)(1) (2007).
24 C.F.R. § 965.201(a).
24 C.F.R. § 990.160.
24 C.F.R. § 903.13(c) (2008).
24 C.F.R. § 966.4(a)(2)(i) (2008).
24 C.F.R. § 966.50 (2008).

26 C.F.R. § 1.42-0 & ff.

49 C.F.R. § 24.2(a)(6)(ii) (2008).
49 C.F.R. § 24.2(a)(8) (2008).
49 C.F.R. § 24.204(a) (2008).
49 C.F.R. § 24.402(b)(1-2) (2008).
49 C.F.R. § 24.402(b)(2)(i).
49 C.F.R. Part 24, Appendix A, § 24.2(a)(14) (2008).

71 Fed. Reg. 32997 (June 7, 2006).

12 U.S.C. § 1715z-1 (2000).

15 U.S.C.A. § 77c(a)(11).

26 U.S.C. § 42.
26 U.S.C. § 9503.

42 U.S.C. § 604(h) (2000).
42 U.S.C. § 1437a.
42 U.S.C. § 1437a(a).
42 U.S.C. § 1437a(a)(3).
42 U.S.C. § 1437a(c)(1)(B).
42 U.S.C. § 1437a(e).
42 U.S.C. §§ 1437c(a)(2).
42 U.S.C. § 1437c(j).
42 U.S.C. § 1437d(c)(5)(A).
42 U.S.C. § 1437d(j)(2).
42 U.S.C. §1437f(a) (2000).
42 U.S.C. § 1437g(e)(2).
42 U.S.C. § 1437f (terminated in 1983, Pub.L. 98-181, § 209(a)(1)).
42 U.S.C. § 1437g(c)(1)(B) (2000).
42 U.S.C. § 1437g(e)(1) (2000).
42 U.S.C. § 1437g(e)(2)(A)(i).
42 U.S.C. § 1437o(d) (repealed in 1990).
42 U.S.C. § 1437p(a) (2008).

42 U.S.C. § 1437p(a)(4)(A-E) (2008).
42 U.S.C. § 1437p(b)(2) (2008).
42 U.S.C. § 1437p(g) (2008).
42 U.S.C. § 4601(10) (2008).
42 U.S.C. § 4601(10)(A) (2007).
42 U.S.C. § 4601(10)(B) (2007).
42 U.S.C. § 4601(10)(E) (2007).
42 U.S.C. § 4601(10)(F) (2007).
42 U.S.C. § 4601(12) (2008).
42 U.S.C. § 4622(a)(1-4) (2008).
42 U.S.C. § 4624(a-b) (2008).
42 U.S.C. § 4625(b-c) (2008).
42 U.S.C. § 4625(c)(3) (2008).
42 U.S.C. § 5301 and ff.
42 U.S.C. § 5304(d)(2)(A)(i) (2008).
42 U.S.C § 12705.
42 U.S.C. § 12741.
42 U.S.C. § 12773(f) (2000).

Act to Secure Homesteads to Actual Settlers on the Public Domain, 12 Stat. 392 (1862) (43 USC 161, was repealed in 1976).
Alaska Admin. Code tit. 15, § 23.103-23 (2006).
Alaska Const. art. IX, § 15.

Cal. Health & Safety Code § 34518.

D.C. Code § 1-309.03(a) (2008).
D.C. Code § 1-309.10(c)(1) (2008).
D.C. Code § 1-309.10(d)(3)(A) (2008).
D.C. Code § 42-3402.3.
D.C. Code §§ 42-3404.02 *et seq.* (2001).
D.C. Mun. Regs. tit. 11, § 2409.9 (2007).
D.C. Mun. Regs. tit. 11, § 3115.2 (2007).

Emergency Economic Stabilization Act of 2008, P.L. 110-343, § 101 (2008).
Emergency Low-Income Preservation Act of 1987 (ELIHPA), 12 U.S.C. § 17151 (1987).
Emergency Supplemental Appropriations Act for Defense, Emergency Supplemental Appropriations Act for the Global War on Terror, & Emergency Supplemental Appropriations Act for Hurricane Recovery, 2006, H. R. 4939, Pub. L. No. 109-234, 120 Stat. 472-473 (2006).

Ga. Code § 8-3-153.
Green Building Act of 2006, D.C. Code § 6-1451.01 (Supp. 2007).

HAW. REV. STAT. §§ 651-91, 92.
Homestead Act of 1862, ch. 75, 12 Stat. 392 (1862), *repealed by* Act of October 21, 1976 Pub. L. No. 94-579, 90 Stat. 2787 (1976).
Housing Act of 1949, Pub. L. No. 81-171, § 2, 63 Stat. 413 (1949).
Housing and Community Development Act of 1992, Pub. L. No. 102-550, 106 Stat. 3860 (1992) (codified at 42 U.S.C. § 853(b)(2)).
Housing and Community Development Act of 1992, Pub. L. No. 102-550, 106 Stat. 3860 (1992) (codified at 42 U.S.C. § 853(b)(3)(D)).
Housing and Community Development Act of 1992, Pub. L. No. 102-550, 106 Stat. 3672, 3859 (1992) (codified at 42 U.S.C. § 5305 (2000)).
Housing and Economic Recovery Act of 2008, Pub. L. No. 110-289, § 1131, 122 Stat. 2654 (2008).
Housing and Economic Recovery Act of 2008, Pub. L. No. 110-289, § 1337 (2008).
Housing and Economic Recovery Act of 2008, Pub. L. No. 110-289, § 1338 (2008).
Housing and Economic Recovery Act of 2008, Pub. L. No. 110-289, § 1339 (2008).
Housing and Economic Recovery Act of 2008, Pub. L. No. 110-289, §§ 1401-1404 (2008).
Housing and Economic Recovery Act of 2008, Pub. L. No. 110-289, § 2301 (2008).
Housing and Economic Recovery Act of 2008, Pub. L. No. 110-289, § 2305 (2008).
H.R. 5475, 103d Cong. (2d Sess. 1994).
H.R. REP. NO. 91-1656 (1970).

35 ILL. COMP. STAT. 200/31-10 (2006).
IND. CODE ANN. § 36-9-38-8 (West, WESTLAW through 2002 1st Spec. Sess.).
I.R.C. § 38.
I.R.C. § 42.
I.R.C. § 121.
I.R.C. § 163 (2002).
I.R.C. § 164.
I.R.C. § 165.

Louisiana Recovery Authority Act, Acts 2006, 1st Ex. Sess., No. 5, § 2 (codified at LSA – R.S. 49 §§ 220.1- 220.7).
Low Income Housing Preservation and Resident Homeownership Act of 1990 (LIHPRHA), 12 U.S.C. §§ 4101-4125 (1990).

MASS. GEN. LAWS ch. 44B, §§ 3–7.
MASS. GEN. LAWS ch. 188, § 1 and § 1A.
MO. ANN. STAT. § 59.319.2-3 (West 2007).

Mo. Rev. Stat. §§ 215.034 – 215.038.

National Historic Preservation Act, 16 U.S.C § 470 (2000).
N.Y. Gen. Mun. Law § 980-a (McKinney, WESTLAW through 2002 legislation).

Pub. L. No. 90-448, 82 Stat. 476 (1969).
Pub. L. No. 98-181, 97 Stat. 1153, 1172 (1983) (codified as amended at 42 U.S.C. § 5318 (2000)).
Pub. L. No. 105-276, § 519(a), 112 Stat. 2461.
Pub. L. No. 110-289, § 2804, 122 Stat 2654.

Quality Housing and Work Responsibility Act of 1998, Pub. L. No. 105-276, 112 Stat. 2518 (codified at 42 U.S.C. § 1437g).

Revenue Act of 1978, Pub. L. No. 95-600, 92 Stat. 2762, 2893 (1978).
Robert T. Stafford Disaster Relief and Emergency Assistance § 403, 42 U.S.C. § 5170b(3).

Tenant Opportunity to Purchase Act (TOPA), D.C. Code § 42-3404.02 *et seq.* (2001).

Uniform Relocation Act, P. L. 100-17, § 418 (codified at 42 U.S.C. § 4621(a)(5) (2008)).
Uniform Relocation Assistance and Real Property Acquisition Policies Act of 1970, Pub. L. No. 91-646, 84 Stat. 1894 (1971) (codified as amended at 42 U.S.C. §§ 4601 – 4638).
United States Housing Act of 1937, ch. 896, Title I (codified at 42 U.S.C. §§ 1437 and ff (2000)).

Miscellaneous Websites

AARP.org, Home Design, http://www.aarp.org/families/home_design/ (last visited September 22, 2008).
ADA Accessibility Guidelines for Buildings and Facilities (ADAAG), http://www.access-board.gov/adaag/html/adaag.htm#4.13 (last visited September 22, 2008).
Alaska Permanent Fund Corp., The Permanent Fund Dividend, http://www.apfc.org/alaska/dividendprgrm.cfm (last visited October 19, 2006).
Canadian Centre on Disability Studies, Visitability Canada, http://www.visitablehousingcanada.com/ (last visited September 22, 2008).
Castle Coalition, Eminent Domain Map, http://maps.castlecoalition.org.
Center for Community Change, Housing Trust Fund Project, www.communitychange.org/housing-trust-funds/ (last visited September 22, 2008).

Check for Safety: A Home Fall Prevention Checklist for Older Adults, http://www.cdc.gov/ncipc/pub-res/toolkit/checklistforsafety.htm (last visited July 10, 2006).

Citizens Campaign for the Environment (NY), Campaigns: Community Preservation Funds, www.citizenscampaign.org/campaigns/cpf.asp (last visited September 29, 2008).

CityFirst Enterprises, www.cfenterprises.org/cityfirst.html (last visited November 6, 2008).

Community Preservation Coalition (MA), The Community Preservation Act, www.communitypreservation.org/index.cfm (last visited September 29, 2008).

Corporation for Supportive Housing (CSH), Research and Evaluation: Using Evidence to Advance Systems Page, http://www.csh.org/index.cfm?fuseaction=page.viewPage&pageID=3749&nodeID=81 (last visited May 6, 2008).

Council of Large Public Housing Authorities (CLPHA), http://www.clpha.org/page.cfm?pageID=659 (last visited November 11, 2008).

Develop Don't Destroy Brooklyn, Response to the Atlantic Yards Arena and Redevelopment Project Blight Study Contained within the General Project Plan, at 3 (September 26, 2006), http://www.dddb.net/documents/environmental/DEIS/testimony/DDDBBlightResponse.pdf.

District of Columbia Housing Authority, http://www.dchousing.org (follow hyperlink to "view projects") (last visited February 11, 2009).

East of the River Community Development Corporation, Ward 8, http://www.ercdc.org/ward8.html (last visited February 11, 2009).

Facilitating Leadership in Youth, http://www.flyouth.org (last visited February 8, 2009).

GQGP Toolkit, http://www.dca.state.ga.us/toolkit/toolkit.asp (last visited April 19, 2008).

Housing Choice Voucher Program, http://www.hud.gov/offices/pih/programs/hcv (last visited February 11, 2009).

Housing Crisis Center, http://www.hccdallas.org/index1.html (last visited September 12, 2008).

HUD USER Data Sets, U.S. Department of Housing and Urban Development, Low-Income Housing Tax Credits, http://www.huduser.org/datasets/lihtc.html (last visited November 16, 2007).

Illinois Tenants Union, http://www.tenant.org/about.htm (last visited September 12, 2008).

Information from the Universal Design Alliance, http://www.universaldesign.org/ (last visited September 22, 2008).

Joint Center for Housing Studies of Harvard University, The State of the Nation's Housing 2007, http://www.jchs.harvard.edu/publications/markets/son2007 (last visited November 11, 2008).

Local Initiatives Support Corporation (LISC), Organizational and Professional Development Programs, http://www.lisc.org/section/areas/sec5 (last visited January 12, 2008).

Market Creek Plaza website, Community Teams, http://www.marketcreek.com/mcp_teams_co.html (last visited February 11, 2009).

Multifamily Housing Guidance for Disaster Recovery, http://www.hud.gov/offices/hsg/mfh/disasterguide.cfm (last visited February 11, 2009).

National Alliance of HUD Tenants, http://www.saveourhomes.org (last visited September 12, 2008).

National Association of Home Builders, Government Support for Affordable Housing, http://www.nahb.org/generic.aspx?genericContentID=79486 (last visited April 19, 2008).

National Center for Employee Ownership, How an Employee Stock Option Plan (ESOP) Works, http://www.nceo.org/library/esops.html, (last visited October 16, 2006).

National Federation of Community Development Credit Unions—About Us, http://www.natfed.org/i4a/pages/index.cfm?pageid=256 (last visited October 19, 2006).

National Housing Trust Fund, http://www.nhtf.org/template/page.cfm?id=40 (last visited October 21, 2008).

NeighborhoodInfo DC, Data: ZIP Codes, ZIP 20020, http://www.neighborhoodinfodc.org/zip/nbr_prof_zip18.html (last visited February 9, 2009).

NLIHC, *National Housing Trust Fund News*, http://www2398.ssldomain.com/nlihc/template/page.cfm?id=75 (last visited October 17, 2008).

PolicyLink, Market Creek Plaza: Overview, http://www.policylink.org/Projects/MarketCreek/ (last visited October 21, 2008).

The Campaign for Affordable Housing, About Us: About the Campaign, http://www.tcah.org/about_us.cfm (last visited May 5, 2008).

The Center For An Accessible Society, http://www.accessiblesociety.org/topics/housing (last visited September 22, 2008).

The Housing Trust of Santa Clara County, http://www.housingtrustscc.org/ (last visited January 12, 2008).

Town of Southampton, Community Preservation Fund, www.town.southampton.ny.us/listing.ihtml?myid=1957&id=170&cat=Land%20Ma (last visited November 6, 2008).

Urban Land Institute, Market Creek Plaza, http://www.uli.org/AM/Template.cfm?Section=Home&CONTENTID=109950&TEMPLATE=/CM/ContentDisplay.cfm.

The U.S. Consulate General Toronto, Exchange Rates for 2007, http://toronto.usconsulate.gov/content/uscitizens/pdfs/exchangeRates2007.pdf (last visited July 10, 2008).

Vermont Housing & Conservation Board, http://www.vhcb.org/ (last visited January 12, 2008).

Visitability, http://www.visitability.org (last visited September 22, 2008).

Index

For Product Safety Concerns and Information please contact our EU representative GPSR@taylorandfrancis.com Taylor & Francis Verlag GmbH, Kaufingerstraße 24, 80331 München, Germany